GHANA ON THE GO

T0305363

GHANA ON THE GO

African Mobility in the Age of Motor Transportation

Jennifer Hart

Indiana University Press

Bloomington and Indianapolis

This book is a publication of

Indiana University Press
Office of Scholarly Publishing
Herman B Wells Library 350
1320 East 10th Street
Bloomington, Indiana 47405 USA

iupress.indiana.edu

Library of Congress Cataloging-in-Publication Data

Names: Hart, Jennifer A. (Jennifer Anne), author.
Title: Ghana on the go : African mobility in the age of motor transportation / Jennifer Hart.
Description: Bloomington : Indiana University Press, 2016. | Includes bibliographical references and index.
Identifiers: LCCN 2016022407 (print) | LCCN 2016023335 (ebook) | ISBN 9780253022776 (cloth : alk. paper) | ISBN 9780253023070 (pbk. : alk.
paper) | ISBN 9780253023254 (ebook)
Subjects: LCSH: Transportation, Automotive—Ghana—History. | Transportation,
Automotive—Social aspects—Ghana. | Transportation, Automotive—Government policy—Ghana. | Automobiles—Social aspects—Ghana.
Classification: LCC HE5707.8.A6 H37 2016 (print) | LCC HE5707.8.A6 (ebook) | DDC 388.309667—dc23
LC record available at https://lccn.loc.gov/2016022407

1 2 3 4 5 21 20 19 18 17 16

Contents

Acknowledgments

KENT MAYNARD—A THOUGHTFUL anthropologist, gifted poet, and dedicated mentor and teacher—told me to always think of everything like a book. He offered this advice while I was in the throes of writing my honors thesis at Denison University. Though I might have failed to craft a monograph-worthy thesis as an undergrad, that advice stuck with me through graduate school, dissertation research and writing, and the long process of revision that resulted in this final product. Kent's wisdom and kindness as a mentor and friend and his skill as a writer and scholar influenced my development as an academic, a teacher, and a person. This book is dedicated to his memory.

This book was supported by Foreign Language and Area Studies Fellowships and a Fulbright-Hays DDRA fellowship, as well as funding through the Indiana University Program on African Expressive Traditions, the Indiana University Office of International Programs, the University of Michigan Eisenberg Institute, the Wayne State University Humanities Center, and the Wayne State University Research Grant. But financial support would have been insufficient—and never possible in the first place—without the guidance and encouragement of a large network of colleagues and friends.

I was fortunate to begin my academic career surrounded by people who were both excellent scholars and kind and generous people. At Denison University, Susan Diduk, Kent Maynard, Sita Ranchod-Nilsson, Pamela Scully, Jim Pletcher, and Joanna Grabski provided a firm foundation in interdisciplinary African studies, which placed state politics and the cultures and practices of everyday life in the same frame. The questions provoked in their courses and through their research continue to inform my work as a teacher and scholar. Susan, Sita, Pam, and Joanna have often gone beyond the call as mentors and friends, for which I continue to be grateful. Barbara Fultner, Steve Vogel, Jonathan Maskit, and other members of the Philosophy Department encouraged and guided my interest in social theory and challenged me to develop a critical voice. Belinda Andrews-Smith helped me find a singing voice, which has enriched my life in numerous ways. They all shaped my development as a complete person. What is truly extraordinary, however, is that they continue to do so. This book is, in more or less direct ways, a product of their influence; it began with them.

At Indiana University, John Hanson provided a warm welcome. John's dedication to his students and his generosity as a scholar and a human being is inspirational. His guidance was essential in obtaining grants and jobs and book contracts. But John also taught me the importance of humor, humility, loyalty, discretion, honesty, sincerity, and kindness. Gracia Clark, Lauren Morris Maclean, Beth Buggenhagen, Marissa Moorman, Michelle Moyd, Claire Robertson, Dorothea Schulz, Maria Grosz-Ngate, Marion Frank-Wilson, Phyllis Martin, and many others created a vibrant intellectual community within the African Studies Program. They have, at various times, served as teachers, friends, and advocates. In the History Department, Michael Dodson, Konstantin Dierks, Sarah Knott, Dror Wahrman, Peter Guardino, Jason McGraw, Pedro Machado and others encouraged my interests in world history and imperial history and provided feedback and references that shaped the parameters of this project in important ways. Seth Ofori, Hannah Essien, and Charles Owu-Ewie guided me through the study of Akan/Twi. Fellow graduate students Kate Schroeder, Nate Plageman, Elizabeth McMahon, Matt Carotenuto, Hannington Ochwada, Cyprian Adupa, Ebenezer Ayesu, Muzi Hadebe, Craig Waite, Vaughan Love, Sara Miller, Fred Pratt, Afra Hamid, Shannon Smith, Kathi Fox, Sandrine Catris, Jennifer Cavalli, Kyle Liston, Devy Mays, Susan Ecklemann, Tanisha Ford, Erin Corber, Fabio Zoia, Nicole Mares, Arwen Kimmell, Katie Boswell, Katherine Wiley, Elizabeth Perrill, Abbie Hantgan, Allison Martino, Megan Hershey, Kitty Johnson, Jennifer Boles, Katie Ottaway, and many others challenged me within and outside of the classroom. Kate, Arwen, Katie, Nate, Tanisha, Susan, and Liz have all supported this project directly by reading drafts, sharing resources and contacts, and providing moral support and opportunities for distraction.

At Goshen College, Jan Bender Shelter, Steve Nolt, and John Roth gave me opportunities to teach. Jan, Marcia Good, and Regina Shands-Stoltzfus provided a safe social and intellectual space within which I could grapple with writing problems and experiment with ideas. At Wayne State, Tracy Neumann, Paul Kershaw, Carolyn Loh, Marsha Richmond, Alex Day, Abdullah Al-Arian, Andrew Port, Eric Ash, Kidada Williams, Janine Lanza, Elizabeth Faue, Marc Kruman, Andrew Newman, Krysta Ryzewski, Chera Kee, Liz Reich, Bryan Mack-McCann, Sharon Lean, Irv Reid, Julie Thompson Klein, and Karen Marrero have all supported and commented on my work in some form. Tracy and I worked on our books together, and I am grateful for her willingness to serve as both a signpost and sounding board. Africanist colleagues at the University of Michigan and Michigan State University welcomed me into their intellectual communities and provided me with opportunities to present my work.

Within the broader community of Africanists, Jeffrey Ahlman, Joshua Grace, Lindsey Greene-Simms, Katie Rhine, Bianca Murillo, Alice Wiemers, Lauren Adrover, Samuel Ntewusu, and Gabriel Klaeger have been both colleagues and friends. Jeffrey and Lindsey both read full drafts of this manuscript and provided insightful feedback that pushed the writing forward in important ways. Steve Feld was an important ally in the context of fieldwork and writing, vouching for me, sharing materials, and advocating for the importance of my work. John Parker, likewise, asked important and critical questions that strengthened this work and laid the intellectual foundation for this and future projects. Countless others have provided feedback by reading drafts of articles or chapters, asking questions in conference presentations, and sharing resources and contacts. In addition to annual association meetings in African studies, history, anthropology, and labor studies, this research has been presented at the University of Florida, Rice University, Texas Southern University, the School for Oriental and African Studies, King's College London, the University of Illinois (Urbana-Champaign), the re:Work International Research Center, the Kellogg Institute for International Studies at the University of Notre Dame, Indiana University, the University of Michigan, and Wayne State University. I am grateful to the conveners of these various workshops, lecture series, and conferences for allowing me the opportunity to present my work and to the participants for their many productive questions.

I am grateful for the interest that Dee Mortensen has expressed in this project over the last four years and for her wisdom and guidance in transforming a dissertation into this book. I am very grateful for constructive and encouraging reviews prepared by William Bissell and Jamie Monson, which provoked me to think about this project in new ways, even if that meant that I had to acknowledge its limits and my own. I greatly appreciate the work of Sarah Jacobi, Paige Rasmussen, David Miller, and Melissa Dalton for their help in ushering this manuscript toward publication and ensuring the quality of its final product.

Of course, none of this research would have even been possible without the enthusiastic support and cooperation of Ghanaian drivers and passengers, who welcomed me into their homes, offices, and cars. Al Haji Tetteh and the rest of the leadership of the Ghana Private Road Transport Union endorsed my project and encouraged driver participation. However, those at local union branches helped us with the bulk of this work. Particularly, members of unions in La (Quarshie Gene), Teshie (Abraham Tagoe), Salaga, Korlebu, and Madina helped us identify some of the oldest drivers and passengers who were able to shed light on their profession's development over much of the twentieth century. Many others answered questions, shared photographs and stories, translated interviews, and provided refuge from the dust and heat of the lorry park or the street. Drivers in La, in particular, welcomed me into their community and invited me to accompany their Por Por Group to performances, festivals, and funerals all over the city. They made possible my only ride in a mammy truck, and in one extraordinary incident, they bandaged wounds incurred during a particularly rough commute to their office. I look forward to delivering this book to them. Unfortunately, many of the older drivers, who passed away during and after my initial period of research, will not see the end product. However, their words appear throughout this book and shape the story I was able to tell.

Apetsi Amenumey served as my research assistant throughout this project. I am grateful for his assistance in obtaining and translating interviews, which often required creative work on his part. But I am also grateful for his friendship. Apetsi has long welcomed us into his family and his home, and he has remained a powerful advocate and protector.

At the National Archives in Accra, Killian, Bright, Florence, David, and others provided a warm and welcoming place to work and, through the many months of my research, we became not just colleagues but also friends. Staff at the Ministry of Transportation, the National Archives in Kumasi, and the Padmore Library also provided assistance in obtaining documentation, often in unexpected places. Prof. A. A. Alemna provided crucial support at the Balme Library at the University of Ghana. At the University of Ghana, Kofi Baaku and Robert Addo-Fening provided introductions and historical context, and they welcomed me into the History Department's community of graduate students and faculty. Mr. Nat Amarteifio provided important introductions in Accra. Prof. Kofi Agyekum taught me Twi and helped me to translate the songs and slogans that form such an important part of this book. Members of the Ghana Dance Ensemble and the National Dance Company proved to be true friends and served as part of my family away from home. Jo Reynolds, Andrea Bergart, Matthew Coryell, Linnet Taylor, Jamie Goodwin-White, Nina Larsen, Hannah Warren, Aileen Few, Akordy Abinga, Karen Attiah, Nicole Miller, Samuel Ntewusu, and SK Kakraba have all encouraged me to have fun in the midst of fieldwork. Jeff Cochrane and Lisha and Karl Kronmann gave me a place to live, and Accragio gave me a chance to do something other than research.

In London, thanks go to the staff of the Public Records Office, the School for Oriental and African Studies Library, and the British Library. Jo Reynolds, Matthew Wheeler, Linnet Taylor, Jamie Goodwin-White, and Nina Larsen made London feel like home. Lauren Hall-Lew and Aileen Few hosted excursions to Oxford and Manchester. Anusha Jogi, Jo Reynolds, and Matthew Wheeler housed us in transit and came to visit when I was just passing through.

In Detroit, Jeremy David Tarrant, Jacob Krause, Kanishk Sen, Steven Davis, Katie Else, Mike Shalast, Elizabeth Lyons, Stephen Lyons, Tina Hunter, Scott Hunter, and Paula Styer all provided support and encouragement as I struggled through this process. Sometimes that meant telling me to suck it up and get to work; other times it meant considerate questions, celebratory dinners for minor achievements or happy distractions from frustrating chapters. We went for drinks, cooked meals, made music, and laughed through much of the last five years. Particularly at the end, Jacob made phone calls and sent text messages that assured me I could do this, and Jeremy ate junk food with me and gave me "busy work" that kept me sane. Friends like Anthony and Rebecca Guest-Scott and Mary Boutain and Colleen Haas ensure that Bloomington always feels like home. Elaine and Lynn Shurley have always seen me as I am, and they continue to support my work and life even as I live much farther away.

My grandparents, Dennis and Arzetta Armstrong, made higher education not only a possibility but also an expectation, and they invested in the futures of their children and grandchildren before we were even able to talk. Their lives continue to inspire me. My parents realized early on that I would carve my own path, and they allowed me to pursue opportunities and possibilities that were unconventional in our small community. My mother, Judy Hart, who taught middle-school English for nearly thirty years, provided a model of tough, dedicated, and compassionate teaching, which continues to inspire my conduct in and out of the classroom.

My husband, Paul Schauert, has been here for all of it. He introduced me to Apetsi and to the archives, he showed me how to do an interview, he suffered through illnesses and exhaustion in the field with me, he believed I could get funding, he read drafts of this book in various forms, he showed me that it was possible to write a book through the wonderful example of his own, and he talked with me about what I wanted to do with this book, with my career, and with my life. We experienced Ghana and graduate school together, we moved more times than I wish to recall, we withstood distance and separation, and we came out the other side smiling. It has been a true blessing to have him by my side.

GHANA ON THE GO

Introduction: Auto/Mobile Lives

In 1902, THE first motor vehicle arrived in the Gold Coast. The fragile and finicky vehicle, a paraffin-fueled and steam-driven French Gardner-Serpollet car that cost £543, was intended for Governor Matthew Nathan.[1] The car was a symbol of luxury and Western modernity in the West African colony, but Nathan's vehicle was also an experiment. British Secretary of State for the Colonies Joseph Chamberlain had suggested two years earlier that "it might be advisable to employ a motor car as an experiment on the roads near Accra and Cape Coast."[2] British colonial officials like Chamberlain believed that motor vehicles would revolutionize imperial governance across the continent and encouraged their incorporation as tools of governance, enabling colonial officials to move more easily throughout their colonies.[3] As a military engineer, Nathan was eager to take up Chamberlain's suggestions. However, the poor conditions of Gold Coast roads limited the degree to which he could use the car. For the next six years, it sat unused before it was finally thrown into the sea in a massive cleanup of Accra in 1908.

In that same year—1908—the first Ford Model T rolled off of the assembly line at the Piquette Plant in Detroit, Michigan. That these events occurred in the same year was no coincidence. The first decade of the twentieth century marked the beginning of profound changes in the technology of motor transportation, which reshaped the politics of mobility in communities around the world and heralded a new age of automobility. Produced using the technology of assembly line mass production and interchangeable parts, the "Model T" was hailed as the world's first affordable automobile, opening motor transportation and vehicle ownership to new portions of the population and democratizing automobility. The influence of Ford's innovation was global in scope, as motor transport technologies spread across the Atlantic and through the networks of trade and empire.

As they spread, the technologies of motor transportation influenced the development of new forms of sociability, cultural practice, and economic exchange. Africans were certainly not exempt from these processes of global transformation. As the Governor's car slid beneath the waves off the coast of Accra, it represented the end of an era. The fragility of Nathan's car marked it as a luxury object and a status symbol, impractical given the limited infrastructure of the West African colony and inaccessible to all but the wealthiest African and European residents. A new age of democratized automobility was emerging in its wake, "creating possibilities and setting in motion forces that cannot quite be contained."[4] As early as the 1910s, African drivers in colonial Ghana seized on the possibilities that technological change afforded, using imported motor transport technologies to further the social and economic agendas of a diverse array of local agents, including chiefs, farmers, traders, fishermen, and urban workers. Drivers built on the older mobility systems of trade routes and head carriers. However, the speed and scale of motorized travel enabled new forms of labor migration, economic enterprise, cultural production, and social practice that were defined by autonomy and mobility, shaping practices and values that formed the foundation of a twentieth-century Ghanaian society.

This book traces the contestations and transformations that were at the center of this emergent automobility in twentieth-century Ghana. It situates the actions of otherwise unremarkable or "average" individuals within a century of social, cultural, and technological change, and seeks to understand the ways in which these individuals made new technology meaningful in local communities and mobilized the culture and practices associated with that technology to realize the visions and aspirations of a wide array of African residents. African entrepreneurs—drivers, traders, farmers, and others—who appropriated motor transport technologies and infrastructures used these tools for their own purposes. But, in pursuing their own needs and the needs of their customers, they also shaped the emergence of an increasingly mobile society, defined not by the static backwardness often associated with the African continent but rather by the frantic and kinetic energy of a country "on the go."

Auto/Mobile Arguments

This introduction and the chapters that follow explore what it meant to be "on the go" and "auto/mobile" in twentieth-century Ghana through a social and cultural history of commercial motor transportation. The history of automobility has remained curiously marginal to most narratives of Africanist social history or the history of technology, and African histories of motor transportation have also been absent from broader theoretical discourses about automobility, which constitute the core of the "new mobilities" scholarship.[5] This scholarly oversight belies what anyone living in Ghana today could tell you: motor transportation is not just an important means of physical mobility, but it also shapes the values, experiences, and possibilities of everyday life. Ghanaian commercial drivers crowd lorry parks and streets in major urban centers, and individual passengers board trotros (mini-buses) and taxis. Drivers and passengers travel across the city to work, to church, and to leisure activities and across the country to trade or to visit natal villages for weddings and funerals. People shop, eat, listen to music, read the newspaper and sleep in transit.

Unsurprisingly, motor transportation is a constant topic of conversation on the street, in homes, in the media, and in the halls of government. Through debates over traffic regulation, vehicle safety, traffic accidents, and congestion, Ghanaians engage in what Rudolf Mrazek calls a "language of asphalt"[6]—a discourse of modernization and technological development, which uses the language of technology, speed, and progress to evaluate the present and envision the future. As government reports, oral histories, historical photographs, and the editorial pages of newspapers show us, the prevalence of automobility in shaping the politics of progress, development, and everyday life is far from new. Asphalt language, and its associated narratives of aspirational modernity and technological development, connect Ghanaian cultures of automobility across the twentieth century, from the procurement and ultimate disposal of Governor Nathan's car in the early 1900s to the development of bus rapid transit systems and debates about new licensing regulations in 2015.

As a technological object, the automobile connected African drivers and passengers to broader conversations about what James Ferguson calls "expectations of modernity."[7] Young men and women crafted new social, cultural, and economic identities and possibilities for themselves in the increasingly mobile society of the late nineteenth and early twentieth centuries.[8] Motor transport technology was essential in shaping this new society. By embracing new auto/mobile technology, Africans engaged directly in global debates about autonomy, mobility, and development that redefined twentieth-century politics in Africa and around the world—a form of vernacular politics that was rooted in technological practice and economic enterprise. But, unlike Western consumers and factory workers, who viewed motor transport technologies and cultures of automobility as harbingers of *industrial* modernity, African drivers and passengers in twentieth-century Ghana viewed these new technologies as a means of achieving a prosperity rooted in *entrepreneurial* mobility. Men and women alike used motor transport technologies to pursue work in urban areas, moving away from family and elders and creating their own communities and networks of support and kinship. Men sought alternative forms of prosperity outside of the control of elders, working for wages, purchasing land and planting cocoa, purchasing vehicles and starting commercial motor transport businesses. Women moved into markets, taking advantage of the more efficient transport provided by the automobile to engage more directly in long-distance and wholesale trade while still maintaining their family and household responsibilities. Motor transportation facilitated the movement of passengers, goods, and ideas between rural and urban areas, inspiring new forms of cosmopolitanism and engendering new debates about the meaning of respectability, masculinity, and modernity in the context of widespread social, cultural, economic, and political change.

This book argues that Africans in twentieth-century Ghana were, in many ways, united through the aspirational modernity of automobility and the developmentalist promises of a language of asphalt. By grounding the visions and aspirations of twentieth-century Africans in the practices of everyday life, auto-mobility pushes us to think beyond colonial categories that were intended to divide or differentiate African communities—"educated elite," "wage laborer," and "farmer"; "formal" and "informal"; "modern" and "traditional"—and which have often been reproduced in scholarly literature and postcolonial political dis-course.[9] Auto/mobile Africans often transcended, transgressed, blurred, and complicated prevailing categories of difference to craft a system that was rooted in the needs, values, and demands of a diverse constituency. But the promise of *individual prosperity* implicit in automobility also guaranteed that the new technology would engender debates and disagreements about its practice and purpose. African drivers, passengers, and state officials negotiated demands for access to infrastructure, freedom of movement, standards of practices, forms of regulation, and the cost of work. In particular, this book traces the experience of drivers and passengers over the course of the twentieth century—from the intro-duction of motor transport technologies and the consolidation of a commercial motor transport industry in the 1920s and 1930s through the criminalization and regulation of more recent decades—to shed light on the shifting values and prac-tices associated with automobility in Ghana. As detailed in the chapters that fol-low, the history of drivers and driving and the cultures of automobility that their work made possible were subject to significant debate and contestation as gov-ernment officials, chiefs, traders, farmers, drivers, and market women all sought to define what Ghanaian automobility would look like.

Vernacular Politics

In its most general sense, automobility "involves the powerful combination of autonomous humans together with machines possessing the capacity for autonomous movement along the paths, lanes, streets and routeways of each society"[10]—"the combination of autonomy and mobility" facilitated by automo-tive technologies and roads.[11] It is, in other words, the technology and infrastruc-ture that facilitates autonomous movement. As imperial historians of technology have long shown, the late nineteenth- and twentieth-century technological devel-opment often associated with the industrial revolution was part and parcel of a larger social and cultural system that simultaneously saw "machines as the mea-sure of men"[12] and "tools of empire."[13]

This certainly holds true for the automobile, which is most commonly asso-ciated with American narratives of technological achievement, freedom, and mobility. Perfected in Detroit (the "Motor City"), the popularization of automo-bile technology and culture not only "coincided with, facilitated, and illustrated the United States' spread across its continental borders and its imperial rise" but it was also "essential to shaping the dominant meanings of 'America' and

'American' in the twentieth century."[14] Cotton Seiler argues that automobility was a particularly *American* form of subjectivity, which reached its zenith with the high modernism of the 1950s and 1960s and the introduction of the interstate system.[15] In Western culture more generally, as Lindsey Greene-Simms notes, the motor vehicle was the symbol of a new industrial age—the automobile was "the epitome of 'objects,'"[16] "the sovereign good of alienated life and the essential product of the capitalist market,"[17] "the central vehicle of all twentieth century modernization,"[18] "the ur-commodity of industrial capitalism"[19]—and the "commodity *par excellence* of post-war modernity."[20] Initially in North America and Western Europe and eventually also in various parts of Asia, individuals engaged automotive technology as both producers and consumers, working in automotive plants in order to afford the family car and the mobile, suburban life that such a car made possible.[21]

European colonial officials similarly fetishized the automobile as both a tool of governance and a symbol of autonomy, freedom, and modernity. Chamberlain's call to introduce cars to the Gold Coast was part of a larger project in which colonial governments and missionary societies across the continent imported vehicles as "an indispensable tool in the enforcement of colonial rule."[22] The motor car was only the most recent in a string of technological developments that gave rise to the industrial age, inspired European notions of technological and moral superiority, and motivated the expansion of colonial rule.[23] Motor transportation itself was the extension of a nineteenth-century colonial technopolitics in which "the comings and goings [of] trains (and steamships) proclaimed the Europeans' mastery of time and space and demonstrated their capacity for precision and discipline."[24] Colonial officials and missionaries toured their districts in motor vehicles, displaying the awe-inspiring technology to African subjects. Settlers and tourists, likewise, went on expeditions and caravans in the motorcar, which included ingenious adaptations to facilitate camping. Yet others engaged in motor rallies and races that traversed the continent, challenging expert drivers—both men and women—to navigate difficult terrain and demonstrate not only driving skill but also mechanical knowledge and survival strategies.

As the story of Governor Nathan's motorcar attests, African automobility in twentieth-century Ghana had its roots in this history of colonial technopolitics and industrial modernity. But the culture and practice of African automobility also differed substantially from its American and European iterations. While new technologies of mechanized speed like the train and the automobile provoked fear and anxiety in Europe, Africans in colonial Ghana embraced the social and economic possibilities of the new technologies.[25] African drivers and vehicle owners purchased vehicles in large numbers in the first decades of the twentieth century. Wealthy cocoa farmers were some of the earliest vehicle owners, investing their profits in technology that would increase their control over the cocoa trade.

By the 1920s and 1930s, motor transport drivers had expanded into other parts of the colonial economy, transporting goods and passengers throughout the region. Some members of the African elite were able to purchase and regularly use private cars. However, these "myself" drivers (i.e., "I drive myself") were concentrated in urban centers. The majority of the population experienced automobility as passengers, subject to the structures, organizations, values, and practices of a commercial motor transport industry dominated by African owner-operators.

In shaping an economy and culture of automobility, drivers and passengers drew on older mobility systems, which connected communities well into the interior and along the coast as part of long-distance trading networks. African states in the southern Gold Coast had been building strong internal markets for products such as salt, fish, kola, palm nuts and palm oil, European goods, gold, and produce since at least the seventeenth century, distributing a diversity of commercial products throughout a vast territory and connecting rural hinterlands to external trading networks across the Sahara and at the coast.[26] Footpaths followed these major trade routes, which connected centers of production with internal and external markets, and traders, local food producers, cash crop farmers, and fishermen supplied and transported goods through these overlapping trade networks.

By the early nineteenth century, the Asante state's dominance in the region attracted traders to the Asante capital, which placed Kumasi at the center of a series of north-south trade routes. Traders from Kumasi served as brokers between two regions, the produce and goods of which were highly valued. Head carriers transported salt from Salaga through Kumasi to areas throughout the southern Gold Coast, while smoked fish from Accra was transported to the north by Asante royal traders. Imported goods also increasingly found their way into Kumasi through this series of footpaths. By the nineteenth century, observers at Kumasi's large central market noted the regular presence of mirrors and silk among produce and indigenous goods such as sandals, beads, and woven cloth.[27] Asante's trade network connected Kumasi to a number of other large regional markets and trading centers, such as Mankessim, as well as the rich gold-mining areas around Obuasi. Similar parallel trade routes facilitated the north-south exchange, such as those routes followed by Ada traders, who used canoes to travel up the Volta River to Kete Krachi, where they traded fish for northern salt. Other traders used canoes to transport goods along the coast. While local markets facilitated the trade of foodstuffs, regional and periodic markets and long-distance trade were dominated by gold, slaves, ivory, and kola, as well as the products of craft industries such as iron.

Far from the timeless, backward, provincial villagers of colonial reports, many Africans in the Gold Coast lived relatively cosmopolitan lives of mobility and prosperity. Thus, the technological changes of the twentieth century were "not a rupture with the past but a metamorphosis from it"[28]—a change in the speed and scale of movement. The industrialized mobility of the railways, which arrived in the Gold Coast in the late nineteenth century, drew on preexisting African networks of agricultural production and trade. However, British officials who encouraged and funded railway construction sought to shape what Brian Larkin calls the "colonial sublime": "the use of technology to represent an overwhelming sense of grandeur and awe in the service of colonial power."[29] Infrastructural technologies provided evidence of the supposed superiority and power of European science by reordering and controlling the natural world. In employing these technologies, British officials sought to fundamentally reorder African social and spatial relationships to nature and, thus, to the economic and political life of the colony. By bypassing regional networks, the railway certainly did centralize trade in railway termini at coastal trading ports, drawing agricultural produce, valuable minerals, and other resources from the interior for export and securing increased British control on trade and profits. But the success of the railway also required the cooperation of Africans, who controlled the particularly profitable cocoa industry and who themselves were part of a much older culture of cash crop production and trade in palm oil, rubber, and other commodities.

African interest in the technologies of motor transportation at the beginning of the twentieth century was rooted in precisely these tensions between African and British demands for control and profits over local and international trade. Unlike the railways, which traveled *through* rather than *in* local communities, motor transportation enabled Africans throughout the region to control the transport and sale of their own produce. However, in transporting both goods and passengers, motor transport drivers also enabled a diverse array of Africans—villagers and urban residents, commoners and chiefs, farmers and wage laborers, women and men—to participate in a twentieth-century society and economy that was increasingly defined by mobility and autonomy. New conditions of work increasingly "took people out of the village, away from the daily round of farming, and paid them a wage." As McCaskie argues, "those who took part remembered the experience as their initiation into the emerging colonial regimes of mobility and money."[30] New forms of cultural expression followed in the wake of mobile capitalism, as Africans sought to make sense of their own lives in a new auto/mobile society. In other words, by facilitating the movement between rural and urban areas, drivers not only engaged in a form of mobile capitalism themselves, but they also facilitated the participation of others, using the technologies of twentieth-century industrial modernity to craft new identities for themselves and their communities as part of a "periurban" sphere of circulation and exchange.

This book traces the shifting politics and publics that developed around the infrastructure and practice of African automobility in Ghana throughout the twentieth century, which were rooted in the technopolitics of British colonial rule, but which also continued to persist and transform well after independence into the first decades of the twenty-first century. Automobility provided a new means through which Africans could engage with the political economy of the twentieth century, facilitating new debates about the meaning and significance of autonomy and belonging. In many ways, these debates were profoundly local and material. Chiefs constructed roads to connect disparate villages; drivers and traders sought new connections with farmers in production zones; urban residents demanded public transport services that would allow them to navigate expanding cities; property owners claimed that road construction damaged the value of their land; passengers complained that high fares imposed an unreasonable economic burden; and drivers organized their industry to resist government attempts at regulation and reform, protesting and striking to secure better working conditions and more equitable treatment. And yet often, as Brian Larkin argues, the "immaterial experience" is as important as the technology or infrastructure itself—a fact which both colonial and postcolonial government officials clearly understood as they sought to regulate the culture and practices that emerged around and through automobility.

By "arranging and rearranging the mundane spaces of everyday life,"[31] roads provided a venue through which the state could exercise and institutionalize governance. That form of technopolitics was most clearly witnessed during the colonial period, when British officials sought to limit access to roads and regulate road transport practice. Nationalist appropriation of motor transportation as a part of an economy of self-help, authoritarian crackdowns on the profitability of motor transport work, and contemporary debates about fuel costs and fares suggest that, while technopolitics may be less overt, it still remains tied to a persistent faith in the rhetoric and policies of modernization and development. Even as those policies and ideals fray in the face of the realities of everyday life in the postcolony, postcolonial leaders continue to use their control over infrastructure and trade in an attempt to reshape the meaning and practice of auto/mobile life in Ghana.

I argue that these relatively mundane debates about the construction of roads, the cost of transport, or the regulation of drivers were also forms of vernacular politics. Motor transport technology and infrastructure were "the material articulations of imagination, ideology, and social life"[32] and "the built forms around which publics thicken."[33] Those publics included government officials, but also engineers, planners, scientists, drivers, vehicle owners, farmers, traders, chiefs, wage laborers, and many others who shaped a new form of public defined by interaction and exchange and debated the meaning of automobility and infrastructure.[34] Conversations about automobility and infrastructure had profound implications for broader, interconnected discourses about autonomy, mobility, citizenship, and development that were at the center of a twentieth-century liberal project. These debates had significance in Ghana and across the continent, connecting local African practices with global processes of social, economic, cultural, and political transformation in the twentieth century.

Automobility, then, had profound effects on the political, social, economic, and cultural life of Africans in Ghana and across the continent, even if those transformations did not follow colonial plans. Jan Bart Gewald argues that the automobile was the single most important invention to twentieth-century Africa.[35] John Iliffe goes so far as to suggest that the scope of transformations that occurred through the colonial period can be traced through the motorcar.[36] By the middle of the twentieth century, Ghanaian drivers and passengers seemed to agree with Gewald and Iliffe. On the eve of independence in the mid-1950s, Ghanaian journalist Moses Danquah claimed, "We are riding confidently on the crest of the wave to greater economic prosperity, to greater social and cultural achievements, and to eventual independence. We have reached this glorious stage largely through our progressive and efficient facilities for transportation—through our progressive, almost dramatic change from a static society to a mobile society."[37] Ghanaian nationalists, led by Kwame Nkrumah and the Convention People's Party, sought to capitalize on the broader culture of automobility by employing mobile vans that took films and political propaganda into villages throughout the country, incorporating rural populations into the larger nationalist project. The idea of mobility became a metonym for the promise of the nationalist project, embodied in Nkrumah's popular slogan, "Forward Ever, Backward Never." Drivers themselves seized the possibilities of automobility to craft identities as "modern men" in the midst of an increasingly diverse transport scene that now included not only mammy trucks, but also taxis, municipal buses, company cars, and trotros. Their prominence is expressed, in part, through the popular culture of the period. While novels like Ayi Kwei Armah's *The Beautyful Ones Are Not Yet Born* cast private automobile ownership as a symbol of postcolonial corruption, midcentury films like *The Boy Kumasenu* portrayed commercial drivers as both the representatives and agents of an age of modern prosperity and cosmopolitanism.

Scholars of automobility have often assumed that the story stops here in a kind of apotheosis of mobile modernization, the ultimate expression of commodity fetishism. Edwards, for example, argues that while the arrival of motor transport technology was spectacular and the pace of change extraordinary, by the mid-twentieth century roads had become the "invisible, unremarked basis of modernity."[38] But persistent and vibrant African debates about motor transport infrastructure and practice across the continent suggest that, far from over, automobility was central to postcolonial imaginations. In twentieth-century Ghana, the political independence and economic modernization of the 1950s and 1960s was only the beginning. Viewed through the lens of nationalist politics and post-colonial economic decline, the same issues of risk and profit, shortage and prosperity took on new significance. In the process, the entrepreneurial prosperity associated with automobility was recast in the postcolony. Drivers were either criminals who continued to pursue their own prosperity or agents of development, coopted into the neoliberal politics of national and international governing bodies.

Despite this, Africans continued to pursue motor transportation as a source of income and status. By the end of the twentieth century, though, the persistence of economic decline and widespread unemployment meant that automobility was more a means of survival than prosperity. Young men who flocked to lorry parks and taxi ranks seeking some form of income in an increasingly difficult economic climate diluted the concentration of passengers and profits and the rigor of standards and status among drivers. The ever-increasing numbers of drivers shaped a late twentieth-century automobility that was defined just as often by its lack of movement as it was by the risks of speed.[39] Particularly in urban areas, Africans sat in suspended motion amid pervasive traffic congestion. Drivers, passengers, and state officials all seemingly agreed that the answer was better roads, even if it was still unclear what that meant or how it would be achieved.

Beyond Technology

In facilitating an array of social and economic circulation and exchange, Ghanaian automobility was, like its American and European counterparts, what John Urry calls a "mobility-system": "a powerful complex constituted through very many technical and social interlinkages with other institutions, industries and related occupations."[40] The technologies and commodities associated with that mobility system have what Igor Kopytoff termed "cultural biography";[41] they are not merely the products of industrial manufacturing. The meanings and values associated with those commodities are a product of "prior meanings"—"the cultural and social raw material from which 'the social life of things' was shaped."[42] The automobile is a prime example of this process of commoditization, which I argue can be traced not only in particular moments, but also over the course of the twentieth century, through an examination of the lives of drivers. However, I also argue that automobility cannot be understood through the process of commoditization alone. As Larkin argues, "The meanings attached to technologies, their technical functions, and the social uses to which they are put are not an inevitable consequence but something worked out over time in the context of considerable cultural debate. And even then, these meanings and uses are often unstable, vulnerable to changing political orders and subject to the contingencies of objects' physical life."[43] The automobile was not only a commodified canvas onto which sociocultural aspirations were projected. Motor transport technology also reshaped Ghanaian culture and society itself. In other words, automobility is a complete system, linking social and cultural practices of work, family, and leisure with the economic structures of capitalist production and consumption and the political realms of regulation and planning.[44]

In constituting both a set of social and cultural practices and a system of technological and infrastructural tools, automobility in Ghana represents only one manifestation of a global system. The conditions of poverty, weak infrastructural development, and underfunded public services across the African continent shape a more general culture of African automobility that is defined by its reliance on commercial motor transportation rather than private cars, and which largely operates outside of the structures and support of the state. *Matatus* in Kenya, *dala dala* in Tanzania, *car rapide* in Senegal, or *combi* in South Africa are all forms of public or commercial motor transportation that dominate their respective markets, providing access to automobility for the large portions of the population who cannot afford private cars. And yet, the particular social, cultural, and economic conditions in these countries also shape unique forms of automobility, varying in their forms of organization and ownership, traditions of decoration, technological appropriations, and patterns of movement. Unlike in Ghana, where the independent wealth of cocoa producers allowed some Africans to purchase vehicles and control the growth and development of a motor transport industry, in colonies like Southern Rhodesia, South Africa, and Kenya, many Africans did not have the resources and/or freedom to invest in motor transport technology and infrastructure and, like much of the rest of the colonial world, relied on railroads to transport goods and move people well into the twentieth century.[45] Even in Nigeria, which also had a large class of African entrepreneurs who were early investors in motor transportation and trade, drivers were slow to professionalize, and, particularly in northern Nigeria, railways remained crucial to trade and transport.[46]

The history of automobility in Ghana also seems both typical and exceptional when situated within the global history of automobility. Early and widespread Ghanaian appropriation of motor transport technologies seemed to echo global trends. By the late 1910s, cultures of automobility were already reshaping European and American fashion. The trade in luxury goods like ostrich plumes collapsed, as newly auto/mobile populations sought forms of adornment that were better suited to riding in an automobile.[47] In America, there were over seventeen million cars on the road by the mid-1920s, with growth spurred by the affordability of mass-produced cars from companies like Ford.[48] Among Britons, who had been amazed and terrified by the transformations brought through the mechanized transportation of the railway only a century before,[49] automobility was embraced first by the upper-classes and gradually by other portions of the population who aspired to socioeconomic mobility and status. But this growth in automobility was not disbursed evenly even in the West. As Kristin Ross argues, within some Western imperial powers like France, automobility was not embraced fully until after the Second World War.[50] Those who did drive often did so in private cars, eschewing public transportation in favor of the luxury of autonomy and mobility. Africans in colonial Ghana who embraced motor transportation as a form of popular mobility in the early decades of the twentieth century challenged European experiences with the technology, reframing the automobile as a tool for commercial use rather than a symbol of personal autonomy through private car ownership.

Thus, Ghanaian automobility, like automobility elsewhere on the continent, is at once local, national, regional, and global; it is part of both a larger history of technopolitics, industrialization, modernization, and liberalism, as well as the mundane demands of everyday life. By exploring the ways in which African drivers negotiated these multilayered processes to secure the conditions of possibility for both themselves and their passengers, this book seeks to redefine our understandings and assumptions about automobility as both an African and a global phenomenon. An emerging scholarship on the history of African motor transportation highlights that automobility is central to any understanding of twentieth-century African experience. And yet, we should not simply insert the history of African motor transportation into globalizing scholarly discourses of technology, which Clapperton Mavhunga argues too often take for granted the imperializing rhetoric and intent of technological expansion without thinking carefully about the context in which technology is experienced and made meaningful. This book follows Mavhunga's call "to account for 'the process of globalization and the multiplicity of individual temporalities and local rationalities that are inserted into it.'"[51] In doing so, it moves away from an analysis of the "spectacle of technology" and more toward a history of "technology-in-use," away from "the promise of technology on paper" and more toward its meaning and practice in context.[52] In Ghana and across Africa, motor transport technology increased the speed and scale of movement and, in the process, transformed the cultural, social, and economic possibilities associated with mobility, but it did not create mobility or mobile values. Nor did it force Africans to abandon traditions of mobility wholesale. Automobility marked not so much a break as a bend, which often subtly reframed old debates and old questions and sparked new conversations about what, exactly, mobility meant.

Although difficult social and economic conditions throughout the twentieth century have rendered family car or private car ownership impossible for many Africans, Africans throughout the continent secured their participation in the global culture of automobility as passengers. In Ghana, then, it was public transportation, not the family car, that represented the newly auto/mobile age—a history that challenges assumptions about the commodity fetishism of the automobile and redirects our attention instead to the practices and cultures of automobility itself. At the same time, the history of African automobility challenges us to think about the profound and particular ways that twentieth-century technological innovation reshaped African mobility practice, as well as the degree to which Africans reshaped what those technologies meant and how they were used. Automobility enabled African entrepreneurs to protect, preserve, and extend systems of circulation and exchange that had long defined the social, economic, and cultural life of the region. At the same time, however, motor transport technologies created new social and economic possibilities for an emerging occupational category of drivers as well as their passengers.

Aspirational Modernities and Entrepreneurial Histories

While the value attached to automobility varied significantly throughout the twentieth century, the future envisioned by Ghanaian drivers and passengers was rooted in the promise of entrepreneurial prosperity. Entrepreneurial activities provided both a language and structure through which individuals could deploy motor transport technologies and mobilize the rhetoric of aspirational modernity, autonomy, and mobility that were part and parcel of an emerging culture and practice of automobility. In doing so, drivers and passengers situated themselves as part of a much longer tradition of economic activity in the region, through which individual men and women negotiated two competing but tightly interwoven concepts: the state's effort to maintain social order and protect public interest and the individual's pursuit of private profit and socioeconomic status.

This occupational tension reflected the population's prominent role as producers and traders in both the trans-Saharan and transatlantic trading networks, dating back well before the arrival of Europeans. The states and societies of southern Ghana gained wealth and power through their ability to control both resources and trade in the region over the course of several centuries, crafting a distinct social and economic culture that rewarded entrepreneurial prosperity. The promise of entrepreneurial prosperity did not go completely unchecked. The centralized states of southern Ghana had long placed controls on the economic activities of their citizens. And yet, Kwame Arhin argues that even in politically centralized states like the Asante, "There were . . . no landlords and tenants, owners of capital and labourers. There were husbands and wives as owners of farms, master craftsmen, and long-distance traders, and their nnipa (sing. onipa), lit. 'human beings,' but in this context dependants, who did not belong to socially or politically opposed groups."[53] For some members of Asante communities, small-scale economic activities enabled them to enact their place within a relatively hierarchical Asante state and society.

However, for others, the relative autonomy of the Asante economy made it possible to establish themselves as "indigenous entrepreneurs."[54]

These "indigenous entrepreneurs" played a significant role in shaping the social, political, and economic possibilities of societies in southern Ghana—a significance acknowledged by their distinguished status as *obirempon* (Asante Twi: "big men"). Unlike other categories of distinction in Akan society, which were determined by birth and age, the title of *obirempon* and the social and political power that accompanied that title reflected and encouraged economic achievement. For many, these aspirations were achieved through agriculture and trade, and Akan populations took advantage of the shifting demand of the regional and international market to accumulate wealth and prestige through the trade in salt, gold, slaves, and palm oil. Raymond Dumett argues that the category of "entrepreneur" should not be casually applied to every small-scale economic agent. However, "An entrepreneur certainly does not have to be an industrialist; he can be a trader, farmer, or skilled craftsman." Entrepreneurs were and are "change agents" who organized production and distribution in novel ways.[55] Entrepreneurial traders in the eighteenth and nineteenth centuries responded to shifting demands, building on existing networks while introducing new products and redirecting trade routes from gold to slaves to palm oil. In the process they shaped an economy that simultaneously reflected the needs of local communities and foreign markets, of individual economic agents and large systems of trade.

African drivers in the early part of the twentieth century articulated their own aspirations and the services that they provided their passengers through the language and practices of entrepreneurialism. In doing so, they drew on both this longer history of entrepreneurial economy and the discourse of modernity and modernization that grew out of late nineteenth-century European Enlightenment and circulated through the institutions of colonial rule. Young men and women took advantage of new wage labor opportunities in the colonial economy to accumulate cash and other forms of wealth. For most young African men, wage labor was not a permanent condition of work, but rather the means to a more valued end of self-sufficiency and autonomy. As numerous scholars have shown in Ghana and across the continent, young men used their newfound wealth to establish families and purchase imported, manufactured goods.[56] Many others carefully saved their income, using wages to purchase land and establish cocoa farms or to invest in large-scale and long-distance trade. In other words, wage labor served as an early form of investment that made later entrepreneurial prosperity and self-employment possible. Drivers were certainly no different. Prospective drivers entered apprenticeships, where they received minimal compensation in exchange for training over the course of several years. Even after receiving their licenses, young men often stayed and worked with their masters or took up employment as a driver for a trading company or colonial office, saving their wages to purchase a vehicle of their own.

Drivers acted as "change agents," altering the economic and social landscape of southern Ghana, providing a new way for Africans to realize their desires for mobility and prosperity. In establishing their own commercial motor transport industry, these drivers facilitated the growth of other entrepreneurial economic activities. Drivers carried passengers and goods through forests, farms, and coastal plains; beside railways and rivers; between and within growing cities and towns. As the transport network expanded, they increasingly traveled to the northern part of the colony, which differed in both its landscape and in the level of state investment in infrastructural development. The frequent movement of people, goods, ideas, and cultures between rural and urban areas fostered the development of a periurban community, connected through the technology and practice of automobility. As such, automobility was fundamental to the survival and growth of the region's economy of small-scale entrepreneurs, enabling individual farmers and traders to assert control over their products in the field or the market and throughout the process of transport and sale. Entrepreneurs of all sorts used these new motor transport technologies to maintain their economic autonomy and increase the profitability of their business.

At the same time, for drivers, much like other young men and women, the new possibilities of motor transportation also facilitated a process of "endless self-fashioning."[57] Particularly for boys like Shadrak Yemo Odoi who did not complete school, motor transportation provided an alternative path to prosperity and respectability as indigenous entrepreneurs and modern men. Odoi was born in 1925 in Aburi-Effiduase, but his parents, who had relocated to Aburi, were farmers from Labadi. Odoi's father supplemented his farming work as a driver, using his vehicle to transport produce from farms around Aburi to the large urban markets in Accra and Kumasi. Odoi's father's vehicle inspired him from a young age, but it also took his father away from the family. When his mother and father ultimately divorced, financial pressures on his mother meant that Odoi had to leave school after completing standard five. In search of additional training and work, Odoi followed in his father's footsteps, entering into an apprenticeship with his uncle to become a driver. Odoi entered his apprenticeship in 1944 as one of two mates in a 1.5-ton Bedford truck. Upon receiving his license in 1948, he stayed with his master for another year, saving money to purchase his own car. For Odoi, driving work was "in his heart"; it was a source of happiness, because "if you are a driver and you have a car, you are working. By all means at the end of the day, you get money in your pocket. So anytime you have money in your pocket, you will always smile."[58] That money enabled Odoi to take care of his house and his family and expand his business, responsibilities that reflected both self-respect and the admiration of the broader community. The allure of money

Fig. 0.1 "Mammy Trucks," photographer George A. Alhassan, July 18, 1968 (Ministry of Information, Information Services Photographic Archive, Ref. no. R/R/9175/13).

also inspired Odoi to travel, relocating to Labadi in pursuit of a stronger base of customers, and driving to Tamale, Asesewa, and elsewhere to transport tomatoes. Odoi's experience was remarkably similar to that of other drivers during the period, who saw the autonomy, mobility, and prosperity of commercial motor transportation as an alternative pathway to respectability and status.

Odoi adorned his vehicle with the slogan "Be Sure," he explained, "because everything I do in my life, I make sure it will be well for me."[59] This confidence in the power and possibilities of automobility resonates with a narrative of aspirational modernity—an "asphalt language" which associates technology with progress, emancipation, autonomy, and prosperity. And yet, as Marian Aguiar has argued in India, the pervasive transformations that resulted from the spread of mechanized mobility had uneven effects on people's lives.[60] While automobiles did not have the same association with the power and dependence on a colonizing power as the railway, automobility was also not always emancipatory. Rather, the future enacted through automobiles existed within and between what David Scott argues are two sides of modernity: the rhetoric of "romance" encapsulated in colonial and postcolonial visions of progress as "an uninterrupted movement forward" and the "tragedy" of reality "as a slow and sometimes reversible series of ups and downs."[61] Some of the instability and uncertainty of progress was a reflection of the failure of states to carry out their visions of modernization and development—failures that are often rooted in the very structures of states and the institutions of governance.[62] The history of automobility in Ghana is certainly dominated by debates over the state's failure to provide and maintain infrastructure. But the unevenness of technology's effects and the difficulties encountered by drivers and passengers who sought to realize aspirations for the future also reflect what Brian Larkin calls "technologies' autonomous power,"[63] or the often unintended technical and social consequences of technological development, which often elude the control of both the "sponsor" and the user.

Odoi's display of confidence and control, thus, seemed more hopeful than reassuring in the constant flux of the twentieth century. He was not alone in his attempt to negotiate the instabilities and insecurities of auto/mobile life. Drivers, passengers, and state officials all attempted to assert their vision of auto-mobility onto the technology, infrastructure, and practice of twentieth-century Ghana. The history of drivers and driving reminds us that the value and status associated with auto/mobile life was constantly shifting—contemporary conditions in the Ghanaian motor transport industry tell us no more about the conditions of driving work or the culture of automobility in the 1970s than it does about the cultures and practices of the earliest African drivers at the turn of the twentieth century. They are part of the same story and, as such, are connected through the values and cultures associated with automobility, but this is not a progressive narrative of unencumbered experience or persistent historical continuity.

Drivers and passengers, who sought to protect their own social and economic interests, constantly negotiated the changing values and status associated with automobility. These shifts were most evident in changing public perception of drivers' identities and socioeconomic status. The prosperity and security of driving work, which drivers used to make claims to respectability as indigenous entrepreneurs and modern men during good times, were the target of public condemnation and government critique during periods of economic stress and political instability. Drivers attempted to reorganize their industry and practice in response to those critiques, casting themselves as honest laborers or agents of development working in cooperation with the state and in the service of the people. And yet, those same efforts often went unrewarded, as drivers were condemned as criminals and bad citizens. These identities, which were multiple, overlapping, and contradictory, existed in tension within driver practice and public discourse. But these negotiated identities also placed drivers at the center of conversations about the meaning of development, the morality of accumulation, the responsibilities of citizens, and the autonomy of individuals in twentieth-century Ghana.

As a result, in order to understand the narratives of drivers like Odoi, we must step back from the "language of asphalt" that assumes the triumph of progress and modernization. Drivers and their passengers certainly engaged with these narratives and appropriated their technologies. But they were made meaningful through a series of practices that often lay outside of the modernizing infrastructures of the colonial and postcolonial state. Drivers used available infrastructures, but they also created their own, building roads and crafting networks that supported the auto/mobile society.[64] Drivers used roads and furthered the development of trade networks, delivering goods for export and supporting a cash crop economy. In other words, the activities of drivers and passengers reflected the growing influence of a capitalist world system in the twentieth century, but this culture of automobility was not a mere byproduct of capitalist expansion and Western hegemony. Rather, automobility emerged out of much longer traditions of entrepreneurial economy and mobile accumulation in the region. Motor transport technologies provided new tools, which drivers and passengers used to further their goals of aspirational modernity and to symbolize their newfound status.

It is tempting, then, to label motor transportation as part of the "informal economy." However, "informal economy" or "informality" as an analytic fails to capture the actions of drivers and passengers who frequently blurred the dichotomies of formal/informal, regulated/unregulated, legal/illegal, licit/illicit. I argue that motor transportation operated in the interstices of these binaries, often forcing a reconsideration of basic assumptions of mobility and governance. These forms of economic activity—and the individuals who pursued them—have often escaped scholarly attention in favor of wage laborers and other formal sector workers, who occupied the attention of colonial officials and postcolonial leaders. After all, entrepreneurial workers appear less frequently in government archives, and the entrepreneurial nature of driving work also means that there are few private archives of substance available. Where drivers and passengers do appear in the archives, they are often the subject of regulation and criminalization. Their voices are rarely heard directly, and their actions are filtered through the lens of government officials who complain about practices that confound the logic of urban planning, modernization, and neoliberal development policies. Government collected little information about fares, cost, or wages, and they failed to consistently collect information on the number and types of purchased and registered vehicles or distinguish between the different purposes behind vehicle ownership. But archival silences belie what was a robust sector of African social and economic accumulation and exchange—one that not only made money for vehicle owners, but which also facilitated the aspirations of a wide variety of passengers and connected all parts of an increasingly auto/mobile society. In order to understand what this society looked like and what significance it had in the context of twentieth-century Ghanaian history, we must look to the spaces of auto/mobile life itself. In streets, vehicles, lorry parks, and markets Ghanaians from all walks of life could work together to imagine and enact new futures for themselves and their country.

Vehicular History

The identities and practices of drivers were closely connected to their vehicles, as both means of movement and profit as well as expressions of personal identity and socioeconomic status. The earliest vehicle owners purchased imported metal engines and chassis, shipped from Britain and assembled after their arrival in Accra. Africans who purchased vehicles took this metal shell to a carpenter, who constructed a wooden body that included a driver's seat, benches, and cargo space that were adaptable to the demands of passengers. A painter decorated the vehicle, often painting the body solid colors, accented by colorful slogans on the front "signboard" and rear gate, and drivers added accessories like tarpaulin shades to cover the open sides and trailers affixed to the back of the vehicle to carry excess cargo. Passengers entering the vehicle either sat in the front seat with the driver or climbed through the open sides of the vehicle using footholds constructed by carpenters.

Fig. 0.2 Carpenters construct the wooden sides of a mammy truck (Ministry of Information, Information Services Photographic Library, Ref. no. GT/9(a)).

These wooden-sided vehicles dominated the motor transport industry through the 1960s—a form of mechanized mobility that not only facilitated the circulation of people and goods but also served as a social and cultural canvas onto which both drivers and passengers projected their identities, values, hopes, and aspirations. While drivers often identified vehicles by their manufacturer (i.e. Bedford, Albion, Benz, Chevrolet, Ford, Morris, Austin, etc.), among members of the African public, these vehicles were closely associated with the experiences of traders (i.e., "market women" or "market mammies"), who made most frequent use of the vehicles. Nicknames like "mammy wagon" and *watonkyene* (Akan/Twi: "You have gone to buy salt") highlighted the integral role of these lorries in long-distance trade between coastal areas and the distant interior. Other nicknames like *tsolole*, a Ga transliteration of the British word "lorry," suggests the centrality of these vehicles to highly mobile communities like the Ga in the coastal south, who saw mechanized mobility not only as a tool of trade, but also increasingly as a way of life and an integral part of their community.

Likewise, for many drivers, the painted inscriptions that decorated their vehicles were, in part, advertising and marketing strategies that made their vehicles easily identifiable to passengers and conveyed a cosmopolitan confidence to those on or alongside the road. Drivers like Shack Marlow, whose name was inspired by a film he saw in the late 1940s, adopted these slogans as nicknames and important forms of social and economic identification.[65] But for others, inscriptions and other forms of vehicular decoration also served as a form of social and cultural commentary, in which drivers made statements about their place in the world and the general conditions of their life and work. Abraham Tagoe explained that he wrote "Owoo se efie" (Ga: "Death spoils the house/family") on his vehicle because "if you are alive you can do something, but if you are not alive—what you have to do, you can't do it."[66] Such slogans not only reminded him to be careful in his work, but also to be diligent in that work, taking advantage of the time available to engage in profitable pursuits. These statements represented a personal philosophy of life and work in an age of mobile prosperity, and they served as an important statement to passengers, pedestrians, and other drivers. They constitute a "philosophy of the street"[67] and a "sign of the times."[68]

Although cocoa farmers and other early vehicle owners often used their automobiles for private commercial pursuits, the technology quickly spread to other industries, and owners began hiring out their vehicles to other farmers and traders. Drivers took advantage of this new commercial industry, purchasing vehicles of their own and extending their services for hire. By the 1930s, roads in colonial Ghana were traversed by a growing population of drivers of African-owned and operated mammy wagons, often based near major markets in urban centers but frequently traveling to every corner of the country. Although they were the most prominent, mammy wagons were not, by far, the only vehicles on the road.

By the mid-twentieth century, they shared lanes with company cars, municipal buses, privately owned taxis, and a government transport service. Drivers often moved between these commercial categories, pursuing profit and economic opportunity and managing risk. However, these different transport sectors were relatively distinct, defined by geography and utility. Company cars—like mammy wagons—carried cargo, but they were not for public hire. Buses and taxis, which were designed specifically for passenger transport, operated primarily in cities and along major roads. In the years immediately after independence, a new form of public transportation appeared on Ghanaian roads, which blurred these boundaries. Named *trotro* for the three-pence fare they charged for travel within the boundaries of metropolitan Accra, these new vehicles utilized the technology of the mammy wagon for urban passenger transport, catering specifically to market women who needed to move not only themselves but also their goods between their homes and the markets. Initially associated only with Accra, by the 1980s, *trotros* were found in urban areas throughout Ghana.

This book primarily focuses on what I call "entrepreneurial mobility"—the sector of drivers who operated these privately owned mammy wagons, trotros, and taxis, transporting goods and people within and between the villages, towns, and cities of twentieth-century Ghana. In some ways, this categorization flattens important distinctions of expertise, technology, and space that were central to drivers' occupational training and practice. However, I argue that it is the experience of entrepreneurial mobility, more than any particular technology or expertise, that defined twentieth-century automobility. At its most basic level, entrepreneurial mobility meant that drivers used new motor transport technologies to provide a public service for private profit. For many drivers, this meant that they owned and drove their own vehicle. However, even those drivers who did not own their vehicles were not strictly wage laborers. Rather, drivers still had considerable control over the conditions of their work and the daily structure of their accumulation—an experience distinct from that of company or government drivers who were paid a biweekly or monthly salary.

Entrepreneurial mobility also focuses attention on the role of small-scale owner-operators who dominated the Ghanaian motor transport industry throughout the twentieth century. In contrast to other parts of the continent, where government, companies, or wealthy individuals controlled a large proportion of the transport sector, Ghanaian vehicle owners who hired out their cars to drivers rarely owned more than a few vehicles.[69] Rather, vehicle owners were often farmers, teachers, professors, policemen, or other drivers who used vehicles to obtain additional income, supplementing existing wages to support their household. Drivers who did not own their own vehicles paid a portion of their daily income (either a fixed amount or a percentage of their earnings) to the vehicle owner. However, those drivers were still responsible for most of the conditions of their work. They maintained vehicles; took care of registration, licensing, and fees; and dictated the geographical and temporal boundaries of their work. Those who drove for others could choose to work longer, charge higher fares, take better care of their vehicle, or work on more lucrative routes in order to maximize their profits, even as they surrendered some of those profits to a vehicle owner.

As this book demonstrates, within this broader category of "entrepreneurial mobility," understandings of who drivers were and what they could and should do varied widely, articulated through debates over the construction of roads, the regulation of driver practices, the conditions of vehicles, and the standards of driver expertise. These debates touched almost every community in twentieth-century Ghana, including those in the often-neglected northern half of the country, where traders traveled for salt, tomatoes, and yams. However, conversations about the meaning and significance of entrepreneurial mobility were particularly concentrated in the more densely populated south, where cash crop production, urbanization, trade, and wage labor meant that automobility was a necessity rather than a luxury. These debates also varied over time, as concerns about public safety led state officials to ban mammy wagons from carrying passengers in the late 1960s. When import restrictions were relaxed in the late 1970s and early 1980s, the flood of new vehicles into the Ghanaian market presented new possibilities and challenges for a younger generation of prospective drivers who crafted new practices and cultures in order to reflect the realities of technological, political, and economic change.

Mobile Histories: Sources, Evidence, and Methodology

This book originated in an oral history, collected from a driver in Madina (a suburb of Accra) as part of another project on the public culture of religion in late twentieth-century Ghana. In 2007, I was interviewing drivers whose religiously tinged car slogans brought religion onto the streets of the capital city. Most of my interview subjects were young men, who told interesting and inspiring stories of struggle and survival that seemed to resonate with a wider experience of life in contemporary Ghana, but whose limited experiences were confined to the economic decline and religious revival of the twenty-first century. Then I met Musa, a Muslim taxi driver in his midseventies, also known as "Feel Free," who operated out of a taxi rank at Atomic Junction in Madina.[70] Musa came of age in the years surrounding independence, first learning to drive as an employee of the Public Works Department (PWD) and later driving for himself. In its various forms, his work presented new and interesting social, economic, and cultural possibilities that aligned closely with the promises and possibilities of the new nation. Playing for the PWD football team as part of a semiprofessional league in Accra, he soon rose to prominence as a football player and earned himself a spot on the national team that won the Africa Cup of Nations in 1963. In his driving work, Musa became an indirect participant in other events of national significance, transporting African leaders who gathered in Accra for the summit of the Organization of African Unity in 1965. His mobile life, in other words, provided narrative and experiential connections between events that seemed otherwise disparate in the historical literature. He was a twentieth-century man whose life captured the complex contradictions as well as the possibilities of the age. As I interviewed other older drivers, it became clear that Musa was not exceptional. Drivers' experiences provided a critical connecting thread between many of the events of the twentieth century, highlighting the role of "everyday" people in events of national and international significance through their own mobility and the role they played in facilitating the mobility of others. As Musa's life demonstrated, in order for us to understand the ways that Ghana was "on the go" in the symbolic sense, we must better appreciate the ways in which its citizens were "on the go" in a quite literal and physical sense—a form of democratized mobility that was simultaneously unique to the twentieth century and yet also deeply rooted in longer local histories.

This interview suggested important and exciting new research, which I pursued through interviews and archival research in 2009, 2011, and 2012. But Musa's oral history also hinted at the challenges that lay ahead. The automobility, which shaped Musa's life history, was difficult to narrate. He and I both struggled to fit his narrative into a conventional chronological framework, because, of course, individuals and objects in constant flux do not have a fixed story or even a clearly delineated one.[71] And those experiences are often overlapping, multilayered, and sometimes even contradictory. Unlike the men interviewed by Stephan Miescher, whose Presbyterian educational and religious training taught them to think about and define their lives as a series of recorded, chronological events—the unfolding of a grand plan that was at once individual and collective—for drivers like Musa, life was often defined by contingency and flexibility. As I witnessed in greater detail in 2009, drivers' lives were also the subject of serious political debate, and older drivers who narrated their lives also sought to distance themselves from the contested and contentious present. Setting up a contrast between "our time" and "these days," drivers not only evidenced nostalgia, but they also continued to engage in a process of "endless self-fashioning." Thus, their oral histories were contingent both in the past (a reflection of their life and work) and in the present (an attempt to situate themselves in a contemporary mobile politics that castigated drivers). If, as Urry argues, (auto)mobility is a *system*, however, drivers' physical mobility is only one part of a much larger and more complex set of economic, social, political, and cultural phenomena that are at once structural, technological, and experiential. Thus, this book does not claim to narrate mobility itself. Rather, it explores the experiences of drivers and passengers through the infrastructures and institutions, practices and possibilities, technologies and regulations that constitute the physical, social, economic, and cultural detritus of mobile lives. These, I argue, constitute the "conditions of possibility" for their life and work.

Oral histories, then, lay at the heart of this book. I formally interviewed ninety drivers and twenty passengers, who ranged in age from fifty to ninety. I engaged in informal conversations with countless others while sitting in lorry parks or riding in taxis and trotros throughout southern Ghana. Interviews began in Madina and New Town among a group of middle-aged drivers with whom my research assistant and I had connections. Conversations spread out from there through the recommendations of drivers and passengers. While most drivers were, by that time, living in Accra or Kumasi, they came from all over the country, and, as mobile workers, they had traveled nearly everywhere. This diversity was reflected in the languages of interviews. When possible, interviews were conducted in English or Twi; however, many were also conducted in Ga, Ewe, and Hausa, with the help of my research assistant, Apetsi Amenumey, and other drivers or family members. They were recorded and later transcribed and translated with Apetsi's help. The initial set of interviews attempted to survey this diversity of motor transportation. However, in later stages of research, we focused our attention on Ga communities that had historically been identified with the motor transport industry—Teshie, Mamprobi, Korle Bu, and most importantly, Labadi. It is, perhaps, not surprising that a history of motor transportation in Ghana would be rooted in Accra. It was the colonial and national capital, as well as the region's largest market and port for most of the twentieth century. However, as drivers' experiences made clear, it was also the center of a mobile culture that was led, but certainly not dominated, by Ga people.

The oldest drivers and passengers began their work in the late 1930s and, thus, directly experienced many of the twentieth-century transformations detailed in this book. Yet others, who came of age in the years immediately surrounding independence, spoke directly to the mundane politics of those otherwise turbulent times. All drivers, including the youngest who were still operating their vehicles or who had just entered the industry, were invested in the contemporary politics of the road, and they were highly attuned to the potential of this project to speak to popular narratives of drivers as criminals and cheats. As such, their recollections are undoubtedly shaped by the conditions of the present and a nostalgia for better times, as they engaged in that process of "endless self-fashioning." But does this make their remembrances any less valid? I would argue that in this self-fashioning, drivers are engaging in a process that has a much longer history that is not only essential for their own social and economic lives but is also central to the very experience of twentieth-century automobility itself. Capturing and contextualizing that process became my task.

My efforts to understand and interpret the "endless self-fashioning" of drivers and passengers was supported by a large archival record. Motor transportation figured prominently in colonial archives, which are housed at the National Archives of Ghana in Accra and other regional branches, as well as the British National Archives in Kew, the British Library, and the Basel Mission Archives. Many documents were found in obvious places such as the Ministry of Transportation and the Public Works Department. However, the infrastructures, practices, and policies of motor transportation also showed up in less obvious places, buried deep within Native Affairs Administration files, Accra Town Council reports, or court records. Finding these records required casting a broad net. In many cases, I excitedly requested a file on, for example, the Ghana Motor Transport Union, only to be told that it was missing. In other cases, fellow researchers or archives staff found or suggested new sites of discovery. This was particularly true in the case of court records, which were impossible to assess based on file names alone. These colonial sources play a prominent role in the book's first three chapters.

The National Archives of Ghana was less productive as a source of postcolonial archives. Due to the political and economic instability of the decades following independence, as well as the declining resources of the NAG itself, many of these files have never been transported to NAG or catalogued in any systematic way. This does not mean, however, that postcolonial archives do not exist. As Jean Allman recently noted, many are held in ministry offices or in private collections, which require slightly more creative archival research.[72] This project utilizes files from the Ministry of Transportation, as well as the Photographic Archive at the Information Services Department. Other sources like newspapers were accessed at the Padmore Library. Ultimately, however, some gaps remained. I could not locate any extensive collection of archival files on the period of greatest political instability, between 1966 and 1983. Thus, chapter four relies primarily on drivers' narratives and newspapers to reconstruct the debates of the period. There are obvious limitations to these sources, but they do convey the contestations between passengers, drivers, and the state during a period that completely redefined the socioeconomic status of drivers and, thus, cannot be ignored.

In utilizing a wide array of archival documents, newspapers, photographs, and popular culture, this book situates drivers' actions and experiences within a broader historical context, enabling us to better understand the significance of their lives and work in twentieth-century Ghana. The political, economic, and social events and processes of the twentieth century undoubtedly circumscribed drivers' choices, sometimes enabling drivers' work and, in other cases, limiting it. However, the everyday life of drivers—the individual experiences that shaped driving practice and the mobility of both drivers and passengers—was often defined by choices that were not directly connected to or informed by the events and processes of "big" history. In taking drivers' perspectives seriously and in acknowledging and validating their own intentionality, this book seeks to understand how history was *experienced*. That does not mean, however, that the state disappears. Rather, the state was integral to the self-fashioning of drivers, creating conditions of possibility for their work and often spurring new forms of professionalization among drivers. Where possible, I attempt to humanize "the state" as a set of institutions staffed by individuals and shaped by their own form of internal politics. However, as is clear in the chapters that follow, changes in state politics were not necessarily always the drivers of change.

The Roadmap

This book, then, explores the history of automobility in Ghana at two different levels. It is, first and foremost, a social history of drivers, tracing the ways in which motor transport technology shaped the possibilities and practices of drivers' lives as indigenous entrepreneurs, honest laborers, public servants, modern men, criminals, and agents of development. Since drivers were an important social and occupational class in twentieth-century Ghana, their experiences were, in many ways, unique to the twentieth century, shaped by the promises, possibilities, and pitfalls of automobility. Where possible, I attempt to allow drivers and passengers to speak for themselves, describing their own experiences in their own words. Likewise, chapter titles are drawn from a large collection of vehicular "signboard" inscriptions or slogans, which, as Ato Quayson argues, represent "Signs of the Times,"[73] capturing the priorities and practices of drivers in particular historical moments. However, I also argue that drivers' identity politics and changing economic and cultural practices help us understand the significance of autonomy and mobility in the twentieth century. By tracing debates between three different but powerful constituencies—drivers, passengers, and the state—this book argues that motor transportation was central to the development of a twentieth-century mobile society, in which technology served as a tool through which individuals envisioned their future. In the process, they engaged in discourses of citizenship and development as a way to shape debates about the changing meaning of autonomy and mobility in twentieth-century Ghana. Throughout the book's chapters, these issues are manifested through debates over road construction, motor traffic regulation, public safety, and fares—relatively mundane debates that shaped a twentieth-century mobility politics.

The chapters that follow trace this history of mobility politics both chronologically and thematically. The first three chapters explore what drivers classified as the "golden age" of motor transportation, 1901–1960, tracing the ways in which drivers used new technologies to negotiate colonial and early postcolonial technopolitics and establish themselves as a social and occupational class. Chapter one,

"'All Shall Pass': Indigenous Entrepreneurs, Colonial Technopolitics, and the Roots of African Automobility, 1901–1939," details the emergence of cultures and practices of African automobility in the first decades of the twentieth century, shaped by the new technologies of motor transportation, the priorities of colonial governance, and the indigenous cultures of circulation and exchange that defined the social and economic life of the region. Chapter two, "'Honest Labor': Public Safety, Private Profit, and the Professionalization of Drivers, 1930–1945," argues that the consolidation of motor transportation in the mid-1930s not only solidified the industry, but also raised new questions about the regulation of their work. Colonial attempts to define "the type of man who should be a driver" highlighted a tension between public service and private profit, which lay at the core of the new industry, but these attempts at regulation also motivated drivers to engage in a process of professionalization and formalization of their occupational practice by forming unions that protected and represented driver interests. Chapter three, "'Modern Men': Motor Transportation and the Politics of Respectability, 1930s–1960s," traces the ways in which drivers used their new occupational status to make claims to modernity and respectability. In doing so, I argue, they highlighted both the fundamental continuities and changes of a period that saw the end of colonialism and the rise of a new nation-state.

The last two chapters and epilogue explore the history of postcolonial automobility, detailing the ways in which drivers' lives complicate the narratives of political instability and economic decline that are often used to define this period. These chapters suggest that the everyday or mundane experiences of postcolonial instability were far more ambivalent that political histories suggest. Chapter four, "'One Man, No Chop': Licit Wealth, Good Citizens, and the Criminalization of Drivers in Postcolonial Ghana," uses debates about driver practice to explore shifting understandings of citizenship and economic morality in the decades following independence. Public discourses and state policies increasingly cast drivers as criminals and cheats, which drivers identified as the root of their declining socioeconomic status. Drivers' ability to "make money" in the context of widespread political, economic, and social decline put them on the wrong side of a postcolonial discourse about belonging, respectability, and development. Chapter five, "'Sweet Not Always': Automobility, State Power, and the Politics of Development, 1980s–1990s," details the significance of neoliberal development policies for driving practice. In particular, it argues that policies of "decentralization" seemingly placed more control into the hands of drivers at the same time that it increased their vulnerability in the context of the broader economy. Thus, in endowing drivers with the responsibility to regulate and police their own industry, the state seemingly gave drivers what they had been fighting for since the beginning of the century. However, decentralization also meant that drivers no longer benefitted from state protection that had long guaranteed the conditions of possibility for their work. Economic and political reform, then, placed drivers at the center of an entirely new set of debates about the meaning of development at the end of the twentieth century. The brief epilogue follows these debates into the first decades of the twenty-first century, using recent projects of urban transport reform to think about the ways in which motor transportation shaped the social, cultural, economic, and political life of twentieth-century Ghana and the ways in which it continues to articulate visions for the future.

1 "All Shall Pass": Indigenous Entrepreneurs, Colonial Technopolitics, and the Roots of African Automobility, 1901–1939

On January 28, 1930, Lord Passfield, the head of the Colonial Office, sent a circular dispatch to the "Officers Administering the Governments of Britain's Colonies" expressing grave concern about increasing reports of "road vs. rail competition."[1] Colonial governments throughout the British Empire had invested heavily in rail transportation as a symbol and tool of the ideological underpinnings of colonial rule in the late nineteenth century—the often-conflicting goals of resource extraction and development.[2] However, as Passfield noted, "the introduction of the internal combustion engine has resulted in direct competition for similar traffic between road and rail which did not exist at the time when the main lines of communication were originally laid down in many territories."[3]

In ordering colonial administrations to report on the development of internal communications in their colonies and to propose strategies for responding to the new challenges to the railways that resulted from the rise of motor transportation, Passfield's circular represented the apotheosis of anxiety that had been growing throughout the administrative offices of the British Empire since the early twentieth century. Hundreds of files on "road vs. rail competition" highlight the degree to which the growing importance of motor transportation at the turn of the twentieth century presented a fundamental challenge for colonial governance in African colonies like the Gold Coast and throughout the empire. Colonial attempts to control infrastructure were part of what Bissell calls an "imperial impulse: the will to power and pursuit of mastery in situations marked by high degrees of complexity, fluidity, and unpredictability."[4] It was a form of technopolitics, through which colonial officials hoped to establish their hegemony in the Gold Coast and, by extension, throughout the empire. And yet, as Passfield's concern about competition suggests, the goal of hegemonic control over circulation and exchange was much more distant than most colonial policies and rhetoric would publicly acknowledge.

The parameters and practices of colonial technopolitics were shaped by British conceptions of mobile modernity. Officials in both Britain and the colonies

understood railways as the material and technological symbol of British dominance. Passfield, Chamberlain, and the succession of governors and other officials
who circulated through the Gold Coast Colony in the early part of the twentieth century were the products of a British industrial age that had been indelibly
reshaped by railway technologies. Entrepreneurs invested in railways, constructing tracks and moving trains through the British countryside in the late eighteenth and nineteenth centuries. Those trains introduced a new speed and scale
of movement, transporting raw materials and manufactured goods to facilitate
the country's growing industrial economy and expanding the wealth-generating
potential of industrial development into the British countryside. But trains also
produced psychic and social changes among the British populace, who were both
awestruck and anxious about the changes that this new technology wrought.
Women fainted at the rapid pace of movement, authors described the ways in
which passing scenery abstracted individuals from the landscape, and painters
depicted romanticized images of an idyllic, pastoral rural landscape increasingly
scarred by the infrastructure of mechanized mobility.[5] New cultures developed
around the railways, which seemingly erased distance and brought ever-greater
numbers of citizens together in a system of modern, mobile interaction.[6] More
than ever before, the British population of both city and countryside moved as
"travelers," moving through the landscape while removed from the surrounding
environment, focused on the endpoint rather than the spaces between.[7] By the
end of the nineteenth century, the British railway was the preeminent symbol
and infrastructure of a modern culture and economy.

It is no surprise, then, that European colonial officials at the beginning
of the twentieth century viewed the railway as a "mobile memorial to British
power."[8] Like the railways, that power was far from static. As Aguiar notes, the
rhetoric of nineteenth-century modernity "connoted by a moving train pointed
always towards a possible future, a destination toward which one ideally moved
quickly."[9] Such a future required imperial expansion. New colonies would simultaneously project and reinforce the social, cultural, and economic authority of the
British state as it expanded across the globe. Within colonies, railways served as
the infrastructure of a highly centralized political and economic system, defined
by an extractive command economy and a hierarchical bureaucratic state. Railways were central to both communications and transportation, moving goods
between production zones and coastal ports, and enabling the efficient administration of far-flung territories by facilitating the movement of administrators (or,
at least, news of their directives).

Colonial officials sought to reshape the social and economic landscape of the
colony through investments in railway construction. In moving goods and people
through rather than *in* local communities, railways represented the expansion of
what Tilley calls the "development state," which "viewed African populations less

as prospective political actors and more as potential producers."[10] The development state sought to simultaneously disrupt old systems of social and economic exchange and implement new networks of extraction that channeled the efforts of African producers away from local and regional economies into the imperial networks of global capital. In this context, colonial investment in railways was a "technopolitical strategy,"[11] which sought to undermine the power of African producers and traders while consolidating British control over the resources of African colonies like the Gold Coast.

Viewed through the lens of colonial technopolitics, Passfield's concern about road vs. rail competition highlights the centrality of railways to both the symbolic and material expressions of colonial authority and the significant and varied challenges to railway construction and administration in Britain's colonies. Engineers debated the more material or technical challenges of adapting railway construction techniques to new environments, and the British engineering community adapted quickly to the new realities of imperial construction and development.[12] The political, social, and cultural roadblocks to railway expansion proved much more difficult to overcome. In the Gold Coast, colonial leaders insisted that the state finance and construct railways as part of an effort to control the colony's economic development. Obtaining consistent profits from the railways proved much more difficult to achieve. Challenges to colonial railway profits were, in part, the result of inefficient and ineffective government planning. Railway construction was slow to respond to the development of new production zones, and roads were often built in parallel with major railway lines.

These mundane debates about financial investment and economic development dominated administrative reports and public statements from the offices of colonial administrators in the Gold Coast. But in the minutes of those files and in internal memos, colonial officials also expressed frustration over their inability to reshape African social, cultural, and economic lives. The frustrations of Gold Coast colonial officials and imperial bureaucrats like Passfield were symptoms of "the incapacity of legal and bureaucratic instruments to reorder the totality of everyday life."[13] British policies of indirect rule limited resources available to colonial governments throughout the empire. Sara Berry characterizes this limited government as "hegemony on a shoestring";[14] however, Berman, Bissell, and others argue that the skeletal presence and limited resources of British indirect rule undermined the ability of these colonial states to achieve their goals of capitalist transformation in the colonies and effectively project and police hegemonic control.[15] Certainly in the Gold Coast, colonial officials viewed road vs. rail competition as a symbol of larger failures in this capitalist transformation. But, when we look beyond the narratives presented by British administrators in the files of the colonial archive, we see that African investment in road transport did not represent a challenge to capitalism, but rather its widespread embrace.

By embracing motor transportation, Africans certainly challenged the supremacy of the railway as a symbol of mobile modernity and the infrastructural technology of trade. But African entrepreneurs also used motor transport technology to expand participation in the global capitalist system, connecting even the most remote villages and farms to global networks of circulation and exchange. In other words, auto/mobile Africans used new technology to extend participation in the capitalist system even as they operated outside of the structures and expectations of colonial capitalism or rejected the technological infrastructure of industrial capitalist development.

Road vs. rail competition, then, was about more than the colonial railways. It was also about the persistence of African mobility systems and the emergence of an African automobility. African entrepreneurs exploited "cracks in the imperial façade,"[16] using economic resources obtained through the expanding cocoa economy to pursue alternative infrastructural and mobile technologies like motor transportation. The earliest motor vehicles were considered novelties, owned by elites and politicians as symbols of status and imported by European trading firms to transport goods between railway stations and commercial facilities. By the 1920s, however, indigenous entrepreneurs in the Gold Coast had fully embraced the new technology, transporting goods between rural production zones, regional markets, and urban ports. Africans utilized colonial trunk roads constructed in parallel with railway lines to bypass railways and transport their produce directly to the coast via increasingly accessible motor vehicles. Even when the colonial state sought to limit African access to roads, road users including drivers, chiefs, traders, and farmers simply ignored colonial regulations, empowered by their own economic power as producers and traders as well as the skeletal police and military personnel's limited ability to enforce regulations and punish offenders.

In the context of colonial technopolitics, African embrace of motor transport technologies had insurrectionary potential. African drivers, farmers, traders, urban residents, and chiefs petitioned the colonial state for the right to roads and circumvented colonial regulations and stagnant infrastructure by constructing and maintaining their own roads. Colonial officials created policies that assumed Africans were incapable of guiding their own development; however, in harnessing their economic power and technological ingenuity to demonstrate otherwise, Africans challenged not only colonial economic control but also the very ideologies that undergirded colonial assertions of power and the right to rule. In other words, auto/mobile Africans acted outside of colonial expectations. In doing so, these entrepreneurs challenged colonial attempts to control African production and trade, undermining the profitability and power of the railway and raising important questions about the limits of colonial authority and the autonomy of African subjects.

But African embrace of motor transport technologies cannot be understood as a mere reaction to colonial power (or its failure) or a simple extension of technological hegemony. Rather, African automobility emerged out of the interstices and tensions of overlapping concerns: the colonial technopolitics of railway construction and economic hegemony, the social and economic possibilities of technological innovation, and the cultures and practices of indigenous entrepreneurs. In constructing their own roads and creatively adapting motor transport technologies to suit their own social and economic agendas, African entrepreneurs engaged in a form of grassroots development that provided powerful alternatives to colonial models. African networks, practices, and cultures of automobility, which emerged in the first decades of the twentieth century, were built on much older systems of social and economic exchange. African farmers and traders invested in motor transport technologies as a way to ensure the survival of these networks while also enhancing the profitability and efficiency of production and trade. Roads often followed the paths of head carriers and cask rollers, connecting farms and villages with coastal ports through a series of regional markets and trading networks. The flexibility of the automobile allowed farmers, traders, and chiefs in the most remote villages or farms to engage directly in the world of global commerce and modern technology. In doing so, African entrepreneurs did not merely appropriate the cultures and values associated with the Western technologies.[17] Rather, motor transport technologies gave rise to a uniquely African culture and practice of automobility that provided a new language for African aspirations.

In this context, the arrival of the first motor vehicles in the Gold Coast represented both a threat and a promise in the first decades of the twentieth century. The debate over "road vs. rail competition" was shaped not only by colonial economic agendas symbolized by the railway, but also by indigenous practices of cash crop production and trade and the technological advancements of motor transportation in the first decades of the twentieth century. Furthermore, "road vs. rail competition" was not merely an issue of infrastructural development and trade. It was also a debate about the fundamental ideals and practice of the colonial project itself: the nature of colonial governance, the limits of African autonomy, and the meaning of auto/mobility in the Gold Coast. By asserting control over their movements and the transportation of their own produce, entrepreneurs in the Gold Coast embraced the lorry slogan "All Shall Pass," evoking the demand for freedom of movement along colonial roads and expressing faith in a more prosperous (and less contentious) future.

Indigenous Entrepreneurs and Mobility in the Southern Gold Coast

British colonial authorities and European merchants arriving on the Gold Coast in the late nineteenth century encountered thriving local markets in the port cities that dotted the Atlantic coast. These new arrivals were certainly not the first to note the significance of urban markets. In the early seventeenth century, European traders like Pieter de Marees noted the vigor of trade in coastal ports. Writing of women in a market near Elmina, de Marees remarked that:

> These women are very eager traders: they are so industrious in their trade that they come here every day, walking five, some of them even six miles to the place where they do their trade, laden like Asses; she carries her child tied to her back and in addition a heavy load of fruits or *Millie* on her head. Laden in this way they come to Market and in turn buy Fish to carry home. Thus they often return home from the Market as heavily loaded as when they set out.[18]

In the eyes of Europeans, these urban markets seemed like the end points of African trade—spaces where raw materials were loaded onto cargo ships and exported to Europe. The presence of European traders on the coast beginning in the late fifteenth century certainly created a new demand for goods, which redirected patterns of trade and long-distance trading networks. But for African traders and producers, coastal ports were merely nodes within a comprehensive system of internal trade routes and pathways. Head carriers and cask rollers facilitated the circulation of goods within complex networks of local and regional markets, transporting produce and manufactured goods throughout the Gold Coast and within the broader West African region. Those urban markets, in other words, were only one part of the infrastructure of an indigenous mobility system.[19]

The economies and cultures of the region, which were caught up in this larger system of circulation, interaction, and exchange, were often highly sophisticated and cosmopolitan.[20] The mobility system of the nineteenth-century Gold Coast had been shaped by the increasing European presence on the coast since the late fifteenth century as well as African traditions of long-distance trading. Before advances in maritime technology enabled Europeans to travel along the African coast, Africans in the resource-rich interior traded gold and other goods over large parts of the continent and, through the trans-Saharan trade, into Europe and Asia. Beginning in the late fifteenth century, interactions with European traders and African middlemen from throughout the region connected Africans residents on the coast and well into the interior with an emerging transatlantic world of goods and culture and redirected major trade networks to the coast. However, early modern European interactions with African communities bore little resemblance to the narratives of hegemonic domination that would accompany the colonial expansion of the nineteenth century. The Portuguese, who built Sao Jorge da Mina ("Elmina") Castle in 1482, used their position to assert control over the seagoing trade, using their caravels to transport gold, slaves, ivory, and some agricultural produce from the Guinea Coast. On land, however, Portuguese soldiers, sailors, traders, and government representatives were heavily dependent on local African leaders and economic agents. The chief of the adjacent village of

Amankwa famously rejected Portuguese requests to move freely throughout the region, confining them to the walls of the trading fort and restricting their claims to sovereignty over the region and its population. The Dutch, the Danish, and the British, who began arriving in the seventeenth century, faced trading restrictions that were similar to their Portuguese competitors nearly two centuries earlier.

In this context, European traders relied heavily on African intermediaries who negotiated access to goods and labor and facilitated long-distance trading relationships. European traders married into powerful African families and their EurAfrican descendants, who had access to labor and knowledge of interior trading networks, mediated most commercial transactions well into the nineteenth century.[21] These "professional traders"[22] or middlemen organized large-scale transport of kola, palm oil, and slaves by connecting producers and internal markets with coastal European commercial agents. Middlemen, who were often headquartered at major coastal ports such as Cape Coast or Accra, hired carriers to transport goods along indigenous footpaths and trade routes.[23] Throughout the eighteenth and nineteenth centuries, their control over interior trade allowed African middlemen to accumulate significant wealth, which they used to expand their trade businesses and to establish themselves as coastal, urban elites. The most successful of these traders, such as the Brew and Sarbah families, rivaled European commercial firms in their size and influence by the nineteenth century.[24]

Based primarily at coastal ports, these EurAfrican intermediaries figured prominently in European records and coastal newspaper and literary culture, and have thus often received more scholarly attention. But the activities of EurAfricans also give us a glimpse at the complicated interior communities and networks of which they were only a part. Individuals and communities throughout the region were part of transnational networks of trade, which connected Africans throughout the western part of the continent and spurred local economic production. Local leaders, who sought to profit from trade networks, engaged in often large-scale mobilization and organization of labor for agriculture, trade, mining, and other pursuits.[25] Labor organization and resource allocation for both local production needs and long-distance trade throughout the southern Gold Coast inevitably varied between economic sectors and ethnic groups. Among politically centralized Akan communities in the forests of the interior, agriculture and gold mining tended to be more directly controlled by chiefs, who mobilized the labor of villagers to tend their own farms or work in mines and controlled access to land and at least a portion of the produce of individual effort in the form of tribute and/or taxes.

Much of the profits of agricultural produce like palm oil and cocoa remained with entrepreneurial cash crop farmers. These cash crop farmers were part of a larger community of indigenous entrepreneurs, who used available resources to achieve individual accumulation and participate in a broader world of export-oriented trade and production. When cocoa production surpassed palm oil as the colony's major export in the nineteenth century, cocoa farmers also had to mobilize and control labor to work their rapidly expanding farms, often accumulating multiple wives and children to provide farm labor and employing local youth and women to tend farms and help with harvest and transport.[26]

The state often maintained a much tighter control on the activities of traders, who generated significant wealth. In Asante, for example, individuals had to obtain the permission of the *Asantehene* in order to travel for the purposes of trade. "Artisans" within the Asante state—including weavers, blacksmiths, goldsmiths, and musicians—were employed directly by the royal court, which regulated access to royal symbols and the technical knowledge and skills passed from through formal apprenticeships.[27] Among less centralized societies like the Ga, commercial activities like fishing and the trade in smoked fish were often also organized at the household level, as both men and women collected, processed, and traded the coastal commodity.[28]

Entrepreneurs worked with African political leaders and local populations to create and maintain trading networks and physical infrastructure. The extension of British political and economic hegemony over the interior of the Gold Coast was hampered by the persistence of chiefly control of these major trade routes. Through the nineteenth century, the Asante Kingdom policed trade routes and carrier paths in the southern half of the Gold Coast, creating what Dickson describes as an "orderly economic and political organization with Asante as the nerve centre."[29] To some degree, raiders and bandits from rival African states turned trade routes into nodes of indigenous competition and contestation over political control and economic resources. However, the persistent British military and political assault on the Asante state throughout much of the nineteenth century more fundamentally destabilized this trade and transportation network. Until the 1880s and 1890s, very little was done to provide a substitute to this Asante-dominated system, much to the chagrin of merchants, traders, and commercial organizations. Roads, railways, and navigable rivers were extremely scarce in the colony in general throughout the nineteenth and early twentieth centuries, and the narrow footpaths followed by carriers served as the main transport and trade arteries well into the colonial period.

Building Railways, Moving Produce: Colonial Infrastructure and Economy

Debates about the infrastructure of trade were situated within the broader politics of nineteenth-century colonial expansion and consolidation. For centuries, rival European powers competed for access to interior African markets along the coast. By the mid-nineteenth century, however, the British increasingly pushed out their European rivals, purchasing and incorporating Portuguese, Dutch, and Danish forts along the coast. These combined territories of British, Portuguese, Dutch, and Danish interest were consolidated as the "Gold Coast Colony" in 1867, and Accra was designated the colony's new capital in 1874. The extension of British authority over larger sections of the interior was not merely a political act. The British administration used its newfound political authority to exert new forms of economic control over the colony's networks of production and trade, building infrastructure and encouraging the production of cash crops.

This form of "economic imperialism" was not unique to the Gold Coast, of course. Across the continent British colonial administrations competed with rival European powers to establish control over raw materials and open new markets for European goods.[30] The motivations behind such policies were practical. Secretary of State for the Colonies Joseph Chamberlain, who began his life as a metals industrialist before he became involved in the politics of empire, understood economic imperialism as an extension of industrial capitalism.[31] In particular, Chamberlain argued in 1893, Britain had to "gain control over new markets and sources of raw materials in the hinterlands of the colonies" if it was going to compete with the rising industrial power of Germany and America, both of which had much larger domestic resource bases and aggressive overseas marketing strategies.[32]

Early imperialists and explorers, who were inspired by theories of cultural and economic superiority, often assumed that European methods could be imported and applied directly in the colonies. The language of "civilization" and "progress" projected the assumed, inherent worth of British values and practices.[33] Political organization, industrial capitalist development, cultural production, and social values were not merely aspirational desires; they represented the very pinnacle of human achievement. Europe, then, served as a model for colonies abroad and a methodological and semantic toolkit for would-be imperial agents. In Europe, the production, collection, and transportation of raw materials were in the hands of entrepreneurs and local farmers, who used their accumulation of private profit to employ laborers and expand their businesses while also supporting their own increasingly lavish lifestyles as members of an upwardly mobile bourgeoisie.[34] Particularly in early colonies like America, India, or South Africa, British officials sought to encourage British settlement as a means to remake colonies in similar spatial, social, cultural, economic, and political terms.

In much of Africa, however, these same "civilizing" goals inspired a different set of strategies, filtered through the lens of racism and the shifting economics of nineteenth-century imperial expansion. Despite centuries of evidence to the contrary, administrators argued that African producers and traders were incapable of engaging directly with the global economy and required guidance in order to modernize or "develop" their systems of production and trade. And yet, colonial officials in the late nineteenth century found themselves with fewer resources available to effect such change. British governance in colonies like the Gold Coast was organized around a policy of indirect rule, which simultaneously sought to limit the cost of empire and mitigate the resistance and rebellion of local populations by co-opting African leaders into the political and economic structures of the colonial state.[35] As a result, production remained in the hands of Africans in colonies like the Gold Coast.

The discourse of European imperialism presented this strategy as part of an epochal shift, transitioning African societies from premodern, precapitalist economies to those of modern industrial capitalism. As such, European economic policies were bound up with justifications for colonial expansion: to "bring light to the darkness" through the saving grace of legitimate commerce. In practice, however, these distinctions were far more ambiguous. The industrial capitalist state in Britain, the development state in the colonies, and the entrepreneurial capitalism of African communities were all shades of the emerging global capitalist system. African producers, who had accumulated significant wealth and power through centuries of export-oriented production and trade of palm oil, gold, slaves, and other products, controlled both land and labor and reinvested accumulated capital back into their businesses in order to respond to changing markets. The limited British presence in the Gold Coast required colonial officials to collaborate with these entrepreneurs. The centralization of trade under colonial authority, then, sought not to usurp African producers but rather to dismantle existing networks of distribution and streamline transportation in order to guarantee high profits and cheap goods for European companies and keep in check a class of African entrepreneurs who provided a significant challenge to colonial authority in the Gold Coast.[36]

Railways, which played a central role in colonial economic strategies, were the preeminent symbol of both the achievements and the structure that lay at the core of the industrial capitalist society that had coalesced in Europe by the end of the nineteenth century. Railways represented not just mechanized mobility and technological advancement; they were synonymous with nineteenth-century notions of progress, civilization, and development, as an emblem of the very notion of a modern, capitalist society. In uniting the political and economic interests of the colonial state, the railways "provided a key component of the civilizing-mission ideology that both justified Europe's global hegemony and vitally influenced the ways in which European power was exercised."[37] The centrality of railways to colonial "technopolitical strategies"[38] was certainly not unique to the Gold Coast. British imperialists like H. H. Johnston declared, "There is no civilizer like the railway."[39] Michael Adas argues that "More than any other technological innovation, the railway embodied the great material advances associated with the first Industrial Revolution and dramatized the gap which that process had created between the Europeans and all non-Western peoples."[40] This faith in science and technology drew on ideas of "improvement" that date to the earliest days of European overseas expansion.[41] By the late nineteenth century, these policies had been refined into programs of "systematic development."[42] In the minds of European imperialists, railways (and other industrial communications technologies like the steamship and the telegraph) were simultaneously tools of political consolidation, means of commercial development, and a justification to rule.[43] The railways were the mechanical and technological harbinger of the industrial age to come. In the process, early twentieth-century railways realized a vision of colonial government that "was focused on resources, revenue, and production rather than political participation," providing the physical and symbolic infrastructure of what Helen Tilley calls the "development state." [44]

These discursive strategies did not always translate directly into action in the often contradictory systems of the colonial bureaucracy. The Colonial Office was slow to respond to demands for railway construction in West Africa. Mining companies headquartered in Tarkwa had been petitioning the government for railway construction since the 1860s and 1870s. In 1879, Fitzgerald, who was the editor of the *African Times*, and Mercer, who was the former Director of Public Works in the Gold Coast, sought to establish a company that would build three railway lines in the Gold Coast. Their plan focused railway construction in important mining and cash crop production zones, including the palm oil and cotton districts of the East (Accra to Kpong), palm oil and rubber districts in the Central Province (Saltpond), and the gold mines of the Western Province (Shama to Wassau).[45] Despite support from Parliamentarians and forty-eight prominent West Africans merchants, the plan was never approved. In part, government resistance was influenced by concern about the long-term costs of privatized infrastructure, which required guarantees of government subsidy and interest on capital investment—a policy that was being abandoned around the empire and within Britain itself by the 1870s. Furthermore, companies that invested in railway construction would control not only the route but also the means of transport, undermining any government control of trade and communications.[46] But concerns also arose out of the particular political conditions of the Gold Coast Colony. Chiefs still controlled land, and large-scale land alienation by private companies would undoubtedly upset the prevailing political equilibrium in the colony.[47]

The unsuccessful proposal of the forty-eight Gold Coast merchants did spur new conversations about the railways within the offices of colonial governance. The Secretary of State for the Colonies suggested that "if a private company could construct and operate railways profitably, then the Colonial Government would do well to do so itself."[48] Government-run railways would garner revenue that could help finance further development projects, serving both the administrative and strategic needs of the colonial state. As such, they reflected Secretary of State for the Colonies Joseph Chamberlain's call for "state-directed development and imperial assistance so that 'those estates which belong to the British Crown may be developed for the benefit of their population and for the benefit of the greater population which is outside.'"[49] In the Gold Coast, government-run railways allowed the colonial state to profit more directly from the produce of cocoa farmers and other cash crop producers, controlling the movement and market of goods throughout the colony. By the late nineteenth century, Britain's competitors in West Africa also began their own projects of infrastructural development, which threatened British commercial influence in the region. The Lome-Kpando-Kete Krachie road in German Togoland was successfully competing with trade routes along the Volta River for the Salaga and Kintampo markets by 1890. In the same year, German administrators granted concessions for the construction of a railway system. The French government in Cote d'Ivoire also engaged in extensive road construction.[50] Infrastructure plans in the Gold Coast took on a new urgency by the close of the century, shaped by domestic, regional, and imperial concerns.

Control over trade in the Gold Coast became increasingly important with the expansion of cocoa production as a primary export crop for the colony in the late nineteenth and early twentieth century, and colonial technocrats sought to centralize the colony's mobility system to control the movement of cocoa. Introduced widely in 1878–1879, cocoa was first listed as an official export of the Gold Coast Colony in 1885. In contrast with agricultural production in other colonies, which was often introduced and managed exclusively by European farmers (e.g., coffee and tea in Ceylon, rubber in Malay), African farmers quickly embraced the cultivation of cocoa in the Gold Coast.[51] African cocoa farmers and traders built on traditions of cash crop trading, following patterns of trade and transportation that had proved successful in the kola and palm oil trade that had connected both African and European commercial interests since at least the eighteenth century.[52]

Cocoa became the leading agricultural export by 1906 and the most valuable export of any category by 1910.[53] African entrepreneurs embraced the economic possibilities of cocoa farming, and prosperous farmers used their profits to engage directly in the expanding cash economy, purchasing imported goods, investing in new business opportunities, and using their newfound economic power to place pressure on a state that was increasingly reliant on revenue from the cocoa trade. The expansion of cocoa farming and the wealth that resulted from its production and trade resulted in profound social and economic changes among Africans in the southern Gold Coast.[54] The injection of cash from cocoa led to the expansion of both rural and urban infrastructure, as colonial and commercial interests attempted to secure transport of cocoa to the coast for export, and this new category of wealthy African entrepreneurs sought to expand their commercial opportunities and to secure and display their newfound wealth.

In 1893, the Colonial Office authorized surveys of the colony as part of a general scheme for the whole of British West Africa.[55] Railways were planned through densely populated and agriculturally rich or promising areas of the interior, including Accra-Kpong, Accra-Apam, Accra-Kumasi, and Sekondi-Tarkwa. The colonial legislature approved funding for the railway in 1896 and construction began in 1898. While early railways were focused on mining regions such as Tarkwa (1901) and Obuasi (1902), the incorporation of Asante into the Gold Coast Colony after 1902 required that the railroad be extended to Kumasi (1903) in order to facilitate administration of the new protectorate. These railways further integrated Asante into the economy of the Gold Coast Colony and allowed the colonial state to assert control over internal communications by providing alternatives to the Asante-dominated trade networks.

The expansion of the railway network was aimed not so much at creating a capitalist system as it was seizing control of it. In constructing railways and reorganizing the mobility system of indigenous entrepreneurs in the Gold Coast, colonial officials sought to undermine the economic power and autonomy of African economic agents. For African residents, it became immediately clear that Gold Coast railways constituted what Tim Ingold terms "lines of occupation": pathways that are surveyed, designed, and built to connect "nodal points of power," "built to restrict movement rather than to facilitate it."[56] These lines of occupation rejected preexisting patterns of movement through which indigenous entrepreneurs had long defined the circulation and exchange of goods in the region, in favor of mechanized railway lines that would "facilitate the outward passage of personnel and equipment to sites of occupation and extraction, and the return of the riches drawn therefrom."[57] In the West, railway systems were "built primarily to serve the interests of expatriate mining capital."[58] Railways in the east would tap oil-palm production and cotton cultivation and facilitate the transport of government goods to the Northern territories. Eastern lines also improved access to the Government Sanatorium and Botanical Station at Aburi so that "Europeans will be able to reside in this delightful spot, coming daily to their offices in Accra."[59] However, this connection between transport and commerce also created opportunities for manipulation and influence among an emerging class of indigenous entrepreneurs. Although colonial officials and European observers at the time heralded the railway as an engine of economic growth and development controlled and nurtured by colonial technocrats, in practice, railway construction followed the movement and settlement of African cash crop farmers who produced and transported cocoa.

Farmers in the Eastern and Central Provinces of the Gold Coast Colony were the first to take up cocoa. As cocoa production spread north and west toward Ashanti and Brong, railways followed, with a railway line being built between

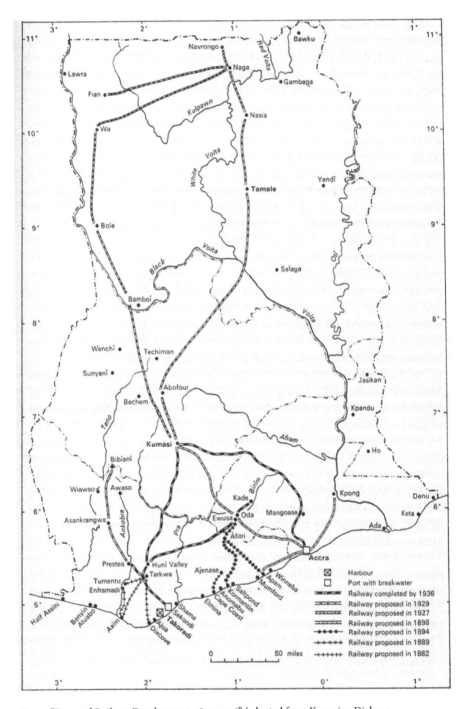

Fig. 1.1 "Port and Railway Development, 1850–1936" (adapted from Kwamina Dickson, *A Historical Geography of Ghana* [Cambridge: Cambridge University Press], 1971: 231).

Accra and Kumasi beginning in 1909.[60] By the 1930s, the Eastern Province and Central Province railways were the most extensive and profitable in the colony. Farmers hired carriers (or used family or slaves) to transport cocoa to the closest commercial outpost or railway station, where the African middlemen of European trading companies would purchase the cocoa and arrange for its transport by rail back to the coastal ports for export to markets in Europe. In order to maximize profitability, farmers clustered their farms near railway stations and commercial outposts, if possible. Those farms situated along the railway line but far from a station or outpost were clearly disadvantaged by a higher cost of transport.

The introduction of the railway revolutionized transport in the Gold Coast by allowing large-scale transport of produce and machinery from interior to coast without extensive labor requirements and at a much lower cost than the older tradition of head loading. However, it also marked a departure from the entrepreneurial networks of indigenous mobility systems, which were symbolized by the tangle of footpaths throughout the interior of the southern Gold Coast. Although the construction and expansion of railways was clearly driven by the local practices of production among African cocoa farmers, the extension of colonial railways placed the state—and, more broadly, foreign interests—in a position of more direct influence over longer-distance trade and transportation, undermining the control of African farmers and traders over the distribution and profitability of their produce. The role of government in planning, building, and maintaining the railways further reinforced colonial control over the dual concerns of transport and commerce.

Controlling Roads, Building Colonies

Given the extensive indigenous networks of carrier paths and traditions of head porterage that had long dominated the region, roads in many ways seemed like an easier and more obvious form of infrastructural development in the Gold Coast. And yet, before the advent of the motor vehicle, nineteenth-century colonial officials considered roads built in the countryside to be experimental and costly, particularly when it seemed unlikely that they would see traffic heavy enough to justify the public expenditure. In a Legislative Council debate on September 30, 1870, the Gold Coast government concluded that "good carriage roads were too expensive to build and were, in any case, undesirable."[61] The lack of a steady supply of labor and the difficulty of keeping roads clean from quickly growing brush made investments in road construction difficult and unprofitable, particularly since the presence of disease-bearing tsetse flies in large parts of the colony made draft animals scarce and limited horse-drawn carriages to the urban areas of the coast.[62] In the absence of any extensive system of wheeled transport, traders continued to use carriers and cask rollers to transport goods through the network of pathways that constituted the infrastructure of indigenous mobility systems. As late as 1899, colonial officers reported that, "Except in the immediate vicinity in the largest coastal towns, there were not roads in the country. The so-called roads are mere footpaths 12–18 inches broad, with the high bush on either side torturous, blocked with falling trunks flooded with water in the rainy season, interrupted by bridgeless rivers."[63] Those roads that had been constructed (such as the Cape Coast-Anomabu road) deteriorated too rapidly to be effective, and the construction of wider roads proved useless when Africans using the road preferred to continue walking single file along the narrow path that had been worn down from use in the center of the road.[64]

By the late nineteenth century, however, engineers developed new technologies that allowed them to build sturdier road surfaces, which could withstand the deterioration resulting from use and weather.[65] While road building remained expensive, the decreased cost of maintenance was appealing to British officials who viewed infrastructure as a tool through which they could reinforce their control over the colony. In 1890, Governor Sir W. B. Griffith appointed an inspector of trade roads who supervised the construction of roads to connect the small port towns that dotted the coast and to link ports to the interior. In 1895, all road construction and maintenance was placed under the control of the Director of Public Works, who proceeded with a program to construct trade roads. These early road-building efforts established a pattern of decentralized road construction and maintenance, rooted in the structures of indirect rule. But colonial infrastructure policy also echoed a general British preference for localism, which had been guiding infrastructural policy in Great Britain itself since at least the 1860s.[66] Urban roads and trade roads were maintained by the colonial government, while bush paths and feeder roads remained the responsibility of chiefs, who were paid ten shillings per mile per quarter to keep them clean and clear.[67]

In his 1901 address to the Legislative Council, Governor Matthew Nathan outlined a new policy for road construction that emphasized the building of roads that could support motorcars and traction engines.[68] Much like the justifications for railway construction, Governor Nathan's vision of a colony-wide commercial road network would free up much of the labor for "other essential occupations" (including the expanding cocoa industry) that had, until that time, been occupied as carriers for the transport of goods between the interior and the coast.[69] The use of motorcars and motor lorries, it was hoped, would not only reduce the cost of transport, but would also "increase our knowledge of the colony and therefore our power of administering it,"[70] thus extending colonial practices of technopolitics. New roads were meant to complement the expanding rail system. Trunk roads built alongside rail lines were intended to bring people and goods to the railway rather than compete with it. Arterial feeder roads connected villages and small towns to the main line, funneling goods to railway stations where they could be loaded and transported to the coast. This interconnected system of road and rail echoed infrastructural development policies in Great Britain itself since at least the 1860s, both in its function and in the patterns of infrastructural investment.[71] Much like the railway, this new system of motor lorries was premised on government control and ownership rather than individual entrepreneurship. Motor transportation was, in the age of commercial firms and middlemen, a potentially new tool in the exploitation and control of the interior.

Early motor transportation, much like the railways, was firmly in the hands of government and European commercial firms, who controlled the means of transport and dictated the development of the emerging networks of roads. European commercial firms had taken up the use of motor lorries soon after their introduction in 1902.[72] By 1903, a German merchant firm (Messrs. Schenck and Barker) had begun importing lorries to be used in their business. Despite increased government investment in road construction after 1901, vehicles only trickled into the country. Only eleven cars and sixteen lorries were registered under the first Motor Traffic Ordinance, passed in 1908, and a year later, only twelve of those were in operation. In 1914, numbers had actually decreased to only fourteen cars and two lorries.[73] In 1909, W.S.D. Tudhope noted that motor vehicles were "largely utilized in conveying cocoa and trade goods to and from the port of Accra and the trading centers of Nsuam (*sic*) and Dodowah" in the years preceding the opening of the Nsawam train station.[74] By the 1910s, companies like Swanzy's were importing vehicles for use in more distant regions.[75]

Early commercial motor lorries were a poor fit for early twentieth-century road conditions in the Gold Coast. At a time when few roads were metalled,[76] the heavy weight of imported European lorries caused dirt and gravel roads to deteriorate quickly. However, it was the low axles of imported vehicles that raised the greatest concern among vehicle owners, drivers, and colonial officials. The low clearance made it difficult for motor lorries to traverse the potholes and obstacles of rural trade roads, and repairs were made difficult by a lack of spare parts and the high cost of maintenance.[77] Compared to the system of feeder roads and railways, early motor transportation proved too costly to make its widespread use commercially viable.[78]

Technological limitations meant that the challenges of motor transport development in the Gold Coast were not altogether different from that experienced in Britain itself, where only the wealthiest members of the population could afford the high cost of the seemingly frivolous and fragile luxury of early motorcars. Henry Ford unveiled the much stronger and more affordable Model T in Detroit in 1908, but protectionist policies limited imports of foreign cars in

British territories.[79] However, when the economic demands of the First World War restricted the availability of British technology, Gold Coast merchants began importing American Ford vehicles in large numbers in order to respond to the growing demand from cocoa producers.[80] Much like the spread of Ford vehicles in the United States and Western Europe, the unique innovations of Ford popularized motor transportation and expanded its role in daily life in the Gold Coast throughout the early part of the twentieth century.[81]

The affordability and strength of the new technology proved popular among African entrepreneurs. Originally developed in the 1910s and renowned for their lighter and stronger chassis, interchangeable parts, high clearance, easy maintenance, and durability, the Ford lorry quickly became the lorry of choice for transport owners, farmers, and traders in the Gold Coast after its introduction in 1913. As Governor Hugh Clifford noted in 1920–1921:

> The appalling conditions of the road surfaces . . . so shortened the lives of motor lorries which floundered over them that it was . . . a too expensive substitute for head carriage. The introduction of the light Ford chassis, however, has completely revolutionized the position. The standardization of their parts and the simplicity of their construction render it easy and cheap to maintain these vehicles in a good state of repair.[82]

The affordability of the lorry facilitated the development of a new form of entrepreneurship that was accessible to Africans in the Gold Coast, but it also allowed farmers and traders to assert greater control over the production and trade in primary commodities such as cocoa.[83] As Polly Hill argues, lorry ownership and operation were some of the only "common forms of economic enterprise which sprang directly from cocoa farming."[84] Cocoa farmers used their growing profits to purchase lorries. In the absence of government-funded road construction, chiefs and prominent cocoa farmers built their own roads as early as 1908. By 1920, as many as 1,300 miles of local roads had been completed in the colony. Without government oversights, roads were built "as and when they were felt to be necessary," often in opposition to government policy and in direct competition with the railways.[85] As transport owners, these African entrepreneurs could transport their own produce to coastal ports, using the network of feeder roads to bypass the colonial railway. Motor roads, which were built parallel to long stretches of railway, connected the cocoa-producing regions of the Eastern Province to the minor but still functioning ports of Cape Coast, Saltpond, and Winneba.[86] These new strategies were appealing to cocoa farmers and other producers and traders who not only sought to maximize profits but also pursued more reliable alternatives to the railways, which were plagued by insufficient rolling stock and poor maintenance as early as 1904.[87] By the beginning of what Hill characterizes as the "lorry age" in 1918, "it became the fashion, for those who could afford it, to travel by lorry for most of the way" during their migrations as cocoa farmers.[88]

The investments of cocoa farmers signaled the emergence of a culture and practice of automobility among Africans in the Gold Coast. This expansion of technology built on preexisting mobility systems while also creating new pathways to prosperity. Roads in rural areas often followed carrier paths, connecting farms and villages with an expansive network of local and regional markets.[89] Farmers, traders, and chiefs were attracted to the alternative possibilities that motor transportation presented, using the new technology to ensure their participation in the growing colonial economy. As the General Manager of the Gold Coast Railway observed in 1930:

> Generally speaking, motor transport in this Country is in a more favourable position to compete with the Railway than is the case in England, in that the vehicles are owned in many cases by Africans or Syrians who obtain them on the hire purchase system and who in many cases actually live in them. Their overhead costs therefore are practically nil, the result being that the larger motor transport organizations find it difficult to compete with them. This being the case the impossibility of quoting rates for goods carried by them is evidence. They charge what they can get and if an instalment on their cars is due they reduce their prices in order to obtain the necessary funds to pay it.[90]

The small-scale nature of the motor transport industry in the Gold Coast by the 1920s and 1930s made it extremely adaptable and reasonably priced. The decreasing costs of road transport in the 1920s and 1930s made it more economical than the railway. In contrast to the railway system, which required farmers and traders to arrange their own transport between railway stations and their farms or markets, motor transport provided door-to-door conveyance of goods and passengers.[91]

Technological and infrastructural change enhanced African participation in external as well as internal trade by extending trade linkages, making it possible for new populations, including women, to participate in trade over longer distances.[92] After World War I the Gold Coast was also home to a much larger population of drivers. Young men in the Gold Coast and Asante took advantage of the war to pursue new, mobile occupations. While deployed in East Africa during WWI, half of the Mechanical Transport Unit of the Gold Coast Regiment received training as drivers. In the 1910s, European observers like W. D. Waghon noted that "the natives of the Gold Coast unlike those of Nigeria and Sierra Leone turn out, I am told, very efficient drivers, fitters and mechanics . . . which would elsewhere on the Coast be left to white men."[93] Many of those who returned found work as drivers in the booming cocoa industry of the 1920s. In 1921, there were 586 lorries and 214 in Accra alone; in the rest of the Eastern Province, there were 303 cars and 860 lorries.[94] By 1930, 4,987 vehicles were licensed in the Gold Coast Colony.[95] By reconnecting farmers and traders, rural and urban areas in systems of entrepreneurial circulation and exchange, motor vehicles quickly became the symbol of African mobility and autonomy in the colony.[96]

Road construction did increase during this period. Sparked by the excess revenue resulting from the economic boom that began in the late 1910s, Governor Frederick Gordon Guggisberg inaugurated a Ten-Year Development Plan in 1919. On the surface, road building seemed to play a central role in this development program, and Guggisberg considered the development of transportation, generally, as a crucial factor in any future economic progress. In the financial distribution, however, road transport was allocated only 1 million pounds, which paled in comparison with the 14.5 million pounds allocated to the construction of railways. Guggisberg's plan did ultimately triple the colony's previous road mileage to 4,648 miles by the end of his term in 1927.

Guggisberg's road construction projects belied the degree to which new road construction was constrained by the organization and goals of the railway. As an enormous financial investment, the Gold Coast government needed the railway to run a profit in order to pay back the debts incurred in its construction and the expenses resulting from its operation.[97] While the railway could be taxed in order to recover its costs, the emerging road network and the vehicles that used those roads proved more difficult to regulate and tax. The General Manager of the Railway argued that, while the proceeds from the railway paid for the cost of its construction and maintenance and provided additional revenue for the colony, roads—which competed with the railway—were costly to build and maintain. Users themselves were directly financially responsible for the maintenance of railway infrastructure through the fees and fares paid. However, the colonial state had to raise taxes on all inhabitants of the colony to cover the heavy cost of building and maintaining roads. Roads, he argued, placed an undue financial burden on the colony, draining colonial coffers, cutting into the profits of the railway, and forcing the general population to fund infrastructure that was only used by a segment of that population.[98] Not only was road transport a form of private enterprise, but it was also largely small scale. Individual or small-scale ownership of vehicles by Africans and Syrians challenged the model of larger companies dominating private transportation, which was familiar in Britain.[99] Enforcing regulations on individual owner-operators required increased police presence along roadways and increased paperwork for colonial officials collecting taxes.[100]

Railway managers found it difficult to compete with the ever-decreasing cost of motor transportation that the expansion of these small-scale transport providers made possible.[101] Tsey notes that the railways were operating at low levels of profitability or in deficit by the 1920s, even with the growth

of operational efficiency and rising revenue.[102] In 1924, the government established a Roads Department that sought to reorganize the road network in the
Colony and Asante.[103] A number of different strategies were adopted to limit
the use of newly constructed roads for the transport of produce, which might
compete with the railway.[104] These policies were part of an empire-wide campaign to address the problems of road and rail competition. Road policies from
East Africa, the Caribbean, and the Middle East were exchanged and circulated
throughout the British Empire, providing a number of possible policy alternatives for Gold Coast government officials.[105] Existing roads that provided direct
competition with the railway were allowed to deteriorate to a dangerous degree
in order to discourage use among lorry drivers. In 1919, Guggisberg instituted
a policy of road gaps that broke up otherwise continuous roads, making them
impractical for long-haul transport.[106] Government also established a system
of scheduling roads, which forbid produce lorries from plying the newly constructed roads at the expense of the railways.[107] These policies had implications
for internal communications as well as trade. Throughout the 1920s and 1930s,
government officials and commercial interests complained that road gaps made
it impossible to move through the colony in an efficient manner.[108] The General
Manager of the Railway argued that "The policy is intensely unpopular with
the unofficial communities, distasteful to the administrative state, and I trust
that you agree that it should be abandoned. Admitting fully that it is the duty
of the government to see that its railway, on which some £8 million of capital
have been spent, are not allowed to become an undue burden on the taxpayer,
it cannot, I think[,] be contended that government can properly continue to
bolster up railway traffic by retarding the normal development of cheap communications . . . a policy of road gaps which prevents the development of normal connecting roads is, in my opinion, indispensable."[109] By attempting to
hamper the growth of independent road transport and redirect produce traffic
and transport of passengers and goods onto the railway, road policies intended
to strengthen colonial control ultimately undermined the enactment of that
power and authority.

The global depression that began in 1929 put a halt to Guggisberg's development plans altogether. Due to reasons of "economy," the colonial state in the
1930s proved either unable or unwilling to do more than basic maintenance on
the colony's roads, even in urban areas.[110] With very few exceptions, the colony's
transportation network, as it had developed by 1930, would remain fundamentally unchanged through the 1950s. The depression, and the resulting decline of
road building, did not, however, dissuade African lorry owners, drivers, farmers, and traders. The effect of the general economic decline of the 1930s on these
indigenous entrepreneurs motivated them to seek out new ways to cut costs and
expand profits.[111]

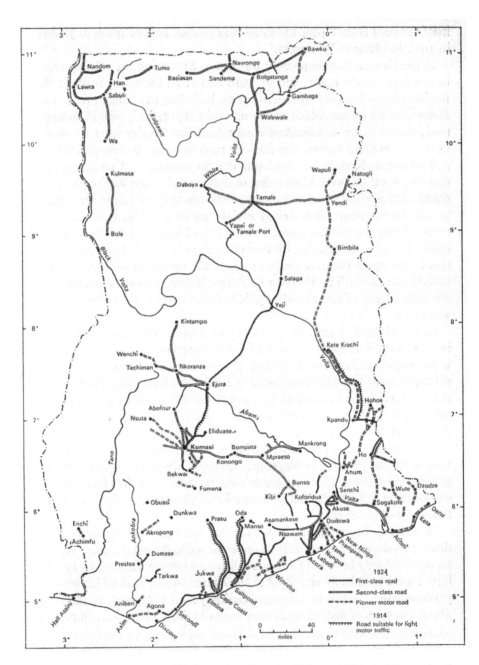

Fig. 1.2 "Motor roads, 1914 and 1924" (adapted from Kwamina Dickson, *A Historical Geography of Ghana* [Cambridge: Cambridge University Press], 1971: 223).

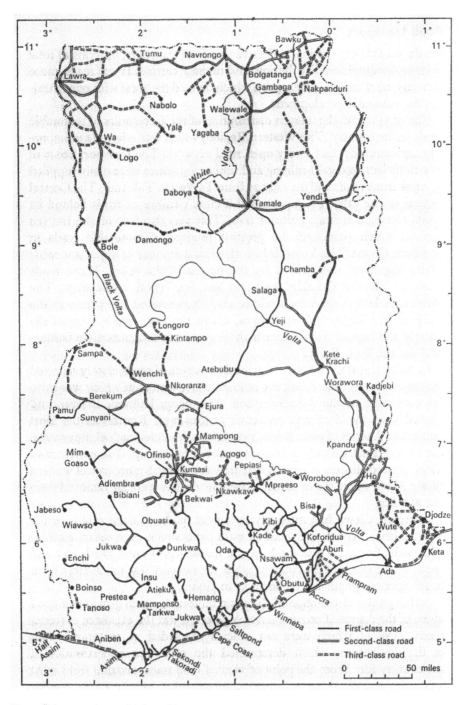

Fig. 1.3 "Motor roads, 1939" (adapted from Kwamina Dickson, *A Historical Geography of Ghana* [Cambridge: Cambridge University Press], 1971: 330).

African Automobility and the Infrastructure of Colonial Rule

Debates over roads and railways were much more than mere discussions about differing visions of technological advancement or economic development. Insufficient infrastructure, slow construction, and inadequate maintenance created a "thickening of publics."[112] Communities coalesced around road and rail, forced to slow down or stop due to the road gaps, railway stoppages, potholes, and other forms of "breakdown" that resulted from both willful and unintentional shortcomings in maintenance and repair. The failure and fragmentation of colonial infrastructure engendered new opportunities, new conversations, and new understandings of space that transcended divisions between rural and urban, village and town. Colonial officials and African residents alike discussed visions for a mobile future. Of course, those conversations were to some degree uneven. Africans had little control over road construction and little direct representation within the political institutions of the colonial state. And yet, in the context of the Gold Coast "development state," the economic practices of African entrepreneurs could provide a powerful check on that state. In raising "questions about the way the state works," Africans in the Gold Coast engaged in a fight over infrastructural change and road design and, in the process, made larger political claims.[113] Thus, when Passfield sent his circular to colonial officers warning about the dangers of "road vs. rail competition" in 1930, he expressed concerns about technological change that cut to the very core of the imperial project. The right to the road, in other words, was not merely a claim about infrastructural technology; it was also a right to mobility and autonomy. African drivers and passengers who asserted their right to the road articulated an alternative vision of grassroots development and localized economic practice that had profound political implications in the context of the economic imperialism of British colonial rule.

Colonial officials were well aware of African discontentment over stagnated road building and increased road traffic regulation.[114] Even as new regulations were debated, which would limit access to roads, British officials suggested that Africans would engage in "legitimate and illegitimate methods of evasion" in order to frustrate the implementation of policy, imagining scenarios in which African drivers would obtain special licenses that would allow them to operate shuttle services on scheduled and restricted sections of road or run goods at night in order to take advantage of limited supervision and enforcement.[115] It is unclear whether those particular fears were realized, but Gold Coast Africans did directly defy government regulations, carrying out maintenance on parallel roads themselves and building new feeder roads that connected villages to the larger road transport infrastructure.[116] In one particularly spectacular example, Akwapim people spent £47,500 to hire an Italian contractor to build access roads connecting Akwapim villages to major trunk roads, markets, and ports over a span of ten years in the 1910s and 1920s.[117]

The extensive community support, labor, and financing willingly mobilized by African political leaders and entrepreneurs in order to complete and maintain these road projects highlighted the degree to which motor transportation was an integral component of African social, political, and economic life, facilitating the continuation and extension of indigenous mobility systems and protecting African autonomy in the context of colonial rule. However, the autonomous mobility of motor transportation also highlighted the ambivalent role of African political and economic life in relation to the logics and priorities of the colonial state. On the one hand, filling gaps in colonial investment in the infrastructure of rural areas by building and maintaining roads, chiefs and entrepreneurs seemed to play their appointed role in the "bifurcated state" of indirect rule.[118] Upon completion of the Larteh-Ayikuma road in Akwapim road, Governor Guggisberg presented Benkumhene Nana Okanta Ofori III (chief of Larteh) with a Ford car in recognition of the extraordinary efforts of the community, stating that "these unaided efforts of the Chiefs and the people showed a belief in the future of the country and a determination to take advantage of new systems of transport that would prove a stimulating example to future generations."[119] Over the ten-year period of Akwapim road construction, governmental attitudes toward these types of indigenous road projects changed significantly. As Hill notes, "An earlier Governor, Sir Hugh Clifford, had shown so little appreciation of the position that, in *German Colonies*, 1918, he had commented that the roads had been built 'to enable the cultivators to spend their weekend in the bosoms of their families' rather than in their 'cocoa-gardens' in the plains (*sic*).'"[120] Clifford's comments may have betrayed widespread British stereotypes about the work ethic of Africans and his own prejudice against road construction, but they also suggest that roads had multiple functions and significance in African communities. While European officials privileged the economic function of infrastructure in the colony, African residents saw roads as a way to connect not only trade networks but also communities.

Indigenous efforts at road construction reflected the private investment practices of rural capitalists.[121] However, these attempts to manipulate and extend colonial networks of infrastructure and communications also constituted a direct engagement with the colonial state, as African entrepreneurs intervened in the public discourse and policies of transportation, mobility, and trade in order to reshape them according to their own interests. The challenge of African mobility highlighted the clear tension between intention and implementation, ideology and reality in colonial policy.[122] Particularly in the Gold Coast, where Africans controlled the production, transport, and trade of major cash crops, the mobility of everyday life was not just a matter of social and cultural circulation, but was also a defining feature of economic exchange. By demanding the extension of infrastructure in the name of economic development and commerce, Gold Coast Africans—both individually and in groups—undermined colonial images of an African subject population and used petitions to make claims to economic rights.

Among state agencies, debates over allocation of responsibility for infrastructural development and maintenance further reflected the cracks and tensions of colonial rule in the Gold Coast. Colonial regulations and ordinances were enacted to define authority and responsibility for various elements of governance. Regulations such as the Native Jurisdiction Ordinance and the Town Councils Ordinance decentralized colonial authority in the late nineteenth and early twentieth centuries, placing chiefs and newly formed town councils in charge of welfare and development in defined colonial spaces. The allocation of responsibility for road construction and maintenance closely followed the decentralized governmental structure and colonial ideology of indirect rule. "Public" roads, the maintenance and construction of which was the responsibility of the Public Works Department, were primarily trade roads, connecting the colony's export-producing areas (cocoa farms, mines, banana plantations) to ports, railways, and markets.[123] The "political" roads, or chief's roads, which connected the Gold Coast's rural population to these main trunk roads, were, by contrast, the financial and physical responsibility of village chiefs and the people they governed.[124] The fundamental difference between public roads and political roads was one of interest. Colonial officials dismissed requests for funding of road construction in rural areas that would "serve only local interests."[125] However, the definition of "local interests" was complicated by larger policy debates over the role of communal labor in the colony. The Roads Ordinance of 1894 dictated that "bush paths" should be cleared quarterly by chiefs, who would be paid ten shillings per mile per quarter. While slavery was outlawed in the Gold Coast in 1874, the Public Labor Ordinance of 1882 protected chief's rights to mobilize communal labor for public works. Even after the Legislative Council passed a new "milder" Compulsory Labor Ordinance of 1895, chiefs continued to utilize compulsory or forced labor to maintain and build roads through their community. In preserving the decentralized systems of road maintenance and construction, which relied on forced labor, representatives of the British colonial state sought to accommodate or reconcile British anti-slavery rhetoric and policy with the political and economic autonomy of chiefs within the context of indirect rule.[126] In order to justify the labor practices deployed in road building, colonial officials declared that short roads connecting villages to main roads were exempt from rules about paid labor because of their "purely local interest." In practice, however, this view was complicated by the reality of the benefits associated with access to roads:

> As soon as a lorry loaded with goods for sale passed over the road to the village, or a lorry loaded with produce left the village for the main road, an avenue to relations with the outside world is opened up, and any work done

on such a road would be work which is of interest to other communities than those performing the work, and would therefore come outside the definition of "minor communal services."[127]

As conduits for trade, traversed by the public and connecting villagers to an "outside world," these political roads prove to be more like the public roads than is indicated in the responses of colonial officials to the petitions of chiefs such as the Temma Manche and the Effutu Omanhene. The blurred and ambiguous distinctions between public roads and political roads created spaces through which rural residents and their leaders could challenge the logic of colonial political and economic order.

In villages some chiefs and their people protested directly to the colonial government, exploiting the ambivalence of colonial legal categories and distinctions to argue that the provision of roads was necessary in order for them to fully participate in the social and economic life of the colony.[128] The Temma [*sic*] Manche[129] recognized the social and economic significance of roads in his 1935 petition to Governor Hodson:

> On behalf of the people of Temma in the Ga State, we have the honour most respectfully with the advice and concurrence of the Elders, Councillors, representatives and leading members of the community to submit the following proposals for your favourable consideration with a view to meeting the people of Temma as far as possible:—
>
> That the road leading to the Temma junction be taken over by the Public Works Department who will, we are confident, keep it in a perfect motorable condition as we are financially embarrassed to meet the up-keep thereof, owing to the poor state of the people. . . .
>
> As regards the road we are prompted to make this request in view of the fact that sometime in the year 1929 the Government was very kind enough to construct culverts along the road to the junction, with a view probably to enabling the townspeople to build up the road leading to the town by themselves to build up the road leading to the town by themselves. This, we respectfully beg to remark, cannot be accomplished by the people successfully and satisfactorily. The reasons are easy to see. The clearing of weeds on the main route for the road can be done by the people but the rest of the work in connexion with the consolidation of the road, as the transport of gravel, which involves the expenditure of money is absolutely beyond the means of the people and it is for this that we write to beg you for assistance so that the Public Works Department can help as was done in the construction of the main road. . . .
>
> There are 8 lorries permanently stationed in the town which are owned by people from Labadi and Accra respectively and during the "Homowo" and Kple Dance festivals, the average number of lorries plying in the town during the period varies from 20–30 a day, bringing in foodstuffs and passengers from the outlying villages and villages along the Railway line and on return they convey fish—besides these lorries, Sir, Cars belonging to both Europeans

and Africans are also plying to the town during the day and especially Sundays and holidays—all these facts make it very essential for the road leading to the junction to be constructed—with due deference, Sir, we beg to mention that these lorries and cars which ply between Temma and Accra are all licensed and the consumption of petrol by these vehicles is a boon to the merchants and therefore in our humble opinion, the little village of Temma contributes her share towards the general revenue of the Colony. We therefore feel that the town should also be given some of the amenities which are accorded to similar villages of its size and importance. This request would have been avoided Sir, had the Accra-Ada Road been constructed nearer to the town, but this was not so, the road having left the town at a distance of 5 miles—therefore lorries from and to Ada do not as a matter of fact halt at Temma and even if one joins a lorry going further east it would not branch at Temma owing mainly to the bad condition of the road.[130]

By reneging on his responsibilities for the maintenance of "political" or chief's roads, the Temma Manche challenged the extension of the political structure of indirect rule to the economic development of the colony, acknowledging the colonial state—not chiefs and other "native authorities"—as the proper source of infrastructural development. The Temma Manche argued that the development of roads was owed to the village of Temma by virtue of its political position as well as its economic and cultural contribution to the colony. Proximity to main roads, which were maintained by the government, highlighted for villagers the sharp contrast with locally constructed and maintained feeder roads. As conduits for trade and economic exchange, motorable roads connected villages and communities and made possible their participation in a broader world of trade, mobility, prosperity, and economic development. Undoubtedly, these roads between Temma and Accra would connect the small village to the colony's capital city and major coastal market and port, providing important economic opportunities for Temma villagers in the colonial economy. However, the Temma Manche's demand for roads connecting Temma with its neighboring city was also rooted in indigenous mobility systems that connected the communities of the Ga littoral in systems of social circulation as well as economic exchange.

While such petitions increased with the growth of motor transport during the 1930s, for some the fight for roads had begun years earlier. The Ayirebi Acquah III, Omanhene of the Effutu State, reminded new Governor Arnold Hodson:

Vis:—Winneba Accra Motor Road. That the Chiefs being convinced of the economic benefit that will accrue with the Winneba-Accra motor road, have proposed to undertake the construction themselves and that Your Excellency's humble Petitioner begs to direct your attention to the following statements made by the late Governor Sir Gordon Guggisberg during an interview Your Excellency's humble Petitioner had with him and respectfully prays for your Excellency's kind assistance and encouragement in the scheme: "I told him that I would make no promise whatever to include the Accra-Winneba Road in the Estimates, although I believe it would be a good thing for general coast traffic to build it when the Estimates come up. It is not likely that the money will be available. . . . A great necessity is felt for good motorable roads to connect the three Efutu-speaking towns of Winneba, Senya Beraku and Obutu Beraku which had already engaged the attention of the people concerned and who had made a start already."[131]

The lack of continuity between colonial administrations meant that priorities and promises often did not translate. The Omanhene's petition makes claims not only to rights to main motor roads that would connect Winneba and the Effutu people to ports in Accra but also to motorable roads connecting different towns in the Effutu state. In contrast to government calculations of profit and loss, through which colonial officials concluded that there would not be sufficient trade on an Accra-Winneba Road to merit constructing a "first-class Public Works Department road," the Omanhene, like the Temma Manche, argued for the road in the name of the public good of his community and the prospects for future economic development for the community at large as well as the individual economic agents within the population.

The petitions of the Temma Manche and Efutu Omanhene were ultimately declined. Colonial officials argued that the distance was not enough to be a burden and asserted that the people of Temma and Efutu ought to be able to construct and maintain their own road. Despite this ostensible failure, the Manche and Omanhene's petitions were part of a large and increasingly powerful movement among rural populations to argue for their right to the road. Social and economic mobility highlighted the false spatial and legal distinctions of colonial governance, connecting rural and urban communities. By claiming rights to the road and using their economic influence to demand that the colonial state provide motor transport infrastructure throughout the colony, local political elites and indigenous entrepreneurs sought to reshape colonial infrastructure to the demands and interests of their people. Protests and petitions for greater access to roads were central to a twentieth century politics of mobility. In the Gold Coast, at least, where indigenous entrepreneurs and African economic agents played a central role in the economic life of the colony as well as indigenous mobility systems of social and economic circulation, these political debates formed the foundation of a powerful critique of the colonial state.

In urban areas, the distinctions of indirect rule were equally ambiguous. The establishment of town councils in the 1920s and 1930s allowed for the provision of some degree of autonomous government. By removing urban areas from the control of "native authorities" and allowing urban residents some degree of self-government, the colonial state transferred responsibility for the public health of urban areas such as Accra, Kumasi, Sekondi, and Cape Coast to the town councils, which were largely elected bodies comprised of both European and African members.[132] As a crucial element of public health in urban areas, the construction and drainage of roads not only facilitated the movement of goods and people throughout the town but also prevented development of malarial mosquito larvae and communicable diseases in collecting water throughout residential areas of the town. In light of a decrease of government funds due to the depression of the 1930s, colonial officials appealed to section 40(1) of the Town Councils Ordinance of 1894, which more specifically empowered the Accra Town Council to construct and maintain streets in the municipal area, while Proviso (f) empowered the Director of Public Works to carry out the work if the Town Council was unable to do it.[133] Such an ordinance did not, however, translate into a complete transfer of responsibility for infrastructure. Members of town councils in urban areas like Accra took advantage of the ambiguity of legislative language as they attempted to balance limited revenue, public interest, individual economic interests, and legal responsibility. In 1931, the Governor instituted annual road maintenance fees of 250 pounds for the Cape Coast and Sekondi Town Councils, which would help pay for the upkeep of town roads.[134] By 1934, the Accra Town Council was contributing as much as one thousand pounds to the construction of roads in the municipality. However, these fees quickly proved insufficient to cover all of the road construction and maintenance necessary in the expanding capital. In 1934, at least twenty-three roads in Accra were in serious disrepair or had never been properly constructed, posing a threat not only to the mobility of urban residents and the appearance of the city but also to general issues of public health.[135] In response to petitions from within the council and from within the general urban population, the Accra Town Council sent letters to the Director of Public Works and the Governor, requesting the allocation of additional government funds for the construction and maintenance of town roads:

> I have the honour to call attention to the dangerous condition of the uncompleted section of Boundary Road. The two ends of this road have been completed for some time, leaving the middle section. Attention has also to be called to the fact that certain sections of Castle Road which have not been drained are causing considerable damage to private property through the collection of rain water, particularly that portion in Adabraka where it crosses the Nsawam Road. At the last meeting of the Council it was decided that representation should be made to Government with a view to asking for action to be taken for the completion of these roads. It was mentioned incidentally during the discussion that the layout of the uncompleted portion of Boundary Road would affect Mr. Kojo Thompson's land. Mr. Thompson, however, stated that in the event of a piece of his land being required for the road, he would be willing to grant the land to Government without compensation.[136]

For residents alongside urban roads, unfinished roads were more than a personal irritation or an eyesore, and, while some African residents like lawyer and politician Kojo Thompson were happy to provide land and other assistance to aid the government's road-construction initiatives, those same residents expected the government to fund the construction itself. The colonial government refused the Town Council's requests in light of the economic depression, citing Section 40(1) of the Town Council Ordinance and instructing the Town Council to fix the problems themselves.[137]

In the context of economic hardship, the principles of indirect rule proved useful in limiting the financial responsibilities of the colonial state. The Public Works Department proved unable to maintain existing roads, much less engage in new road construction. However, in the aftermath of the significant colonial investment of the 1920s, government reluctance to finance construction and maintenance of basic infrastructure in the 1930s was conspicuous. While the unfinished roads provoked protests from urban residents whose private property was damaged as a consequence of slow construction and thus added greater urgency to the request, African members of the Accra Town Council worried that assistance in necessary road construction during a period of economic crisis would sanction a broader decentralization of government responsibility over infrastructural development in cities.[138] The hesitance of action among Town Council members because of fear of "setting a precedent" reflected an attempt to balance the demands and responsibilities of autonomy from the colonial state with their rights as urban residents and ratepayers.

Like their fellow citizens in rural areas, both European and African urban residents also claimed rights to road access based on their social and economic contributions. In controlling the production and exchange of cash crops and other exports essential to the success of the Gold Coast economy, rural residents made important, if slightly more indirect, contributions to the economic vitality, success, and stability of the colony. While rural entrepreneurs paid some fees to participate in this colonial sphere of economic exchange, most of the political and economic regulation of the rural parts of the colony were controlled by chiefs, who were compensated for their work by the colonial government and who used their position to collect taxes from rural residents. However, Africans living in urban areas were subject to the more direct rule of colonial governments. Property owners paid taxes directly to the colonial state, constituting a class of "ratepayers" whose financial contributions supported urban infrastructure.[139]

Many Gold Coast Africans were attracted to the prestige, opportunities, wealth, and resources available in major towns such as Accra, Kumasi, Cape Coast, and Sekondi. Elite Africans, merchants, and commercial firms located in emerging cities like Accra eagerly embraced projects of colonial restructuring and town planning, which would make a modern, Westernized lifestyle possible.

Surrounding themselves with imported commercial goods, driving around town in cars, supporting a large retinue of family and employees, living in grand houses, and participating in the politics of colonialism, these merchants, commercial interests, and urban elites were concerned that their houses and businesses and the roads leading to them befit their status.[140] In a letter to the Colonial Secretary in 1935, representatives of the Rumball Trading Company Limited complained:

> The conditions of Orgle Street can only be described as scandalous, and the fact that nothing has been done to effect essential repairs since the MCR's very urgent recommendations to the Town Council in May 1934, implies gross neglect on the part of Authority. As will be seen from the Town Engineer's letter, no reason is offered for the continued neglect of the street. We are told by Mr. Sutherland that the matter will be tabled at the meeting of the Town Council on 12th instant, but it remains to be seen whether any constructive action will immediately follow. The rights of ratepayers are secondary to the considerations of health, and we do assure you that in the rainy season, Orgle Street is a menace to the entire town, being a vast area of breeding pools for mosquito larvae.[141]

Much like the chiefs' petitions, the Rumball Trading Company articulated their grievances in terms of their economic contributions to the colony. In the same way that village proximity to a main road motivated petitions for state-sponsored road improvement, urban residents demanded equal distribution of infrastructure and the guarantee of a certain quality of life as a right conferred on ratepayers. As the Rumball Trading Company argued, "Quite apart from considerations of health, the residents of Orgle Street have equal rights with those here fortunate rate-payers who have houses and stores in those thoroughfares which are blessed with constant attention by leveling and tar-spraying squads."[142] The Rumball Trading Company proved dogged in their pursuit of road construction, sending a number of letters to members of the Accra Town Council and the Governor and using their contacts within government in an attempt to realize their demands. While concern over sanitation led to the filling of potholes with ashes and gravel, officials at various levels of the colonial state appeared unconcerned about the improvements requested by the company.[143] Lack of action became even more apparent to urban residents when they witnessed road repairs on main thoroughfares and in European residential areas, which were considered more important in the colonial state's scheme of infrastructural development and town planning, while their own residential roads in the newly emerging African suburbs remained uncompleted.

As the colony's cities expanded, concerns about infrastructural development and road construction increasingly consumed the attention of the state. The Public Works Department was unable to keep up with the rapid pace of growth of the residential areas in colonial towns.[144] By the 1920s and 1930s, migrants increasingly favored the major coastal towns of Accra and Sekondi-Takoradi, where railway, road, and port construction concentrated almost all of the colony's business and entrepreneurial opportunities, over the older ports such as Cape Coast.[145] As the colonial capital, Accra had a population of only 17,892 in 1901, significantly less than the population of Cape Coast, which had increased to 28,984 by 1901. By 1931, however, Accra's population had increased to 61,558. Sekondi-Takoradi's population grew at a similar rate after the construction of the railway, and in 1931 it had a population of 26,041.[146] Urban growth transformed Accra and Sekondi-Takoradi into cities, with newly developing residential suburbs connected via roads to an urban center. In Accra, a European residential area known as "Ridge" was established in the 1910s, and African suburbs such as Adabraka, New Town, and Riponsville were also developed in the 1910s as Africans began settling outside of the old urban center and town improvement projects attempted to decongest the old Ga towns.[147] These new residential settlements and neighborhoods solidified before roads and drainage could be constructed. The lack of funds in the interwar period made planned development sporadic and gradual, and urban residents became increasingly frustrated that their investment in a modern, urban life was being hampered by a financially paralyzed colonial state. When the residents of Kofi Oku Road witnessed improvement in their neighborhood, they used this information to make their own claims on the state:

> We the undersigned, owners and occupiers of houses in Kofi Oku Road in James Town, beg to invite your attention to the condition of this road which has apparently escaped the notice of those responsible for its maintenance. The importance of the Road can be appreciated from the fact that it runs from the Horse Road near the Palladium to the London Market, but for a number of years no repairs have been done to it and at every rainy season old cavities are deepened while new ones are cut and the road has consequently become dangerous not only to pedestrians but also to vehicles especially at night. The Road also boasts of a number of modern buildings and a few motor vehicle owners but the approaches to some of the houses, particularly those on the West of the Road are rendered increasingly dangerous year by year by surface rain water owing to the absence of proper drainage and it is feared that the safety of the houses themselves is likely to be affected. We respectfully ask therefore that this road be now given the attention it deserves; if it cannot this year be made a tarmetted[148] street with side gutters, it should at least be made safe for those who use it. A year or two ago we were glad to notice the improvement to the neighboring Adedenkpo Road and we expected that a similar improvement would be extended to Kofi Oku Road but we were disappointed.[149]

As the experiences of the residents of Kofi Oku Road suggest, the inhabitants of cities like Accra pushed the development plans of the colonial state just as much as the commercial interests of village dwellers. The increasing prosperity of some Gold Coast residents and their desire for colonial markers of modernity such as mobility challenged the façade of colonial power and control over both urban and rural spaces. By appropriating the modernizing language and practices of the colonial state, Gold Coasters asserted their economic rights and contributions to the colony and demanded that their interests be represented in colonial policy.

Conclusion

Despite colonial efforts to inhibit the growth of "road vs. rail competition," by the time Passfield sent his circular in 1930 it was clear that motor transport technologies had become an important part of the social, economic, and political climate of the Gold Coast Colony. On the most practical and material level, roads and automobiles connected communities and markets, facilitating the movement of goods and people throughout the colony. African chiefs, farmers, and traders who adopted these new infrastructural technologies built on preexisting networks of mobility and economic exchange. After all, people in the region had been engaged in export-oriented farming and trade for centuries as part of indigenous mobility systems and long-distance trade networks. African entrepreneurs used new technological tools like motor transportation to enhance these systems. Producers could move their products faster, traders could travel farther, and communities could engage more directly in the processes of global capitalism. But motor transport technologies and infrastructures also had social consequences. Distant communities were connected in new ways through more regular interaction. For young men and women, lorries laden with cocoa increasingly represented new occupational possibilities as drivers and traders, pursuing lives defined by movement. By the 1930s, African entrepreneurs participated in an emerging culture and practice of automobility, which was subtly reshaping social and economic opportunities in the colony.

In the context of British colonial rule, this form of grassroots development had profound political consequences. Infrastructural technology was more than a form of economic development or investment for British colonial rulers in the Gold Coast. Colonial investment in the railways was a technopolitical strategy, which sought to undermine the power of African producers and traders by centralizing the movement of goods throughout the colony. Railways were a powerful symbol of European technological, economic, and cultural superiority. When African entrepreneurs pursued alternative technologies and developed their own form of road transport infrastructure, then, they not only challenged colonial visions for economic development but they also raised questions about the colonial project itself. As chiefs constructed roads that competed with railway lines, local communities maintained roads when the colonial state left them to deteriorate, and drivers negotiated their way around "road gaps," these African entrepreneurs highlighted the limited power of the colonial state to enforce their authority and the power and resources of local communities to pursue and protect local interests. Rural and urban dwellers who petitioned the colonial state for the right to the road provided a more direct challenge to colonial governance, demanding access to resources and representation.

The infrastructure and technology of mobility provided a powerful new language through which both Africans and Europeans contested the terms of colonial presence in the Gold Coast. Colonial concerns about "road vs. rail competition" highlight the degree to which the rhetoric of the "civilizing project" and concomitant notions of progress, development, and European superiority obscured the frequent failures and contradictions of the colonial project on the ground. Those failures were no less obvious to colonial officials and African subjects than they are to contemporary scholars who reassemble those contradictions through the archives. By the 1930s, officials at every level—from the General Manager of the Railway to the Secretary of State for the Colonies—acknowledged that the railways were, essentially, a lost cause. Chiefs who constructed roads in rural areas, drivers who dodged road blockages, local communities who maintained deteriorating roads, and rural and urban dwellers who petitioned the colonial state for the right to the road simultaneously exploited these "cracks in the imperial façade" and widened them. In doing so, African entrepreneurs did not reject participation in the economy of colonial capitalism or reject industrial technologies. Much like individuals throughout the Gold Coast and across the continent, automobile Africans "did not experience these developments in a reactionary fashion, but rather they actively sought to understand and affect them."[150] As such, their actions cannot be merely understood as either resistance or appropriation. Rather, in establishing a culture and practice of automobility in the Gold Coast, African entrepreneurs were "active progenitors of transition and change."[151]

African automobility challenges us to reframe the politics of colonialism as a series of self-interested contestations, negotiations, and investments.[152] But debates about "road vs. rail competition" should also remind us that African success in reshaping colonial social and economic structures did not guarantee that British colonial officials gave in to African pressure or gave up their visions for a hegemonic colonial state. African political leaders and urban residents who petitioned the colonial government demanding better road construction and maintenance often found that their requests were ignored. Even as late as 1939, British officials continued to seek out new ways to inhibit African motor transport and funnel traffic and trade into the railways. In other words, African demands often motivated European colonizers to create new strategies and suspend assumptions in order to more productively and successfully execute their visions in the colonies.[153] In the Gold Coast, the growing realization of the power of automobility sparked new conversations about regulation and control of the African industry.

2 "Honest Labor": Public Safety, Private Profit, and the Professionalization of Drivers, 1930–1945

In 1935, EXPERIENCED drivers, local politicians, and religious officials gathered under palm trees along the beach in La, an eastern suburb of Accra, to inaugurate a new drivers' union. The new members designated a chief driver and a linguist (with his own linguist's staff, topped with a lorry), who were to facilitate the work of the union, and the new officers swore an oath on a steering wheel.[1] In some ways, this was an extraordinary event. La was widely considered to be the headquarters of driver training in the colony. Nearly every La household was connected to a driver, and the skills of driving were passed down from generation to generation. Drivers from all over the city still maintain that La could lay claim to "License No. 1," or the first driving license granted to an African driver, and the training provided by master drivers in the town was well respected by colonial officials and passengers alike. The structure of the union highlighted the social and cultural significance of driving in La, drawing from practices of chieftaincy that were widespread throughout the southern Gold Coast by the early twentieth century. The community elected the "chief driver" from among all eligible master drivers, and he worked with the linguist and other master drivers to ensure order among entrepreneurs and mediate between workers and the public. In forming the La Drivers' Union, the community of drivers and passengers in La highlighted the increasing need to regulate otherwise entrepreneurial driving work.

The language of chieftaincy employed by the La Drivers' Union was relatively exceptional.[2] The creation of the union itself, however, was not unique. Throughout the 1930s and 1940s, drivers organized themselves into countless local professional associations, such as the Bekwai Transport Union and national umbrella organizations like the Gold Coast Motor Union. These unions were institutions of professionalization and respectability, where drivers sought to standardize training and regulate the behavior and practices of individuals who were simultaneously entrepreneurs and public servants. In doing so, drivers' unions established themselves as both part of and distinct from the broader labor union movement in the Gold Coast, which organized African wage laborers to protest the conditions of their employment and their place within the society and economy of the colony.

In establishing institutions of self-regulation and professionalization, unionized drivers were part of a much broader conversation about public safety, public interest, and the dangers of the road in the Gold Coast. This politics of mobility was rooted in conflicting visions of the role of motor transportation in the social and economic life of the colony. In securing their dominant economic position over the colonial railways, African drivers and their passengers endorsed a new form of entrepreneurial mobility. For drivers, the dominance of motor transportation expanded the social and economic possibilities of their work as profit-seeking entrepreneurs and facilitated the emergence of new economic opportunities for their passengers. In the eyes of colonial officials, however, the public's increasing dependence on motor transportation highlighted the degree to which drivers were increasingly more than self-interested and profit-driven entrepreneurs. They were also providers of a public service, essential for the social and economic life of the colony. This vision of drivers as public servants prompted new state attempts to control the industry on behalf of passengers and the broader public. Beginning in the late 1920s, drivers experienced a dramatic expansion of the regulatory power of the state, culminating in the 1934 Motor Traffic Ordinance. As the first comprehensive regulatory policy, the 1934 Ordinance sought to place limits not only on the technological and infrastructural dimensions of the motor transport industry, but also to define proper driving practice.

These regulatory and reform measures spoke directly to demands from a broadly constituted "public," including passengers, African and European political elite, and others, working to ensure "public safety"—regulatory debates that echoed emerging global conversations about how to govern the culture and practice of automobility. In the Gold Coast and throughout the auto/mobile world, political elites often framed strategies of regulation around public concern over the risks of the road.[3] Indeed, the danger of accidents on the increasingly bustling rural and urban roads of the Gold Coast Colony was real. The inherent risks of finicky early automobile technologies and poor road conditions were exacerbated by the practices of drivers, who engaged in overspeeding[4] and overloading[5] in order to meet the demands of passengers and increase their profit. For drivers, these practices reflected what Jeremy Packer characterizes as the "productive tensions between safety and automobility" or what Adeline Masquelier argues are the "contradictory aspects of the road as a space of both fear and desire."[6] African drivers and passengers perceived motor transportation as "a process fraught with risky and contradictory possibilities."[7] Drivers in the Gold Coast embraced this risk of the road as a reality that required professionalism and skill—"pathways to wealth and status for those who know how to use them."[8] "Good drivers" did not avoid risk; they "managed" it through expert knowledge of the vehicle, patience with passengers, and extensive experience on the road.[9]

Within the offices of colonial governance, however, the fear of accidents and the risk of the road provided opportunities to assert control over an increasingly auto/mobile society. Early "tactics for governing mobility" included police and technological enforcement of regulations that sought to limit African access to roads—a manifestation of "infrastructural power" and colonial technopolitics.[10] However, as access to motor transport technologies expanded, British officials increasingly redirected regulatory scrutiny and surveillance toward the practices of drivers themselves.[11] Colonial officials who sought to define "the type of man suited to be a driver" were part of global conversations about the governance of newly auto/mobile populations.[12] As American traffic safety pioneer Albert Whitney argued in 1936, "Being a good driver requires the same qualities that are needed if you are to be a good citizen, a good neighbor, a good son and a good brother. That would mean that *learning to drive must be closely connected with learning to live.*"[13] Regulation, in other words, was not merely a mitigation of risk, but rather a way to shape the boundaries of acceptable living in the modern world—strategies that excluded and marginalized minority populations in new ways and made them targets of government surveillance and discipline.[14]

These strategies of social and cultural regulation, articulated through the technology of the automobile and the risk of the road, took on new significance in the context of colonial Africa. Regulations that sought to define "the type of man suited to be a driver" were couched not in the language of public safety, which justified technological and infrastructural regulation, but were rather glossed as "public interest." Tactics for governing mobility in the Gold Coast were part of the broader "quest for the knowable civil and fiscal subject" which "was predicated on fixing African bodies and movement in governable spaces."[15] The language of "public interest" and the infrastructural power of road traffic regulation, in other words, was another gloss for the civilizing mission of British colonial rule rather than any form of essential public safety. The weak practical justifications for this new type of motor transport regulation, which were fully realized in the 1934 Motor Traffic Ordinance, were transparent to African drivers who argued that many of these reforms severely impinged on their ability to conduct business by failing to recognize the realities of their work as well as the broader labor conditions in the colony. Drivers regularly sought to "subvert the infrastructural governance" of new regulatory regimes, and, in the process, negotiated the new risk associated with punishment for regulatory violation.[16]

In the eyes of the British colonial state, drivers who flouted road traffic regulations were not only irresponsible; they were also criminal. And yet, in organizing unions that defined standards of professional skill and social responsibility for the emerging industry, commercial drivers provided a powerful challenge to the rhetoric and enforcement of colonial authority in the Gold Coast. The unionization of drivers, then, does not merely reflect efforts to justify entrepreneurial driving work within the realms of formal sector waged labor. Rather, this chapter explores the ways in which drivers created and mobilized institutions and practices of professionalization, using the language and structures of trade unionism to negotiate the unfolding regulatory policies in the Gold Coast throughout the 1930s and 1940s. Particularly in the aftermath of the 1934 Motor Traffic Ordinance, African practice and colonial regulation came into ever-greater conflict over the rules of the road. As is clear in prominent vehicle slogans from the period—"Honest Labour," "Fear Not," and "Safety First"— pragmatic concerns among African drivers and passengers concerning trade, profit, and safety influenced the emergence of a distinct transportation culture that emphasized respect, responsibility, and skilled training. Through negotiations over motor transport regulation, entrepreneurial drivers created organizations and structures of professionalization that provided new spaces of debate and negotiation between drivers, passengers, and the state.

"Good Driver": Expertise, Regulation, and Professionalization

By the 1930s, a technology that was once a private investment among cocoa farmers had transformed from a private enterprise to a commercial industry. Undoubtedly, drivers' working lives were still largely defined by practices of entrepreneurialism and autonomy. Indeed, many young men were attracted to driving work because of the private capital accumulation entailed. Young men like Joshua Maama Larbi left occupations like carpentry to work as drivers. Defying his parents, Larbi recalled, "I had to hold my driving work properly because if I drive I'm the only person who will be on the steer, and if something happens I am the only person who is going to solve it, so if money comes, I am the only person who is going to handle the money. That is why I prefer driving more, so that is what I tell my parents."[17] For Larbi and many other young men, the autonomy of motor transportation meant not only freedom of movement and control over the conditions of their work; it also meant daily profits, which were widely preferred over wages. Daily profits gave drivers personal and financial security and enabled them to adjust to shifting economic conditions. While their fellow countrymen employed in wage labor occupations saw their buying power decrease throughout the early twentieth century as global depression and global conflicts strained imperial and colonial finances and produced widespread inflation and wage stagnation, drivers continued to profit, adjusting their prices with the changing capital requirements.[18]

Much like the apprenticeship systems that had traditionally served to train young men in adult occupations, drivers developed systems of training through which apprentices (or "mates") would learn the craft and skill of driving work.[19] If possible, fathers or family members identified qualified drivers to serve as

Fig. 2.1 "The driver, Murphy, waits patiently for his turn while his mate cleans the bonnet," *A Day in the Life of a Tro-tro Driver*, photographer Ben Kwakye (Ministry of Information, Information Services Photographic Library, Ref. no. PS/1877/6).

masters for young men. In some cases, families identified masters through family connections. In other cases, a master's reputation as a driver attracted the interest of families and their young men. However, by the mid-twentieth century, apprenticeships also reflected the growing influence of the cash economy, more clearly quantifying, standardizing, and commodifying training and fees. Families often presented masters with drinks (beer, gin, and/or akpeteshie[20]), cigarettes, and cash in payment for their services, which then indentured the young man to the master.

Being a mate entailed a number of responsibilities, including the basic maintenance and cleanliness of the vehicle (washing the vehicle, checking vehicles' fluids, etc.), loading and unloading goods, obtaining passengers (i.e., fighting for passengers) in lorry parks, aiding the master in repairing the vehicle, and other domestic responsibilities in the master's household, including ironing, pounding fufu,[21] sweeping, and cleaning. In exchange, mates were often given lodging and food, as well as training in driving work.[22] In performing these tasks,

young mates embodied what Bourdieu termed "habitus": the practices and structures that defined the "everyday life" of drivers.[23] Through seemingly menial
tasks, mates learned basic problem-solving skills and social practices essential
to successful driving work, while also observing the technical skills of driving.
In emphasizing respectful interactions with passengers, diligent care of the vehicle, and responsible personal practice, masters emphasized the degree to which
driving required much more than technical skill. Rather, masters integrated their
mates into the social and economic world of driving work much as young men
were socialized into their social and economic responsibilities in local communities. Drivers with a good foundational training in technical, professional, and life
skills were more successfully able to adapt to the constantly changing demands
of twentieth-century economy and society, building social and cultural capital
alongside their economically profitable businesses.[24]

In the first several decades of the twentieth century, as drivers were defining the practices and organization of their occupation, the conditions of mates
varied widely and depended both on the practices and beliefs of the master and
the social connections of mates. Those young men who had family connections
in their areas of training often lived with relatives rather than with their master.
Accordingly, payment of mates also varied. As apprentices, there was no obligation by the master to pay his mate. Some mates were, however, given "chop
money"—small amounts of money for food and/or lodging. The most industri-
ous mates saved this money for future expenses, including licensing fees and car
payments. Mates who did not receive adequate training from their masters often
sought out help and advice from other drivers in the lorry park. For some drivers,
these interactions proved crucial in enabling them to develop the skills necessary
to pass the driving test and obtain their license.

Private companies and government ministries employed a number of drivers, and many other young drivers worked for their masters after receiving their
license; however, drivers preferred owning their own vehicles, saving money
while working other jobs or purchasing vehicles on a "work-and-pay" or hire-
purchase system from Lebanese, Syrian, or European importers. Drivers purchased imported engines and chassis from companies and then took the vehicles
to carpenters to construct the wooden body, and then to painters who decorated
the vehicle. For many African drivers and passengers, the hybrid vehicle—the
product of both foreign manufacturing and local construction—symbolized the
economic creativity and autonomy of the African entrepreneur, physically transforming foreign technologies to serve local economies rooted in African mobility practice. The body of the vehicle also became a literal canvas onto which the
driver projected his own identity, values, philosophies, and practices. For many
drivers, the slogans painted on their vehicles came to define their professional and
personal lives, replacing their given names and serving symbols of the intimate

connection between drivers and their entrepreneurial labor.[25] As a driver's wealth and prosperity increased, he might purchase additional vehicles, which he would hire out to other drivers. But the purchase of their first car—and their identity as an owner-operator—served as the foundation for future success.[26]

Drivers adjusted their practices throughout the early part of the twentieth century to meet the demands of the emerging industry and the interests of their passengers. The movement of passengers and their goods was intimately linked to the market, and drivers followed major trade routes that connected productive interior zones with coastal ports and major urban centers. Cocoa farmers, who had been the first to recognize the potential of motor transportation, remained important to this system. But by the 1920s and 1930s, market traders from Accra, Kumasi, Sekondi, Cape Coast, and other major towns also joined cocoa farmers on the road, taking imported goods and other commodities to rural markets to exchange for produce like salt, tomatoes, and yams.[27] Rural-urban trade was so essential to the Gold Coast economy that by the mid-1930s driver W. W. Taylor could argue that "our lorries supply all the foodstuffs for the town of Kumasi."[28] In carrying both market women and their cargo, African drivers blurred the boundaries and strict separations that the colonial state sought to create between goods and passenger transport. The close association between lorries and market women also led to a new nickname: "mammy wagon." However, other rural residents often also joined vehicles as they regularly passed through villages and small towns throughout the interior.

Within urban areas themselves, lorry parks popped up beside central markets, providing a place to offload goods. These parks quickly became gathering places for increasingly mobile urban residents.[29] For drivers, however, lorry parks were tense, as drivers fought for passengers and sought to increase their profits. In many cases, drivers engaged in a literal tug-of-war over passenger cargo or physically removed cargo from a competing truck. For colonial officials, fighting in lorry parks was the most immediate symbol of the disorder in driving work. However, drivers understood fighting as a professional obligation—part of a broader set of practices or values that dictated how to be a good driver.[30] In placing value on characteristics like patience, carefulness, and skill, drivers did not aim at perfection or the elimination of the risk and danger of the road. Rather, these characteristics represented a driver's ability to manage risk, overcome adversity, and negotiate dangerous situations, both in their interactions with passengers and in the act of driving itself. In light of the increasing congestion on Gold Coast roads, such skill was essential. If vehicles numbered only 16 in 1908, by 1932 there were 4,141 commercial motor vehicles and 1,618 private cars and taxis registered in the Gold Coast. By the end of the 1930s, there were over 5,501 commercial vehicles and 2,076 private cars and taxis.[31] The number of drivers in the colony also grew and, in fact, even outpaced the number of

registered vehicles. By 1945 a single vehicle could have well over twenty-five different licensed drivers associated with it, as well as a likely much larger number of
mates (or apprentices) who helped the driver take care of the vehicle and its cargo
(goods and/or passengers).[32]

"The Speed of Change": Public Safety and the Dangers of the Road

The expansion in the number of vehicles and drivers in the colony established
driving as a dominant occupational and economic category. However, this expansion also led to an increase in the number of accidents. By the 1930s and 1940s,
many in the Gold Coast clearly identified driving as a dangerous profession, and
parents often attempted to dissuade their young sons from pursuing driving as an
occupation because, as Joshua Maama Larbi recalled, "some of our parents think
driving is a dead work—like if you are driving, you will die or something. So if
they have children that want to go and learn driving, they won't allow them."[33]
Young men who successfully entered driving work often prided themselves on
their ability to manage the risks and dangers of the road, but the prevalence of
accidents—and fatal accidents in particular—also often put the lives and well-
being of drivers, passengers, and pedestrians at serious risk. In 1940 alone, there
were 651 accidents in the Gold Coast, 74 of which resulted in fatalities.[34]

　　Among drivers, the dangers of the road were real, but they were just as often
the result of failing infrastructure and technology as they were driver error. For
drivers like Anum Sowah, such unpredictable conditions required patience or a
cool head in dangerous situations. A "tire blast" on a hill or some other sudden
mechanical malfunction could be negotiated, but only if you "know how to hold
your steer and the number of speed you're supposed to go."[35] A driver who exhibited patience, in other words, was able to more effectively use his training and
knowledge of the vehicle to travel on the road safely. Of course, patience alone
was not sufficient protection. Rather, the skill detailed by Sowah assumed an intimate knowledge of the vehicle, both in terms of its operation and its mechanics.
Drivers were trained as mechanics or "fitters" as well as drivers, and they performed much of the basic maintenance on their vehicles.[36] In rural areas where
resources were sparse, a driver's mechanical knowledge and creativity could be
particularly important. Drivers like J. F. Ocantey creatively adapted available
materials to survive the long journeys between urban centers:

> I even had to use a plantain skin to repair my water tank before. On old Bed-
> fords, the water tank was like a rubber hose. One time when I was driving
> from the north, I reached Kumasi when the rubber in the water tank broke, so
> I had to park the car. I was trying to search for a fitter (mechanic) to buy a pipe
> and fix it, but I couldn't find anyone. So, I found someone carrying plantain.
> I begged him to give me one. I wrapped the plantain skin around the rubber
> hose and used sealing tape to hold it tight. Then, before I even put any water

inside, I went and started the car and let it run until the bandage was hot and dry. Then I put water in the tank and started the car again to see if the tank was still leaking. When I saw that it was okay, I began my journey again. I managed to drive all the way to Nkawkaw, where I found a spare parts store to properly repair the tank.[37]

Ocantey's experience was in some ways extraordinary (and perhaps even fanciful), but in many ways it highlights the creative adaptation that was essential to all driving work. However, no amount of skill or creativity could eliminate all risk of their work. From mechanical failure to the insults of passengers to the danger of passing wildlife in the event of a breakdown,[38] drivers widely understood that skill, patience, and creativity could only mitigate the danger and unpredictability of the road.

Within colonial institutions the threat of accidents and danger on Gold Coast roads led to calls for new strategies of restriction, regulation, and punishment. These efforts were not merely coercive policies imposed in the name of preserving a colonial social order.[39] Rather, motor traffic regulation grew out of popular concerns about the dangers of the road, and various levels of colonial administration implemented new regulations in the interest of protecting public safety. In the Gold Coast, motor traffic regulation reflected the interests of a diverse, if still relatively elite, constituency in the colony. Colonial officials, members of the press, chiefs, and African members of the Legislative Council all increasingly voiced concern over the dangers of the road and demanded that actions be taken to decrease the number of motor accidents. Public safety, they argued, was in the public's interest.[40] While the state's desire to protect "the public" reflected a broader paternalistic approach to governance not only in the colonies but also in Britain itself—what Lynn Thomas calls "moralizing projects"[41]—concerns about accidents, in this instance, also reverberated in many corners of colonial society by the 1930s and 1940s. A number of prominent social groups, from cocoa farmers to merchants to the educated elite, also relied on automobility in order to access and participate in the social and economic life of the colony. Such concern clearly motivated the creation of new colonial policy as "representations made in the Press and by the Chiefs in the matter of the increasing number of motor accidents and road fatalities throughout the Colony made it clear that some action of a more or less drastic character would have to be taken."[42] However, if the danger of motor transport was easy enough to identify, the cause of that danger was less obvious and easy to define. All of these different constituencies—colonial officials, members of the press, chiefs, African members of the Legislative Council, passengers, drivers, and drivers' associations and unions—voiced their opinion in a vibrant debate about the cause of accidents (i.e., who or what was responsible) as well as the regulatory measures introduced in an effort to decrease the prevalence of accidents (i.e., what could be done about it).

To a large degree, the risk and danger of the road was the product of poor colonial infrastructural planning. Much of the existing road infrastructure in the Gold Coast was built before the 1930s,[43] and the persistent lack of maintenance on old roads resulted in dangerous conditions for drivers. Although these efforts had been intended to dissuade drivers from using the roads, in practice, drivers continued to use the poorly maintained roads, often carrying out basic road repairs themselves or with the help of community members living along the roadside. Even though the state had begun to reverse its position on road construction and maintenance by the 1910s, the financial impact of the global depression of the 1920s and the First and Second World Wars limited the availability of state funds for anything other than basic maintenance.[44] The shortsightedness of colonial development policy in the early part of the century directly contributed to the dangers of the road by the 1930s. Road conditions were further complicated by the persistence of decentralized road maintenance systems. While "political roads" or "chief's roads" in rural areas provided crucial connections for many villagers, farmers, entrepreneurs, and others to the rest of the colony—and in particular to the Gold Coast's major commercial centers—the lack of standardization in rural road construction and maintenance meant that the conditions of these roads varied widely.[45] Government-funded roads also varied in their basic construction. The lack of available state funding meant that the width of roads and the sturdiness of road surfaces, in particular, failed to keep pace with the changing size of motor vehicles and the loads they were able to carry.[46]

In the face of an overwhelming need to restructure and reconstruct the Gold Coast's road transport infrastructure, the colonial government first attempted to impose regulations on vehicles themselves. Unable to keep pace with the changing technology of motor vehicles through road construction, early regulations reflected an attempt by colonial officials to neutralize the impact that these new technologies would have on the transportation infrastructure that did exist.[47] Motor vehicles were bigger, faster, and stronger; "the speed of change" itself contributed to accidents, clearly outstripping the state's ability to respond to technological advancement.[48] Colonial officials noted that the new vehicles with bigger engines, lighter chassis, and greater towing capacity were unsuited to the poor conditions of Gold Coast rural and urban infrastructure. In response, the Legislative Council imposed regulations that attempted to control the vehicle itself and its impact on the road—and, by extension, the public on and alongside the road.

In imposing these regulations, state officials failed to take into account the economic motivations of drivers.[49] As entrepreneurs, drivers wanted to secure greater profits, and the greater load-carrying capacity of new vehicles such as Ford, Chevrolet, and Bedford made them more efficient and, thus, more economical. Regulations that limited the weight and speed of vehicles prevented vehicle owners from capitalizing on advanced technology, undermining investment in the new vehicles and the profitability of their business. In protest, drivers like W. W. Taylor organized to petition colonial government officials. As early as 1935, Taylor, the Secretary of the Ashanti Motor Union, wrote to the Chief Commissioner of Ashanti, complaining that "police have been harassing and instituting a host of prosecutions against motor drivers for the most trifling technical offenses, and heavy fines have been meted out to the unfortunate drivers."[50] For many drivers, these restrictions were "unbearable," highlighting the degree to which drivers were "dependent for our livelihoods on earnings derived from road transport operations."[51] The fines, regulations, and restrictions prevented drivers from profiting from technological advances that made vehicles faster, stronger, and more efficient, and drivers claimed that the consequences of these policies impacted not only the profits of drivers, but also the broader colonial economy, which relied on drivers to cheaply transport foodstuffs from rural markets to major urban centers like Kumasi and Accra.[52]

The governing of vehicles, in particular, attempted to mechanically limit the speed at which lorries of a particular size could travel. While in theory, the use of governors would help preserve road surfaces from the deterioration caused by speeding lorries without requiring tremendous exertion or additional resources on the part of the colonial police to monitor roads and drivers, in practice, vehicle owners and drivers became experts at manipulating the governors and avoiding detection. Drivers (and likely also fitters and mechanics) altered or disabled the governors without breaking the seal used by colonial officials to prevent against such tampering.[53] Additionally, colonial officials observed, drivers of vehicles going downhill would simply place their vehicles in neutral and gather greater speed through force of gravity alone. By 1938, when the Governor of Somaliland wrote to the Governor of the Gold Coast requesting information on their experience with the use of governors to control the speed of vehicles and their effects on road surfaces, the Governor and the Colonial Secretary admitted that governors had failed as a policy and had been discarded in 1935.[54]

"The Type of Man Suited to Be a Driver"

The 1934 Motor Traffic Ordinance reflected a fundamental shift in colonial approaches to accident prevention and motor vehicle regulation. While maintaining regulations on vehicle weight and other mechanical issues, the 1934 Ordinance exemplified an increasing concern about the behavior and knowledge of drivers as a primary cause of accidents. How an individual drove their vehicle; how people rode in a vehicle; how the driver of the vehicle interacted with other drivers, passengers, and pedestrians; and who was qualified to be a driver all came under increasing state scrutiny as colonial state sought to regulate and organize motor transport practice. As such, the Ordinance represented the first comprehensive system of motor traffic regulations.

At the center of this new approach was a concern about African driving practices. Individual African "owner-drivers or small syndicates" dominated the motor transportation industry in the Gold Coast.[55] The competition that resulted from the increase in the number of registered vehicles in the colony in the 1920s and 1930s led transport owner-drivers to further cut their prices to "uneconomic" levels and placed them at significant financial risk. While the mobile public appreciated the low prices generated through competition, the financial pressures that competition placed on owner-drivers also forced them to drive vehicles far longer, faster, and with heavier loads than was safe.[56] Nicknamed "boneshakers" by their passengers, the wooden lorries (or *tsolorley*, in Ga) became legendary for their rough ride and cramped, uncomfortable conditions. However, beyond issues of basic discomfort, the questionable safety of these "old" vehicles and their wooden bodies clearly increased the risk of accidents—and fatal accidents in particular.

The most careful and well-trained drivers approached their work with a high degree of respect and concern for the safety of themselves, their passengers, pedestrians, and other drivers and represented careful driving as an accident-free record as a badge of honor.[57] As Kofi Attah bragged to the Colonial Secretary, "my driving career is 12 years and [I] have only one endorsement i.e., 'driving without light' which in my opinion is the common crime that drivers used to commit."[58] The petitions and protests of drivers like Attah, who responded to the new regulatory climate embodied in the 1934 Ordinance, highlighted a fundamental tension between colonial attempts to ensure "public safety" and drivers' attempts to protect the conditions of possibility for their work as entrepreneurs. Skillful and careful drivers attracted loyal paying clientele. The respect that their skill and care engendered among passengers and other drivers also attracted apprentices, who paid for the pleasure of learning to drive and who provided cheap labor for the driver and/or vehicle owner both on the road and in the home.

Drivers demonstrated their skill not through the avoidance of risk but rather through its management; however, they were also pragmatic entrepreneurs whose desire for profit often led them to engage in otherwise risky behavior. "Driving without light,"[59] overloading, and overspeeding constituted "common practices" among African drivers who weighed the danger of these practices with the potential for financial reward. While some drivers engaged in these calculations merely to enhance their own profits, most were motivated by the need to pay credit installments to the commercial firms that sold vehicles on a "work and pay" (or hire-purchase) system with high rates of interest and high monthly or quarterly payments.[60] These credit systems—with their low overhead or capital input requirements—made motor vehicles available to a wider range of consumers and enabled many drivers to realize the dream of owning their own vehicles. However, credit systems also placed difficult long-term financial pressures on drivers, who had to pay off their vehicles while also providing for what was often a large family including both their own children as well as their siblings and one or both parents. Risky behaviors such as overloading and overspeeding not only had implications for road surfaces and for passenger safety but also for the livelihood of drivers. By pushing their vehicles to the limit in order to squeeze the greatest amount of profit out of the vehicle when it was newest and, thus, most efficient, drivers also exposed the vehicles—their investment and financial security—to the risk of breakdown and accident.

Both master drivers and colonial state officials sought to establish systems of training and regulation that ensured that licensed drivers possessed the skill to manage risk. The transition from mate to driver was represented both in personal recognitions of responsibility and skill between masters and apprentices as well

Fig. 2.2 "An applicant answering questions from a testing officer after he has been tested on the trunk road," *To Receive a Licence*, photographer P. K. Alale, October 10, 1962 (Ministry of Information, Information Services Photographic Library, Ref. no. R/R/3437/7).

as bureaucratic and governmental processes of licensing. The license test marked a threshold for young men—often difficult to pass—which validated their training and skills, opened the possibilities of accumulation that driving promised, and integrated drivers into the bureaucracy of late-colonial modernity. However, for many mates, their masters held the key to the license test.[61] In most apprenticeships, masters determined when their mates were ready to learn driving (rather than merely carry out mundane tasks of cleaning and maintenance) and when they were ready to take the test. Taking the car back and forth to the river to wash, moving the car from the house to the station, and helping with repairs all provided apprenticed young men with opportunities to learn driving work. However, formalized training in the mechanics of driving—lessons from the master—rarely came until the master recognized that his mate was ready for the license test. Mates trained for specific parts of the test, honing their skills in starting vehicles, climbing hills, turning, and stopping.

Many drivers remembered their training and testing as a rite of passage—a momentous event marking their transformation from mate to professional driver—recounting events in strikingly similar narratives:

So we are doing this thing for some time, up to about a year. After a year, we are there one day and he asked me, right now if he gave me the steering, can I drive? And I say, oh, once I have been seeing the way he had been controlling the steering and everything, I'm sure I can also drive. After that day, because I also make my mind that I want to learn the driving, so I started watching him very carefully any time he's driving. So one day, we close from work and we are going back home, and then we reach some place and then he stop and asked me to come and take over. So he get down and go to the back and left me alone on the front. So he asked me to move the car to the house. I'm not sure of myself, and even my own self I hope I can do it, so I spark the car, and when I spark the car and I try and I move it, and when I move it because I know I'm not perfect, I'm not rushing the car, so I am moving it slowly. From Oda to our house it would be about 2.5 miles. While we were moving, the first time I stopped, I made a mistake. Instead of me to put my leg on the clutch before applying the brake, I just put my leg on the brake straight so the fire go off and the car jerked stop. He just didn't say anything. He just get down and say I tried but I should watch him carefully. But truly, it is not easy because when I hold the steer, the steer is throwing me around, but I am also careful and I throw it very hard. We are on it like that, and after one week we close to the worksite again going back home when he gave me the steering again. But this time when he give me the steer, he didn't get down to go to the back, he is sitting behind me and he ask me to move the car. So I move the car, and when we are going, there is a hill that I have to climb before we get home. So at the top of the hill he asked me to stop and I stopped. So he make me stop at the top of the hill—a place that if you want to move the car again, the car will move backwards. So I stop over there, and when I stop the car, it didn't make like the first time when everything went off—I was able to stop it correctly because I was learning and I correct the mistake. So he ask me to get down and I went down, and we went to the back of the car, and he asked me to take a small stone, so I take the stone. I gave him the stone and he put it under the back tire. And he asked me to go and move the car—he's here watching, but I should make sure that if I move the car, I should make sure the tire didn't touch the stone.[62]

Parking and starting on a hill, in particular, was an important milestone for many drivers, who recounted very similar stories of their masters placing stones or chalk behind the wheel and ordering them to move forward. Master drivers used these exercises to train their mates in the essential skills of driving work; however, the exercises themselves also mimicked the driving test, preparing young men to pass the formal evaluations of colonial licensing officers. Simultaneously, young men also learned the rules of the road—when and how to stop, how to prepare the vehicle for departure, proper levels of fluids, when and how to signal turns, and so on. However, for masters and professional drivers, social training or "habitus," which required years of observation and instruction, was just as much, if not more important than the technical skills of operating a vehicle and reading road signs and motor-traffic regulations.[63] While technical skill-training sessions closely mimicked the rigors of the driving test, masters often offered these sessions only near the end of an apprenticeship, after their mates had mastered other social skills necessary to conduct themselves professionally as drivers and to manage the risks of the road.[64] Licensing tests, by contrast, only evaluated the technical skills and knowledge of vehicle operation and regulation. Young men who sought to obtain their license and engage in driving work found themselves caught in between two competing systems of knowledge and occupational training, both of which were necessary to secure their profession's promises of respectability and profitability.

The majority of offenses prosecuted under the Motor Traffic Ordinance of 1934 exemplified the "minor" or "common" offenses (i.e., driving without light, overloading, and overspeeding) committed by drivers—their willingness to risk the dangers of the road in the name of greater profit, relying on their skills and training to ensure safety. If drivers considered these offenses minor or common, colonial officials viewed them as contributing factors to the general and increasing danger of the road.[65] In particular circumstances, colonial officials argued, the accumulation of "minor" offenses reflected a lack of care and attention to driving that resulted in serious and often fatal accidents. The experiences of drivers like Yaw Kumah seemed to justify colonial fears.[66] When Kumah's Chevrolet lorry struck a group of boys and girls who were in the street performing the dance Buntuku in the Asante town of Effiduase on March 26, 1929, the accident resulted in the death of two children—Abena Yawa and Yaw Mensah—and the injury of twelve others, who had to be rushed to the hospital in Koforidua.

Kumah was clearly aware of his mistake and its potential consequences, running away to the nearby town of Asokore. In driving through the streets without lights and in failing to blow his horn when approaching the children, Kumah exhibited a general disregard for the conditions and dangers of driving or the safety of pedestrians.[67] In both rural and urban areas, roads functioned not merely as the infrastructures of travel, but were also integrated into the social life of communities that lived alongside those roads.[68] Kumah's actions were risky not only because they violated colonial law, but also because they failed to recognize the realities of the road as a space of interaction and exchange by both drivers and pedestrians. After his arrest in Asokore, Kumah was convicted of manslaughter, sentenced to eighteen months in prison, and faced five years with a suspended license. While the sentencing court did not disqualify him from holding a license in the future, the broader circumstances of Kumah's case raised concern among colonial officials about his qualifications as a driver. In 1936 and 1938, when Yaw Kumah petitioned the government for the return of his license, the consequences of his otherwise minor offenses constituted the actions of "a most dangerous driver" whose possession of a license "would undoubtedly cause grave risk to other road users."[69]

The seemingly minor offenses that contributed to Kumah's tragic accident were far from exceptional. However, police reports, African petitions, and drivers' oral histories also testify to the prevalence of the more "serious" and "grave" offenses that constituted careless and dangerous driving. "Driving to the common danger" encompassed a wide range of driver practices, many of which often resulted in accidents.[70] Erratic behavior, like that of driver Davis Kofi, defied explanation and often resulted in both serious accidents and serious punishments. Kofi was driving between Koforidua and Koukrom when he took his hands off the steering wheel and began clapping. The five passengers in the vehicle reportedly begged Kofi to stop, but Kofi quickly lost control of the vehicle, jumped out, and allowed the vehicle to crash, killing one passenger and injuring four others. Colonial officials, and drivers themselves, understood drivers like Kofi to be poorly trained and "not serious," and, as a result, severe punishments were considered warranted in an effort to keep them off the road. Kofi himself was convicted of manslaughter and negligently causing harm, sentenced to five years' imprisonment with hard labor, and barred from holding a driving license in the future.[71] While colonial action was motivated by a general public concern about accidents, drivers themselves saw such careless individuals as a stain on the profession, negatively impacting their own ability to make a living and endangering the lives of all.

Drunk driving proved to be a particular problem, even among well-trained and experienced drivers. By the late nineteenth century, drinking had emerged as an important social activity in coastal towns, where "drinking circles replaced the family and kin networks abandoned in rural areas, and provided a platform for demonstrating their newly acquired wealth" among young, male migrants.[72] As active participants in the cosmopolitan culture of Gold Coast urban areas, the status of drivers was closely associated with alcohol. As responsible professionals, drivers received bottles of schnapps as part of apprenticeship agreements.[73] While the presentation of schnapps—with its parallels to the long-established traditions of chieftaincy and religious practice in the Gold Coast—clearly identified drivers as respected and knowledgeable elders, their consumption of alcohol also contributed to their image as "cool" and worldly men. In their leisure time, many drivers joined their friends in drinking spots, bars, and clubs where they told stories about their adventures on the road and participated in popular music and dance.[74] For some, however, the social practices of drinking spilled over into the workday, which had profound consequences for not only the driver's safety but also the safety of his passengers, fellow drivers, and pedestrians.[75] The behavior of drunk drivers such as John Kwadjo were considered most outrageous not for their injury of pedestrians and passengers, per se, but rather for their blatant disregard for human life. After Kwadjo knocked down and injured a pedestrian while driving drunk in Accra in 1935, he failed to stop and assist the person and then went on to crash his vehicle and injure himself. Such behavior reflected an abdication of the responsibility inherent in driving work,[76] and drivers like Kwadjo received serious punishments, including fines, imprisonment, hard labor, and license suspension.

Despite the urgency expressed by colonial officials, African chiefs, the press, and others, the need for regulations to control transport had to be balanced with the ability of the colonial state to enforce regulations.[77] The financial constraints in the early twentieth century, which limited the ability of the state to construct and maintain roads and keep pace with the technological change of motor transport development, also placed limitations on the resources available to the police, the judicial system, and other agents of regulation.[78] Debates over the creation of regulations such as speed limits and the ability of police to enforce those limits reflected tensions between colonial desires for efficient and effective governance and the realities of limited funding, infrastructure, and personnel in the context of indirect rule. In colonial discourses, speed was one of the most important contributing factors to accidents.[79] Officials posted notices and used white paint to encourage drivers to slow down on particularly dangerous sections of road; however, drivers were widely understood to ignore such signs.[80] The abandonment of governors as a means of speed regulation in 1935 placed greater focus on the issue of speed limits and speed enforcement. Colonial officials weighed the increased power of new motor vehicles and their capacity to travel safely at higher rates of speed against the conditions of roads and the safety of the general public, particularly in urban areas.[81] Furthermore, the tensions between the need and desire to protect public safety and the financial resources available ensured that protection motivated the development of creative and sometimes contradictory policies. By failing to change speed limits to reflect the modern capacity of vehicles, for example, colonial officials reasoned that the overspeeding that was already being practiced by drivers likely reflected the maximum safe speed for colonial roads. Increasing the speed limit to an enforceable and reasonable number would place greater pressure on the police to monitor speeds and would likely result in an even greater increase in the speed of drivers.[82] In other words, colonial officials intentionally maintained outdated policies in order to maximize resources while still achieving the desired effect. However, outdated policies also made the colonial government the focus of driver complaints and created an image of a state that was simultaneously crippled and crippling.[83]

While the most serious offenses resulted in the revocation of licenses by magistrates and the refusal of principal licensing officers to renew licenses, prosecutions took on additional significance after the passage of a 1937 amendment that allowed colonial officials (police commissioners, certifying officers, electrical and mechanical engineers, district commissioners, regional commissioners, etc.) to confiscate the drivers' licenses of those who were considered particularly dangerous due to their record of driving offenses. These new powers meant that drivers who had long been calculating the risk of punishment with financial reward and who had accumulated a number of convictions for minor offenses, could now find their motor license confiscated without warning if they committed a very minor offense or in some way incurred the wrath of a colonial official. This diverse range of colonial administrators and officials possessed the power to revoke licenses outside of the judicial system, and their decisions could be appealed only directly to the Governor.

Some officials expressed concerns about their new powers and the ways in which they had been enacted. As one Executive Council member argued, the lack of clear rules to establish when and under what conditions a license could be revoked and a lack of warning for drivers that their accumulation of offenses would make it likely that their license would be revoked placed an undue burden on drivers.[84] Individual officials often had varying interpretations of what offenses or actions constituted a "dangerous driver" and justified the revoking of a license. For some members of the Executive Council, the revoking of a license was only justified when a "serious" offense was committed.[85] For others, consistent and long-term accumulation of minor offenses demonstrated a disregard for public safety. For still others, disregard for police (failing to stop), the personal or social reputation of drivers (reputation as a drunkard), or non-driving-related offenses such as forging a license or erasing endorsements from a license also reflected an individual's ability to drive and their responsibility as a driver.[86]

In a generally ambiguous and contested regulatory environment, it is perhaps unsurprising that the personal power the new amendment gave to individual officers gave rise to abuses of power and complaints by drivers of unfair and discriminatory treatment. Some complaints, however, predated the 1937 amendment. As an engineer transport officer and a Certifying Officer, A. H. Cruickshank had long been the subject of these complaints. As early as 1934, numerous drivers complained that Cruickshank imposed unfair burdens in the examination of drivers. Trained drivers like Adjei Badoo and Kotey Nikoi prepared extensively for the driving test with their masters, who only released them to take the test when they felt they had achieved the appropriate level of knowledge and skill. They were also well aware of the requirements of the test, having gone through preliminary examinations by their master. However, Badoo and Nikoi wrote to the governor complaining that Cruickshank had failed to fulfill their expectations, ignoring basic questions about road signs and signals in favor of thought experiments. Some of those questions seemed more directly relevant to the skills of drivers. Badoo reported that Cruickshank asked: "If a clutch and engine are removed and affixed to a trailer could that trailer move?"[87] While Badoo speculated that Cruickshank had been intoxicated at the examination, it was Nikoi who experienced the more bizarre interrogation. Nikoi reported that "Mr. Cruickshank who was then in charge of the Transport put before me that if 2 sparrows walking on the street how could I identify the male from the female bird."[88] These interactions were not only frustrating for unlicensed drivers who were not allowed to demonstrate their skills, but they were also expensive, requiring entrance fees for every visit. Clearly such complaints (and accusations of drunkenness and physical abuse) did not impinge on Mr. Cruickshank's career advancement—by 1937, he had been promoted to Chief Transport Officer. Even as the 1937 amendment empowered individual officers in assessing the abilities of drivers, complaints about Mr. Cruickshank, in particular, continued. Syrian merchant Latouff Amin, for example, complained to the Governor that Cruickshank was brusque and discourteous, refusing to examine him on multiple occasions.[89] Despite the very accusatory depictions in driver petitions, drivers generally remembered Cruickshank as a "tough" officer who held drivers to high standards.[90] While it is possible that his communication style did not reflect the expected rhetoric of Europeans in colonial society and did cause offense to drivers and betray some degree of prejudicial attitudes toward Africans (or non-Europeans, more broadly), these complaints about Cruickshank also highlight the degree to which the dramatic changes in Gold Coast motor regulation and the ambiguity of colonial regulatory efforts exacerbated preexisting tensions between African (or non-European) drivers and the colonial state.[91]

African resistance to colonial regulation and, in particular, the new powers embodied in the 1937 amendment reflected the seriousness and severity of the consequences that colonial regulations had on the lives and livelihoods of drivers. Even the best-prepared and most skilled mates feared the license test. Such fear was often a combination of a fear of the financial loss of failure and the rigorous standards of colonial law and bureaucracy. As Abraham Tagoe recalled,

> They make sure they test you very well in Accra before they give you the licence, and those testing officers—they are whites. You can't just go to driving school and go and say you are a driver and they give it to you. And even if you fail—they will give you some months before you can come again. Even some companies, if you were not mate before you get your licence they will not take you because you don't know any place. That is the reason why you have to be a mate so that you learn the work very well and you know every place.[92]

The high cost of the test and an understanding of its rigors and high standards made most young men and their masters cautious and hesitant in approaching the testing officer. Many drivers either saved money they received while working as a mate or did other work after their apprenticeship to save money to pay for the test. For example, one driver wove baskets in his hometown and sold them through his sister at Makola Market. Young men would often tell their masters or other members of their family (especially sisters and/or mothers) to save the money for them so that they would not spend it.[93] Drivers' willingness to invest in the professional and financial requirements of the licensing test highlighted the degree to which, for many young drivers, passing the test brought about a transformation both in legal recognition as well as personal status. Unsurprisingly, many drivers remembered the name of their testing officer many decades later and would describe their testing experience, detailing their successes, failures, and the commentary of the testing officer.[94]

Government crackdown on motor traffic offenses led to higher fines, which surprised and inconvenienced drivers. J. B. Cobblah, for example, was fined £11.5 (11 pounds 5 shillings) for overloading his vehicle. Having been fined five times for overloading since he began driving in 1915, Cobblah was shocked by this much more severe punishment and became "mentally unbalanced in the dock when such a heavy fine was imposed on me."[95] Further, the financial burden of the fine brought "hard times" for his family, which included a wife and five children.[96] While driving was seen as a guarantee for steady income, the profit margins of individual owner-operators were small (even smaller for those who drove a vehicle owned by someone else and had to pay a portion of their earnings to the owner). As a result, significant fines could bankrupt a family or place them in serious debt.

The loss of a license was perhaps even more detrimental to a drivers' welfare. While young men could—providing they could access resources that would enable them to be trained in another profession—undergo another apprenticeship, for older men and more experienced drivers, the loss of a license resulted in psychological, emotional, social, and financial challenges.[97] These "old drivers" not only lost their job, but they also lost their livelihood.[98] Those drivers who were oldest sons were expected to support not only their own wife and children but also often their mother and/or siblings upon the death of their father.[99] The loss of a license later in life could have greater implications for a driver when the demands of family and restrictions of age made it impossible for a driver to devote the additional time and resources required to be retrained through a new apprenticeship. Since, for many, apprenticeship had served as a substitute for more formal education (i.e., school), many drivers had little to fall back on, and the relocation that was necessary to pursue apprenticeships meant that many lacked the social and financial resources to pursue such training. They also faced a difficult economic climate, in which the number of skilled and educated workers had far outstripped the available employment opportunities as young men left agricultural communities to be trained as artisans and entrepreneurs. Even standard VII graduates—the *krakye* ("scholars") of colonial society—had difficulty finding work.[100]

"School Boy": Literacy, Competency, and Care on the Road

The embrace of education—both through schools and through vocational training—had, by the 1930s, raised the standards for employment in the Gold Coast. The access to cash in rural areas, which was made possible through the cocoa boom of the 1920s, enabled many families to send children to school. As a result the number of educated Africans in the Gold Coast expanded rapidly.[101] The job market in the colony, however, failed to keep pace with the expansion in the available educated workforce. Once the core of the colonial workforce and the center of the middleman middle-class that were in high demand, by the 1930s and 1940s even those Africans with a standard VII (elementary school) certificate were faced with few available job prospects. Traditionally employed as clerks and storekeepers in the offices of commercial merchants and the colonial government, *akrakyefo* like Ismael Shah increasingly turned to apprentice-based occupations like driving, carpentry, fitting, and tailoring.[102] While Ismael Shah, who had completed his degree, was relatively extraordinary, many drivers belonged to a group of school-leavers or ex-schoolboys. Often drawn to the driving profession through family misfortune or the death of a parent, many drivers were oldest sons who were withdrawn from school in order to earn income. As the petitions of the drivers above demonstrate, leaving school left drivers with restricted options that depended heavily on their skills as drivers. However, the limited schooling that these drivers did receive set them apart from the older drivers who trained them. In particular, literacy (however limited) became an important marker of this emerging class of school-leavers.

This new generation of drivers was the product not only of the increased social and economic importance placed on education in the Gold Coast, but also of the colonial government's attempts to make literacy a central characteristic in an emerging definition of "the type of man who should be a driver." Literacy constituted one of a number of physical, social, and intellectual characteristics of "competency" that were central to the new licensing process that the 1934 Ordinance introduced. "Certificates of Competency" were required before prospective drivers were allowed to take a road test. The expansiveness of "competency" allowed great leeway among certifying officers to define who was "suited for a driver's license."[103] According to Chief Transport Officer Cruickshank, the examinations through which applications for certificates of competency were evaluated were "held with a view to make sure that the applicants are familiar with the control of a Motor Vehicle and also that they know the Road Signs. This will eventually reduce the number of serious accidents on the roads where many passengers are injured."[104] However, in practice, issues of health and physical fitness,[105] height,[106] disposition (i.e., "nervous"), language (i.e., ability to speak English), and intelligence (or seeming lack thereof) heavily influenced such examinations.[107] The vagueness of the new tests and the additional level of bureaucracy highlighted concerns about who was qualified to ascertain the "competency" of drivers as dozens of new certifying officers and transport officers were appointed to fulfill the demands of the new licensing process.[108] This expanded bureaucracy also gave rise to corruption, as some of the expanded number of certifying officers required to implement the new restrictions took advantage of their position to sell licenses for personal profit.[109]

The new literacy requirements, in particular, significantly redefined the accessibility of driving as a profession. Before 1934, the skills of drivers were defined by their ability to handle a vehicle. While this required an ability to "read" (or identify) road signs, functional literacy was not expected.[110] This new literacy requirement—and the broader conversations about competency of which they were a part—reflected an expansion in the understanding of what it meant to be a driver. At the core of this shift was an increasing appreciation of drivers as businessmen and professionals, which not only elevated their prestige and respectability in colonial society but also placed them in positions of greater legal responsibility. In other words, by professionalizing drivers, new regulations made drivers directly and personally responsible for the "public interest," as defined by colonial officials.

For colonial officials, literacy was seen as a necessary characteristic of a good, responsible driver. The new literacy requirements ensured that licensed drivers could read the Motor Traffic Ordinance—the ability to follow the rules required the ability to read the rules.[111] Drivers were now expected to not only follow basic rules of the road but also be conversant with the Ordinance itself and the shifting boundaries of colonial regulation. The increasing focus on the legal responsibility of drivers reflected the priorities of a colonial educational system, which emphasized the importance of "obeying the rules." Educational institutions such as boarding schools and the Boy Scouts attempted to socialize young men (and women) into a discourse of obedience, responsibility and respectability. In the process, these social institutions attempted to shape model subjects that were guided by the "public interest" or "public good." Similarly, by refocusing the expectations of drivers through literacy requirements—and in particular, by making drivers legally responsible for knowledge about the Motor Traffic Ordinance—colonial officials attempted to reassert their control over drivers and passengers.

In attempting to control drivers and make them legally responsible for their actions, the new licensing practices also reflected colonial concerns about increasing numbers of accidents. Many officials saw the literacy requirement in and of itself as the answer to the problem of accidents and the danger of the road.[112] Chief Transport Officer Cruickshank argued that illiterate drivers should not be allowed on the roads, as they would be unable to read booklets that provided the limits and requirements of safe lorry operations or road signs that designated safe speeds.[113] However, some colonial officials as well as African drivers protested that literacy was not a guarantee of a knowledgeable and responsible driver. Literate drivers like Ismael Shah were unable to even pass the driving test because of a lack of basic knowledge about the operation of a motor vehicle. More broadly, the distinction between literate and illiterate drivers was not indicative of the quality of drivers. In fact, as one colonial official noted, "a large percentage of dare-devil drivers are semiliterate, in fact most of them belong to the class of 'never-do-well' ex-school boys"[114]:

> Drivers in this country may be put into two categories: the careful and the careless. The number of the latter is roughly about 9 to 2 of the former. It is not merely a question of illiteracy but the lack of an adequate sense of responsibility and respect for human life and for another's property. . . . I would not go so far as to restrict the grant of driving licenses to only Standard VII Certificate, but rather to <u>sober-minded persons of good character and physical fitness</u>, preferably educated. Full control of nerves, a clear vision and a sense of responsibility are indispensable to all drivers, educated or not.[115]

While the semiliterate "dare-devil drivers" and "'never-do-well' ex-schoolboys" engaged in risky behavior that was seen to increase the danger of the road, colonial emphasis on responsibility, carefulness, good character, physical fitness, calm, and patience reflected the values and systems of training and self-regulation among many drivers. Codes of responsibility and respectability within driving work applied to literate and illiterate drivers alike. While the danger of driving made it an exciting profession with social prestige, for many drivers the regular news of accidents was a sober reminder of the consequences of risky and irresponsible behavior. If young ex-schoolboys had little to lose (other than their own life), older drivers understood their actions to have broad implications not only for themselves, passengers, and pedestrians, but also for a social network of family, friends, and admirers.

The experiences of drivers themselves, thus, directly challenged the clarity and appropriateness of the new literacy requirements. While, as is noted above, drivers had long been responsible for knowledge of road signs, many of those licensed before 1934 were classified as "illiterate." The new ordinance grandfathered in these older drivers, stipulating that any driver who had obtained his license before the 1934 Ordinance was enacted was exempt from the literacy requirement. The continuing operation of old, illiterate drivers alongside the more recently licensed literate drivers provided a direct challenge to colonial justifications of the literacy requirement. As members of the Ashanti Motor Union argued, "many of our best drivers are illiterate."[116] Furthermore, the new ordinance failed to take into account the scores of illiterate mates who had already entered their apprenticeship before the Ordinance was enacted.[117] Still others who had finished their apprenticeships and had been driving without a license for a number of years (likely for their apprenticeship master) now found themselves unable to receive a license.[118]

The internal ambiguity and inconsistencies in the literacy requirement were highlighted through external comparisons. Movement between colonies, in particular, meant that many drivers were aware of alternative systems of transport regulation and licensing. Drivers who moved between the Gold Coast and Nigeria or Togo found that licenses were not equally valid throughout the colonial system.[119] Colonial officials cited different licensing standards in colonies like Nigeria and Togo as insufficient proof of competency. The Commissioner of Police argued that drivers like Codzo Agbeli, who possessed a Nigerian driver's license, should obtain a new certificate of competency to prove his awareness of motor traffic laws in the Gold Coast and his safety as a driver on Gold Coast roads.[120] After 1934, regardless of their previous driving experience, licensed drivers from these colonies had to obtain new certificates of competency. Drivers who protested these variable colonial standards pointed to colonial policies that recognized driver's licenses from other European countries without the requirement of an examination.[121] Still others challenged colonial definitions of literacy that were intended to mean "literacy in English." Prospective Hausa and Syrian drivers, in particular, protested such definitions of literacy, which demeaned their educational and social status.[122] These inconsistencies in colonial policy highlighted inequalities within the colonial system—between Europeans and Africans, between different colonies, and between different classes and ethnic groups within the Gold Coast itself. In the face of mounting challenges and inconsistencies, colonial officials resisted making further exceptions. In the Northern Territories, in particular, sparse educational facilities and widespread poverty limited the ability of many to achieve literacy.[123] However, such exceptions were seen as dangerous to colonial officials, who argued that the mobility of drivers opened up possibilities for the abuse of exceptions and an increased danger to other drivers.[124] Indeed, rumors that illiterate drivers in the Northern Territories were exempted from the literacy requirement attracted a number of illiterate drivers from other regions to Tamale, where they received illicit licenses from corrupt certifying officers.[125]

A more fundamental challenge came from the military, which had served as a training ground for drivers and mechanics throughout the first half of the twentieth century. Military bases in Cantonments and Burma Camp attracted young men who enlisted as mechanical drivers and mechanics in the Gold Coast Regiment. During World War II, as many as one-third of all Gold Coast Regiment soldiers were trained as mechanical drivers, and these soon-to-be ex-servicemen provided a significant challenge to the colonial system of regulation and control of motor transport. In particular, many of these military drivers could not fulfill the literacy requirement of the Motor Traffic Ordinance—the standard for driver "competency" in the Gold Coast Regiment was clearly not the same as it was for the civilian population of the Gold Coast. Facing the impending demobilization of soldiers in 1943, colonial officials relented, passing a concession that would waive literacy requirements for those ex-servicemen who had been trained as drivers in the military. This concession reflected a broader concern among colonial officials about the impact that demobilized soldiers would have on a Gold Coast economy that was already experiencing job shortages and cost-of-living increases.[126] The large number of soldiers who had been trained as drivers would return with few occupational options other than driving. Mobile certifying and licensing boards, which were set up throughout the colony to license demobilized soldiers, highlighted the internal consistencies in colonial understandings of "competency" within the colonial state itself and undermined arguments about the connection between literacy and effective driving.

Colonial Authority, Driver Autonomy, and the Conditions of Possibility for Driving Work

New literacy requirements and state regulatory efforts sought to supplement, and in some cases correct, emerging standards of driving work in the late 1920s and 1930s. Drivers began to institutionalize these standards of driver practice in drivers' associations and unions, and as government regulatory efforts expanded, drivers sought formal recognition of their unions. By 1935, a wide range of drivers' unions existed, from local unions in small trading towns like Bekwai, to the more powerful locals like the La Drivers' Union and Ashanti Motor Union, and umbrella organizations like the Gold Coast Motor Union. Traditions of organization and discipline in drivers' unions were heavily influenced by the practices of ex-servicemen who had learned to drive while serving in the Mechanical Transport Unit of the Gold Coast Regiment during the First World War.[127] In addition to identifying clear leadership under a chief driver, union members also established rules of personal behavior (i.e., how to drive, how to conduct yourself with passengers, how to dress, how to maintain your vehicle, etc.) as well as rules of procedure (i.e., training drivers, resolving disputes, punishing bad behavior, organizing in the lorry park, setting the prices of fares, interacting with the police, petitioning the government, etc.).[128]

In forming unions, drivers drew on a long tradition of labor organizing in the Gold Coast, rooted not only in indigenous systems of apprenticeship, guilds, and secret societies, but also in older forms of union organizing.[129] Gold Coast miners first went on strike in 1919, and a number of unions, including the Gold and Silversmiths' Association and the Carpenters and Masons' Union, formed in the 1920s. Motor unions themselves were part of this early labor movement as drivers organized the Gold Coast and Ashanti Motor Union in the 1920s. However, the aims and practices of organizations like the La Drivers' Union and the Ashanti Motor Union that were forming by the 1930s spoke directly to the changing regulatory landscape in the Gold Coast. The culture of drivers' union and work lives differed substantially from the unionized railway workers, dock workers, civil service employees, and other waged laborers who followed more conventional models of union organizing and participated in forms of waged work defined by British colonial capitalism.[130] By transporting goods for trade, drivers were central to systems of exchange and accumulation in the colony, facilitating the expansion of a colonial capitalist economy. Drivers derived socioeconomic benefits from this system, which they used to establish lives of masculine respectability and prestige in colonial society, but they did so with significantly greater autonomy than other African workers in the colonial economy. Most drivers owned their own vehicles and controlled the profits from their business. In transporting both goods and people throughout the colony, drivers operated as indigenous entrepreneurs, facilitating the connections and mobility of overlapping entrepreneurial networks of farmers, traders, chiefs, and others. Unions represented drivers' efforts to self-regulate and define the standards of professionalism in their work. However, in the wake of the 1934 Ordinance, drivers increasingly used the union framework to protect the values of autonomy, mobility, and entrepreneurialism, which were important to both them and their passengers, from the manipulations of colonial officials.

As individuals and through their union representatives, drivers petitioned chiefs, regional commissioners, the Colonial Secretary, and the Governor in an attempt to protect what they understood as the conditions of possibility for their work. Provision of roads and other relevant infrastructure and technology of motor transportation were, of course, essential for their work, and representatives of the Ashanti Motor Union's 1937 petition to the Colonial Secretary complained that the institutions of the colonial state in Kumasi, including the Kumasi Public Health Board and the police, were limiting access to important roads and were unfairly applying the law to African drivers. Likewise, they complained that local commercial firms were artificially inflating the price of petrol above government control prices. But, for drivers, those conditions could not be disconnected from the autonomy and mobility inherent in driving work. Union Secretary W. W. Taylor argued that while Asante drivers were "dependent for our livelihood on earnings derived from road transport operations carried out *under the laws of the Government*," those laws often did not take into account the realities of driver practice.[131] Drivers in Asante and elsewhere increasingly found themselves subject to laws that criminalized practices that had once been common, and often even necessary, to driving work. Some practices like overspeeding and overloading were indeed calculated risks that often increased the danger of the road. However, as Asante drivers complained, police also charged drivers with "obstruction" when they stopped in the streets to load goods for their passengers in front of stores and homes. Taylor and others argued that these types of laws, which were enshrined in the 1934 and 1937 Motor Traffic Ordinances, empowered harassment by "ignorant and overzealous constables," and he begged "for the Motor Driver to be treated as a friend of the police and not as an Ishmael to be harassed and suppressed by every means at their disposal."[132] Drivers, in short, should be left to do their work.

Unions were not always successful in their petitions—the 1934 Ordinance stood, Chief Transport Officer Cruickshank kept his job (and was even promoted), and literacy requirements remained in force throughout the colonial period, even as some exceptions were made. And, for some drivers, obeying the law became just as important a part of the definition of a "good driver" as apprenticeship or fitting or fighting.[133] But drivers' petitions were considered and provoked serious conversation among colonial administrators seeking to understand and implement the new ordinances under strict budget constraints and popular calls to ensure public safety. For many of those administrators, unions appeared to be an ideal manifestation of indirect rule among the increasingly urbanized population of workers—decentralized authority even at the centers of colonial capitalism. However, drivers' appropriation of the union model and their attempts to negotiate with the state highlight the ambivalence of their position and the tension between driving as an entrepreneurial activity and a public

service. Particularly as motor transportation replaced other forms of commer-
cialized mobility, it became clear that driver practice could not be motivated
by profit alone. Much like chiefs, clerks, and other intermediaries who engaged
with the colonial state in order to protect their interests, unionized drivers found
themselves increasingly beholden to the colonial state even as they tried to limit
its influence.[134]

The formal recognition of drivers' unions fundamentally altered their role
in colonial politics and gave drivers more direct access to state officials and the
power to negotiate or bargain on behalf of their members. However, more explicit
acknowledgement and engagement with unions was also part of a broader colonial or imperial strategy. Concerned about the strikes of railway workers and
other types of labor unrest across the continent in the 1930s and pressured by a
British Labour Party government, colonial officials in the Gold Coast and elsewhere brought trade unionists to train workers in union organization.[135] Government officials in Britain and the Gold Coast argued that the labor unrest was
the result of lack of organization and training among early unions in the art of
collective bargaining, which lay at the foundation of British trade unionism.[136]
Eager to curb strikes that were crippling the colonial economy, trade unionists
arranged "education" sessions for African union officials and sponsored representatives of the largest unions to travel to Britain for more advanced training.[137]
In order to facilitate collective bargaining and to maintain some control over
emerging workers' organizations, colonial officials encouraged the centralization
of smaller unions into larger umbrella structures, which were then registered
with the government beginning in the early 1940s.

Such efforts were geared toward limiting the influence of the radical politics
of people like Bankole Awooner-Renner and I.T.A. Wallace-Johnson, who sought
to organize workers into unions as part of a broader political project of antico-
lonial resistance.[138] However, the formal recognition and registration of trade
unions also enabled colonial officials to better control and influence the politics
of labor organization in the colony. Colonial officials would negotiate only with
those unions officially registered with the government, making it difficult for new
unions to influence negotiations and enabling the colonial state to marginalize
more radical unions in the bargaining process.[139] Entrepreneurial drivers, who
directly experienced the consequences of government reforms and regulations,
constituted two of the first four unions to register with the government in 1942.[140]

Much of the collective bargaining and union organizing of workers in the
colonial economy involved the state directly. Colonial capitalism, which centralized economic authority and wealth, privileged the state as the primary source
of both jobs and capital.[141] For state employees, like railway workers, collective
bargaining over wages, benefits, and working conditions required negotiations
with colonial officials. Drivers, by contrast, represented a very different kind of

worker in the colonial capitalist economy. As self-employed entrepreneurs, drivers were not "employees" and received neither wages nor benefits directly from the colonial state. However, state actions often produced dramatic changes in the working conditions and profit margins of drivers. As the first real attempt to regulate driver practice, the 1934 Motor Traffic Ordinance marked one of the earliest examples of this relationship, mobilizing drivers across the country to protest government regulations.[142]

Out of frustration, all drivers in Accra finally went on strike in 1938. Chief among their complaints was the inadequate provision of lorry parks, which reflected neither the extent of the driver population in the city nor the ways in which people in Accra used lorries.[143] The mobility made possible by motor transportation resulted in increasing numbers of traders bringing goods to sell in the large markets of major urban centers such as Accra.[144] These traders and the mammy trucks/wagons that bore them overwhelmed existing lorry parks, forcing drivers to park illegally in the streets surrounding the city's major market.[145] Furthermore, alternative markets such as London Market and Salaga Meat Market developed in various parts of the expanding city, and traders in these new markets demanded motor transport to carry their goods.[146] The colonial government quickly responded to the striking motor drivers' demands—seeking out land for new lorry parks and expanding existing lorry parks. Not all strikes were successful, however. As Joshua Maama Larbi recalled, Atta Odai, the Chief Driver of the Gold Coast Motor Union, rallied drivers to protest increases in the price of petrol by refusing to drive in the late 1940s. When some drivers refused to participate, Larbi and others went to a road outside of town to stop vehicles. The drivers stopped one vehicle driven by a British man, who reported them to the police for intimidation, and they were quickly rounded up and taken to the Cantonments Police Station in Accra, where Odai arranged for their release. While Larbi's strike action was less successful, these sorts of activities brought the unions to the attention of government officials and police. As Larbi recalled, "Before he [Odai] bailed us out, the Chief Driver let the policemen know that a union had been formed, so that the policemen understood his position before they talked about the issue at hand."[147] Thus, while union organizing among drivers did not necessarily result in profound policy changes, it did imbue their leadership with a degree of legitimacy that could facilitate new cooperation between drivers and local government officials.

Colonial officials considered these early strikes troublesome because of the economic impact of the strike—a clear indicator of the degree to which the colony had become reliant on motor transportation to facilitate movement both between and within rural and urban areas. The success of the strike required a strong network of social support from passengers and the broader community.[148] Social sanction of driver protests was rooted in their identity as representatives of working-class African communities as well as the role that motor transportation played in facilitating the growth and prosperity of local economies in both rural and urban areas. Unions in La and Teshie appropriated the symbols of chieftaincy, and the social and political legitimacy that such symbols implied, to highlight the public responsibilities of drivers and the importance of their role in local communities. The head of the union was known as the "chief driver." Chief drivers were confirmed in their office through a public ceremony, in which the La Manche (chief) (and sometimes even also the Ga Manche or Ga paramount chief), colonial government officials (such as the District Commissioner of Accra), and the larger La community gathered at union offices to witness the new chief driver swearing an oath on a steering wheel.[149] This very public investiture emphasized the responsibility that drivers—and in particular the chief driver— had to protect and ensure the safety and interests of the larger community.[150] Chief drivers also appropriated the material culture of chieftaincy, appearing in photos wearing leopard hats and fly whisks, and speaking through a "linguist," who represented the chief driver in public appearances and carried his own linguist's staff at public ceremonies, topped with a wooden image of a mammy truck to represent the "clan" of the drivers.[151]

The La Drivers' Union's structure drew directly from the structure of chieftaincy, which, as an "invented tradition" among Ga communities, had characterized political organization in La and greater Accra since at least the mid-nineteenth century.[152] By appropriating and mobilizing the language and symbols of chieftaincy, motor transport unions in La and Teshie explicitly allied themselves with the people—establishing themselves as the guardians and protectors of the community and their interests. Colonial state regulations of motor transportation that were enacted in what colonial officials understood as the "public interest" failed to grasp not only how drivers were trained and ran their business but also what kind of services the public valued. However, the appropriation of the material and symbolic culture of chieftaincy was only the most superficial and visible example of a much broader connection between drivers and local economic and cultural practice. As is clear in the 1938 strike, in organizing themselves into unions and protesting these state regulations, motor transport drivers acted to protect not only their interests but also, perhaps more indirectly, the economic interests and values of their passengers and the broader culture of work of which they were a part.

Conclusion

By the 1930s, drivers were firmly established as a major professional class in the Gold Coast, central to both indigenous and local economies. Over the course of several decades, driving work shifted from a disorganized, decentralized entrepreneurial activity to a thoroughly professionalized and unionized public service. The "honest labor" of drivers was not merely a question of hard work. Rather, the regulation of motor transportation highlights the degree to which both of these terms (honest *and* labor) were contested in the Gold Coast by numerous competing and overlapping constituencies. Drivers themselves sought to professionalize their work, creating cultures, economies, and institutions of driving that standardized and regulated their interactions with both passengers and the state and established broad-based understandings of what it meant to be a "good driver." However, in providing a public service, drivers also found themselves subject to public debates and state regulation. In asserting "the type of man who should be a driver," state regulations attempted to limit driver autonomy in the name of public safety.

Drivers' unions were, in many ways, the products of these debates. Drivers formed unions in an attempt to contest colonial regulations and protect the conditions of possibility of driving work. Unions, which were formally recognized by and registered with the colonial government, used their position to negotiate the boundaries of crime and punishment, accumulation and dispossession. These negotiations were not always successful, but the very inclusion of drivers in the negotiating process was a reflection of the degree to which commercial automobility had become such a central part of the social, cultural, and economic life of the colony. However, the unionization and broader professionalization of drivers also highlighted that motor transportation was no longer a purely entrepreneurial activity. In securing the right to roads, drivers transformed themselves into public servants and, in many ways, reluctant intermediaries. In vigorously debating public safety and the regulation of drivers, the colonial state, the African public, and drivers' unions all implicitly recognized that drivers provided an essential public service at the same time that they pursued private profit.

In forming unions, registering with the government, and engaging in negotiations over regulation, drivers acknowledged the increasing role of the state in shaping driving practice. The autonomy of drivers was, in very real ways, circumscribed by a series of colonial laws that dictated driver behavior and punished risky and dangerous drivers. Many drivers who failed to adjust to changing regulation lost their profit, their freedom, or their livelihoods, and drivers' petitions through their unions often did not result in significant changes to colonial policy. However, unions also drew on deep connections within societies and economies of entrepreneurialism. When drivers chose to strike, their actions were often backed up by broad social sanction, which highlighted the degree to which drivers were not merely autonomous capitalists. Rather, drivers were also an important part of the social and economic fabric of African communities.

3 "Modern Men": Motor Transportation and the Politics of Respectability, 1930s–1960s

For a young Inussa al-Haji, the appearance of motor vehicles in his village in the late 1940s and early 1950s was a revelation:

> At those times, we are young and our eyes are not open, we don't know anything, so sometimes if you hear the sound of the cars or you see some car is passing, sometime we used to run and go and stand on the roadside, and say oh, for this car, it is very nice, it is beautiful, and we'll be talking talking talking. So at that time, Austin and all those cars we had been seeing at those times—they don't spark it. They used to put an iron at the front, and they wind it before the car would spark, so we would be looking at those things and we are surprised, so we are on it like that until we are also grown and we are also knowing something.[1]

For young men and boys like al-Haji who observed motor vehicles and drivers as they passed through or near rural villages and farms, automobility represented an "eye-opening" or *anibue*. Equated by early colonial missionaries and translators with European concepts of "civilization," Gracia Clark has more recently argued for a translation of *anibue* as "modernity" or "modernization."[2] Such modernity implies worldliness, sophistication, and cosmopolitanism, as well as knowledge and/or wisdom. The worldliness and sophistication of drivers was clearly not the same as "been-tos" who traveled and lived abroad. But for many young men, experiences of mobility through driving work expanded their horizons in significant ways. Travel within and beyond the Gold Coast/Ghana—and the worldliness and cosmopolitanism that such travel made possible—connected rural and urban areas and facilitated a process of *anibue*.[3] In driving, young men embodied the aspirational ontology of modernity, seeking out new opportunities and possibilities for engagement with/in the world.[4]

Drivers identified *anibue* simultaneously with their experiences as drivers and with the processes of modernization of the late-colonial and postcolonial era, representing "a social state or process of increased knowledge and awareness which is a condition of greater effectiveness and prosperity."[5] For Ghanaian drivers, access to the city, mastery of mechanical knowledge and skill, and access to wealth helped their "eyes open" to what they understood as a new world of possibility and opportunity. Driving, in short, represented an alternative path to socioeconomic status in the twentieth century, particularly for those with limited education and resources—a means through which young men could claim their place in the modern world. *Anibue* was simultaneously a symbol of mature status and a sign of the times, and through *anibue*, young boys like al-Haji became men and rural villagers became modern cosmopolitans.[6]

The "eye-opening" of drivers' work had consequences not only for their own lives, but also for the broader communities in which they moved. For drivers, the outward symbols of their work and status—engagement with technology and mobility and the consumption of wealth and goods—were intimately interconnected with social conceptions of a "good man," a twentieth-century politics of respectability. The *anibue* of driving work attracted young men like Inussa al-Haji to the profession, and the worldliness, cosmopolitanism, wisdom, and prosperity of *anibue* was central to drivers' self-fashioning as respectable, modern men. The ability of drivers to negotiate the bureaucratic, legal, and regulatory structures of the colonial state and the demands and criticisms of the public engendered the emergence of a culture and socioeconomic class of drivers in the mid-twentieth century. That status enabled young men to purchase property, support families, expand their businesses, and engage in conspicuous consumption, establishing themselves as respectable, modern men. However, the mobility and economic utility of motor transportation ensured that drivers' lives had consequence far beyond themselves and their families. The self-fashioning of drivers, who used autonomy and mobility to construct identities as respectable, modern men, enabled them to engage with colonialism and capitalism and to facilitate the creation and expansion of new occupational categories opened to new populations in the twentieth century.

Drivers often characterized this period—1930s–1960s—as a "golden age," a title that highlights the degree to which many drivers were able to realize the promises of *anibue* through their life and work, using automobile technology to pursue alternative paths to respectability and prosperity. These individual experiences of *anibue* resonated with the politics of a period marked by the aspirational visions of modernization, nationalism, and development. However, this period was also marked by significant political and economic changes that shifted the parameters of gendered respectability, and required constant renegotiations of identity and practice in order to preserve status and prosperity. The consolidation of drivers as a professional class in the 1930s and 1940s raised the expectations of both drivers and the public. The rhetoric and politics of nationalism, independence, decolonization, and modernization that emerged in the 1950s, to some degree, reframed these expectations but did not fundamentally alter the *anibue* of driving work or the gendered respectability of drivers' status.

Drawing on drivers' narratives, newspapers, songs, and vehicle slogans, this chapter explores the ways in which drivers negotiated the complex social, cultural, economic, and technological demands of twentieth-century Ghana to claim status as respectable, modern men. Far from an unproblematic account, the occupational and life histories recounted by two generations of drivers—the first who began their careers between 1932 and 1949, and the second who began driving between 1952 and 1965—do, however, provide us with an opportunity to view a period of marked political change through the lens of individual experience. In doing so, the significant continuities between these two generations' occupational and life histories highlight the degree to which everyday life existed within and often outside of the processes of historical change that have marked the historical record of this period. This does not mean, however, that drivers' lives were static or ahistorical; drivers were both subjects and agents of many of the changes that defined African experience in the twentieth century. As a new *kind* of work, drivers in the first half of the twentieth century struggled to find their niche in the broader socioeconomic scene. Drivers were both mobile and liminal. As auto/mobile men and entrepreneurs, drivers defied conventional categorization, and thus, perhaps even more than the technologies they appropriated or the commodities they consumed, drivers themselves embodied the promises and challenges of the new "modern man" of the twentieth century, exemplifying the complexities and tensions of colonial modernity, the politics of respectability, and the fundamental continuities that underlay a period that was subject to significant political change.

Colonial Modernity, Mobile Capitalism, and the Rise of a New Respectability

The professionalization of driving work in the 1930s and 1940s coincided with a broader attempt by drivers to define their socioeconomic status as respectable, modern men. Drivers' self-fashioning was part of a twentieth-century identity politics that raised new questions about the meaning of respectability in the context of an emergent colonial modernity. New occupations, technologies, and values reshaped the possibilities and opportunities for Africans in the Gold Coast in the first half of the twentieth century. Some of those changes were rooted in or resonated with precolonial practices and values. As McCaskie and others have noted, precolonial African societies "possessed ideologies of wealth and technologies of accumulation," a legacy that was "drawn upon, reconfigured and mobilized . . . in meeting the challenges posed by colonial capitalism."[7] In Akan communities, respectability was defined by indigenous conceptions of "power," which permeated the cosmologies of various ethnic groups in southern Ghana before the nineteenth century. Power was understood as "'the ability to produce change' (Twi: *tumi*)," and was intimately connected to and defined by access to knowledge.[8] Multiple social, political, and economic groups sought to claim or mobilize tumi, establishing institutions and positions of distinction, achievement, and accumulation. However, tumi alone was not a sufficient indicator of status; respectability also required good character (Twi: *suban*)—the deeds and actions, habits and conduct of an individual.[9] While chiefs and other political and spiritual figures commanded authority that was often inherited, many of these communities also recognized "big men" (Twi: *abirempon*), who were distinguished by their ability to accumulate wealth and mobilize social, political, and economic resources.[10] These individuals of elevated status were complemented by people of more humble, but no less respectable, occupations as fishermen, farmers, and traders, as well as specialized artisanal occupations like weavers, blacksmiths, goldsmiths, and musicians, who were often attached to royal courts. For many of these occupations, access to land was key, and elder men who controlled that access used their power and authority to dictate the terms of respectability along the lines of gender, age/maturity, and ethnicity.[11]

Drivers who sought to define their socioeconomic status in the first half of the twentieth century were part of a broader conversation about the consequences of what McCaskie terms "colonial modernity" for Gold Coast communities that had long defined respectability through access to land and power.[12] The growth of commerce and the market economy in coastal trading communities, which led to the rise of a new class of merchants and middlemen in the eighteenth century, also revolutionized agriculture and spawned new opportunities in cash crop farming, wage labor, and trade well into the interior by the nineteenth century.[13] Cocoa farmers and traders grew in wealth and prestige throughout the southern Gold Coast and used their accumulated wealth to influence local politics. At the same time, Christianity, Western education, and the expanding colonial bureaucracy facilitated the rise of a new class of "scholars" (Twi: *akrakyefo*) and "gentlemen" (Twi: *akonkofo*)[14] whose status was tied directly to their participation in the emerging colonial culture and society of coastal towns and urban centers, serving as translators, clerks, teachers, journalists, and lawyers. In both rural and urban areas, *akrakyefo* and *akonkofo* distinguished themselves through their choice of housing, dress, language, religion, and entertainment. These new colonial gentlemen attended church; lived in nuclear family units; wore European clothes; resided in square houses with corrugated iron roofs; possessed chairs, tables, beds, radios, bicycles (and sometimes, in rather extraordinary cases, carriages or cars);[15] consumed tinned or imported foodstuffs; spoke English (and often also French and other languages); joined social clubs and literary societies;[16] and attended formal dances.[17] This same culture of consumerism and colonial capitalism also drew young people to urban centers as wage laborers in emergent colonial industries and public works offices. The high demand for unskilled laborers—painters, carpenters, drivers, fitters, and others—allowed employees to change jobs frequently in search of higher wages. By the beginning of the twentieth century, the enticements of the colonial cash economy reshaped understandings of the "sweet things in life" among a wide swath of the African population of the Gold Coast.[18]

Young men like Inussa al-Haji, who were enchanted by the technology and opportunities of motor transportation, thus were part of a larger process of transformation, both as agents and subjects of change.[19] New forms, technologies, structures, and institutions of mobility in the twentieth century profoundly altered the way that many Africans viewed the possibilities of their lives and the standards by which those lives were lived and judged. Many young people took advantage of this new knowledge and mobility to pursue and redefine traditional symbols of respectability—work, marriage, status—outside of the control of parents, elders, and chiefs. The strain that new paths to wealth and marriage had on traditional social relations were manifested in chiefs' attempts to "round up spinsters" and accusations of witchcraft or "juju" as leaders attempted to reassert control over social order.[20] As the centers of this new colonial economy, coastal towns witnessed some of the most intense contestations over status, authority, and control, manifested in debates over the use of alcohol[21] and the development of new leisure practices (popular music and dance).[22] However, in practice, these changes did not represent a wholesale rejection of "traditional" values, but rather a careful calibration of past, present, and future by individuals who sought to secure status for themselves within the new society.[23] Drivers, who embodied the fluidity and mobility of modern technologies and economies, sought to situate themselves and assert their status within a society that had more options, but also fewer certainties. The automobility that defined drivers' lives placed them in constant interaction with both rural and urban communities. While their work enabled young men and women to participate in the possibilities and opportunities of mid-twentieth-century mobile capitalism and colonial modernity, the automobility inherent in their work also meant that drivers were directly subject to the full range of values that defined twentieth-century identity politics. Drivers, thus, engaged in a form of self-fashioning that embraced a plurality of these values and identities. In doing so, they were certainly not alone—young men and women throughout the colony had multilayered and coexisting identities that were highly contextual.[24] However, the liminality of drivers' socioeconomic position, defined by the necessities of their work, meant that drivers' self-fashioning had profound consequences for their relative economic prosperity and respectability.

"Good Boy": Mates, Mobility, and Gendered Respectability, 1930–1945

While young men and women both engaged with the processes and possibilities of colonial modernity and mobile capitalism, the identity politics or politics of respectability in the twentieth century were gendered in often striking ways.

Driving, which remained a male occupation throughout the twentieth century, provided opportunities for young men to negotiate the plurality of masculinities in operation in the Gold Coast in order to establish themselves as respectable, modern men. This wide array of masculinities available to drivers differed significantly from that of previous generations. Standards of Akan masculinity dominant before the nineteenth century were defined through the roles of warrior, husband, father, farmer/fisherman, elder, big man (Twi: *obirempon*), and chief (Twi: *ohene*)—roles that were contested not only along the lines of class and lineage but also in terms of maturity.

The expectations and opportunities for men changed significantly as they aged. "Adult masculinity" was marked by marriage and children, while "senior masculinity" was accompanied by an acknowledgement of a man as an elder, with additional responsibilities and privileges in the social, political, and cultural life of the community.[25] However, nineteenth-century colonial conquest, which introduced new forms of respectability, also altered local conceptions of masculinity. Beginning in the 1820s, British governors on the Gold Coast sought to break the power of major kingdoms like the Asante, limiting warfare and ending the slave trade.[26] At the same time, traders took advantage of the increased commerce of the new colonial economy, surpassing the wealth of chiefs. Mission societies, which often served as a vanguard for the expanding British colonial state, also introduced Western education and Victorian norms that privileged the nuclear family and created new categories of privileged masculinity in the *akrakyefo*, who asserted their newfound status by participating actively in new colonial social and economic organizations, including literary societies and newspapers, the Boy Scouts, and the colonial civil service.[27] Urban wage laborers held less prestigious positions in colonial society, but they did use their wages to participate actively in the cash economy as consumers and engage in popular culture and leisure activities afforded by cosmopolitan city life. Masculinity and respectability, then, were inextricably intertwined in the lives of men in the first half of the twentieth century, structuring drivers' experiences of *anibue*. Rather than one hegemonic masculinity, drivers in the first half of the twentieth century negotiated a number of competing masculinities and embraced many of the new opportunities and possibilities of colonial modernity, connecting rural and urban parts of the colony.[28]

While women had historically served as long-distance carriers, the mechanics of motor transportation and the physical strength required of drivers were seen to be exclusively male.[29] Drivers noted that driving work required "all of your body—your legs, your head, everything—so it is not easy."[30] Poor road conditions outside of the cities (and even within them) and an absence of power steering indeed demanded great physical strength of drivers in order to keep their vehicles safely on the road. Men also believed that the thoughtfulness inherent in driving work was beyond the capabilities of women.[31] Being able to adapt and deal with any situation—particularly, to protect yourself and your vehicle, goods, and passengers, and carry out repairs during breakdowns in rural areas—was seen to be an inherently masculine trait. Physical strength was also required to load and unload produce and other goods from vehicles at points of departure and arrival. The competitiveness of driving and the ability to attract and maintain passengers required another kind of strength—a willingness to fight and a confidence and strength of will to enforce good behavior among passengers. The respect that drivers experienced as a defining characteristic of their work was tempered by the often-heavy criticisms and insults of passengers and the general public. On some occasions, drivers would fight verbally with passengers before forcibly removing them from their vehicle for bad behavior or turning them in to the police station.[32]

Drivers' masculinization of their work reflected broadly held stereotypes about the roles of men and women throughout the southern Gold Coast. To some degree these stereotypes—which, Clark argues, men also used to justify the feminization and gender segregation of the market—represented attempts by men to claim power and authority over more privileged or lucrative occupations.[33] However, gendered occupational roles were also deeply engrained in the social and cultural life of the community. Work (Twi: *adwuma*) was the central experience of childhood in societies of the southern Gold Coast, through which children learned patterns of appropriate behavior and mastered the necessary skills to pass through the rites of passage into adulthood.[34] Children who grew up on farms, for example, were responsible for gender-segregated work that reflected adult responsibilities. Children also acted out gendered divisions of labor and domestic arrangements through play. As children grew into adulthood, they took on new roles of gendered respectability as husbands and wives. Some of the occupational training that defined the experiences of those who pursued specialized skills created and sharpened further gender differentiations.[35]

As part of a new community of "modern" entrepreneurs in the first half of the twentieth century, both drivers and the traders who served as their primary customers also sought to define their spheres of access and accumulation along gendered lines. Women's participation in the market expanded in the first half of the twentieth century in conjunction with the expansion of motor transportation as a commercial enterprise. As men left market trading to seek wealth and accumulation through cocoa farming in the southern Gold Coast at the beginning of the century, women quickly took their place, dominating most parts of the market by the 1940s.[36] Women like Felicia, a trader from a village outside Keta, used motor transport to travel further distances in shorter amounts of time, enabling them to both take care of their families and engage in local and long-distance

Fig. 3.1 Women climb through the open sides of a tro-tro in Accra. *Feature Stories on Transportation in Ghana*, photographer George Alhassan, June 2, 1966 (Ministry of Information, Information Services Photographic Library, Ref. no. R/R/7179/10).

trade. By the 1960s, Felicia had lived in Keta, Kumasi, and Accra, traded in a number of different sections of the market, and regularly traveled to Boduase, Kasoa, Wenchi, and Effiduase.[37]

The gendered expectations that distinguished traders from nontraders by the beginning of the twentieth century also distinguished them from drivers. While their spheres of work were relatively strictly defined by the mid-twentieth century, both drivers and market women were part of a larger culture of entre-preneurial respectability that emphasized accumulation, autonomy, and mobil-ity and facilitated the care of extended family and access to imported goods and other commodities. Women were largely excluded from driving work, and female traders and farmers were dependent on male drivers in establishing prof-itable businesses. However, drivers also relied on those entrepreneurial women to guarantee the success of their driving work, and they sought to attract women as passengers and regular customers. Becoming a driver entailed its own process of socialization, maturation, and skills development through apprenticeship and licensing—a process that not only taught them technical skills, but which also helped young drivers develop social, economic, and cultural capital that would enable the success of their business. Drivers' training, then, was not merely an occupational or vocational activity. Rather, drivers understood both their skills and their lives as privileged domains, and apprenticeships were a central way in which young men established themselves as respectable drivers and community members, mastering the skills necessary to conduct business with efficiency, profitability, and honor. The formality of driving apprenticeships themselves made them largely unavailable to women, by contrast, whose parents rarely invested in formal or institutionalized occupational training.[38]

"It's In My Heart": Technology, Vocation, and the Appeal of Driving Work

Mates' experiences of training were remarkably similar throughout the mid-twentieth century; however, the paths by which young men came to apprenticeship and driving work varied greatly. Place of residence, family situation, and access to resources all shaped young men's experiences as mates—and later as drivers—in profound ways. For those who grew up in driving communities, such as La (a suburb east of Accra), where motor transportation had long been established as a dominant occupation, young men saw driving as a desirable and respected family tradition. As J. F. Ocantey describes his own early experiences in a house and community of drivers:

> As for me, the house that I come from, there is a lot of cars in the house so since we are going to school we are learning driving because we're always washing the car. And once we're washing the car, that means you are on the way trying to be a driver. Since 1947, we were doing those things in the house. Every weekend, we take the car—my father or brother will take the car and I will be inside and we go to the riverside and we wash the car and we bring it back. Sometime I got and fetch water and wash car. So that make me choose driving as my hobby, that I would like to be a driver. So when I was in school I said no, school will not help me. It's wasting my time. I can also see that my father is getting old, so I go to my father and say I want to take driving as my profession. So when I tell my father that, he says no problem, you know the driving already, but that those time you don't call that a driver because you don't work under anybody. So they took me to a master and share drink to ask permission from the master that I would like to work with him, so my master accepted, and that is where I started learning as a mate. So my father tell me I have to learn the driving well and make sure I know it and so he send the drink here in La somewhere, so they take me to my master called NV Labad and then they give him a drink that I would like my child/son to learn driving under you, so he accepted me so from there I started working with my master.[39]

A senior brother served as an inspiration and model for Mr. Ocantey; however, the tradition of driving in his family also influenced his family's support and encouragement of his occupational decisions. Those who grew up in La, for example, felt that driving was in their blood:

> For the driving, they born us in the driving work because where we were born from, driving is the work that most of the people have been doing. That is the reason why—our area here in La, we like driving. You should understand that La people are the people who brought driving into the system because the first driver in Ghana here, he come from La. Before it spread around the whole of Ghana—it's La it started from. The thing is, this man sitting here—his father is a driver, so he was born in the driving work because his father is driving, and I myself too, my senior brother was a driver so any time he always bring cars to the house so even if he's not there and I enter the car, once you spark the car and you accelerate it, the car will move. So that is what we've been doing—once our fathers or brothers brought the cars to the house for us to wash, we would be sparking the cars and that brought our interest, so that make us to have the interest of the driving work.[40]

La itself was seen as a major center for driving. If you were deemed suitable to be a driver by standards in La, then you were seen to be a driver of significant skill, and young men from throughout the colony came to La to train as mates and drivers. Drivers argued that the quality of driving and driver training in La was recognized not only by other drivers but also by the colonial state and the various commercial firms that operated throughout the Gold Coast. The first African driver, initially working for a European company (Bartholomew) and later driving Governor Gordon Guggisberg, was said to come from La, and the La Drivers' Union, which was established in 1934, was one of the earliest and most influential unions throughout the middle of the twentieth century.[41]

For those young men who didn't have family connections to the driving profession or come from a community of drivers, driving work was appealing because of what it offered. Young boys in farming and fishing communities like Coblah Nimo often stopped work to watch as mammy trucks and other motor vehicles passed. The fascination with cars extended into play, as boys pretended to be drivers, improvising imagined vehicles and "blowing" horns (*porpor*) as they traveled back and forth to collect water.[42] When motor vehicles arrived in their villages, children swarmed around the vehicle, looking at themselves in the reflection of the metallic chassis and sitting behind the steering wheel pretending to drive.[43] Many of those who ultimately became drivers described themselves as completely occupied, if not spellbound, by the vehicle and its driver, and they saw driving as a calling or vocation that was "in their heart."

Both the work and culture of driving proved appealing to boys and young men who followed drivers. The loading of goods and interactions with passengers that young boys witnessed in villages and markets in rural areas highlighted the independence and respect of drivers. Their command of the machine and its horn further added to the allure of skill and prestige. The inherent mobility of driving—the ability to travel to new and diverse places—was particularly appealing to rural young men.[44] As Abraham Tagoe noted:

> I like the driving, and the reason why I choose driving instead of goldsmithing is that I wanted to travel to different-different places and go far from Accra so that I could know places. That is the reason why I choose driving, but not because of money too much. Because goldsmith too—if you do it, you can get money, but I don't prefer goldsmith. I prefer the driving to the goldsmith.[45]

Travelling was an important means of eye-opening—as drivers, as men, and as citizens. The privileging of travel among young men in explaining the appeal of driving corresponds with traditions throughout the southern Gold Coast, which equated travel with respect, status, and wealth. By the 1930s, "been-tos" became increasingly recognized as important figures of cultural sophistication and social status in the Gold Coast, as a result of their international travel.[46] For rural boys and young men, motor transportation and driving work provided an accessible way to participate in this new culture of prestige and mobility. Not only did they see new things and have their eyes opened themselves, but they also facilitated the movements of others (and their goods)—a responsibility that was undertaken with a fair degree of reverence.

In some cases, young boys refused to leave the car when the driver began his return journey to the city, forcing himself onto the driver as a mate. However, for most boys enamored with the life and work of drivers, their careers as drivers began in apprenticeships as mates. The support of family, however, varied significantly. The inherent danger of driving work caused some parents to discourage their young sons from pursuing driving. Drivers cited the reactions of their mothers, in particular, who feared for the safety of their sons, and the very real danger of accidents made driving a risky and sometimes deadly occupation. For others, parental resistance was motivated more by disapproval of the young man's choice of profession. Fathers who had already chosen their son's profession were sometimes resistant to alternative ideas and bristled at their son's rejection of their chosen path.[47] For many, however, families supported these occupational decisions and followed the traditionally structured apprenticeship system to seek out respected masters (through family and social connections or otherwise) to train their sons.[48] The willingness of many families to embrace their sons' occupational choices, taking them away from their families and communities for long periods of time, highlights the degree to which mobile capitalism had pervaded communities throughout the Gold Coast by the 1930s, drawing young men from throughout the colony into the new mobility system of motor transportation and accepting their work and training as a new sign of respectability defined by that very mobility itself and the wealth and autonomy that it made possible.

"Oh to be a man . . .": The Rewards of Prosperity, the Allure of
Leisure, and the Value of Hard Work, 1945–1960

As mates became drivers, their experience and relative success or prosperity as
workers and entrepreneurs had implications for their identity as respectable,
modern men. For many drivers, accumulation through driving work enabled
them to establish independence and self-sufficiency, acquire specialized skills,
and attain relative social and economic status. Their establishment as a socioeconomic group was influenced as much by their shared social experiences as
men as any particular degree of accumulation or class consolidation. That their
economic prosperity made such social experiences possible, however, meant that
accumulation, modernity, and masculinity were intimately connected in the
lives of drivers.

Accumulation and wealth, facilitated by driving work, helped drivers realize adult status as respectable men and the maturity and independence that such
status implied. For young men who grew up on farms, adulthood was connected
to their work on the farm. Helping their father and contributing to the household
highlighted the maturity of young men.[49] However, for many others, the delayed
adulthood brought about by extended apprenticeships meant that attaining their
license and becoming a driver created new possibilities and opportunities for
establishing themselves as respectable, modern men. Most notably for many,
driving work meant making money. In many ways, drivers were part of an urban
scene of young men who used the income obtained through their engagement
with the cash economy to create new lives for themselves, obtaining the markers
of adulthood outside of the control of elders. Early highlife songs of the era captured the connection between wealth, youth, and masculinity—one such song
declared, "*sika fata merantee*" ("money benefits young men")—and many young
men spent their newfound earnings on luxuries, such as alcohol, which elders
had restricted in their home communities.[50] However, drivers were also distinct
among the larger mass of young men who migrated to cities in increasing numbers in search of work in the first half of the twentieth century. The autonomy and
mobility of their work facilitated the new forms of sociability and social possibilities central to the experiences of their fellow urban dwellers, but it also provided
great flexibility in a late-colonial economy characterized by relatively unpredictable cycles of depression and growth.[51]

In contrast to the wage labor and factory work of many urban residents who
were paid salaries according to weekly, biweekly and/or monthly pay schedules,
drivers controlled their own business and collected daily profit. Daily income limited the need for budgeting and insured that "drivers always had something in
their pocket."[52] Drivers themselves saw this is a personal benefit, using their earnings to purchase "fine dress" and imported goods that attracted the respect and

patronage of passengers and enabled them to participate in the "sweet things in life."[53] The "luxury" consumption that defined the elevated status of drivers was embedded in daily practice. Drivers like Simon Djetey Abe and P. Ashai Ollenu loved driving work because "at that time, corned beef—nobody could eat it, but when you go to the city and see city drivers, they eat corned beef and sardines and so many things."[54] Driving work was guaranteed "quick money" that drivers controlled; however, daily income also attracted women who saw drivers as sources of financial stability.[55] Many drivers acknowledged that "we loved women and women loved us."[56] By the 1950s and 1960s, popular highlife songs like "Driver ni" ("The Driver")[57] highlighted some of the appeal of drivers. The flexibility of driving work as an income-generating occupation based on skill rather than resources provided security as well as obligations in the face of the threat of financial ruin or traumatic event. "If I marry a man and he loses his job, how will he take care of me?" reasoned the fictionalized and generalized woman in the song. Drivers, however, could always find some work at the station, even if their vehicle was in disrepair or they did not have a vehicle of their own. Helping other drivers load and unload vehicles at the station or driving the spare vehicle of a friend or other vehicle owner enabled even formally out-of-work drivers to earn income. The daily income of drivers also guaranteed that women would receive more regular "chop money."[58] Furthermore, the role of drivers in the transportation of foodstuffs guaranteed a steady supply of food, even in times of economic distress or drought.[59]

Drivers used their earnings and financial stability to establish homes and families in urban centers, which served as the headquarters of the colony's emerging commercial transport industry by the 1940s. In addition to maintaining their extended family (parents, siblings, uncles, cousins, nieces, and nephews), drivers' wealth enabled many to "do something small" for themselves and their immediate family—accumulating property and vehicles, building houses, and having children who they were able to send to school. Particularly for drivers like Shadrak Yemo Odoi, who was forced to leave school in the early 1930s when his father left and his mother was no longer able to pay his school fees, the ability to secure higher education for their children was an important outcome of their work.[60] These markers of masculine status and respectability established drivers in their urban communities, and more permanent settlement and connection to particular communities enabled many drivers to establish regular business arrangements with traders and other passengers that guaranteed steady work. However, mobility was much more central to drivers' lives than that of most urban dwellers. Rather than an occasional occurrence defined through the experience of labor migration, mobility for drivers was a daily reality, and their social and economic lives were intimately connected to both rural and urban communities. Drivers who traveled throughout the interior regions of the colony/country also attracted a number of additional girlfriends and wives, who cooked food and provided housing and other services at regular stops along their routes. These additional relationships also bore children, connecting drivers to an extensive family network spread throughout the colony.[61] While these dispersed families highlighted the mobility of drivers, they often did not impact their life in their urban bases. In other words, these families existed in a discrete world shaped by mobility, in contrast to more formal "wives" for whom houses were built by drivers and a settled life was established.

The benefits that their prosperity afforded—family, property, status—also came with obligations, which profoundly shaped drivers' experiences. In contrast to some of the stereotypical "youngmen" of late-colonial and postcolonial public discourse,[62] drivers worked long hours in order to make their vehicle profitable and to enable them to fulfill the social and financial obligations that accompanied their new status as "modern men." Despite the wealth that drivers' social and personal lives and occupational success suggested, driving was not an inherently profitable occupation. Drivers who owned their own vehicles often obtained them from European, Syrian, or Lebanese import companies through a lease system popularly known as "work and pay," which required high monthly payments. Those who did not own their own vehicles paid a portion of their daily earnings to the vehicle's owner. As a result, profit was obtained only through hard work. Those for whom driving did result in profits often had aspirations for their wealth, either in the form of car ownership or property and building. For most drivers, this meant working from sunrise until 8:30 in the evening, six or seven days a week.

While the emergent popular culture of the working class in African cities—both within and outside of the Gold Coast—has often been characterized as a central part of the urban experience, among many drivers, work and family took precedence over leisure. Many drivers who had relocated to Accra explicitly for the purposes of work saw the city as an economic and occupational base rather than as a social scene.

> At a certain point in time when we have off days, we don't have particular days for rest. If you choose to rest today, you rest. Because within all your [work] you be going up and down. Sometime you have arrangements—every Monday there is a market you have to go; every Wednesday there's a market you have to go. It's an economic venture, so every Friday I have to go here. So those off days, then you come back for your car to be road worthy, you take it to the workshop. After the workshop, then you enjoy. You take a little rest and then the following day you go. Normally it doesn't have drivers resting because their hard work—drivers are hard workers. As fishermen and the farmers, too. They are hard working people, so they have little time to enjoy. It is not as much. But if you fall into this category of factory workers, that place is an establishment, so everything have been arranged orderly. You work 11 months, and the 12th month, you go on leave. You rest and come. But here we don't have it like that. Because it is self-employed.[63]

For many drivers, days entailed rising at sunrise, driving until evening, returning home to wash their cars and perform basic maintenance, and then retiring to the house to eat with their wives. "Days off" often required more extensive car maintenance. In other words, many drivers defined success by an individual's ability to refrain from what they saw as the income-draining distractions of leisure. Unlike wage laborers who were "caught in a 'net' of urban time," which identified leisure in opposition to work and associated it with the consumerism of mobile capitalism, drivers' practices reflected the persistence of precolonial forms of leisure as *afoofi*—"a term translated by Christaller as 'keeping at home resting or doing domestic work; refraining from plantation work.'"[64]

In focusing their attention on work and domestic life, many drivers challenged assumptions and anxieties about the impact of mobility and urban life on young African men, which dominated colonial discourses on "youngmen" in the late-colonial Gold Coast. Although motivated by different interests, the colonial state, African elites, and rural elders were concerned that the concentration of aimless "youngmen" in cities, alienated from the control of elders and families in rural communities, posed dangers not only to other urban residents but also to the young men themselves.[65] This anxiety prompted colonial attempts to control African leisure time in urban space, encouraging the development of organized sports and introduced new forms of social organizations like literary clubs, dance clubs, and the Boy Scouts.[66] As the Gold Coast Film Unit's 1952 film *The Boy Kumasenu* cautioned, even the best-intentioned or guileless young men could fall victim to the temptations of the city without guidance.[67] As the labor migrations of young, male wage laborers that were once thought to be temporary turned into permanent occupations and wage labor positions failed to realize the dreams of prosperity that had drawn many young men to the city, these issues became less abstract concerns.[68] Drivers, however, who were both autonomous and mobile, often defied the expectations of their parents and the colonial state, pursuing lives of respectability and prosperity, while facilitating a regular interaction between urban and rural communities through trade and travel.

"Accra Boy": Urbanization, Mobility, and the Politics of Autonomy

The type of work in which drivers were engaged—the kind of cars they drove and where they drove—had consequences not only for their social status but also for their status among fellow drivers. The establishment of driving as a recognized occupational category in the 1930s not only consolidated drivers into unions and other professional organizations but also spawned a period of increasing differentiation and innovation among drivers. Possession of a license did not necessarily establish oneself as a driver by profession. By the time the 1934 Motor Traffic Ordinance was passed, taxi drivers as well as long-distance cargo drivers (mammy trucks) had come to define the commercial motor transportation market, while an ever-increasing number of private drivers (or "myself" drivers) drove personal vehicles particularly in urban areas. Drivers themselves often subscribed to a sort of hierarchy of driving in which "professional drivers" were only those who drove long-distance cargo trucks. Private drivers, taxi drivers, and others who were located solely in urban areas were not considered professional and, thus, did not receive the same degree of recognition as the drivers of mammy trucks. Long-distance driving required more specialized skills, training, and knowledge. As drivers carried goods and passengers between farms, villages, and urban areas, the ability to negotiate rough rural roads and to maintain and repair vehicles required a higher degree of training than urban taxi driving (or, for that matter, private driving).

Drivers' debates about the meaning of "professional" simultaneously echoed and challenged colonial concerns about driving that had motivated the passage of motor traffic regulations in 1934 and 1937. These debates were most heavily concentrated in urban areas like Accra, where both local populations and colonial government officials sought to define the space of the city through mobility practice. Mammy truck drivers, who carried goods and passengers between villages and cities, highlighted the porousness of the boundaries between rural and urban space. For drivers and their passengers, this periurban mobility was the defining feature of colonial modernity for Africans; the social, cultural, and economic interactions that physical movement made possible facilitated *anibue*.

If drivers and their passengers embraced periurban mobility as a path to modernity, for British and African representatives in colonial institutions, the constant movement of drivers and passengers and the circulation and exchange of goods and ideas that accompanied them raised serious questions about colonial conceptions of ordering and governing of a "modern" society. Particularly in the colonial capital, the mobility of drivers and passengers was seen to challenge colonial models of modern, urban mobility, but their movement also undermined the economic and political organization of the Gold Coast. Beginning in the mid-1930s, members of the Accra Town Council, the Legislative Assembly, and the Colonial Governor expressed concern over the increasing prevalence of "pirate passenger lorries" on the road between Labadi (an eastern suburb) and Accra.[69] Mammy truck drivers, who entered the city limits from the agriculturally productive eastern interior carrying goods, often offloaded goods at the first major market in Labadi. Rather than driving into the central lorry park in Accra with partially empty loads, drivers in the mid-1930s began picking up market women along the roadside who were traveling to the central market just near the lorry park with their goods.[70] While both drivers and market women saw this arrangement as mutually beneficial, members of the Accra Town Council raised repeated concern, accusing the drivers of "piracy."

In blurring the boundaries between goods and passenger, rural and urban transport, the drivers of these "pirate passenger lorries" unintentionally highlighted the tension between African practices and colonial visions of modern mobility and urban space. The Accra Town Council alleged that mammy truck drivers who picked up passengers along the roadside undermined the profits of the Municipal Bus Service, which had a monopoly on passenger transport since its founding in 1927.[71] The language of "piracy" spoke to the financial challenges presented by these entrepreneurial drivers. Their increasingly successful business threatened the profits of the Municipal Bus Service, which served as the primary source of revenue for the Accra Town Council.[72] However, attempts to limit the ability of mammy trucks to pick up and carry passengers within city limits also reflected the degree to which these practices challenged a colonial "plan for the town," rooted in modernist visions of regularly spaced bus lay-byes and stops, ticketing agents, and street lights throughout the city's major streets.[73] The Municipal Bus Service connected the city in a system of urban mobility in which white-collar workers and waged laborers moving between home and office. However, these visions ignored the realities of many urban residents, the most mobile of whom were women who moved back and forth to the market to buy and/or sell goods. Buses, which had individual seats and little storage space, provided challenges for both traders and shoppers, who had to carry their goods on their laps.

At the urging of the Accra Town Council, the Legislative Assembly ultimately passed new regulations outlawing any private passenger transport services in the city and guaranteeing the monopoly of the Municipal Bus Service by the mid-1940s.[74] Independence, however, provided new opportunities for entrepreneurial African transport workers. In the late-1950s, driver Anane purchased a mammy truck to follow municipal buses and pick up the overflow of passenger who couldn't find a seat.[75] Nicknamed "trotros" for their three-pence fares that covered transport within municipal boundaries, this new passenger service competed directly with municipal buses, extending passenger service to new parts of the city and providing faster transportation. Trotro drivers responded directly to the needs of urban African residents and passengers who appreciated the increased cargo space of these converted cargo trucks, which allowed passengers like market women to transport goods to and from neighborhoods and markets. Trotros were particularly appealing in outlying suburbs like Labadi, which did not benefit from frequent bus service. Labadi drivers quickly established a vibrant trotro business including six vehicles, which attracted passengers from nearby communities like Teshie.[76] To further serve the needs of their passengers, trotro drivers added trailers to the back of their vehicle, which carried excess goods.[77] Unlike long-distance mammy trucks, which carried both passengers and goods between rural and urban areas, these new trotros carried passengers exclusively within the city. By the 1960s when the municipal bus service was disbanded due to lack of funds, trotros had become the exclusive form of passenger transport in the capital.⁷⁸

The emergence of trotros in the 1950s challenged the dominance of long-distance mammy truck drivers. Trotro drivers maintained similar standards of training and practice, working through the apprenticeship system as mates before ultimately gaining their license. Because they drove large trucks similar to those of the long-distance cargo drivers, their success required many of the same skills and strength. The categories of mammy truck driver and trotro driver also frequently became blurred as drivers moved back and forth between the two occupational categories, often in response to financial setbacks. Similarly, the training of mates through apprenticeship served as a requirement for those hired as "company drivers." Working for commercial companies and the state, such drivers worked on salary using company or state-owned vehicles. Furthermore, much like the ambiguous boundaries between mammy truck and trotro, drivers often moved in and out of company work, supplementing and substituting their company salaries with earnings as mammy truck and/or trotro drivers.

However, the increasing diversity of commercial motor transport options also led to professional competition and distinction among drivers. Mammy truck drivers insisted that trotro drivers, taxi drivers, and "myself" drivers were not *real* drivers. As driver Justice John Bay argued, "A driver who will go to Asesewa, go to Boku, go to Tamale and go and load food and bring it—that is a driver! There are some drivers, they can't drive in the night. They can't even drive from here to Kumasi. But you can't say that you drive from here to Quarters and back again and say that you are a driver!"⁷⁹ To some degree, this "mobile hierarchy" reflected the relative difficulty of work and the requisite skill of the driver. Drivers of mammy trucks were not only responsible for larger vehicles, which were more difficult to maintain, but they also drove much longer distances over difficult terrain. The more extensive mobility systems, which took mammy truck drivers into rural areas with weaker road infrastructure, required expertise in negotiating the dangers and risks of the road. In successfully transgressing the boundaries between urban and rural spaces and moving through unsettled rural areas, mammy truck drivers had to mobilize a large body of technical, spiritual, commercial, and social knowledge. Trotro and taxi drivers, who were located exclusively in cities faced fewer risks and thus needed less specialized training, moving passengers along the city's streets. Furthermore, trotro drivers, who were motivated by many of the same issues as drivers of "pirate passenger lorries" of the 1930s and 1940s, were not only tolerated, but they were also lauded by the postcolonial state as providing an essential public service for the city's workers. Trotro drivers and their vehicles symbolized a new vision of autonomous mobility, rooted in the politics and rhetoric of independence—decolonization of mobility in the center of colonial power.

Automobility in the Age of Nationalism and Decolonization

The transition to self-government that culminated in independence in 1957 introduced new forms of *anibue*, encouraged by the state and couched in the language of decolonization. Ghana's new president Kwame Nkrumah warned of the threats of neocolonialism in the years immediately after independence and attempted to reorganize Ghana's economy to encourage African enterprise and facilitate rapid industrialization. Nkrumah, who sought to create not only an independent state but also a coherent nation, embraced motor transport workers as both literal and figurative drivers of this new national project. Drivers, who had effectively decolonized their industry by the 1930s, were exemplars of the "African genius" that Nkrumah and other nationalist leaders sought to harness.[80] The decolonization of the motor transport industry was obviously only partial. Drivers were still dependent on imported vehicles, spare parts, and petrol, and they were subject to government regulations that sought to impose new expectations and standards for their industry. However, the very act of driving was subversive. African men and women who embraced the possibilities of motor transportation, in the process, rejected colonial plans for the physical, economic and social mobility of Africans in the Gold Coast. And, as small-scale entrepreneurs, drivers created institutions and practices of organization and professionalization that preserved the autonomy of their work and protested attempts at regulation.

At the same time, drivers were essential to the work of postcolonial modernization, achieving Nkrumah's "high modernist visions" by moving workers and goods throughout the newly independent country.[81] In establishing physical, social, and economic connections, drivers helped to establish a sense of national belonging. Drivers proudly stated that "Nkrumah loved drivers!"[82] That affection was mutual among many drivers in the years immediately following independence, both symbolically, as union branches participated in independence-day parades and other public celebrations, and practically, as union leaders worked closely with the Nkrumah government to provide effective transportation services for the new country.[83] For many young men in the years following independence, driving government leaders and providing transportation services for major summits and conferences in Accra was both a privilege and an honor.[84]

Nkrumah's attention to drivers resulted in a number of regulatory changes that further distinguished drivers from the general population. Immediately after independence, Nkrumah lifted literacy requirements for drivers' licensing, reopening the industry to a broader population of Ghanaians. At the same time, a series of independence-era regulations sought to categorize and physically mark different types of vehicles and their drivers. In the early 1960s, Nkrumah introduced legislation that mandated uniforms for commercial drivers. The "khaki-khaki" (khaki shirt and pants) and black tie of trotro drivers distinguished them as professionals at the same time that it distinguished them from other types of drivers. Mammy truck drivers wore white shirts and khaki pants, while taxi drivers wore black pants, white shirts, and black ties.[85] While these different uniform configurations seem to more closely reflect Western cultures of commercial driving, which privileged taxi drivers over bus drivers, such uniforms failed to challenge the established hierarchy among drivers themselves. Differences in dress were mere differentiation rather than symbols of alternative status. More generally, uniforms were seen to enhance the respectability and professionalism of driving work. Reflecting experiences of colonial culture, in which uniforms symbolized privileged access and prestige for men and boys,[86] for drivers and their passengers, uniforms identified drivers as respected professionals of status and skill. Importantly, now when people saw a driver in his uniform, they knew he was a driver.

Government regulations introduced after independence also sought to physically mark vehicles themselves as commercial or professional. While rules governing the appearance of mammy trucks and trotros remained relatively unchanged aside from new requirements for "trafficators" or traffic signals, regulatory efforts were made to more clearly differentiate commercial taxis from private vehicles.[87] In the 1960s, Minister of Transportation and Communication Krobo Edusei announced that taxis were to be painted "yellow-yellow," which, in addition to the light on the top of the taxi, required drivers to paint the front and back portions of their vehicle a bright yellow color.[88] Such policies not only brought Ghanaian taxi services more closely in line with international practices,[89] but they also helped to differentiate taxis from the increasing numbers of private vehicles on urban roads. Rumors circulated that the policy was the result of an unfortunate encounter in which a mistaken passenger seeking a taxi flagged down the car of Krobo Edusei himself, who was driving his own private car in Accra.[90] While these policies undoubtedly further highlighted the professional nature of driving work, in the context of broader attempts by the Nkrumah government to control economic activities through price controls, marketing boards, and other state-run enterprises, such regulations also reflect an attempt by the state to assert some degree of control over a fiercely independent, but vital, profession. In Accra, such control was seen as a reflection not only of economic centralization but also of Nkrumah's larger project to "modernize" the first capital of a newly independent African country as a showpiece and exemplar for Africa and the world.[91]

Nkrumah and other CPP leaders were much more comfortable with workers who could be molded than with entrepreneurs whose profit-driven work was at odds with nationalist rhetoric about shared sacrifice and national development. Unlike cocoa farmers, whom the government taxed in order to fund national

Fig. 3.2 "All About Mrs. Gladys Korkor Agbozo, Govt. Transport Lady Driver," *Government Transport Lady Driver*, photographer P. K. Anane, January 1, 1962 (Ministry of Information, Information Services Photographic Library, Ref no. R/R/2440/6).

development projects throughout the late 1950s and 1960s, drivers were mobile and, thus, more difficult to control. However, through organizations like the Builder's Brigade, Nkrumah sought to redefine the gendered respectability of commercial driving work. Young female members of the Builder's Brigade were taught to drive, and some were employed as government transport workers, driving officials in government vehicles.[92] The significance of women as drivers was part of a broader rhetoric about the gendered expectations and possibilities in an independent Ghana, highlighting the country's embrace of new principles as they entered a new age of modern self-government.[93] The numbers of women trained through the Builder's Brigade or employed in government service are impossible to ascertain, and drivers asserted that women's opportunities for driver training did not lead to work in the private commercial motor transport sector. However, these women drivers figured prominently in government rhetoric. The Information Services Department collected information and ran stories about Mrs. Gladys Korkor Agbozo, a woman who worked as a government transport driver, using pictures to document her life as both a mobile worker and a wife and mother. National newspapers regularly reported on women who drove tractors and other heavy equipment in the Builder's Brigade, and women were increasingly employed in other parts of the motor transport industry, collecting tickets and serving as bus conductors in Accra's Municipal Bus system and Omnibus Service. Nkrumah's attempts to redefine the politics of gendered respectability through work, however, failed to change driver practice. In the post-independence era, private drivers, who still dominated the motor transport industry, refused to apprentice and train women as mates and drivers and insisted on the masculine nature of their work.

Mobility, Autonomy, and Opposition Politics in Nkrumah's Ghana

Debates over the role of women in driving work and the shifting definitions of gendered respectability in the years immediately following independence highlight the degree to which the modernization of Nkrumah's rhetoric and policy both resonated and existed in uneasy tension with the modern mobility of drivers and passengers. For some drivers, the tensions of their work informed broader political critiques. Attoh Quarshie, who was a government driver, led a group of increasingly vocal critics in Nkrumah's own district of Bukom in central Accra who organized an opposition party—the Ga Shifimo Kpee (Ga Standfast Association)—only five months after independence.[94] Although they declared themselves a "nonpolitical association," the Ga Shifimo Kpee represented the interests of indigenous Ga peoples of Accra, who were concerned about the representation of Ga social, political, and economic interests in national policy. Raising concerns first within Nkrumah's Convention People's Party (CPP) in 1956 and later as a critical voice outside of the CPP, the Ga Shifimo Kpee was a powerful force for political, social, and economic opposition in the heart of the national capital and Nkrumah's seat of power.

As a government driver for the Ministry of Transport, Quarshie drove high-level government officials all over the country. The privileges of the governing elite who served as Quarshie's passengers were a marked contrast to the struggles for land, housing, and jobs among his own Ga community. His own politicization was the direct result of the mobility of driving work—a condition that Quarshie generalized to the broader community of drivers in Accra. Quarshie claimed—and Dennis Austen later also argued—that drivers were central to the Shifimo Kpee, using their vehicles to spread the Shifimo Kpee's message throughout Accra.[95] Quarshie's critiques, which raised questions about the meaning and possibilities of *anibue* in an independent Ghana, undoubtedly resonated with many drivers. But in reality, they represented only a fraction of the members actively involved in the organization. Political activity was a personal choice—as Quarshie's brother argued, "everybody with his own choice."[96] Drivers carefully weighed their political interests with the demands of their business. For many drivers, political mobilization remained a professional risk with social and economic consequences. Drivers like Abraham Tagoe refrained from using their vehicles as tools of political mobilization or spaces for political conversation and debate because:

> Passengers used to talk and use some words in the car that is not good. Something like they will start insulting each other in the car—if they start doing that and I hear about it, I don't like it in my car—I don't like people who don't respect themselves in my car. . . . Sometimes there will be a quarrel in the car, so I used to stop and ask them did they know they are disturbing my peace while I'm driving. Then I tell them they should stop—when they get to the place they are going they can get down and continue their fight. But they don't have a right to fight in the car. [97]

For Tagoe and others, politics was a distraction while driving, just like music or other forms of verbal disagreement among passengers, which could distract the driver and endanger passengers. Many drivers refrained from expressing their own political opinions on or in their vehicles out of a fear of alienating potential passengers, who carefully parsed the appearance, character, and behavior of drivers when choosing a vehicle.

These economic and social concerns influenced a political ambivalence among many drivers—an ambivalence that highlights the diversity of driver experience. While Quarshie's experience as a government driver in the Transport Department and his work as a chauffeur for major political figures increased his awareness of political issues, his experience was relatively exceptional. "Ordinary" drivers, who used their mammy wagons to transport goods and passengers between and within rural and urban areas interacted directly with passengers of a similar socio-economic class (e.g., market women, cocoa farmers) and, thus, were not exposed on a daily basis to the same economic disparities and political activity as government drivers like Quarshie. Rather, for many drivers, the changes brought by independence often enhanced their work and enabled them to maintain their position of socioeconomic privilege. Independence brought inevitable change for drivers' experiences. But the fundamental continuities between colonial modernity and postcolonial "modernization" also meant that, while the means by which anibue occurred varied, the conditions of possibility and respectability for drivers' lives remained remarkably stable.

"Trust No Man": Insecurity, Anxiety, and the Limits of Success

The "modernity" of Accra and Ghana more broadly, which both the British colonial state and Nkrumah used as exemplars in discourses of governance and order, was simultaneously embodied in and contradicted by the lives and experiences of drivers. While many men saw driving as a means of becoming modern—having your eyes opened—for others, driving highlighted the tensions of that modernity. The pursuit of driving itself reflected an attempt to evade what drivers saw as a ubiquitous culture of corruption and mistrust.

> You are doing your own thing. Nobody can cheat. Anything at all you go on the road, anyone you get, you know this what and what—car owners' account, you know the balances. So anything at all you go and get, everybody will like the way you drive so that you will do something better with the car. You don't sit down until month end before you get your pay. So when your car is okay, anytime you go, you get your daily chop, your daily bread. That's what we used to look after family.[98]

In the context of what Margaret Field characterized as chronic insecurity,[99] drivers' lives were often consumed by fears of inadequacy, failure, jealousy, and sabotage. Those drivers who had not yet attained financial stability and success confronted anxieties about personal failings, while those who had achieved relative prosperity often found themselves guarding against the threat of jealous retribution and sabotage.

Possession of a license, in and of itself, was no guarantee of prosperity, wealth, or achievement. As noted above, high lease payments placed pressure on the income of owner-drivers, while those who did not own their own car saw their income decrease as owners themselves received a share of earnings. The high dependence on vehicles for work also meant that accidents and breakdowns could have heavy implications for the prosperity of drivers. As the highlife song above illustrates, part of the appeal of driving work was that drivers could still receive *some* income even when their primary means of work was unavailable. However, in reality, such income replacements were more like supplements that provided for only the most basic necessities (food, water, shelter). When vehicles remained damaged for long periods of time, any savings that a driver might have accrued were gradually exhausted by the demands of daily life and social obligation.

The prosperity of drivers also depended on their ability to manage money. While the most successful drivers dedicated themselves to their work and invested wisely in ways that grew their business and did not waste their hard-earned income, others found the allure of leisure to be too tempting. Those drivers who were "not serious" about their work not only sabotaged their own future financial security, but they also engaged in risky behavior that damaged the public reputation of drivers. Drinking, chasing women, attending cinemas and dance halls, and other forms of entertainment and leisure, while important zones for the formation and contestation of identity and status,[100] also required young drivers to spend their hard-earned cash. While they were young, such activities seemed necessary. As they grew older and found themselves without savings or other financial safety nets, drivers increasingly viewed their earlier behavior as a "disgrace" to themselves and their families.[101]

For those drivers who did achieve economic success, the very symbols of drivers' prosperity could also be the source of their downfall. "Fine dress," vehicle ownership, property ownership, and large families all physically and publicly marked drivers as men of relative prosperity. Vehicle slogans like "Fear Women, Save Your Life"; "Trust No Man"; "Enemies All About Me"; "Suro nnipa" ("Fear man"); "Suro nea oben wo" ("Fear the one who is near to you"); and "Friends to-day, Enemies to-morrow" highlight the threat that drivers' success—and the jealousy of others—posed for their well-being and security.[102] Drivers' concerns reflected the tensions and complications of "modern" life in twentieth-century Ghana. Survival and success were clearly bound up with money—van Binsbergen and Geschiere claim that consumption was "the hallmark of modernity"[103]—but, as McCaskie argues, "money itself was something more than substance."[104] The spectral or magical qualities of accumulation and consumption—and indeed of money itself as a form of exchange—further complicated the social tensions inherent in a society that simultaneously preserved the old and embraced the new. Many drivers, who exemplified and constantly negotiated this dual identity, expressed anxiety and fear about the consequences of these tensions in their own lives and sought to protect themselves. Drivers who crafted identities as respectable, modern men were responding to broader public perception, which had profound consequences for their relative success through driving work. However, those very categories of "respectability," "modernity," and "masculinity" produced their own tensions and contradictions that failed to completely erase anxiety and fear. While some drivers obtained charms and amulets to serve as spiritual protection against the spiritual warfare (or "juju") of family, friends, neighbors, and colleagues,[105] others isolated themselves from all but their immediate family. Friends, in particular, were an issue of concern for many drivers:

> My mother tell me that I shouldn't make friends and it's true because maybe I have a friend and he can put me into a trouble. And also maybe I am doing things that he can't do—maybe I buy something that he can't buy and he becomes jealous of me, and if he becomes jealous he can kill me or destroy my life. That is the reason why my mother tell me that one, and I take it very serious. And up to now I don't have friends because I don't know what friend can do for me so I don't have it. Even all my friends that I work with as a driver, now they are all gone. Left with me alone, so who am I going out to see? If you see me going out, I am going to buy something or I am going to town to do something and come back. I'm not going to sit in any friend's place chatting—I don't have any friend.[106]

In some cases, fears were justified as jealous friends directly attempted to sabotage individuals.[107] While, as Margaret Field has noted, such fear was not necessarily unique to drivers, men engaged in driving work seemed particularly prone to such anxieties and represented a significant percentage of those visiting spiritual specialists for protection and defense.[108]

The liminality that was essential to the success of drivers' work and lives meant that they were able to transcend geographical, social, and economic divides, facilitating the circulation of people and the exchange of goods. However, that liminality also left them unmoored from conventional categories of sociability or expectations for prosperity, vulnerable in the face of economic and social uncertainties. While most drivers' anxiety was manifested in concerns about the accumulation of wealth and their own physical safety, the choice of a wife also required careful consideration because, as the song "Driver ni" highlighted, many drivers felt that women's attraction to their relative prosperity raised questions about their trustworthiness as spouses. While some men feared that their wives would leave them when they encountered financial difficulties, others were afraid of the jealous actions of other members of her family (as well as his own). In the context of Nkrumah's increasingly authoritarian rule in the 1960s, jealous friends, neighbors, and colleagues engaged not only in spiritual warfare, but also in physical and political sabotage, often passing false information to government agents in order to get drivers placed in jail.[109] The increasing intrusion of political authoritarianism into the social and economic lives of drivers and the political manipulation of legal structures throughout the 1960s marks the beginning of a slow decline in the socioeconomic status of drivers.

Conclusion

As is suggested here, both the personal experiences and the public image of drivers were complicated and contradictory. What marks this period as distinct, however, is the possibilities available to good drivers, not the condemnation of those drivers who failed to live up to professional, social, and legal standards. While independence did not bring any remarkable improvements in conditions for drivers—in terms of road conditions, numbers or types of vehicles, numbers of passengers, and so on—it also did not result in a dramatic decline in conditions of driving work. As a result, driving during this period presented possibilities for accumulation and prosperity for many young men that lay outside of the traditional paths to status in late-colonial and postcolonial society—chieftaincy, education, Christianity, civil service. Through driving, young men were able to access wealth, marry and establish families, build houses, own vehicles, and establish themselves as people of status in the community. In taking advantage of these opportunities, young boys transformed themselves into "modern men." In working as drivers, they not only made alternative claims to masculinity and defined themselves as men, but they also experienced the "eye-opening" (anibue) of modernity and modernization. As drivers, they participated in this world themselves, but they also made it available to others, connecting and sometimes fusing rural and urban, tradition and modernity in new and innovative ways. In the process, they established themselves at the center of an increasingly mobile world as symbols of both the opportunities and the difficulties that anibue might bring.

4 "One Man, No Chop": Licit Wealth, Good Citizens, and the Criminalization of Drivers in Postcolonial Ghana

In their July 24, 1962, issue, the editors of the *Daily Graphic* channeled the outrage of their readers in a strong condemnation of the country's entrepreneurial class of traders, storekeepers, and transport owners/drivers. They argued that the unwillingness of drivers and other entrepreneurs to lower their "unreasonable prices" was "an indication that there are some people in Ghana today who are determined to exploit their neighbors." While the *Graphic* editors recognized that these small-scale entrepreneurs were invested both in protecting the capital already in their businesses as well as securing profits, those profits, they argued, should be reasonable: "We condemn, in the most severe terms, the practice of exploiting the public in order to make turn-overs which are fantastically out of all proportion to the capital invested in specific business." Any transport owner who attempted to recover the capital they had invested in their passenger lorries within eighteen months or less "should consider themselves public enemies," they declared.[1]

In condemning drivers and other entrepreneurs as "local Shylocks" trying to "exploit their neighbours," the *Graphic* editors voiced the Ghanaian public's frustration with their position in relation to their country's changing economic fortunes. After decades of economic stability and relative prosperity buoyed by high cocoa prices, the significant drop in cocoa prices during the late 1950s and 1960s[2] profoundly altered the economic possibilities of the Ghanaian public and the authority of the postcolonial Ghanaian state. The unfortunate timing of this economic crisis, coming so few years after independence, placed economic development at the center of the broader social and political project of nation building. As bad years turned into bad decades, and as successive regimes from across the ideological spectrum failed to halt steady decline, both the state and its citizens attempted to root out the cause of their misfortune and re-establish social and economic order. In the process, the boundaries between "good citizens" and "public enemies" became ever more starkly drawn.[3]

As mobile entrepreneurs, drivers were caught in the middle of these politics of postcolonial citizenship. In attempting to balance their role in providing an essential public service and in securing private profit, drivers' efforts to "make do" and "make money" in the context of general economic crisis raised the ire of the public and the state. Drivers like Okan Tetteh and Nii Ayi Bule were perplexed and frustrated by the sudden changes in public perception:

> Because of our driving work, the ministers and then the big men in the country, they don't think about us at all. They don't regard us that we are somebody and we sometimes used to pick people who come from abroad, and then we take them rounds. And then some of these people who come from abroad, they come to have talk with some of us because we take them round and what they tell us is driving work is not a small work at all because if you are driving, you use the whole of your body—your hand, your head, you listen to the engine, to your leg—you're using every part of your body to drive. And abroad, when they make exams for all of the workers, doctors are the people who came first, and then the second people are drivers. But this our country, our elders, they don't regard us in anything at all. Instead, if there is a problem, the Prime Minister or the leaders to come and stand for us, they will not do it. What they used to say is "their wife also can drive." But if you yourself, you see what they are saying that their wife can drive in case right they load articulator full of cassava and they say they should drive it to Kumasi, do you think this woman can drive this articulator? Or if they ask a woman to take articulator and go to Navrongo and bring tomatoes to Accra, do you think a woman can do it? Because of all this, now our driving work that we do before, we work with happiness and so much strength and we see that we're working, but now if you see the people that are trying to lead the nation, they don't think about drivers.[4]

The criticisms of government officials like Krobo Edusei, who dismissed drivers by pointing out that his "wife can also drive" in the mid-1960s, marked not only a change in the regulatory climate of the country, but also, more fundamentally, a transformation in the social and economic possibilities of drivers' work.

Drivers like Tetteh and Bule saw themselves as the inheritors of an occupational practice, which their fathers and uncles had used to establish themselves as respectable, modern men. In the midst of declining economic conditions that began in the 1960s, drivers ensured the continued prosperity and security of themselves and their families by exploiting the flexibility and entrepreneurial autonomy of their work. Drivers insisted that they "made money" throughout the long period of economic decline that lasted through the mid-1980s—a statement that contrasts sharply with that of market women and other workers who characterize this period as one of survival, rather than accumulation.[5] The same entrepreneurial autonomy that had established drivers as respectable, modern men in the 1930s and 1940s and enabled drivers to survive the emerging economic crisis of the decades immediately after independence also highlighted the limitations of postcolonial economic stability and control.

During this period, the increasing financial and economic constraints on passengers like market women and waged workers raised new questions about the motivations and actions of the private commercial drivers who had long profited from their dominance in the country's motor transport industry. In undermining state efforts to reshape the country's economic future and assert its authority, drivers unintentionally and indirectly aligned themselves with an emerging understanding of "bad citizens" as "public enemies."

The general shift in public opinion about the respectability and responsibility of drivers were part of a much larger economic crisis that had consequences for the social and economic lives of all Ghanaians. This period of Ghanaian history—from the moment of independence under Kwame Nkrumah in the mid-1950s through the military coup of Jerry John Rawlings in the early 1980s—is conventionally defined by the series of coups and changes in political leadership that characterized early postcolonial state politics. However, for much of the Ghanaian population, these changes in leadership masked fundamental continuities in political rhetoric and economic policy.[6] Unable or unwilling to effectively respond to the economic crisis, a series of postcolonial regimes engaged in a process of "scapegoating," identifying entrepreneurs like drivers and market women as the source of economic crisis. The centrality of drivers to this predicament reflects the degree to which scapegoating happened not only in a top-down fashion but also at the grassroots itself, as various agents sought to make sense of changing social, political, and economic realities. Market women, for example, sought to deflect criticism and justify their own economic strategies by shifting blame to drivers, pointing to the high cost of transport as one important explanation for rising prices and dwindling profit margins.[7] Waged workers, likewise, expressed discontent over rising transport costs as their wages stagnated and their buying power diminished. While drivers were less explicitly targeted as victims of violence during this period (as opposed to market women, who were regularly attacked, particularly during the Rawlings regime), drivers emerged with a new reputation as scoundrels, cheats, liars, and thieves—mobile, autonomous ne'er-do-wells who symbolized economic anxieties and insecurities of both a Ghanaian public and the postcolonial state.

Despite public discourses about drivers as criminal, the emerging critique of drivers was not rooted in any fundamental changes in driver practice. Rather, the incremental nature of this process of criminalization—from "respectable" to immoral to criminal—over the course of nearly thirty years reflects shifting understandings of economic morality, rooted in both the country's changing economic conditions as well as a public rhetoric of citizenship that centralized power and authority in the nation-state. Economic and social crisis raised new questions about the commercialization of automobility, highlighting the limitations of African autonomy and the social and economic significance of mobility in postcolonial Ghana. The social relationships and expectations between drivers, passengers, and the Ghanaian state were effectively reordered as drivers and driving practice were caught up in attempts to (re)define the Ghanaian nation-state as the new institution of social and economic order in the decades after independence. As a result, this chapter argues, the independence and entrepreneurial success of drivers, which had once been the foundation of their respect and status as cosmopolitan, modern men, became their greatest liability during the "era of decline"[8] that lasted from independence through the early 1980s.[9] Their experience highlights the degree to which entrepreneurial autonomy—long central to Ghanaian economy and society—was transformed into a national threat by postcolonial state and society.

"Good Citizens": Risk, Profit, and the Politics of Striking

Although driver practices did not change in substantive ways, the pace of urbanization and economic growth in the 1950s resulted in ever-increasing numbers of cars and pedestrians on Ghanaian roads. Between 1954 and 1955 in Accra alone,

Fig. 4.1 "Old and New Mammy Truck," photographer P. K. Anane, April 22, 1960 (Ministry of Information, Information Services Photographic Library, Ref. no. R/R/9720/5).

the number of registered cars increased by 4,000, from 15,000 to 19,000. By 1957, there were 27,000 cars registered in the capital.[10] Similarly, the population of Accra by the end of the 1950s had tripled from its pre–WWII numbers.[11] In contrast with the scarcity of motor vehicles during the 1930s and 1940s, by independence in 1957, drivers and pedestrians competed for space on the new country's roads, resulting in greater numbers of accidents that greatly increased the risk of motor transportation for both passengers and pedestrians.

The Nkrumah government renewed attempts to regulate and control the motor transport industry in light of the new pressures on the country's roads. Some of those regulations enhanced drivers' prestige and contributed to their image as respectable, modern men. However, post-independence regulation also reflected an attempt by the Nkrumah government to integrate drivers into the new, national project—a shift in focus from individual accumulation to national development. In that spirit, Parliament passed new regulations in 1957 that required drivers to carry "Third Party Insurance."[12] In many ways, new insurance regulations were an extension of colonial efforts to limit the risk and danger of the road through the regulation of driver practice, casting drivers as providers of an essential public service. However, in a newly independent Ghana, these regulations were also part of a new rhetoric of responsibility and shared sacrifice— an attempt to bring drivers into a new national project of development. As part of a broader effort to help protect the health, safety, and prosperity of workers, who were seen as central to the newly independent country's development, third-party insurance would cover the medical costs and/or burial of any victims of accidents while travelling in commercial transportation. Drivers, who had organized themselves into the Ghana Motor Drivers' Union, immediately went on strike in protest against the new regulations, which they argued placed an undue financial burden on drivers who would pay regular premiums to insurance companies.[13] Drivers across the country left the lorry parks, refusing to transport goods or passengers.

Drivers' strikes were not new in Ghana. During the colonial period, drivers had gone on strike several times to protest inadequate lorry parks and undesirable regulations. Furthermore, strikes were an important part of a broader culture of political mobilization in Ghana, helping to secure independence by placing pressure on the colonial economy to guarantee rights for workers and political representation for Africans in government.[14] However, this strike failed to resonate with the general public, who viewed driver unwillingness to take responsibility for the risk of motor transportation as a reflection of their incompatibility with public interest.[15] The editors of the *Graphic* summarized the opinions of many of its readers who had been writing with complaints to the newspaper, arguing, "No reasonable-minded person in the country would sympathize with the Union's line of action."[16] According to the *Graphic* editors, the government was fulfilling its duty to "safeguard the lives of the people by demanding a higher sense of responsibility among drivers and transport owners in the discharge of their duties to the general public."[17] Not only was the drivers' decision to go on strike "not justified," but "the Union's coercive measures aimed at forcing the Government to yield immediately to their demands can only create unpleasant conditions by paralyzing the road transport system, the object being to create a general background of chaos."[18] In light of the insurance scheme's goal "to give protection to innocent parties involved in motor accidents," the unwillingness of drivers to negotiate was perceived by the public to be both callous and dangerous.[19]

The 1957 strike increased public criticism of drivers, who had failed to adequately read the changing public and political sentiments on issues of economic morality and good citizenship. The rhetoric of economic morality and good citizenship in the new country was rooted in much older values and practices. The ability to accumulate through individual effort had long been valued in the states and societies of southern Ghana where *abirempon* (or "big men") were granted special titles and privileges through the accumulation of wealth.[20] However, the morality of their accumulation or profits was assessed based not on "how they are made (for example, through trade or production), but from their results."[21] As the popular slogan "one man, no chop" indicates, when only one person holds wealth, the community cannot survive. Individual economic agents were bound by norms of reciprocity and mutual support, which evaluated their accumulation in light of its benefit on other members of the family and community.[22] "Licit wealth"[23] resulted in the betterment not only of the individual but also of his/her family and community. Those who failed to spread the benefits of their wealth among the broader community were seen to be profiting at the expense of others, and, as a result, were engaging in illicit or "wicked" behavior.[24] During the colonial period, drivers were respected for their ability to respond to passenger demands, protecting and asserting the interests of indigenous entrepreneurs against the actions of a colonial state that sought only to extend its own profits. Passengers and the general public understood driver's strikes as an extension of the social and economic interests of both drivers and passengers. However, independence shifted definitions of "wickedness" and "licit wealth," implicating all Ghanaians in the social construction and economic development of the new nation. The public response to the strike highlighted the degree to which drivers, who had long engaged in strike action that was broadly supported by the public, had clearly misread that public and failed to respond adequately to changing social and economic conditions.

The union was unable to come to terms with the government's representative, Minister of Interior Ako Adjei, after several attempts at negotiation. As the strike dragged on for weeks, passengers began to complain about the inconvenience of the strike as a "footsore nuisance."[25] The resistance of drivers to assume some greater responsibility for the risk of riding in their vehicles led to passenger condemnation of trotros and lorries as "death traps."[26] Meanwhile, the riding public consistently applauded the reasonableness of government demands on behalf of citizens in contrast with the unreasonableness of drivers.[27] In the months immediately after independence, government attempts to regulate and reform the motor transport industry were viewed as part of "the duty of every good government to see that the citizens in the country do not lose their lives in road accidents."[28]

Ultimately, and to the detriment of the union, it did appear that misinformation and misunderstanding about the function of third-party insurance was at the root of the strike.[29] While drivers came away looking foolish, selfish, careless, and unreasonable, the government was widely viewed as efficient and civic minded.[30] In public statements, government officials expressed concern about the hardships the public was facing as a result of the strikes. Resources were redirected to guarantee that essential services and commodities were provided to all of the major urban areas. By the time the union called off the strike on August 1, 1957, drivers had suffered irreparable harm to their relationship with the public, while the Nkrumah government had taken advantage of the opportunity to forge a new relationship between private commercial drivers, passengers, and the state.[31]

This new relationship reflected fundamental shifts in economic morality that were tied to nationalist understandings about the relationship between citizens and the state. The independence and self-reliance of drivers contrasted sharply with Nkrumah's rhetoric of shared sacrifice for the development of Ghana and the benefit of all of her citizens, which, at least initially, was well received. Nkrumah argued that workers' dedication was essential to the success of the five-year development plan, while the entire country was encouraged to participate in community self-help projects.[32] Motor transportation was not ignored in these projects, as roads were widely recognized as a central part of the self-help nation-building movement.[33] However, the consequences of the drivers' strike for the Ghanaian public highlighted for the Nkrumah regime the tensions between a worker-centered economic policy that privileged union organizing, the space that union organizing provided for political dissent and economic protest, the importance of entrepreneurs in providing essential public services, and the value placed on entrepreneurial accumulation.

At least in part in response to the drivers' strike, throughout the 1960s, the Nkrumah government gradually limited the independence and power of the unions. The 1958 Industrial Relations Act placed the Trade Union Congress—the country's largest union organization—under direct government control and coopted unions into the nationalist project. Nkrumah encouraged all unionized workers to act in solidarity with the government and refrain from striking. In exchange for their cooperation and support, the government promised to provide a program of incentives to reward excellent work, increase the purchasing power of workers, and provide "sanatoria and holiday resorts on the seaside" to reward workers and farmers for their shared efforts and sacrifices.[34] However, government officials condemned those workers who did engage in strikes, such as the Railway and Dockworkers Union in 1960, as "politically motivated."[35]

Although unionized, drivers fell outside of the benefits of the government's labor policy, having not yet been incorporated into a TUC that was dominated by public sector unions, waged labor, and industrial labor.[36] Rather, particularly after the 1957 strike, drivers, who were entrepreneurs, were widely viewed as a primary cause for the high cost of living that was impinging the purchasing power of workers.[37] The government increasingly argued that workers needed the cost of living to decrease rather than an increase in wages, shifting the blame for the plight of workers onto drivers, traders, and shopkeepers in the private sector and associating them with the economic exploitation of foreign industries and governments that provided essential processed goods and were viewed as agents of neocolonialism.[38] Throughout the 1960s, drivers were attacked in the pages of the nation's newspapers as "political" and "revolutionary" and accused of fare-cheating,[39] corruption,[40] recklessness,[41] and carelessness.[42] The changing discourse about accidents also embodied broader changes in public attitudes toward drivers as passengers and government officials identified driver's "careless" and "reckless" behavior as the central factors in persistent accidents. Some went so far as to describe accidents as "deliberate murder."[43]

"Poverty is Painful": Morality, Legality, and the Risks of Survival

In the aftermath of the misunderstanding over third-party insurance, drivers found themselves on the wrong side of an increasingly stark dichotomy between "good citizens" and "public enemies" in newly independent Ghana. In failing to prevent accidents and in engaging in behavior that was classified as "economic exploitation," drivers seemed to ignore Nkrumah's calls for worker responsibility and shared sacrifice at the same time that drivers and motor vehicles were increasingly viewed as symbols of wealth and means through which some young Ghanaians sought to "get rich quick."[44] In the context of populist nationalist politics, such action (or inaction) by drivers resulted in profound changes in their public image and raised new questions about the morality and patriotism of their practices. Passengers called on the government to "use the law when injustice is done,"[45] demanding the regulation of lorry fares and condemning the behavior of drivers toward passengers.[46] These critiques were particularly dangerous in the context of an increasingly authoritarian Nkrumah government, prompting previously apolitical drivers to mount huge demonstrations in Accra to establish their loyalty to Nkrumah and the CPP[47] and pass resolutions pledging "their unflinching support to President Nkrumah, the Party and the Government in their effort to transform Ghana into a prosperous socialist state."[48]

Throughout the 1960s, however, the promises of Nkrumahism—the benefits that would result from shared sacrifice—failed to materialize. Industrialization, coupled with heavy military involvement and aid in liberation movements around the continent depleted the country's coffers at the same time that the fall in cocoa prices and the transition to a new national currency, the Ghana cedi, limited the country's access to foreign exchange. By 1965, people throughout the country complained about shortages of imported goods. Drivers suffered from shortages of spare parts and tires,[49] which made it difficult to keep their vehicles on the road and cut into their profits. In many ways, drivers faced the shortages of the 1960s as part of a much longer history of creative adaptation and struggle over spare parts, tires, and petrol. Drivers had dealt creatively with scarce materials and difficult road conditions in pursuing their work since the introduction of the motor vehicle in the 1910s, and many drivers improvised spare parts and held their vehicles together through street-side welding and salvaging used parts from those vehicles beyond repair. Long-distance drivers, in particular, were accustomed to thinking creatively in order to maintain and repair their vehicles on long journeys through rural areas.[50] Rough road conditions and heavy loads made the risk of damage high, and spare parts were not available in smaller towns and villages. Furthermore, drivers had experienced periodic shortages of spare parts throughout the colonial period, most notably during and immediately after the two world wars, when imports were significantly curtailed and petrol was rationed.[51]

The temporary shortages experienced during wartime paled in comparison to the persistent conditions of want that began in the 1960s. While spare parts were the earliest affected inputs, tires represented some of the most significant and dangerous shortages. The persistent shortage of tires highlighted not only the long but precipitous decline in the Ghanaian economy, but also the specific failure of Nkrumah's vision for Ghanaian industrialization. Nkrumah had identified tire manufacturing as one of the central industries to be nurtured in the newly independent country (along with a number of other ventures including vegetable oil production, distilling, metallurgy, boat building, paper mills, vehicle assembly, cocoa processing, footwear production, and pharmaceuticals); however, by the mid-1960s, these new industries were losing money and becoming a drain—rather than a boost—for the national economy. As one Circle Odawna driver recalled, tire shortages also called for creative solutions, as drivers placed oversized tires over top of their regular tires in order to keep their vehicles on the road:

> Even sometimes the lorry tire will become difficult for us to get to buy, but at the time that I am a mate I remember, during Nkrumah time, tires have become difficult for us and we can't find tire to buy. But my master is a fitter-man. Because he was a fitterman so what he did because we don't have tire, we went to take oversized tires that are bigger than our car and then put it on our tire before we use it to work—six-ton car tires is what he went to take and then put it on our tire before we fix it. If the thing happen like that, we also find our own ways and means and then do what we can do to do our work.[52]

Only two decades earlier, such ingenuity had marked drivers as knowledgeable and skilled professionals who were respected by passengers and the general public for their ability to safely operate their vehicles and achieve economic prosperity through work that was widely perceived to be dangerous. However, the implications of driver creativity and economic autonomy had clearly shifted by the mid-1960s, as both the state and the general public held up these practices as examples of risky, profit-driven behavior.

The coup that overthrew Nkrumah on February 24, 1966, reflected the tenuous political and economic climate in the country. The National Liberation Council (NLC), led by Lt. Gen. J. A. Ankrah, promised to "stabilize the economy."[53] The NLC and its later civilian representative, K. A. Busia, implemented new Western-oriented reforms, including currency devaluation and austerity while opening the country to foreign investment and aid. Although the NLC and Busia's strategies to deal with the crisis differed significantly from that of Nkrumah, the state remained at the center of their attempt to re/form the social, political, and economic order. Now couched in the language of "civic duty," the NLC/Busia regime called on Ghanaians to stamp out corruption and be "good citizens."

The fight against corruption established a strong connection between issues of morality and legality in Ghanaian politics and economics, which echoed Nkrumah's earlier calls for shared sacrifice and the collective good.[54] "Cheating drivers"[55] who raised their fares were accused of engaging in a form of corruption that transgressed both the legal and moral expectations of citizens.[56] Government officials and passengers also viewed vehicle condition as a threat to the safety of the general public. By the mid-1960s, mammy trucks—once symbols of Ghanaian ingenuity and entrepreneurialism—were widely condemned in popular newspapers as "death traps,"[57] and their "importation and assembly was banned in 1966 in favor of a new type of customized bus produced by Motorway."[58] While importation and assembly of new mammy trucks was banned, older vehicles were still allowed to operate on the road. They were not, however, allowed to operate as passenger vehicles. In other words, mammy trucks after 1966 were confined to cargo transport (with the driver, his mates, and the owner of the goods as the only allowable passengers). Despite the ban, many wooden mammy trucks remained on the road, as drivers cannibalized old vehicles for spare parts and carried out makeshift repairs in order to keep vehicles operating.[59]

When drivers again went on strike at the end of 1967 in protest against high premiums for third-party insurance, they further transgressed notions of the "good citizen." Despite warnings by NLC-member and Minister of Defence Lt. Gen. Emmanuel Kotoka to avoid strikes in order to enable the country to re-establish itself on the path to economic progress, trotro and taxi drivers across the country and particularly in Accra again took their vehicles off the road. The strike lasted through the end of December 1967. While the government promised to investigate the drivers' claims about insurance-company abuse and established a committee to produce a white paper summarizing the results of the investigation into driver complaints, both the government and the public saw the strike itself as another manifestation of the antisocial behavior of drivers. The strike, which caused further damage to an already struggling economy, justified further criticism of drivers who were seen to be pursuing their own profits at the expense of a public interest in cheaper and safer transportation. In the eyes of both citizens and the state, strikes were no longer seen to be a means of legitimate protest, but rather a tool of political manipulation and economic sabotage. Speaking to the Maritime and Dockworkers Union at the Workers College in Takoradi only a month after the drivers' strike, Col. I. A. Acheampong, then chairman of the Western Region Committee of Administration, "called on all workers to realize that as a result of some strikes in the country, a great damage has been done and unless they refrained from such strikes, the country would not achieve its aim in resuscitating its economy. . . . The chairman said that by acts of indiscipline 'the strikers are unconsciously creating the very climate suitable for the enemies of the state.'"[60]

Defining and Solving the "Transport Problem": Shortages, Corruption, and Crime

While the drivers' strikes significantly damaged the public perception of drivers and their relationship with passengers, the difficulties and inconveniences that resulted when private commercial vehicles were kept off the roads highlighted the inadequacies of public sector transport services and the dependence of the public on the trotros, taxis, and mammy wagons that they now condemned. The rapid pace of urbanization and the national economic crisis that accelerated during the late 1960s made it difficult for government transport services to keep up with passenger demand. Particularly in urban areas, where the general public viewed efficient motor transport as an essential right of citizens and a necessity for the country's workers, municipal and national governments found it increasingly difficult to maintain an operating fleet. State retreat from public sector transport services was coupled with a desire to assert greater control over private sector drivers and commercial motor transportation. Whereas trotros and taxis had been viewed as a supplement to a reasonably well-developed urban transit system at independence, only a decade later, transit agencies like the Omnibus Services Authority (OSA) found it difficult to maintain their vehicles. The result was a near-complete dependence on private sector commercial transportation like trotros and taxis, which many feared encouraged exploitation by drivers. However, these public and state anxieties over potential exploitation by drivers were mere metonyms of ongoing negotiations over the nature and scope of state authority, in which the state saw its power over the nation's economy erode in the face of persistent economic crisis.

When trotro and taxi drivers pulled their vehicles off the country's roads during the strikes, the Ghanaian public found that their ability to obtain essential goods and get to work or the market was significantly constrained. A more financially secure Nkrumah government in 1957 dedicated resources to mitigating the effects of the strike, transporting food to urban centers and setting up additional bus routes to transport workers. However, the country's economic situation had deteriorated significantly by 1967, when the drivers strike disrupted economic activity in Accra and other urban centers and forced those without private cars to walk to work. As one *Graphic* reader noted in the aftermath of the strike, "Workers could but reach their work places late. House-wives, whose husbands had no cars, had to walk long distances to and from the market in order to purchase foodstuffs for their households."[61] As the hardship imposed by the strike demonstrated, what had begun in the 1930s as a private enterprise had become transformed into an essential public service, as trotro and taxi drivers stepped in to fill gaps left by failing government transport services.

The 1967 strike forced the new NLC government to remove import restrictions for spare parts in order to alleviate some of the difficulties faced by private commercial transport drivers. However, the strike also refocused the attention of both the public and the government on the country's "acute transport problem."[62] In the context of a revolution motivated by accusations of corruption and mismanagement, both the state and the public focused significant attention on the inadequacies of state transport services. However, the public identified private commercial drivers as the source of, rather than the solution to, their transport problem. Couched in terms of political rights, some members of the Ghanaian public demanded access to government-funded public transport as an escape from the danger and exploitation of the private sector trotro and taxi drivers. The ever-increasing size of Accra meant that transport problems were particularly acute in the country's political and economic capital. As one *Graphic* reader complained:

> The public sector which should have provided reliable means of transport is now playing a supplementary role to the Private Road Transport Owners Association. Thus workers have been placed at the mercy of private transport owners to charge any fares they life. The "tro tro" strike which took place about two years ago nearly brought the city's transportation system to a standstill and these drivers have come to realize that they are indispensable. Hence they have been exploiting the poor workers.[63]

While such statements clearly critiqued government failure to provide essential public services, drivers, it was argued, had taken advantage of the situation and were not engaging in outright exploitation. The NLC and, later, Busia governments responded by importing hundreds of buses for the Accra-Tema City Council and the Omnibus Service Authority (OSA). The OSA, in particular, publicly announced plans to compete with trotro drivers,[64] and the NLC declared "an all-out war on transport problems" in an attempt to "save the public from the mercenary grips of the 'tro-tro' drivers and their 'Aprankes' [*sic*]."[65] Such public statements amounted to an outright vilification of drivers, who were more explicitly labeled as criminals and public enemies, even if there was no legal code under which they could be clearly prosecuted.

Some members of the Ghanaian public welcomed the introduction of new buses. As Mary Tetteh, a passenger waiting for an OSA bus in 1970 said (with tears of joy): "Thank goodness the buses have started coming on the road. Who wants to use 'trotro' whilst a comfortable bus is available?"[66] At the same time, the public continued to protest the high cost and poor service of trotros, arguing that "some poor conditions in the [transportation] service have become almost a tradition and so strong measures are needed for changes because tradition dies hard."[67] Public protests did not result in any significant changes in the fare structure, but they did focus the government's attention on drivers' reputation for recklessness and indiscipline. As part of a larger "Discipline Campaign," Prime Minister Busia "exhorted [drivers] to discipline themselves, especially about how they handle their vehicles and passengers."[68] He called on drivers—and all Ghanaians—to resist corruption and refrain from bribery, assisting the government in the detection of what were increasingly widespread crimes.[69] Busia's calls for "civic responsibility" echoed Nkrumah's demands for shared sacrifice and allegiance to the nation. However, these calls to end corruption rang hollow in light of daily evidence of bribery, corruption, and theft within Busia's own administration. The OSA itself was racked by corruption, which had resulted in bankruptcy, even as it tried to resurrect the public transport sector.[70]

The inability of the NLC/Busia government to improve Ghana's public transportation and to limit the perceived danger and exploitation of drivers was due in large part to a fundamental shortage of foreign currency, which in turn led to a shortage of essential imported goods like spare parts and tires. The shortages that began during the Nkrumah period persisted long after the coup, as the economic crisis deepened and the "transport problem" was seen a symbol of systemic problems in the Ghanaian economy:

> It's because we have no foreign exchange to order new buses to take our workers to and from their places of work. We have no foreign exchange in order new buses to take our workers to and from their places of work. We have no foreign exchange to order spare parts for the old buses that we have. . . . We need to increase productivity in order to generate enough growth in the economy to give us the resources out of which debt servicing obligations can be met. Yet we cannot carry our workers to work on time and they have, indeed, to spend the greater part of their energies just trying to obtain transportation to get to work! To produce wealth to pay our debts. How do you resuscitate an economy that way?[71]

After the NLC government opened import licenses for spare parts to the general public in an effort to ameliorate the country's transport difficulties, Lebanese and Syrian traders eagerly entered the auto import business, bringing new and used cars and spare parts into the country. Soon, however, their outsider status led to suspicions and accusations of exploitation as prices remained high.[72] In response to public accusations, Busia's 1969 Alien Expulsion Act forced these Lebanese and Syrian traders and transport owners to surrender their businesses to the government.[73] In light of rhetoric that claimed foreign business owners were limiting opportunities for Ghanaians to build their own businesses, the Busia government anticipated that Ghanaians would invest and takeover these surrendered companies. However, unemployed Ghanaians lacked enough capital to invest the large sums required and lacked the foreign connections to make import businesses sustainable.[74]

Private commercial vehicles were, by and large, Ghanaian owned and operated, and thus they fit well within the policy and rhetoric of the Busia administration. However, the shortages of spare parts that resulted from the failed Ghanaian Business Promotion policies severely impinged on drivers' abilities to do their work. Drivers had long been accustomed to operating in situations of shortage and were known as creative and skillful mechanics who were adept at improvising through help from roadside fitters and vulcanizers. But, as became increasingly noticeable to the public, drivers' creative repairs and improvisations made their vehicles more dangerous than ever before.[75] In the absence of spare parts, drivers would ask roadside fitters to weld their vehicles together or to alter used spare parts intended for other vehicles.[76] The need to continue working pushed drivers to find solutions to shortages and use their skills to adapt in difficult circumstances.[77] While some drivers, like Inussa al-Haji, honed their skills in complementary fields like vulcanizing in order to have alternative options when driving work dried up or when their vehicles required unattainable or unaffordable repairs, for many driving was their only option. Those who were unable to adapt to the shortages were forced to abandon their businesses and find new ways to survive.[78]

Both government officials and the Ghanaian public had long rebuffed driver complaints that spare parts shortages limited their ability to both maintain and profit from their vehicles. However, the efforts to fix the "transport problem" and the failed attempts to revive public sector transport in the 1970s highlighted the creativity and ingenuity of drivers who managed to keep their vehicles on the road in the context of shortage. The hundreds of buses imported by the government to improve public transport services in the late 1960s and early 1970s soon were sitting idle in transport yards as a shortage of spare parts and a lack of maintenance made the expensive buses useless. In the minds of the passenger-public, however, the increased danger of vehicles due to the creative adaptations of drivers made ever-increasing fares even more outrageous and cast doubt on the legality of driver practices. The result was a vilification of drivers as active participants in a culture of corruption that both transgressed the norms of economic morality and disrespected and disobeyed the law.

By the early 1970s, the Busia administration's currency devaluation and austerity measures deepened the impact of the crisis on the Ghanaian public. The suffering of the Ghanaian public was made all the more painful in light of widespread corruption within the government ranks of the Busia regime. Despite the administration's anticorruption campaign (complete with a propaganda center) encouraging individuals to eschew corrupt practices, difficult economic conditions led many within and outside of the government to grasp at the dwindling resources.[79] Drivers became one of many targets of corruption accusations and public condemnation as Busia's failure to effectively implement and police anticorruption measures resulted in a profound public disillusionment with government. When the administration attempted to implement economic reforms that were intended to reverse the perceived damage caused by Nkrumah's "socialist" policies in 1972, discontent seemed to boil over.[80] The currency devaluation and austerity measures significantly deepened the financial and economic hardships of many Ghanaians, while Busia traveled abroad to court international donors and further his own academic career.[81]

The military coup of the National Redemption Council (NRC) and Col. I. K. Acheampong that followed in January 1972 further solidified the image of the corrupt driver. In an attempt to reverse the effects of the Busia administration's currency devaluation, the NRC centralized and nationalized the country's major economic sectors. However, at the same time, Acheampong encouraged workers to "take a militant stand" in the revolution and, in the same language as his predecessors, proclaimed that "Workers have been reassured by the government that they occupy an envious position in the framework of the revolution. They must therefore reciprocate this honour done them by eschewing laziness, lateness, apathy, and other undesirable attitudes which militate against the advancement of the country."[82] The NRC had declared "Economic War"[83] and called on the country to embrace the principles of self-reliance and responsible citizenship.[84] "Operation Feed Yourself," which began in 1972, presented perhaps the most complete realization of the NRC's objectives, redirecting farmers' energies toward food crops in an attempt to decrease the reliance on imported foodstuffs and strengthen the country's economic self-sufficiency. However, the rhetoric of responsibility contrasted sharply with the realities of NRC administration, as the centralization of scarce economic resources encouraged the development of a system of corruption at every level of Ghanaian society. "The evils of smuggling, profiteering, and hoarding" dominated national conversations as "the tendency among Ghanaians to 'get rich quick' has become so endemic that people are prepared to risk their lives in the dirty business of smuggling and hoarding, regardless of the baneful consequences such practices have on the national economy."[85]

Drivers, market traders, and storekeepers were frequently associated with *kalabule*, a system of corruption and bribery, which was widely seen to be damaging the economy and exploiting the public.[86] To a large degree, participation in *kalabule* was necessary in order to keep their businesses operating, but the role drivers played in the illegal activities of hoarding and smuggling traders further undermined the public image of drivers. In some cases their involvement was a one-time event. However, more commonly, individual drivers specialized in smuggling, and transport companies emerged in and around border areas, which were dedicated to smuggling both agricultural products and imported goods between Ghana and its neighbors—most notably Togo and Cote d'Ivoire.[87] For many, smuggling was seen as the only way to achieve success as a driver in the context of general economic decline and uncertainty, and some drivers flaunted their wealth obtained through smuggling by buying numerous vehicles. Particularly in the midst of hardship, these displays of wealth caused resentment and often led to drivers being turned in and/or arrested. Smuggling itself was more obviously illegal; however, in the context of the "moral ambiguity that could attach to smuggling,"[88] such antisocial behaviors on the part of some drivers heightened the moral disapprobation of the community at large. More importantly, however, their participation in *kalabule* also placed them in more tenuous legal relationships with the institutions of the state.

Recognizing the danger of this position, drivers' unions took a very public proactive stance against illegal activity among its members and pledged to aid the police in stamping out corrupt behaviors. Drivers' unions made public statements about their efforts to prevent smuggling across the Ivoirian and Togolese borders.[89] These antismuggling and anticorruption campaigns seemed to successfully shift some of the focus of blame off drivers and onto other related social groups (i.e., market women, traders, police, bookmen); however, they were unable to escape the accusations of "profiteering." Public condemnation of high fares had been haunting drivers for decades, and the pattern of behavior and widespread public disapproval of driver fare practices motivated more direct state response. Soon after the coup, Col. W.C.O. Acquaye-Nortey, Greater Accra Regional Commissioner gave all trotro drivers a forty-eight-hour ultimatum to revert to their old fares or have the police and military sent for them.[90] In the Ashanti Region, Ashanti Regional Commissioner Lt. Col. E. A. Baidoo threatened to confiscate the vehicles of any driver charging exorbitant fares.[91] Such threats reflected both the militarization of Ghanaian state and society as well as an increasing frustration with the widespread corruption and lawlessness that challenged the state's ability to maintain (or impose) order on a restless public.

The military regime's condemnation rang hollow for drivers in light of endemic corruption by soldiers and their families in the mid-1970s, and drivers grew increasingly frustrated at the seemingly intractable situation. At the same time that drivers and other private sector entrepreneurs were attacked for engaging in *kalabule*, soldiers and government officials used their privileged access to government resources to enrich themselves, their extended families, and, in some cases, their mistresses, further restricting access to essential goods, including vehicles and spare parts. Endemic corruption resulted in significant inflation and shortages of all imported goods, including spare parts, causing drivers to raise their fares even higher. When passengers complained and protested fares, drivers often verbally abused them or forced them out of their vehicles.[92] While drivers were perhaps understandably irritated at the lack of public understanding of the financial demands of their work and insulted by accusations of "cheating," these interactions with passengers gave them a reputation for insolence.[93] When oil shocks quadrupled the price of petrol, these complaints escalated further, resulting in public calls to further regulate drivers.[94] In 1977, Acheampong accused the Ghana Private Road and Transport Union, the country's largest drivers' union, of contributing "towards the prevailing high cost of living in the country," highlighting the "collaboration of transport owners with 'bookmen' and lorry park overseers to exorbitantly over-charge the conveyance of foodstuffs" and "the smuggling of lorry tyres, foodstuffs, and petroleum products out of the country which lead to the scarcity of those items."[95]

In response, the state criminalized relatively quotidian driver practices. In particular, drivers' refusals to pick up passengers became a subject of both public critique and government sanction:

> It is very disheartening when in the heat of the scorching sun one stops a virtually empty taxi and yet not paying the least attention, a taxi-driver speeds up past one without a word. Or when at night the service e light of a taxi is on, which indicates that he is still working, yet when you stop him, he wouldn't even have the courtesy to stop and inform you that he is not going your direction. That alone is even assuring enough than just to drive off. The behaviour of taxi drivers in this country more especially in the urban centres makes one wonder under which laws they operate.[96]

In other cases, "deliberately obstructing traffic" resulted in the arrest and fine of drivers. While these practices would not be considered the flaunting of wealth and power in better economic times, in the depth of economic crisis of the 1970s, drivers who refused to pick up passengers were seen to be thumbing their noses at the working classes. In many ways, drivers might be considered as belonging to the broader category of "workers." However, their ability to "survive" and, in some cases, "accumulate" despite overwhelming economic hardship made their experience relatively exceptional. By refusing to pick up passengers or deliberately obstructing traffic, drivers further highlighted their wealth by declaring that they did not need the work. This independence in wealth reflected what many saw as the drivers' privileged position in an ongoing struggle for power and control of the nation's economy. In making such practices illegal, the state attempted to reassert control over its citizens and the economy.

"*Sika Nti* (Because of Money)": Professionalism, Respect, and the New Generation of Drivers

The shifting standards of economic morality, which raised calls to criminalize driver practice, were compounded by changing standards of driver training and professionalism within the industry itself. Ambitious young men and savvy investors looked to motor transportation as a means of making "fast money" in the years after independence, buoyed by the increased accessibility of motor vehicles and driver training. Direct access to a vehicle meant that individuals could more easily become commercial drivers, bypassing training as a mate. While individual citizens may have felt that such a system was more just, drivers themselves expressed increasing concern about the professionalism of this new generation of drivers. Apprenticeships had not only trained would-be drivers in the technical skills of driving, but they also taught them the social skills necessary for effective public service work and inculcated in them a sense of respect and responsibility for themselves and their passengers. In bypassing this training, many of these new drivers marked themselves as amateurs among their colleagues. However, among public passengers and government officials, who did not necessarily know either the background of the individual driver or the politics of motor transportation, such distinctions were largely elusive, as all drivers became identified by the disrespectful and insolent practices of these "amateurs."

While some young men continued to pursue driving through the apprenticeship system as mates, the distinction between professional and amateur overlapped with generational distinctions between "old drivers" (i.e., drivers who had received their license before the late 1960s) and "new/young drivers" (i.e., drivers who had received their license after the late 1960s). As this population of new/young drivers expanded through the late 1970s, they increasingly came to represent driving work in the public sphere. Taxi and trotro drivers, in particular, were targeted as the subjects of public ire. Long-distance commercial transport still required significant skill and training to successfully maneuver poorly maintained rural roads and conduct routine repairs; however, taxis and trotros, which were located primarily in urban centers, represented a relatively easy entry for these new "amateur" drivers.

Taxi drivers were seen to embody all of the negative attributes of drivers— immorality, corruption, insolence, cheating, exploitation, and disrespect of self and others:

> The discourteous behaviour of taxi-drivers all over the country, especially in Accra, is surprisingly shocking and one wonders why taxi drivers of all people feel as pompous when it comes to stopping for passengers. It is very disheartening when in the heat of the scorching sun one stops a virtually empty taxi and yet not paying the least attention, a taxi-driver speeds up past one without a word. Or when at night the service light of a taxi is on, which indicates that he is still working, yet when you stop him, he wouldn't even have the courtesy to stop and inform you that he is not going your direction. That alone is even assuring enough than just to drive off. The behaviour of taxi drivers in this country more especially in the urban centres makes one wonder under which laws they operate. A taxi driver can pack as many passengers as he wishes and yet charge each individual as much as he himself likes. Sometimes you might be in a hurry to get somewhere and you hire a taxi ready to pay any amount he will charge you, yet, he will stop on the way to pick other passengers. If you dare challenge him he'll tell you to get down. Sometimes too, unmindful of the passengers, in the car, a taxi-driver without any excuse to his passengers stops on the way or branches elsewhere, talk as long as he so wishes before he comes to drive them off. Maybe one need not blame the taxi-driver that much for his discourtesy to passengers because if the public transportation system in the country was that efficient, if most departments and corporations had enough buses for their workers and if most individuals are owning their own cars, taxi-drivers would rather have begged for passengers. If one talks about economic saboteurs, the taxi-driver is a number one enemy. If one should talk about nation wreckers and cheats in our society, it should be nobody other than taxi-drivers.[97]

Through indiscriminate fares, threats, delays, and overall rudeness, taxi drivers seemed to be betraying the luxury status with which taxis were associated in most other countries. While, for some, the problems associated with taxi drivers was the result of an imbalance of power (i.e., too many passengers for too few drivers, making it possible for drivers to choose whom they drove and how), for others, including many drivers themselves, such practices marked a distinct generational shift:

> In recent years, Ghanaian taxi drivers, especially those operating in Accra, have managed to carve some sort of cheap "professional culture" which is not based on any set of human or ethical principles. By this they have succeeded in putting too much fear into the general public. This fear or "reverence" for Accra taxi drivers is made manifest by the excessively unnecessary respect and humility with which passengers stop taxi cabs and plead to be picked up to their respective destinations. With the greatest respect, I say that I pity the youngmen and women who were not born early enough to enjoy the good old days as far as the prices of taxi cabs were concerned. In those days, which our youth refer to as "colo," we did not have to signal a taxi to a halt in order to enjoy a smooth ride to your destination. As far as the taxi driver was concerned, your physical presence at the road-side was sufficient evidence of your indescribable desire to travel by taxi. Stop the driver would; and politely ask you where you were going. Gracious Goodness! My colo days are palatable!"[98]

Far from being an irrelevant or extraordinary event, the behavior of taxi drivers represented larger and more fundamental distinctions in the experience of urban life. The "colo[n]" (or colonial) days were marked not only by more reasonable prices but also by more reasonable behavior on the part of both drivers and passengers. The widening of these generational divisions in experience and practice throughout the rest of the twentieth century would come to define a new age, characterized by lawlessness, disrespect, corruption, and the declining status of drivers.

These changes in both state and driver practice, which resulted in the increasing criminalization of drivers, was at least in part a reflection of the declining power and effectiveness of driver's unions. Union and strike breaking became a central component of Ghanaian governance as early as the Nkrumah regime. While the colonial government of the 1940s had seen workers' unions as essential tools in the creation of a stable economic and political environment,[99] the increasing protests and strikes of workers throughout the 1960s in opposition to Nkrumah's increasingly oppressive and ineffective economic policies were seen as a direct threat to the stability of the state. By the 1970s, Acheampong had appropriated Nkrumah's antiunion, antistrike language in order to keep a lid on the growing unrest that resulted from lackluster economic improvement. Government threats to arrest striking workers and union officials and government attempts to control both prices and practices of economic agents[100] undermined the collective bargaining and organizing potential of unions. Drivers' unions found their ability to set fares and regulate driver actions increasingly coopted by the state, the police, and the military.

The role of unions, however, highlights the ambivalent relationship that the public and the state had with drivers. At the same time that the power of the unions was being undermined by the state, government officials and the public increasingly looked to the unions to control their drivers. Such control often took the form of regulatory or restrictive policies. Officials of the country's largest union attempted to implement lower fares for vehicles and to prevent drivers from adopting higher fares,[101] ban drug peddlers (and preachers) from vehicles,[102] and chastise drivers who engaged in antisocial behavior. At the same time, however, unions also attempted to encourage responsible driving through competitions to find the best driver and reward those drivers who had gone long periods without experiencing an accident.[103]

Ambivalence toward the drivers' unions paralleled more fundamental ambiguities in public attitudes toward drivers. In the face of mounting criticism, drivers not only defended themselves but were also defended by others. While some people recognized the financial constraints placed on drivers by high prices and shortages of spare parts,[104] others shifted the blame for the inherent problems in the transportation system to other groups who, as outsiders, were seen to corrupt the system. "Aliens," who had become the scapegoat for economic hardship more broadly in the late 1960s, were said to extort drivers through work-and-pay leasing systems and to operate large, corrupt transport businesses, which inhibited Ghanaian access to and profitability from the transportation system. Market women became similar targets of government and public condemnation, widely seen to be taking advantage of their privileged position in the market to manipulate the availability and price of goods. As a result, in the context of smuggling, traders, rather than their drivers, were often the most vilified targets of police action and public denunciation. By the 1970s, "bookmen" became the focus of public outrage:

> The role of transportation in the economy of especially, developing countries, cannot be over-emphasized. That is why the government places big emphasis on opening up new roads to the hinterland and is improving the existing road network. However, the despicable activities of some operators of transport business in the country has created a situation which has seriously affected the whole Ghanaian public. No wonder then, that the Head of State took the Ghana Private Road and Transport Union of the Trades Union Congress to task for their "woeful contribution" towards the prevailing high cost of living in the country. As if these anomalies are not enough, the activities of "bookmen" have not improved the image of GPRTU. We are appealing to the executive of the Union to reappraise its role in the economic war and remove the "chaff" in an effort towards improving the economy. We therefore suggest that

any driver caught in the act of smuggling must be banned from driving by the Union and when proved that the transport owner had previous knowledge of the deal, go further to confiscate the vehicle. A tall order, yes, but a necessary one aimed at clipping the wings of the saboteurs. Finally, the "Bookmen menace" must be solved realistically once and for all. The complaint from the public indicated that their elimination from the scene will not in any way disrupt the smooth operation of the transport business. Let the executive and members of the Ghana Private Road and Transport Union reflect on these important issues.[105]

Lorry parks overseers who were tasked with organizing the activities of lorry parks, helping passengers, selling tickets to passengers, collect taxes and tolls from drivers, and ordering the arrival and departure of vehicles, bookmen were widely seen as corrupt cheats, who used their power over access to motor transportation to steal and extort money and goods from potential passengers. While discontent over bookmen continued to place focus on motor transportation more broadly, the willingness to shift blame from drivers to bookmen represents the degree to which drivers were seen as victims, as well as perpetrators, in the context of economic hardship. Personal attacks, theft, and violence perpetrated against drivers and reported in newspapers further highlighted their own relative victimization.[106] If drivers were participants in one element of the broken economic and social system of the 1960s and 1970s, they were not immune from the ill effects of its more fundamental causes—corruption, shortages, and crime.

"Sea Never Dry": Petrol, Food, and the Survival Strategies of Drivers

Flight Lieutenant Jerry John Rawlings seized control of the country in 1979, vowing to cleanse the country of corruption. After a brief attempt at civilian government under the direction of Hilla Limann, Rawlings retook control of the government in 1981 as the head of the Provisional National Defense Council (PNDC). Rawlings's "second coming"[107] was motivated at least partially by the Limann administration's perceived inability to address what had become, by the end of the 1970s, a catastrophic economic decline.[108] However, Rawlings had little time to implement broader economic or structural changes in light of persistent drought and bushfires, which led to a dramatic shortage of agricultural products (including basic staples) by 1982. Unable to import food due to a lack of foreign exchange, many Ghanaians experienced extreme food shortages, with market stalls often standing empty and the price of those staples that could be found escalating well beyond the income level of most Ghanaians.[109] At the height of this crisis in 1983, more than a million Ghanaians were expelled from Nigeria, increasing the numbers looking for jobs and food. By the time the country began experiencing severe petrol shortages (a consequence of international and external

Fig. 4.2 "Passengers queue for transport at Tema Station" *Transportation Problem in Accra,* photographer Chris Briandt, February 5, 1983 (Ministry of Information, Information Services Photographic Library, Ref. no. PS/2856/8).

"oil shocks") in 1983, the economic situation had already severely deteriorated for all Ghanaians, including drivers.

While one might expect that petrol shortages would severely impinge on drivers' income earning capacity, drivers' perspectives on this period were ambivalent at best. In restricting their ability to move—and thus, to work—petrol shortages profoundly reshaped driving practice. As Inussa al-Haji described, lines formed at petrol stations that were rumored to be receiving shipments. In order to be the first in line, drivers often joined the queue two to three days ahead of time, often sleeping in their vehicles or leaving their mates to watch the vehicles while they went home. Working drivers were constantly on the lookout for a new source of fuel.[110] In light of the aimlessness and frustration of drivers who were kept immobile by a lack of petrol, long queues were unavoidably tense, particularly when waits extended beyond the typical two-to three-day waiting period:

> At that time, when it happen so, everybody make hot because there is not any place that you can even lay your head because if you go lay your head somewhere, how can you get what you're looking for? So it make us make hot at that time. And it spoil so many things for us. Oh, we form line! And I remember

at that time, there was a time when I was looking for petrol seriously to go somewhere and I want to form a line. I can say that I am inside the line for almost two weeks and I can't get petrol. So sometimes I have to leave my mate in the car and tell him to be in the line, f it reach time he should come and call. So when I leave the mate, because the way the line is, everybody if the line is moving you have to push your car forward small small small, so I remember I was in the house and someone come call me that my mate has used by car to hit someone's car in the line. Because I'm not there, he's also forcing to fight for the petrol, so he's also pushing the car and moving the car forward. So when it happened so, I've entered into a death, so I say to myself, ah, me, I no get what to eat and I'm suffering like this, and now they use my car to hit someone's car again. I have to pay for the repairs of that car, so at that time, we are so tired.[111]

The financial burden of repairs and accidents weighed heavily on drivers like Tawiah Adjetey as the inherent risks of motor transportation took on even greater significance. Many drivers were much closer to the poverty line or subsistence level than they had ever been before. Those who were wise enough to save money during good times found their savings gradually eroded by the daily costs of food, water, and shelter when their lack of petrol left them unable to work.

Despite the urgency of this survival mode, the mobility of drivers and the organizational support of their fellow drivers and unions enabled them to weather the crisis much better than some. The ability of drivers to maintain a sense of security and stability was remarkable given the implications that these events had for most Ghanaians. As Adu Boahen recalled:

It looked as if the very elements and gods were enraged against us. The outcome of these two calamities in particular [expulsion of Ghanaians from Nigeria and prolonged drought and bushfires] was the scarcity and escalating cost of basic foodstuffs especially in the urban centres, widespread unemployment, sheer hunger depicted by the famous "chains" which most people came to acquire, and with these all sorts of social evils such as stealing, armed robbery, confiscation of people's cars in broad daylight, and the resort to various devices, fair and foul, just to keep body and soul together. It was a most excruciating and traumatic experience and anybody who lived through and survived must be awarded the Order of the Volta.[112]

While drivers clearly recalled queuing for petrol, the petrol crisis did not make it impossible for them to work or force them to abandon their profession. Rather, the structures and practices of their profession enabled them to weather the crisis with remarkable security.

Mutual support had long been a defining feature of driving work. In the late-colonial period, women were attracted, in part, to the stability of driving work due to a driver's ability to always find some work at the station even when his car was in disrepair, and drivers would often sacrifice some of their income to give money to an ailing or elderly driver who was no longer able to work. Since drivers had no real retirement or health insurance, these mutual support networks were essential to driver survival. In the midst of crisis, mutual support became more important than ever, as drivers attempted to spread the wealth resulting from scarce work in order to enable everyone to survive:

> At that time, we the drivers, we help each other, like example, like I'm sitting here now, it's been some time now I haven't been working, but if my fellow drivers come they say al-Haji, how is the day. I say fine. They say take this one and go and manage things in the house. At that time, that is the way we do it because we know that is the situation. So if you are in the line and your friend get petrol and go work, then if he see that you are still in the line he will say oh, me, today I work small so take this and go and manage. So if me too I see someone who hasn't bee working for some time because he is in the line, I will also give him. So that is the way we had been doing it until the petrol started coming.[113]

Since the scarcity of petrol and the necessity of waiting in line decreased the frequency of driving work, drivers who were able to work shared their profits with colleagues and friends.

For many drivers, close relationships with market women and other traders ensured that they had access to food, even when it was unavailable in urban markets:

> You see something, drivers are the people who travel. They take food, so everybody in the town think if he move with driver, anytime he travel and he come, he will also get something from what the driver brings. Not the women alone—the men too are involved.[114]
>
> To be a driver taking market women to the market then loading from village to town, we don't have problem with food so much because any time we come, we have food in the car that we bring to the house, so food problem, we don't worry about food.[115]

In some cases, drivers were given food as gifts or forms of payment by trader clients. In other situations, drivers took advantage of their ability to travel to production regions in order to purchase foodstuffs themselves. Such privileges allowed drivers to "survive" and "get by" during these extreme shortages.

"Managing" by both drivers and passengers also drew on and elaborated on older models of coping.[116] The 1980s petrol crisis shaped conditions that were simultaneously typical and extreme. Motor transportation in Ghana had long been characterized by scarcity. Although the petrol shortages escalated the scarcity of vehicles to a point of crisis, in many ways, that scarcity was one extreme example of a historical and social reality. In appropriating "articulators" (i.e., articulated trucks) as passenger vehicles, for example, drivers and passengers

Fig. 4.3 "Passengers boarding articulated truck at Kaneshie-Takoradi Station," *Transportation Problem in Accra*, photographer Chris Briandt, February 5, 1983 (Ministry of Information, Information Services Photographic Library, Ref. no. PS/2856/6).

built on a long tradition of creativity and improvisation in motor transportation. Passengers loading themselves and their goods into articulators intended to transport cattle echoed transport practices from the 1930s that confounded colonial officials and blurred distinctions between goods and passenger vehicles.[117] Drivers, too, responded to the scarcity by raising their rates above control prices and adapting their practices to maximize their access to petrol. While drivers' strategies enabled them to survive, the public often saw driver actions as a continuation of the criminalized practices of the 1960s and 1970s. These strategies, which had been characterized as exploitative and careless, further solidified a public image of drivers as corrupt, disrespectful, and dangerous cheats.

Conclusion: Criminalization and the Ambivalence of Decline

Calls for price controls on fares and the criminalization of cheating drivers were realized in the "housecleaning exercises" of the Armed Forces Revolutionary Council (AFRC) and the "people's revolution" of the Provisional National Defence Council (PNDC) in the 1980s. In the midst of a significant drought and famine, the repatriation of Ghanaians from Nigeria, and a dramatic increase in oil prices, "callous drivers"[118] were arrested for profiteering and were given government directives on fares.[119] The "people's revolution" of the AFRC/PNDC's Flt. Lt. Jerry John Rawlings embodied and realized the political, economic, social, and cultural rhetoric of the last thirty years. He called for the "moral upliftment" and "reincarnation of the moral fibre" of Ghanaians, which required "the meting out of deterrent punishments to thieves and economic saboteurs." Conflating categories of morality and legality, Rawlings argued, "It is only when such boldness is displayed in implementing the public tribunal laws, resulting in a decrease in criminal offences, that we can begin to measure the moral achievements of the revolutionary process."[120] Rather than relying only on the power of the military, Rawlings empowered the public to directly confront illegal and immoral activity through People's Defence Committees (PDCs) and criminalized a wide swath of behaviors that were widely seen as immoral and antisocial—most particularly profiteering and hoarding. By 1984, PDCs in Accra had begun arresting trotro drivers who charged above government-stipulated fares, bolstered by new laws that made such offenses illegal and punishable.[121]

Rawlings' explicit criminalization of drivers did not necessarily stop the practices that were now considered both illegal and morally repugnant. As late as 1986, Gerald Okoe of Ghana Commercial Bank complained that

> I shall very much like to call on the authorities to take a country-wide and sustained action on those greedy drivers, for sometime ago every Ghanaian thought "kalabule" could not be eradicated, but under the PNDC Government, "kalabule" has almost died a natural death. The same antidote should be directed against our drivers.[122]

In part, Okoe's statement reflects the fact that drivers did not experience the greatest degree of public condemnation during this period—an unfortunate distinction likely earned by market women who faced regular violent attacks and dispossession.[123] However, unlike market women, who had long experienced criminalization resulting from the imposition and policing of price controls by colonial governments, the criminalization that drivers experienced was relatively new. By viewing this period (the late 1950s through the early 1980s) through their experiences and the public debates about the legitimacy and legality of motor transport practice, we can more clearly see the dynamics of social control at play during what is otherwise viewed as an "era of decline."[124]

Drivers themselves recall this period with an ambivalence that belies the grand narratives of postcolonial decline—corruption, violence, poverty, state failure. Despite the difficult conditions of their work, driver practice did not change in significant ways, and prosperity was still possible. They were able to "make money," and for them, shortage meant profit. However, it was their pursuit of prosperity (i.e., charging high fares, refusing to pay for third-party insurance) during broader conditions of want that led to their criminalization—a shift in their position from an integral part of the Ghanaian social order to its enemy. It is indeed possible that some drivers were guilty of profiteering. It is equally possible that the ever-increasing costs of spare parts, tires, and petrol necessitated an increase in fares in order to maintain particular profit margins. Drivers' expectations of their work as mobile entrepreneurs—rooted in the colonial image of the respected, successful, cosmopolitan, worldly driver—implied some degree of profit, which would allow them to maintain their families. In fact, they and their families valued the independence, flexibility, and mobility of their occupation because of its stable income—the surety of daily income. However, the public viewed the profit of drivers as a conceit in light of their own tenuous economic situations and the increasingly important role private commercial drivers played in providing transportation services for the public. Drivers were caught in the midst of a tension between the necessity of public service and the demands of private profit, and in negotiating that tension, they were not unlike the "average Ghanaian" who, the editors of the *Daily Graphic* observed, only wanted "the basic freedoms: food, shelter, clothing, and a good job for himself and his children."[125]

The risks that drivers took in preserving their vehicles and guaranteeing the financial survival and prosperity of themselves and their families certainly can be perceived as negative—the public condemnation and criminalization of drivers undermined the authority, respect, and status they had secured in the previous generation. However, the assumption that this period was an overwhelmingly negative one belies the ambivalence of the risk and decline of this period for drivers. Economic crisis inevitably impacted all Ghanaians in significant ways, as did the suffering and violence that accompanied such crisis; however, the necessity of managing shortage and risk was not new to drivers, who drew on a long history of practices and strategies to maintain the profitability of their business. And, ultimately, drivers remember this period as one of relative prosperity in which they "made money"—a "good time" in comparison with the slim profit margins of the overcrowded lorry parks and streets of twenty-first-century Ghana. But it was the social order of the period—the normative expectations of community, the definition of a "good citizen"—that defined the debates in the public sphere. While drivers carried on with "business as usual," shifting public understandings of licit wealth and social responsibility and the politics of citizenship and economic control were being reshaped around them. In pursuing their own immediate needs in the context of broader economic crisis, drivers unintentionally transformed themselves into the quintessential "bad citizen," a postcolonial scapegoat, which shaped both the short-term realities of their work as well as its longer-term possibilities.

5 "Sweet Not Always": Automobility, State Power, and the Politics of Development, 1980s–1990s

Inussa al-Haji was born in Akim-Oda around 1953. Al-Haji's family was unable to send him to school, and he lived with his mother in the village. Bored and listless, al-Haji began accompanying his older sister's husband, who ran a mammy truck between Oda and Accra, when he was eighteen years old. Like many other drivers, al-Haji began his work as a mate, but gradually his master gave him the wheel and taught him to drive. When al-Haji obtained his license in Akim-Oda in 1979, he envisioned a prosperous future, because, "if you see the drivers at that time, we respect them, and they respect themselves too."[1] Driving work was an escape for a young man who felt "stranded" by both the physical location and the circumstances of his life.[2] He threw himself into driving work, riding with his brother-in-law/master and honing his craft through extensive training—running errands, loading vehicles, and observing his master for years before he was allowed to attempt driving.

Al-Haji came to Accra in the late 1970s, where he encountered a mobility system crippled by decades of neglect and disinvestment. He was unable to find steady work as a driver, and his lack of education meant that he was ineligible for "company work." And yet, for al-Haji, driving still represented the promises of prosperity. Drivers who purchased and maintained their own vehicles continued to prosper, operating within the cultures and economies of entrepreneurial mobility. He took up work as a vulcanizer, repairing tires and attempting to save money so that he could buy his own car. But al-Haji's attempts to distinguish himself and advance his career through car ownership were futile. When he did begin work as a driver in Accra, he drove a car belonging to someone else in Nungua, using connections he made through vulcanizing work to secure a reputation as a responsible and competent driver. Al-Haji split his limited income between fuel costs, payments to the owner and his mate, and himself, saving small amounts of money that eventually enabled him to afford to get married and establish a household. By that point, he was more than thirty years old—his path to prosperity began much later and seemed much less stable than the previous generation of drivers who inspired his work.

Al-Haji's story echoed that of drivers all over the country, who balanced the risks of precarity, the promises of entrepreneurial prosperity, and the realities of state power. Drivers who had secured continued prosperity throughout the 1970s were able to withstand the vagaries of shifting public opinion, government legislation, and economic insecurity through what Paul Schauert calls "managing": "the ability to 'run things' by navigating economic, political, and social challenges."³ Drivers were not unusual in their managing—traders, musicians, bar women, and others engaged in similar forms of "hustling" that sought to balance individual desire for self-improvement with collective interests in preserving social stability and progress.⁴ But, in controlling the technology and practice of automobility that defined Ghana's social and economic life, drivers had more power and resources than many to negotiate the conditions of their work and secure stability for themselves and their families. Everyone needed to move, and even if that dependence on drivers provoked bitterness among the population and government officials and undermined the respectability of driving work, it did not necessarily cut into profits.

The dire economic realities of the 1980s, however, provided new kinds of challenges that reshaped the role of the state in Ghanaian society. Scarcity increasingly defined all aspects of Ghanaian social and economic life. The collapse in the price of cocoa and other primary commodities, which provided the country's primary source of foreign exchange, meant that neither the government nor private businesses could afford to import goods. Shortages of food, petrol, spare parts, and many other goods were compounded by domestic problems. Drought decimated the country's domestic agriculture industry. The expulsion of Ghanaians from Nigeria flooded the country with young, unemployed men and women. Oil shocks and petrol shortages made trade nearly impossible. Drivers also suffered from these symptoms of broad-based economic crisis. Without oil, petrol, spare parts, or vehicles, it seemed like Ghana was no longer "on the go," and the promises of prosperity that had attracted drivers like al-Haji were ever more difficult to achieve.

The importance of road transportation to the country's economic and social life placed the conditions of drivers' lives and work at the center of national and international debates about the persistence of economic decline in Ghana. Among government officials and international observers alike, this "crisis of the present" prompted new and often contradictory visions of the future, articulated through the language of development.⁵ This language of development was not new, in and of itself. The rhetoric and ideology of development in the 1980s was an extension of colonial projects of "civilization" and "improvement" which shaped the technopolitical strategies of infrastructural development in the early part of the twentieth century. Cooper and Packard argue that, within the realms of late-colonial policy, the concept of development "became a framing device bringing together a range of interventionist policies and metropolitan finance with the explicit goal of raising colonial standards of living"⁶—a discourse that had its roots in the colonial investments and consolidation of the 1920s and 1930s as well as postwar efforts to transform "third world" countries into productive modern economies through state-led modernization.[7] In Ghana and around the world, development experts and government officials sought a path to stability, implementing policies that could mitigate the insecurity and volatility of the global capitalist system and eliminate poverty.

The 1980s, then, did not mark the beginning of "development" but rather a shift in policy—part of a "neoliberal 'counter-revolution'" that sought to correct the global recession and international debt crisis that had decimated the economies of countries like Ghana by the 1980s.[8] For drivers and passengers, the shift in development policy manifested most immediately through the structural adjustment programs (SAP) imposed as a condition for loans from the World Bank and the International Monetary Fund (IMF). SAP reforms, including decentralization of government authority, privatization of state enterprises, liberalization of markets, and devaluation of currency, sought to decrease the power of the state and remove barriers to free trade, ushering in what the Comaroffs call "the second coming of capitalism"[9]: a neoliberal global capitalism that was distinguished from the faith in modernization and state-centered economic development, which had defined global capitalism for decades.[10]

In Ghana, the PNDC government, which formed in the wake of Rawlings' "people's revolution," was reluctant to adopt structural adjustment reforms. But in 1983, in the midst of the worst of the crisis, the PNDC reversed course, announcing a new economic recovery program, shaped by the structural adjustment reforms imposed as loan conditions by neoliberal international financial institutions like the World Bank and the IMF. Structural adjustment constituted a set of policy formulations, rooted in a belief in unfettered capitalism and private investment, rather than the state, as the engine of development. The Economic Recovery Program (ERP) decentralized and privatized much of the state bureaucracy, eliminating a large portion of formal-sector jobs. At the same time, economic activity was deregulated, tariffs and taxes were scaled back, and subsidies were removed, all in the service of foreign direct investment and favorable terms of trade in the global market.

This chapter explores the changing meaning of automobility, the contradictions of development and popular democracy, and the consequences of state retreat in the neoliberal age. Development "experts" were able to dictate policies of economic reform, backed by the power and resources of international financial institutions like the World Bank and the IMF. Viewed through the lens of neoliberal development discourse, public-private partnerships in road construction, the elimination of subsidies on petrol and fares, the empowerment of drivers' unions in the regulation of driver practice and the operation lorry parks, and the expansion of access to vehicles seemed to signal the success of neoliberal reform in Ghana—quite literally paving the way for the growth of an export-oriented economy organized on free-market principles. Ghana was known as the "World Bank's star pupil" throughout the 1980s and 1990s, and in the aftermath of structural adjustment, macroeconomic indicators suggested that the economy was growing and the ideology of development had triumphed.[11] And yet, as anthropological and sociological critiques of development suggest, the outward symbols and public rhetoric of growth represented what Arturo Escobar calls the "colonization of reality"[12]—a distortion of social experience that often obscured alternatives, complications, and challenges to the neoliberal order. Debates over roads, fares, and driver practice highlight both the power *and* the limits of development ideology.[13] Drivers and passengers, road users and residents who engaged with the institutions of neoliberal development encountered a system that was far more complicated than official discourses that touted the efficiency and efficacy of the decentralized state.[14] Rather, as public reaction reports, radio programs, newspaper editorials, and life histories of auto/mobile Ghanaians suggest, the practice of development was shaped by a number of competing interests: international financial institutions, PNDC officials, private investors, land owners, chiefs, unions, drivers, and other mobile entrepreneurs.

On the surface, the political and economic changes of the late twentieth century would expand access to automobility through the spectacle of postcolonial technopolitics—harnessing colonial strategies to project new regimes of liberalization and globalization. Road transport infrastructure investment was central to structural adjustment policies that sought to encourage export-oriented trade, and a large percentage of development money was funneled into road construction. With new access to foreign exchange and liberalized markets, both foreign and African importers began purchasing vehicles in large numbers, flooding the market for both private and commercial cars. Government rhetoric and economic theory suggested that liberalization in all realms would result in freedom of movement and prosperity for all. For drivers like al-Haji, however, this new "development" was highly contradictory—increasing access to motor transportation while at the same time decreasing the profitability of driving work.

The influx of vehicles constituted one of many "paradoxes of prosperity," which characterized the lived experience of Ghana's late-twentieth-century economic development.[15] The construction of roads and the traffic jams in urban centers were mere "signs of development without its substance"[16] or what the Comaroffs have described as "the experiential contradictions at the core of neoliberal capitalism," which "appears both to include and marginalize in unanticipated ways; to produce desire and expectation on a global scale and yet to decrease the certainty of work and the security of persons; to magnify class differences but to undercut class consciousness; above all, to offer up vast and almost instantaneous riches to those who master its spectral technologies—and simultaneously, to threaten the very existence of those who do not."[17] Though not quite as extreme as Nigeria in the 1970s and 1980s, where "conspicuous spending, fleets of hi-tech buses, and the intensified consumption of luxury imports brought the signs of development without its substance,"[18] the physical symbols and macroeconomic indicators of development in Ghana in the 1980s and 1990s masked a declining security in the lives of many Ghanaians including drivers at the same time that the government retreated from any direct responsibility or control of the private sector. The narrative of "crisis," in other words, did not disappear with structural adjustment reform or populist rhetoric. Rather, for many in Ghana around the turn of the twentieth century, "development" evinced a growing vulnerability and insecurity that brought into question the values and practices of autonomy and mobility that formed the foundation of a twentieth-century mobile society. If "anyone" could be a driver in the age of "development," the aspirations of automobility in the postcolony had clearly changed.

"The Road to Success Is Full of Potholes": Modernization, State Power, and the Politics of Crisis

On the street and in the halls of government, debates about development were rooted in overlapping interests in the preservation and exercise of state power, the promise of postcolonial modernization, and the politics of crisis. Nkrumah's own vision of state-driven development borrowed from the technopolitical strategies of the development state that emerged through postwar British colonial policy as well as the socialist ideologies of emerging "third-world" countries. In building new infrastructure, planning cities, and organizing workers, Nkrumah sought to render the nation "legible"[19]—bringing order to the new country for the purposes of governance and creating a new path to freedom. The mechanized mobility and prosperity of motor transportation symbolized these future visions of autonomous and mobile citizens, and auto/mobile Ghanaians seemed to embody the promises of postcolonial modernization.

For Nkrumah, social engineering was part of a larger project of national identity formation, through which ethnic diversity could give rise to a unity of common purpose and a shared set of fundamental values.[20] But Nkrumahist visions of planning and progress also drew on the ideologies of high-modernism and the political and economic theories of modernization. Grand infrastructural projects like the Akosombo Dam, Tema Harbor, or the Accra-Tema Motorway represented not only the power of the state, but also "a strong, one might even say muscle-bound, version of the self-confidence about scientific and technical progress, the expansion of production, the growing satisfaction of human needs, the mastery of nature (including human nature), and, above all, the rational design of social order commensurate with the scientific understanding of natural laws."²¹ In the postcolony, this faith in modernization was rooted in the promise of industrialization as a path away from the dependence and underdevelopment of colonial capitalism and the threat of neocolonialism.

Nkrumah's state-centered economic development fostered a broad social agreement that the private accumulation of national leaders and politicians was accepted as long as they sufficiently redistributed state resources to the population.²² As the literal conduits through which resources were circulated and exchanged, roads symbolized this responsibility for redistribution and figured prominently in government development priorities—a form of postcolonial technopolitics that was intended to project confidence and progress to national and international audiences alike. Road transportation and other infrastructural improvements were at the center of Kwame Nkrumah's "Work and Happiness Plan" and the Soviet-style "7 Year Development Plan," which were dedicated to decreasing Ghana's dependence on foreign capital and building an industrial base, as well as redesigning Accra as a modern national capital.²³ Widening and resurfacing roads, in particular, became important parts of rural development plans, which were intended to jump-start agricultural production in rural areas and connect rural production zones to urban ports.²⁴ In cities, large numbers of buses were imported by parastatal transport organizations in an attempt to address the perennial inadequacies of urban transport, particularly in Accra.²⁵

The politics surrounding road construction and motor transport development also highlight the different interpretations of modernization that existed and competed within a larger set of shared social and political values. In particular, the high costs of modernist projects, the failures of mechanization and scientific development on the ground, and the realities of economic decline and financial hardship prompted visions of "imagined alternative societies"—competing interpretations of the modernist promise and the power of the state—which in turn inspired calls for regime change. Deteriorating economic conditions, which began in the 1960s, often meant that debates about development were structured around what Roitman calls the "politics of crisis."²⁶ Indeed, Nkrumah himself was removed from power, at least in part, because of the financial drain of "prestige projects" like the Accra-Tema Motorway, which would link the capital to the newly developed port and industrial center of Tema.²⁷ The National Redemption Council and the Busia government, which came to power in the aftermath of the 1966 coup, critiqued Nkrumah's expenditures as expensive and irresponsible given the country's deteriorating economic condition.

The "politics of crisis" certainly explain much of the public rhetoric surrounding development and the ensuing political instability that defined the decades after independence. Both military and democratic regimes came to power promising to halt decline and correct the mistakes of the past. But, like the official maps and government reports that James Scott describes, the narrative of crisis also failed to "successfully represent the actual activity of the society they depicted, nor were they intended to; they represented only that slice of it that interested the official observer."[28] Debates about the economic morality of driving work, which began in the 1960s, suggest that, while road construction and infrastructural development were essential parts of the country's overall economic development policy, the entrepreneurial nature of the country's commercial motor transport system existed in uneasy tension with the state-centered models of economic modernization that shaped postcolonial development plans. Infrastructural development was intended to project the power of the state and the economic stability of the country. Like the colonial railways, postcolonial infrastructural development was a form of technocratic spectacle through which African political leaders imagined a prosperous future that mirrored the Western industrial development from which they had long been excluded.[29] But infrastructure alone could not produce development, and many of Nkrumah's expensive prestige projects, which sought to industrialize Ghana through mechanization and scientific development, failed due to lack of spare parts and low levels of local participation.[30]

The most successful postcolonial development schemes sought to build on local systems of production and exchange, articulated through the language of "self-help" or "self-reliance." Some, like Nkrumah's Builder's Brigade, sought to employ the country's youth as a "new type of citizen" at the vanguard of scientific development in mechanized work camps and state farms.[31] Acheampong's "Operation Feed Yourself," by contrast, encouraged all people in the country to participate directly in domestic food production as part of an "economic war" against neocolonialism. Acheampong's project aimed at producing "enough food to feed the nation, to provide import substitutes, to produce agricultural raw materials to feed our domestic factories, and to produce for the export market."[32] Ashanti Regional Commissioner Lt. Col. E. A. Baidoo acknowledged that "The success of the 'Operation Feed Yourself' programme depends on the good conditions of the feeder roads."[33] The final plan, which was drawn up to address persistent transport problems and increase access for workers, farmers, and traders, centered on the construction of roads.

Roads connected producers and consumers, and members of the public pushed the government to increase road construction in the pages of the nation's largest newspaper. Building roads, the editors of the *Daily Graphic* argued, was not merely a means of encouraging trade. Rather, "to rural folk a road is not just an important development project, it is a vital link-up with the world."[34] If self-reliance was supposed to include everyone in the project of national development, roads would need to be extended into the remotest parts of the country, making maximum use of the country's productivity and connecting all members of the country with the national economy. After initially suspending all rural development projects, the NRC called on all regions to submit new plans for the construction and maintenance of the country's feeder roads in May 1972.[35] Other development schemes like "Operation Keep Right" sought to align the country's driving practices with that of their neighbors. In July 1972, a mere seven months after taking over leadership of the country in a military coup, the National Redemption Council and its leader, Col. Ignatius Kutu Acheampong, announced that Ghana was going to drive on the right-hand side of the road. By continuing to drive on the left, Acheampong and the NRC argued, Ghana not only reinforced its history as a British colony, but it also isolated itself from its neighbors and limited its potential for economic growth and development. The "Operation Keep Right" campaign culminated on August 4, 1974, when road signs and drivers switched to the other side of the road in a massive feat of social and infrastructural engineering.

Through these infrastructural projects, postcolonial development regimes sought to improve the country's mobility system while also asserting some control over automobility itself. Mbembe argues that these conflicted visions of postcolonial progress represent "forms of colonial rationality sedimented in the 'globalization project.'"[36] Postcolonial leaders who embraced the modernization project were part of a much longer history of postwar development, embedded in both midcentury visions of an industrial future and colonial systems of extractive capitalism and dependency. More cynical analyses argue that, by perpetuating these kinds of ideological and structural continuities, postcolonial African leaders are implicated in the construction of "gatekeeper states"[37]—an "instrumentalization of disorder" through which "well-organized predatory networks" regulate the circulation of goods and wealth into and out of the country.[38] In the motor transport sector alone, government officials were implicated in *kalabule,* profiteering, and smuggling even as they condemned and criminalized the activities of drivers and traders. The political instability that defined the two decades after independence could easily be seen as a symptom of this larger predatory system. But, at least in Ghana, regime change also suggests a serious engagement with the ideas and practices of development.

By the 1980s, that vision of development was much more contradictory and complex than the narrative of economic decline or the politics of crisis may imply—part of a longer political culture that emphasized centralized state power while also embracing the importance of decentralization and popular participation, empowering African producers while also criminalizing the profit of entrepreneurial effort, encouraging mobility while often restricting autonomy through regulation and surveillance. But the material realities seemed to overwhelm ideological complexity, limiting the degree to which centralized states could effectively enforce regulations, maintain infrastructure, or realize visions of economic development. Despite policy dedication and persistent public pressure, reforms and reconstruction of the 1960s and 1970s were inhibited by the limited availability of domestic resources. By the time that transport rehabilitation was undertaken again in the 1980s, the country's roads had suffered nearly a decade of neglect of maintenance and repair.[39]

"Expect a Miracle": Structural Adjustment and the Infrastructure of Economic Recovery

The failures of earlier development efforts—both generally and in relation to transportation—hit home in the 1980s. Environmental and social crises highlighted the failures of previous efforts as well as the importance of road transportation to any substantive recovery. Changing attitudes in the 1980s toward "development," generally, and transportation, in particular, were manifestations of what Nugent identifies as "an ever-widening gap between the tenets of a dominant ideology and the realities experienced by most Ghanaians during that time."[40] By the late 1970s and early 1980s, the statist model of economic and social redistribution had proven incapable of guaranteeing the security of the country's citizens. Public concerns over *kalabule* and profiteering in the late 1970s and early 1980s, which targeted drivers and others, reflected one manifestation of the anxiety surrounding this growing disjuncture. The 31st December Revolution and the ideology of Rawlings and the PNDC marked another attempt to respond to this anxiety.[41]

By the time that the PNDC came to power in 1981/82, the country's acute fiscal crisis meant that the institutions of the state were "increasingly incapable of maintaining the existing economic and social infrastructure,"[42] much less engage in any new development or reconstruction efforts. Between 1970 and 1982, income per capita fell by 30 percent and real wages fell by 80 percent. The value of exports like cocoa fell precipitously on the world market, and the lack of foreign currency meant that imports also decreased by as much as two-thirds. These economic struggles placed a strain on the country's domestic finances, as the domestic savings rate and investment rate declined and government deficits rose.[43]

Drivers and passengers, who struggled to secure access to automobility, indexed a more fundamental insecurity in Ghanaian social and economic life, as well as the increasingly frenetic nature of government response. As driver Shadrak Yemo Odoi noted:

> Those times, things have become difficult for us because even a tire to put on a car we are not getting it. We are not getting parts or anything that we need to fix in the car is difficult so it makes things have become rough for we the drivers. Even it reach a time that I have to park one of my car because I don't have things to replace things that have spoiled because if I go round to the old places to get things, I can't find them, so I have to park the car.[44]

By 1983, 60 percent of the available vehicles were unserviceable because of lack of tires, batteries, and spare parts, and 40 percent of vehicles were considered old and uneconomical.[45] Drivers were unable to guarantee stable profit from their work in the context of such significant shortages. In many cases, drivers' attempts to "manage" the newfound insecurity of their auto/mobile lives fueled efforts to further criminalize driver practice. But the realities of infrastructural and technological decline also increasingly redirected government attention away from drivers and toward roads—an infrastructural technology that drivers used but did not control. Government officials in the Ministry for Transport and Communications, who sought to combat infrastructural decline, found themselves engaging with a broad section of the public. In some cases, local communities contributed to the breakdown of roads. The PNDC Secretary for Transport and Communications noted the "bad habit of cutting across . . . roads for water mains or electricity connections [had] over the years become one of the major contributory factors to the rapid deterioration of roads in the urban areas."[46] In other communities, local leaders and individuals protested the conditions of roads and the plans for redevelopment.

If Rawlings promised a "people's revolution" that would bring about a new social and economic order, then, it was initially unclear what that order might

Fig. 5.1 "King of Kings buses and workshops at Odorkor," *Transportation in the Economic Recovery Programme*, photographer Ben Kwakye, January 30, 1987 (Ministry of Information, Information Services Photographic Library, Ref. no. PD/73/16).

look like. The breakdown of older models of state-society relations and the per-sistent crisis had created an "ideological vacuum," but the PNDC's adoption of neoliberal reforms in 1982/83 was far from an inevitable result of this transition. Early PNDC rhetoric had, in fact, centered on a critique of dependence, neoco-lonialism, and other forms of foreign interference. Rawlings initially embraced scientific socialism and sought to resurrect Nkrumahist policies that centralized economic institutions in order to limit corruption and facilitate national devel-opment. At least in some communities, early efforts at local social organization did seem to address issues of smuggling and corruption by creating cultures of surveillance and discipline.[47] However, PNDC efforts at economic development through mass mobilization failed to produce significant changes in the economy, and price controls and import-export controls placed pressure on the country's limited foreign currency reserves.[48] In the transport sector, the PNDC govern-ment's attempt to establish new state-mandated, nationwide transport fares in 1981 ultimately proved unenforceable and was repealed.[49] In April 1982, when PNDC officials sought economic assistance from Communist bloc countries, including Libya, Eastern Europe, Cuba, and the Soviet Union, they returned empty-handed.[50]

The PNDC's turn to the World Bank, then, reflected less a shift in their own ideological orientation than it did the desperation of a government with no other options. Dr. Kwesi Botchwey's presentation of the Economic Recovery Program (ERP) in April 1983 announced a formal policy orientation guided by the neolib-eral policies of the IMF and the World Bank. These policies were not completely new in Ghana—Kwame Nkrumah had considered IMF/World Bank–sponsored stabilization and adjustment policies as early as the 1960s, and Busia unsuc-cessfully implemented currency devaluation and austerity measures in 1971.[51] However, even as the new policy was announced, there was still a great deal of disagreement among members of the PNDC, many of whom had approved an alternative economic program that, in particular, did not include currency deval-uation and resisted foreign influence through conditional World Bank and IMF loans.[52] Many PNDC politicians also worried that structural adjustment policies were potentially risky; earlier attempts at reform provoked popular protests that toppled the Busia regime in 1972. Even those who accepted the necessity of neo-liberal reforms sought to situate structural adjustment within a revolutionary ideology that emphasized popular participation and social development.

The ERP included two phases: Phase I (1983–1986) sought to stabilize the economy, halting decline in the industrial and export sectors; Phase II (1987–1989) used structural adjustment policies to grow and develop social ser-vices. These policies were shaped by a number of national goals: the need to increase the production of agricultural products, manufactured goods and raw materials; improvement in the availability of consumer goods; decrease in inflation; increase in the availability of foreign exchange; rehabilitation of physical infrastructure; and the restructuring of economic institutions.[53] However, the ERP was also strongly influenced by neoliberal structural adjustment policies including labor retrenchment, trade liberalization, currency devaluation, and subsidy withdrawal,[54] which sought to decrease the size and influence of the state over the national economy. Both government and Bank officials argued that transportation operated at the nexus of these issues:

> Transport bottlenecks constitute one of the most serious impediments facing Ghana's economic recovery program. Ghana's transport system has nearly broken down over the past few years, for want of regular maintenance, spare parts and other inputs, due to the deterioration of the country's economy and the related shortage of foreign exchange faced by the country during the last ten to twelve years. The present state of Ghana's transport network is dismal. Regarding road transport, only about 20–30% of the annual maintenance needs of the road system have been met during the last 10–12 years, and as a result, even some of the main roads are full of pot holes, and many road sections have become practically unusable, where motorists do not wish to pass for fear of breakdown of vehicles. All these shortcomings have made transport of essential exports, farm inputs and farm products difficult and expensive, thwarting economic recovery programs and raising costs and prices through the economy. Rehabilitation of the road network is of primary importance in removing transport bottlenecks.[55]

Although "transportation" as a broader category also included railways, shipping, and air travel, road transportation figured prominently in government plans and discourses and justified the creation of a separate Ministry within the PNDC government.[56] While roads were central to this vision of transport-driven development, officials also viewed drivers, who transported goods from rural production areas to coastal ports, as essential to the success of reforms and projects dedicated to the externally oriented growth of international trade, export production, and the generation of foreign exchange. By 1992, drivers transported 94 percent of all national freight and 97 percent of passenger traffic on the country's roads.[57]

Reforms targeted both the infrastructure and practices of transportation. As part of ERP I and II, a rolling five-year development plan for the road sector began in 1986, which charged the Ghana Highway Authority with the rehabilitation and/or construction of 3133.5 km of roads at an estimated cost of US $922.9 million between 1986 and 1991.[58] Funded initially by the World Bank, this project was the beginning of an extensive road rehabilitation and construction effort for the country's 14,000 km of roads.[59] By 1991, 30 percent of the national budget was allocated to road maintenance and construction, second only to education in terms of national spending.[60]

In tackling road transport infrastructure, the PNDC engaged technopoliti- cal strategies that had their roots in the modernist imaginings of midcentury colonial and postcolonial leaders. Infrastructural development in the postcolony was shaped around the priorities of global capitalism in strikingly similar ways to that of British colonial leadership more than fifty years before. For Rawlings, his PNDC comrades, and World Bank officials alike, economic development required foreign trade, which focused energies on primary commodities like cocoa in order to minimize costs and maximize short-term profits while deepening Ghana's engagement with and dependency on a global economy still dominated by the interests of Western industrial capitalism. But the PNDC's qualified embrace of neoliberal ideology also marked a departure from these earlier visions of "prog- ress." Reforms that decentralized and privatized many of the functions of the state tied future prosperity to the efforts of foreign capital and private entrepreneurs. Technopolitics was, increasingly, not just a national but also a global issue, which placed auto/mobile entrepreneurs in conversation and competition with multina- tional corporations, as well as national and regional transport syndicates.

The "development plans" in their final form masked an intense debate over funding, control, and priorities. As a broader category, "road transport devel- opment" incorporated a number of disparate but critical projects, all of which clamored for attention, support, and funding. In rare cases, new funding for infrastructural development made it possible for shelved or abandoned proj- ects from the 1960s, like the Accra-Tema motorway, to receive renewed atten- tion.[61] Begun by Kwame Nkrumah as part of his larger project to develop Tema as an international port and industrial center, the project was shelved during the coup as a "prestige" project only to be resurrected during the 1980s. The new motorway project not only rehabilitated and extended the old road in a way that reflected original plans, but it also expanded as a dual carriageway or four-lane highway. Other, less flashy, examples included a multistory car park in front of Ghana House, but the extension of the Accra-Tema motorway consumed most of the funds for new road construction. The remaining available funds were dedi- cated to the reconstruction, resurfacing and maintenance of existing roads— priorities that reflected the importance of crop evacuation and trade from rural areas to urban centers—or, what the Civil Engineering and Building Contractors Association of Ghana (CEBCAG) identified as "an efficient and effective distrib- utive system which is essential to our growing economy."[62] Particularly under the National Feeder Rehabilitation and Maintenance Project, rural roads and bridges, which had in many cases been constructed in the colonial period, were reconstructed and resurfaced.[63]

In urban areas, infrastructural development expanded to embrace provi- sions for pedestrians and the operators of nonmotorized vehicles, as well as an extensive if still inadequate motor transport network that included both publicly and privately operated vehicles. While road construction was still a central concern, the PNDC prioritized issues of traffic congestion, pedestrian safety, and the accessibility of transportation for the city's poorer residents. Zebra crossings for pedestrians, traffic signals, road signs and road markings, as well as bicycle lanes, all held prominent positions in debates about the shape of urban transport projects. Furthermore, in contrast to rural transport and produce evacuation, which was dominated by independent or private transport operators, urban transport networks were amalgamations of national transport companies (e.g., City Express Services; Omnibus Services Authority; State Transport Corporation), municipal bus services (Accra Municipal Assembly bus service), private transport companies (e.g., King of Kings), and independent operators (e.g., individual owner-operators). While rural transportation was crucial to the redevelopment of the country's domestic and international trade, at least 80 percent of Ghana's transport services were based in the country's four largest cities: Accra, Kumasi, Sekondi-Takoradi, and Tema.[64] Urban transport projects, which were dedicated to increasing the accessibility and efficiency of urban transport networks, frequently invested in bus stops and taxi ranks as well as imported buses, which would expand the fleets of parastatal transport companies.[65]

Ghanaian citizens—both drivers and passengers alike—were vocal in expressing their own visions of infrastructural development. To some degree, citizen complaints about infrastructure and suggestions for reform were part of a longer history of petition writing.[66] Much like the chiefs, traders, and urban residents who petitioned the British colonial government demanding their right to roads and complaining about government regulatory efforts, a broad spectrum of Ghanaians wrote directly to the PNDC government to express their opinions on the shape of future development. Their petitions and protests suggest the persistent centrality of roads in the social and economic lives of people throughout Ghana.

Petitions also suggest that local communities continued to struggle in their efforts to secure access to adequate infrastructure and maintain the social and economic security of their population. As chiefs from the Eastern Region complained to the Secretary for Transportation and Communications in February 24, 1992, letter:

> Sir, it may be of interest to note that, people of Adeiso, Obeng Yaw, Kofi Asare to Atimatim, as well as Roll Call to Bebiche has not been able to bring their food items to the urban centres as a result of the damaged culverts as well as the deteriorating roads which need urgent repairs. The inhabitants of the village have mobilized forces to repair the roads but all our efforts have been in vain and we are therefore calling for your immediate assistance before the rains set in. In view therefore of the above, we pray that you use your good office and take the due action and save the people of the villages concerned to enable us also to contribute our quota towards the development of mother Ghana.[67]

These Eastern Region communities' efforts embodied both the rhetoric of local development and the realities of economic crisis. Chiefs, farmers, and traders, who used the profits of the cocoa boom to fund rural road construction efforts in the 1930s and 1940s, had the financial resources and economic power to shape infrastructural development, often in defiance of colonial state priorities. By the 1980s and 1990s, the resources of local communities had diminished significantly in relation to the rising costs of construction materials and other imported goods. Even community leaders in cocoa growing areas, like the chiefs of the Eastern Region, found it difficult to fund road construction projects without the aid of private companies or other organizations.

The PNDC seemed to encourage popular participation in shaping national development priorities. During the 1980s and 1990s, People's and Worker's Defence Councils (P/WDCs), which the PNDC established as structures of popular democratic participation in governance, created new opportunities that magnified local input.[68] Government-sponsored call-in radio shows or "magazine programs" and letters to the editor provided important forums for popular expression.[69] PNDC officials also sent representatives to local communities to collect Public Reaction Reports, through which they gauged the effects of development on local populations. The PNDC government did investigate and respond to complaints that affected the safety of citizens, filling holes near pedestrian flyovers in congested market areas or filling potholes and addressing drainage issues along urban roads.[70] But the rhetoric of popular democracy also redirected local labor and resources in the service of national development—a decentralized form of infrastructural development that echoed both the spatial dichotomies of British colonial rule and the roll back in state power and resources in the neoliberal era.

The PNDC encouraged local development by providing equipment necessary to complete major infrastructural projects. In communities like Wa, a district capital in the Upper West Region, the Department of Feeder Roads released graders used to construct roads linking food-growing areas to the district capital. The project was financed by P &W Ghanem Construction Ltd, a private company, which was interested in extending Catholic educational projects in the region. However, local communities bore the costs of operation, which were often prohibitive. A grader required one drum of diesel oil and a gallon of engine oil per kilometer of road, and each district was allowed to use the machinery for only one month—time constraints that were complicated by the slow pace of fundraising and the difficult working conditions during the rainy season.[71] Individuals and communities submitted a number of requests for projects, but ultimately local communities initially could fund only one feeder road—Charis-Egu—under the program. The difficulties faced by local populations in Wa were not exceptional. Public Reaction Reports from

August 1990 noted that "the laudable efforts of the people to improve the condition of the road through communal labor has not yielded much result since the whole stretch is muddy."[72] Other communities like Pwalworgo and Holimund attempted to raise three hundred thousand cedis to build twenty-five kilometers of road that would link them with the main Wa-Katua-Kundungu road, but they were unable to secure the necessary funds. Failed development seemed to be worse than no development at all. In the aftermath of the failed project, PNDC officials noted that "the poor state of the road has made it virtually impossible for the farmers to send their foodstuffs and other crops to the urban centers for sale."[73] The detritus of these failed development projects was not just a scar, but rather an open wound in the economic and social life of the community, further hampering local participation in national and global economies, rendering local communities immobile.

The complications and failures of local development initiatives reflected the shifting politics of development and reform. Local input now competed not only with national or central government initiatives and priorities but also with the ideologies, policies, and mandates of international financial institutions and bilateral donors. Neoliberal ideology and structural adjustment rhetoric of the World Bank and the IMF shaped the broad goals of the initial economic recovery program. Well after the initial conversations about reforms, donors/lenders continued to have significant voice in the shape and implementation of projects.[74] In addition to their more obvious influence over the selection of projects for funding, organizations like the United Nations Development Programme (UNDP) and the World Bank required approved projects to follow strict procedures for vetting and selecting contractors, mandated the use of external consultants, and made further project funding contingent on periodic evaluations of the implementation and progress of project plans.[75] In some cases, such as the Accra-Tema Motorway, the disjuncture between the purpose or intent of the project and the way that it was used by residents highlighted the limitations of this system, as well as more fundamental tensions between the desire for Western-influenced infrastructural development and the practical demands of Ghanaian citizens.[76]

This tension was most powerfully manifested in citizen complaints about the ways in which construction efforts and the practices of contractors impacted individuals and communities. Particularly in built-up urban areas, road construction and the widening of roads required some degree of demolition. Contractors rarely had to demolish an individual's entire property, and those who did have property demolished were supposed to be compensated. However, citizen complaints about what should be demolished reflected a broader debate about what transportation development (or development, in general) should look like.[77] Mr. Michael Dollah, for example, was extremely concerned not only about the fact that his property in Nima was demolished as part of the Nima Road Works and Upgrading Scheme, but also about the way in which contractors conducted themselves during the process:

> As part of the face lift programme going on in the city, Nima and Mamobi, among other areas, have been earmarked for road constructions and other vital projects. Consequently the Land Valuation Board, in conjunction with other Services came to value and demarcate the area in view of determining structures that have to be demolished. The time came and the demolition went on as planned. The way was paved for the roads to take their planned courses without any future harassment of any landlord or tenants. However, in the case of one such street a curious situation has arisen. Instead of the street taking its normal course, the surveyors have managed to divert it, by-passing two houses that stand right in the middle of the street. As a result, the inmates of the two houses that had not been marked for demolition are now facing constant harassment from the Resident Engineer and his men. They came to mark the house on Friday, 1st November and asked the inmates to move out by Monday, 3rd November for the demolition exercise. On the insistence of the inmates that the street was not taking its normal path due to the bribes that the surveyors had glaringly collected from one of the landlords whose house is blocking the way, the construction work temporarily came to a stop. . . . They say they will demolish the house in a week's time, throwing 36 men and women and children and their property into the streets. Sir, these men want to perpetuate evil because of bribe and more so because we refused to yield to pressure to give bribe.[78]

Here Mr. Dollah's complaint about the "ugly nature of the road" seems to refer both to the unconventional layout of the road as well as the immoral manner in which, he argues, the construction was taking place.[79] Although residents in both rural and urban areas eagerly welcomed road construction, which was seen as an often long-awaited infrastructural improvement, this welcome was tempered by competing local priorities about land usage, layout, and function.[80] Aside from more obvious issues of demolition, contractors constructing roads, bridges, and culverts often rerouted drainage patterns with profound implications for local residents living around the construction zone. Residents of the Monomanye area of Tema along the Ashiaman-Katamanso road pleaded with the PNDC secretary for the Ministry of Agriculture to address the construction mistakes of local officials. Issues as minor as improperly constructed culverts had profound consequences for local residents. When the Tema Municipal Council constructed roads and drains from the Ashiaman main market to Monomanye, they failed to take into account the volume of water passing through the area in constructing the culvert system. Local residents sought out the help of the Municipal Council and the Department of Urban Roads and Highways, and spend over three hundred thousand cedis on machines to de-silt the culvert, but those efforts failed to correct the situation. For many Monomanye-area residents, these construction mistakes resulted in personal loss, flooding local properties, and killing livestock. Roads, they argued, were "sinking many families as well as our livelihood."[81]

While some of these complaints reflected unintended and unanticipated consequences of road construction, in other instances, contractor mistakes led not only to a waste of money in terms of the construction project itself but also the resulting damage to adjacent property. As a result, neither Ghanaian nor expatriate contractors were immune from the expectations of honesty that were essential parts of the new social order of the 31st December Revolution. While the PNDC no longer responded as often with the violent "revolutionary action" of the 1979 AFRC "housecleaning exercise," contractors who were found guilty of committing crimes against "the people" were subject to dismissal, fines, blacklisting, and/or prison.[82]

"Whatever You Do . . .": Deregulation and the Political Economy of Living

While drivers' voices (or the voices of their union representatives) were largely absent from debates over infrastructure construction and financial policy, such reform inevitably had implications for their lives as professional drivers, and the PNDC's dedication to road construction served as evidence of the close relationship between drivers and the Rawlings/PNDC government.[83] The introduction of the ERP in 1983 marked a transformation in government policies toward drivers. This new attitude was embodied in the 1988 establishment of a Transport Policy Review Committee (TPRC), which allowed the government to discuss transport policies and issues with private-sector users and providers of transport services.[84] Bringing together the Ministry of Transportation and Communications; Ministry of Roads and Highways; Ministry of Industries, Science and Technology; Ministry of Local Government; Ministry of Interior; Ghana Chamber of Commerce; Ghana Private Road Transport Union (GPRTU); Ghana Road Transport Council; and the Ghana National Association of Garages, the TPRC reflected not only a government commitment to coordination but it also established the government—and particularly the Ministry of Roads and Highways—as the arbiter of disputes between the public and the transport sector.[85] Such an approach marked a gradual move away from control and regulation, which was influenced not only by free-market ideologies but also revolutionary ideas about economic and social reform.

Just as transport infrastructure development was part of a larger project of infrastructural improvements that were dedicated toward economic recovery in a broad sense, the fiscal and trade dimensions of reform—particularly after the initial phase of stabilization—directly impacted the profitability of transportation and driving work. In an effort to facilitate the importation of essential inputs and new vehicles, government officials introduced and implemented a number of reforms, including a Reconstruction Import Credit Program, a lottery for import licenses and access to foreign exchange, licensed Forex Bureaus, and ultimately a floating currency exchange rate, all of which were geared toward making foreign exchange more accessible and thereby facilitating international trade and imports.[86] While these policies and programs were intended to have broader trade implications, the freeing up of imports and exchange resurrected and reenergized the country's fleet of vehicles. As the PNDC Secretary for Transport and Communications noted in 1988, new economic development institutions and policies like the Reconstruction Import Credit facility brought in large supplies of inputs for road transport, and by 1986 large numbers of previously unserviceable motor vehicles were back on the roads.[87] If licensed vehicles numbered 32,000 in 1984 (the start of the ERP), they had reached 109,000 by 1991. For many, the increasing number of cars on the road was evidence of a marked improvement in the road transport system and in the economy more broadly.[88]

However, the extraordinary growth in the number of cars had incongruous implications for Ghanaian citizens. More vehicles meant more available—and

Fig. 5.2 "A View of Accra Lorry Station," photographer E. S. Boateng, May 29, 1973 (Ministry of Information, Information Services Photographic Library, Ref. no. PS/1365/11).

reasonably priced—public transportation. After decades of transport shortages, passengers no longer had to wait in long lines or leave early in the morning to procure transport. The importation of new vehicles also meant that passengers no longer had to ride in mammy trucks, which, by the 1990s, were considered an unnecessary discomfort for passengers.[89] However, in urban areas, increases in car ownership exacerbated existing problems of traffic congestion, while newly constructed roads in both cities and rural areas were found to be inadequate in the face of the increased traffic burden.[90] As a consequence, the Accra-Tema Motorway, for example, had to be reconstructed twice in response to an unexpected volume of traffic.[91]

The increasing availability of vehicles also had diverse and often contradictory consequences for drivers' lives. Undoubtedly, in making vehicles (as well as spare parts and other inputs) more easily accessible, these new government policies alleviated some of the financial pressures and risks faced by drivers. In the context of shortages and scarcity, drivers whose vehicles went into disrepair often found themselves without work when they were unable to find the necessary spare parts or to pay for the repairs. While increased availability alleviated these problems, it also indirectly cut into driver profits and work, as more drivers took to the road. What state leaders viewed as "necessary competitive pressures," which were desirable to keep prices at an affordable level for passengers, meant declining profits for drivers. As Inussa al-Haji noted the increasing democratization of vehicle ownership undermined not only drivers' profits but also their status. By the 1990s, "anyone" could be a driver:

> Because the nation has developed and also the cars too have become many. So by all means while the nation is developing the cars will be coming more and more. And there is not any good work in town now that if you get money you say you are going to do that business. So that make now everybody—if he is able to raise some money, if he see what to do with the money, then he decide, either he should buy one or two cars, either they should be working for him as trotro and taxi so that they would be making him some money. So even now, if I get some money, because it is driving that I learn, I will buy car and make trotro. Even there are some people in town who have about 20 to 30 cars that are working for them. So the cars will be many like that.[92]

The increased availability of vehicles was accompanied by expansion of "driving schools," which promised to provide training for the otherwise unqualified and uneducated drivers who were seen to be flooding the market. Driving schools themselves attempted to convince the government of their importance to the transportation system. The proprietors of McAshley's Memorial School of Driving argued that "before anybody dreams of becoming a driver he/she":

1. Must have at least attained middle/JSS school certificate.
2. Must have attended driving school.

3. Must have attended a course on selected route, important places, Hotels in the country and their locations, public relationship and some historic places in the cities and towns and to explain to tourists, Road and traffic regulations as it is done in other countries.
4. Must have passed a test conducted by high rank officers of AMA before a taxi licence is issued to anybody. With these measures we can achieve a better and safe driving in the system [sic]. Also the bad nuts will be flushed out.[93]

In other words, McAshley's proprietors argued that "driving school," rather than apprenticeship, should become the primary institution of driver training because "the driving profession is not for drop out, it is equal to that of Pilot, Actors, Shop Captains and all those whose services are concerned with human beings."[94] In doing so, McAshley's and other driving schools sought to bring the motor transport industry in line with other transport industries, with formalized and standardized systems of training that were more closely modeled on schools than apprenticeships.

In providing an alternative form of driver training, driving schools like McAshley's seemed to formalize driver training along Western models, even as they expanded access to driver training for young men who sought to capitalize on the flood of new vehicles that had entered the country. By creating formal institutions, driving school operators presented a clearer set of criteria for evaluating the expertise and skill of driving work—a process of training and evaluation that could be more easily observed and regulated by the state and which mapped more directly onto the processes of licensing that identified and endorsed qualified drivers. The claims of driving school operators echoed that of licensing officers, police, and other regulatory officials of the British colonial state more than fifty years before. Like these earlier attempts to regulate and formalize driver training, driving schools provoked resistance among "professional drivers" and the general public who questioned the skill and professionalism of graduates. Driving schools trained individuals in the basic mechanics of driving and the rules of the road, but commercial motor transportation required a much broader set of skills and expertise, including social skills, business management, and mechanical improvisation, which could not be conveyed through books and classroom training. As Joshua Maama Larbi argued, the instructors at the driving schools were, themselves, amateurs and thus incapable of properly training commercial drivers, and inadequate training led to accidents and other risky behavior.[95] Unqualified graduates, then, endangered the public and other drivers in both a physical and a social sense.

The expansion of the motor transport industry, which emerged in response to liberalized markets, seemed like a realization of free-market principles. But the economic consequences of neoliberal reform also raised questions within the revolutionary rhetoric of popular democracy and moral economy, which informed the PNDC's claim to power and legitimacy. PNDC officials sought to ensure that new populations of drivers did not exploit the passenger-public, limiting the potential profits of drivers through price controls and official fares. The PNDC first established official fares in 1981 as a response to high transport prices.[96] This strategy was far from new. Both colonial and postcolonial regimes used price controls to guarantee economical rates in the market and on the road. Neoliberal ideology demanded a rethinking of this strategy, rooted in the ideals of market liberalization. Structural adjustment reform did not eliminate price controls and official fares; however, in the aftermath of reform, government officials increasingly negotiated fares with transport unions as a way to ensure the sustainability and profitability of the expanding motor transport sector.

New set fares attempted to balance the "public interest" with the real costs of transport operation for drivers. This balance was made all the more delicate in light of a progressive program of deregulation of essential commodities, including petrol.[97] Allowing fares to be raised passed these costs on to the general public without unduly burdening drivers and vehicle owners. Furthermore, at least initially, higher official fares were complemented by more efficient (and centralized) means of distribution of essential inputs (i.e., tires, petrol, engine oil, etc.).[98] Such an approach limited opportunities for profiteering while still allowing for a reasonable profit margin among drivers and vehicle owners.

While this new negotiated approach to fares more fully represented driver interests in establishing policies, their agreement to participate through government channels also bound them to the structures and conclusions of negotiation. Drivers proved particularly resistant to the time lag that resulted between the announcement of a new budget (and thus new prices for essential inputs like petroleum products) and the renegotiation of fares. Despite union commitments to the system of negotiation and government-mandated fares, local union branches and individual drivers who bore the financial burdens of these delays were less patient. When new fiscal-year budgets resulted in increased petrol prices, fares immediately rose in pockets around the country as drivers attempted to respond to the changing costs of their work. Passenger complaints to the central government highlighted the persistence of popular suspicions of driver motivations. Emmanuel Nath complained to the PNDC Secretary for Transportation and Communications in 1984 that the Secretary of the Asesewa Drivers Union displayed a "certain unrevolutionary spirit," setting fares above the government-mandated prices. Nath was concerned that "despite the efforts being made by the PNDC Government to put the country's economy to its feet, some bad elements in the society are making this noble effort a fiasco." However, Nath was also self-interested, writing "as a worker/farmer and a concerned citizen and on behalf of my other workers/farmers especially on behalf of the poor farmers to protest strongly against these arbitrary increases." In raising their prices, he argued, drivers' unions undermined the efforts of workers who relied on transportation to access their farms and contribute to national efforts of economic development.[99]

Although passengers like Nath recognized that new budgets resulted in increased petrol prices, many did not sympathize as drivers attempted to have these new costs reflected more quickly in the fares that they collected. When fares were officially renegotiated several months later, the official fares were remarkably similar to the unofficially raised fares drivers attempted to impose at the beginning of the year. Regardless, those drivers and branches that were found to be charging illegal fares were warned and often punished by union officials. However, the union's control was limited. There was no required union membership, and "floating cars" (i.e., cars whose drivers did not belong to the union and, thus, did not have a station) could not be controlled.[100] Dominated by individual owner-operators, there was also little that the union could threaten for a driver who refused to recognize or accept their authority.

By contrast, employees of transport parastatals were more vulnerable to "revolutionary action" through public tribunals and other sorts of investigations and prosecutions. Employment in formal-sector transport perhaps afforded more opportunities for corruption and other misdeeds, and public transport employees were accused of a number of crimes including stealing oil and spare parts, overselling tickets, and producing fraudulent waybills. Complaints received by national government officials about the fares collected by state transport employees significantly outnumbered those addressing the practices of independent or private-sector drivers.[101] The "corrupt" behavior of government drivers was considered even more egregious than that of private-sector workers, and the high fares collected by government drivers were thought to set a bad example or precedent for others operating in the area.[102] However, public sector transport employees were also vulnerable as victims of the actions of others. Fearing the withholding of salary or being targeted for "redeployment" as a result of an unjust PDC vendetta or personal disagreement with members of management, many of these drivers were forced by station managers to drive overloaded vehicles or remain silent while bus conductors forged tickets or waybills, which could reflect poorly on a driver.[103] When such practices resulted in accidents or complaints, drivers themselves were often held responsible and found guilty by association.[104]

"Had I Known": Decentralization, Privatization, and Control over Drivers and the Road

While revolutionary ideologies gave passengers a new framework through which to evaluate driver practices, in practice, the close relationship of cooperation between the PNDC government and the drivers' unions reflected an emerging trust that empowered the unions and gave them greater authority over public affairs. Whereas drivers in the 1970s had been increasingly cast as the enemies of the state and the people, drivers and their unions had a much more active role in the revolution and reform of the 1980s. As the largest drivers' union, the Ghana Private Road Transport Union (GPRTU) embraced the revolution, its new relationship with the government, and its position of leadership and authority among drivers and within Ghanaian society more broadly.

As the government progressively removed itself from the economy, the GPRTU and other drivers' unions gained more authority and responsibility for the structures of transport and the practices of transport workers. Even when imbued with such authority, the GPRTU was still subject to government oversight, input, and pressure; however, drivers and their unions increasingly dictated the terms of their relationship with both the government and with the general public and protested when individuals or organizations impinged on their authority. Ironically, in taking on these additional responsibilities as informal representatives of government and agents of development, unions also undermined their own independence and autonomy. Under the guise of decentralization and popular participation, government co-option of drivers' unions limited the degree to which drivers' interests (individually and collectively) were represented in the realms of policy and planning.

If the revolutionary ideology of "popular democracy" informed the socialist policy orientation of the early PNDC government, local political and economic organization took on new meaning in the context of structural adjustment reform. P/WDCs, which facilitated popular participation in the revolutionary government of the early 1980s, also provided a framework for decentralization in the aftermath of the ERP. Under the guise of decentralization, the PNDC government restructured its ministries, placing all departments with responsibility for transportation under a single ministry—the Ministry of Roads and Highways. As part of a larger process to streamline the government, the Ghana Highway Authority, the Department of Feeder Roads, and the Department of Urban Roads were consolidated into the new ministry. By the 1990s, the PNDC was increasingly attempting to transfer the responsibilities for urban roads to the various municipal councils, as part of an effort to strengthen "local authorities' ability to maintain and rehabilitate their road networks and develop transport services."[105]

The GPRTU was, in many ways, a less than ideal "local authority" and partner. Building on the early efforts of the Gold Coast (later Ghana) Motor Union (1930–1967); the Teamster's and Private Transport Union (1958–1962); and the Post, Transport, Maritime, Railways, and Dockworkers Union (1962–1966), the Ghana Private Road Transport Union was established in 1967.[106] Drivers' unions had organized drivers since the 1930s to resist government attempts to regulate motor transportation. However, the entrepreneurial nature of motor transportation and the existence of competing unions made it difficult to organize and mobilize drivers for strike action or collective bargaining. While the GPRTU had experienced splintering, which resulted in the foundation of alternative unions (i.e., Co-Operative Transport Society, Progressive Transport Owners' Association), it maintained its dominance throughout the 1980s and 1990s.[107] As a result of this mobilizing force, the GPRTU represented a significant potential challenge to government policies and reforms.

The threat of the GPRTU lay not only in its independent power but also in its connection to other labor movements. By the 1980s and 1990s the GPRTU was one of seventeen members of the Trades Union Congress (TUC), which had developed a tense relationship with the government since the coup. The TUC of the 1980s and 1990s was the most recent manifestation of a strong labor tradition in the Gold Coast. Although workers and union leaders had been instrumental in rallying popular support during the earliest days of the revolution, the PNDC quickly distanced itself from the powerful unions and attempted to pacify the TUC by replacing its leadership with PNDC allies and encouraging the development of WDCs, which would organize workers within the workplace to interact directly with the PNDC government.[108] Furthermore, unions had a long and powerful history of political action and protest, dating back to the colonial period. The Railway Union, in particular, played an important role in nationalist organizing during the 1950s. Undoubtedly by the 1980s, the power of the unions had decreased significantly. The once-powerful Railway Union had declined as the railways lost out to roads and the percentage of the country's labor force engaged in wage labor decreased; however, the unions organized under the umbrella of the TUC still influenced a large portion of the Ghanaian population. By the end of the Acheampong regime in the 1970s, the TUC itself had been taken over by "revolutionary" workers, influenced by Marxist rhetoric and dedicated to the overthrow of the government in the name of the country's workers.[109] While drivers did not have a strong tradition of striking or other forms of public protest or political engagement, the country's reliance on motor transportation—and in particular, the individual owner-operators who dominated the GPRTU—meant that a strike by the GPRTU could damage not only the PNDC's system of reforms but also the country's economy as a whole.

Despite the leverage held by the GPRTU, the union, which represented 85 percent of the nation's drivers,[110] seemed disinterested in an antagonistic relationship with government. Undoubtedly shaken by the previous decade of popular protest, in which drivers and their unions were cast as the enemies of the people, GPRTU officials pursued a conciliatory and cooperative attitude toward government. First with the Hilla Limann government and later with the PNDC regime, GPRTU leaders pledged the loyalty and support of their drivers to the national cause.[111] As a result, the GPRTU maintained its democratically elected leaders and were welcomed to the government's table in negotiations and policy conversations. As early as the 1980s, union leaders could "count on [the government's] usual cooperation."[112] As many drivers noted, "Rawlings—he liked drivers!"[113]

Because of the centrality of transportation to the PNDC's reform agenda, the cooperation of the GPRTU was essential to the smooth enactment of reform and development. Particularly in the era of deregulation and decentralization, the ability of the government to rely on the goodwill of drivers in pursuing their agenda made the reform process easier and freed up government resources. Early disagreements about fares, which were the result of the GPRTU not being included in negotiations and talks,[114] were quickly quieted as the government incorporated unions into the decision-making process. Beginning with the fare negotiations as early as 1983, the PNDC progressively allocated more authority and responsibility to the GPRTU. Not only did the unions negotiate fares and provide the government with information about the running costs of vehicles and the difficulties of driving work, but they also increasingly enforced the official fares.[115] Although citizens protested directly to the PNDC Secretary for Transport and Communications (later the Ministry of Roads and Highways),[116] it was the unions, not the police or the military, which were tasked with correcting driver practice.

In order to enforce order and discipline among drivers, the GPRTU transformed once-derided "bookmen" into a "guard" or police force, which patrolled stations and lorry parks and, if necessary, punished drivers and passengers who were engaged in transgressive, illegal, or antisocial practices. Although the guards were not an officially sanctioned police force, they had wide latitude in carrying out their functions within union spaces. "Stations" within a lorry park, which were dedicated to particular routes, were operated by the unions, which required any driver who used the station to be a union member. As a result, guards chased off "floating cars" who attempted to load near the station, often to the chagrin of passengers who sought lower fares or a quicker ride.[117] Within the station itself, guards monitored the fares charged by drivers, collected taxes and levies, and organized the arrivals and departures of drivers.[118] By the 1990s, union guards were stopping vehicles to check for paid income taxes and to evaluate roadworthiness.[119]

As the GPRTU took on more responsibility in the regulation of transportation, they increasingly came in conflict with groups who disagreed with their tactics or questioned their authority. Rival unions were the most obvious and frequent challengers. Emerging out of fundamental disagreements between members over the union's role in maintaining discipline and order, smaller unions like PROTOA and Co-Operative attempted to establish rival stations and reported the GPRTU to the government for what they saw as illegal abuses of power.[120] However, the most significant challenges to union power came from municipal and district councils. By collecting their union dues at the station in the form of usage fees (rather than annual, monthly, or weekly membership fees), the GPRTU appeared to be usurping the rights and responsibilities of other "local authorities" like municipal and district assemblies, which technically owned the lorry parks and, thus, had the right to any taxes or fees collected on the property. These organizations of local government protested to the PNDC and ultimately took the union to court in order to halt fee collections and better define the responsibilities and authority of the union.[121]

While such a conflict seems to have been fundamentally an issue of misunderstanding, debates over such technicalities highlight an increasing tension between the processes of decentralization and the increasing government interest in privatization. Decentralization was intended to disperse power, authority, and responsibilities to local and regional governments at the same time that the very scope of government responsibility and authority was shrinking. Transport operators certainly felt the effects of these processes. The maintenance and construction of urban roads and other forms of local transportation infrastructure were delegated to municipal and town councils. Given government interests in public transportation—exemplified by their sponsorship of STC, OSA, and CES—decentralization was inevitably a jointly held authority through which both local and national interests were negotiated, rather than a purely local enterprise. Although such interaction between the national and local levels seemed to contradict the PNDC's commitment to grassroots or popular democracy, PNDC leaders increasingly espoused the necessity of some national-level leadership and planning in order to achieve their intended reforms and the broader economic recovery. At the same time, the ERP and other structural adjustment reforms also committed the PNDC to a program of privatization of what had become a large collection of state-controlled enterprises. The PNDC famously dragged its feet in selling off most of the parastatals. It proved less reluctant, however, to yield power over transportation regulation to the drivers' unions. Although the Motor Traffic Unit and other police forces still enforced national traffic laws, the unions increasingly had authority over the behavior of drivers.[122]

Privatization of transport regulation and enforcement marked a significant shift in government relations with transportation. Since colonial-era regulations in the 1930s attempted to define "the type of man who could be a driver," government officials had attempted to enforce discipline and order over a growing population of entrepreneurial drivers. In the absence of any significant transport companies who could, as employers, define and regulate the conditions of their employees' work, the colonial state established itself as the arbiter of transport work and workers. In doing so, it established a precedent that was followed, with few exceptions or alterations, by successive postcolonial governments. In privatizing and decentralizing control over transportation and opening the structures and practices of driving work to market conditions, the PNDC government broke with this long tradition and established a new relationship with drivers and the GPRTU.

"Only God": Survival, Accumulation, and the Search for Security

Even at the height of the crisis, popular representations of drivers, such as the popular highlife song "Adwuma Yi Yε Den" ("The Work is Hard") by Nana Ampadu I and His African Brothers Band Int'l, resonated with an earlier era. The inherent risk of driving work required drivers to exhibit both patience and effort because, as Ampadu sings: "If you make a mistake and God doesn't intervene, you will cause somebody to lose his/her life."[123] And yet, if drivers once commanded respect from passengers on the basis of skill and professionalism, that respect seemed to be eroding in the context of "development." Impatient passengers publicly chastised drivers' speed and made frequent demands that implied a lack of professionalism among drivers. Older drivers, who had been trained to deal with passenger complaints, reacted "cooly."[124] But young men often returned insults. For many older drivers, the increasingly widespread practice of "driving by heart" highlighted the breakdown in training and professionalism among drivers that accompanied the expansion and deregulation of the industry. "Anyone," they argued, might be able to own a car or operate a vehicle, but only those who could exhibit patience, skill, and professionalism should actually work as a driver.

"Driving by heart" also highlighted the increasing frustrations of young and old drivers alike for whom the promises of prosperity seemed increasingly elusive. As Ampadu noted, "All drivers want to be fashionable, and all drivers want people to recognize them. When you wake up in the morning, you go and sit in front of your steering wheel. Everyone sees you and calls you and you also wave at them. When it is so, you are happy. You also are popular, you are somebody."[125] The popularity of drivers and the promise of regular income and economic stability drew increasing numbers of young men like al-Haji to the profession, working for a newly expanded class of vehicle owners. But the financial prosperity on which that status and popularity was based became increasingly difficult to maintain in the aftermath of structural adjustment. Increased professional and personal expenses and increased competitive pressures, which limited the availability of work, placed financial strains on drivers who attempted to find new ways to squeeze money out of their cars. Drivers waited in lorry parks for thirty minutes or more in order to load their vehicles. Less work and lower incomes meant that drivers worked longer hours, had greater difficulty purchasing vehicles, and increasingly relied on the income of their wives and children to maintain their households at a subsistence level.

The frustrations of drivers highlighted the contradictions at the heart of the neoliberal project. Policies of decentralization, deregulation, and liberalization, which were supposed to streamline the economy and improve the economic conditions for entrepreneurs, certainly expanded access to the motor transport industry and gave drivers greater control over their work. But the autonomy and mobility promised through neoliberal reform proved to be a double-edged sword that transformed a culture and practice of automobility, which had once been touted as a path to prosperity, into a means of survival for professional drivers and upstarts alike. Particularly as vehicle ownership became more difficult for young drivers, "small boys" drove with abandon since they did not directly absorb the consequences of damage done to the vehicle due to their reckless behavior—they would simply find another car to drive. The consequences for such behavior were seemingly less severe. Drivers were not taken to court except in the most extreme cases, but the financial cost of recklessness was significant in the context of restricted incomes. Small infractions created opportunities for policemen to collect bribes, which supplemented the declining budgets of their department and their own household. Okan Tetteh and Nii Ayi Bule noted that if police stopped you, "they tried to give a lot of complaint that this thing has spoiled, this thing is not good, this thing is that. They are worrying us with money. When they stop you, money problem!"[126]

These financial risks also exacerbated the physical dangers of the road. Drivers in the 1970s and 1980s sought out "fitters" and improvised solutions to mechanical problems because of a lack of available spare parts; however, by the 1990s, drivers sought out fitters not because spare parts were unavailable but because they were too expensive to afford.[127] The perennial problem of accidents also took on a new significance. While the potential damage to driver and vehicle was clearly identified as an inherent risk in the colonial period, by the 1980s–1990s, drivers took a far greater financial and physical chance on the roads. Driving older vehicles at faster speeds, drivers, many of whom had undoubtedly received inferior training compared to previous generations, were constantly at risk of death and serious injury, particularly when they travelled outside of the cities. Even if a driver was careful and well trained, the increase in the number of vehicles on the road still placed him at risk.

In the face of insecurity, uncertainty, and risk, drivers found their unions ill-equipped to deal with fundamental issues of high petrol prices, standards of training, uneconomic competition, and other issues, which were at the center of driver problems. If driving itself had once been a path to security and prosperity, it now increasingly became viewed merely as a tool for survival. In a lackluster formal-sector job market and a burgeoning urban population, motor transportation increasingly came to be seen as the male equivalent of market trading in the "informal sector."[128] With low overhead (i.e., you didn't have to own a car, you only had to have access to one), few barriers to entry (i.e., as long as one could find a car to drive[129]), and at least some degree of guaranteed income, driving was now a bulwark against starvation.

Conclusion

Driver experiences in the era of structural adjustment highlight the ambiguities of "respect" and the limits of authority. In constructing roads and releasing its control over the conditions of transportation work, the PNDC government's neoliberal policies seemed to be exactly what the country's drivers had been asking for from the beginning. Particularly in the wake of attacks on drivers in the 1970s, the government's trust in the ability and authority of drivers and their unions as agents of development signaled a renewed respect for driving and drivers. However, such respect did not necessarily mean that their lives and work were any more secure or that driving itself began to hold out more possibilities for accumulation and prosperity.

The experiences of drivers in the 1980s and 1990s reflect a fundamental contestation about the meaning of "development." For international financial institutions—and increasingly Ghanaian government leaders—"development" meant improved macroeconomic indicators, increased trade, and new and maintained infrastructure. However, such indicators meant little to those who directly experienced the implications of those reforms and policies. After decades of government intervention and manipulation of the national economy, drivers found themselves subject to the whims of a global and national market economy. While the deregulation and privatization of transportation conformed to World Bank/IMF policy, it did not necessarily result in development in any way that improved in the life and work of drivers—a population and economic sector that was targeted by such reforms. If drivers had come out of the initial period of road construction in the 1930s with a renewed sense of purpose and possibility, driving in the 1990s was increasingly associated with those who had no other options. It had become an economic tool, rather than an occupation or profession.

Epilogue
"No Rest for the Trotro Driver": Ambivalence and Automobility in Twenty-First-Century Ghana

THE CONTRADICTIONS AND complexities of twenty-first-century automobility are immediately apparent to anyone driving through one of the country's major cities. During rush hour at major intersections like Accra's Tetteh Quarshie Interchange or Kumasi's Kejetia Circle, innumerable vehicles sit in unmoving traffic for hours. The teeming masses of the city in all of their variation are united in their im/mobility: wealthy car owners driving themselves in expensive, air-conditioned luxury sedans and SUVs, seemingly untouched and untroubled by their surroundings; members of the middle class whose achievement of vehicle ownership is tempered by the decrepit quality of their vehicles and the need to roll down the window in the absence of an air conditioner; and the masses of others who find vehicle ownership unattainable, sitting in taxis or crammed in trotros, falling asleep in the heat, wiping their brows to remove sweat and dirt or covering their mouths to keep from breathing in ubiquitous exhaust fumes. Immobility has spawned its own new forms of social and economic exchange even as the physical and economic costs of motor transportation increase. People buy food and drinks through their car windows: "pure water" (plastic water sachets), bananas, groundnuts, pineapple, popcorn, ice cream, bread, fried dough, spring rolls, and meat pies. They also shop from the numerous street hawkers who walk between vehicles selling anything from toilet paper to dog chains to posters of Jesus. Such activities reflect an attempt to capitalize on otherwise wasted time on the part of both hawkers and passengers, who regularly travel all the way across the city for work or church.

Sitting in the midst of this traffic congestion on a daily basis, it is clear that automobility remains a very important part of life in twenty-first-century Ghana—highly debated and discussed, central to the daily lives of millions of urban and rural residents. And yet, it also seems clear that the nature of automobility has changed. The increasing numbers of private cars on the road suggest that, far from the democratizing rhetoric of twentieth-century motor transportation, twenty-first-century automobility is a physical manifestation of both local and global income inequalities and capital flows. Both on the road and in the realms of policy, the interests of elite and middle-class drivers, who have been steadily increasing investment in private car ownership since at least the 1990s, have reshaped debates about motor transportation, using their privileged access to social, political, and economic power and the physical presence of their vehicles on the road to dictate a new form of road policy and a culture of automobility. Even as the vast majority of urban and rural residents continue to rely on commercial motor transportation, it is the power of private car owners that has effectively shifted the parameters of the debates about autonomy and mobility in the twenty-first century. The result is a form of postcolonial ambivalence,[1] marked by the contradictions within development discourse and popular culture. On the one hand, automobility in Ghana is central to development initiatives, which seek to improve road transport infrastructure while marginalizing commercial drivers. Such efforts are connected to widespread condemnation of the motor transport industry—the danger of the roads, the practice and training of drivers, the condition of vehicles, the increases in fares, and the congestion of the streets—which have dominated public conversations and debates since the early part of the twentieth century. And yet, in the realm of popular culture, both drivers and passengers continue to idealize an earlier era of Ghanaian automobility, embodied in the mammy truck, which at once symbolized Ghanaian ingenuity in the context of colonialism and the prosperity of the new nation in the years immediately following independence. The interactions of twenty-first-century drivers and passengers are bound up in these continuities and contradictions between development and nostalgia.[2]

Nostalgia for the Road

On a sunny day in April 2009, I emerged at the intersection of Ring Road and Oxford Street from the car of Paa Joe, the famous Ga coffin maker, carrying a rather large wooden replica of a mammy truck. I had asked Paa Joe, an artist and craftsman famous for his "fantasy coffins," to create a smaller model of a trotro, the ubiquitous Ghanaian minibus that serves the motor transportation needs of many in the country. Such a request was not altogether unusual for the artist, whose figurative coffins symbolize or represent the aspirations, obsessions, and accomplishments of the deceased—from the tilapia of the fishermen or the lion of the chief to the Mercedes Benz of the rich businessman. But instead of making a model of the fifteen-passenger vans that served as trotros on the roads of contemporary Ghana, he made a mammy truck. With their imported metal engine and chassis and their locally constructed and decorated wooden body, mammy trucks famously traversed both rural and urban areas carrying goods and passengers throughout the colonial and early postcolonial period, and they were used by drivers in the earliest trotro services of the 1950s. In 2009, however, mammy trucks were rarely seen on Ghanaian roads, having been banned in the 1960s due to safety concerns. It was not the "trotro" I expected. Throughout contemporary Ghana, fabricators perform feats of local engineering and creativity to fit hollowed-out fifteen-passenger vans with locally welded metal and plywood seats designed to maximize the number of passengers, "tropicalized" and "baptized into the system" to better cope with the physical and material conditions of the twenty-first-century Ghanaian motor transport industry.[3] Trotros ferry often-cramped citizens throughout and between municipal areas, bouncing over jarring potholes, speeding around blind corners, and taking shortcuts to avoid traffic. Despite the discomfort of contemporary trotros, they are often noted as a vast improvement over the old "boneshaker" mammy lorries with their wooden bench seats and open wooden sides.

As I passed through the streets carrying my newly acquired work of art, however, people passing remarked, "That is a fine car," and, "That is a proper car." Such attention transcended class, gender, and generation as rich and poor, men and women, young and old stopped to compliment Paa Joe's creation. That this old mammy wagon would receive such attention seemed particularly surprising given the highly critical public discourse on motor transportation and drivers in twenty-first-century Ghana, which had justified development projects like the bus rapid transit (BRT) system and new forms of government regulation. Newspapers were filled with stories about dilapidated vehicles, accidents, and traffic congestion, and passengers and pedestrians alike complained about drivers' seeming disregard for human life as they sped through city streets and rural roads in a quest for profits. I experienced such anxieties directly when a fatal accident occurred right in front of my residence in Accra, and a friend's relatives were hospitalized after a severe accident in the Volta Region. I also began to understand cynical public attitudes toward drivers, as I bargained incessantly with young, male taxi drivers who saw me as a wealthy cash cow, missed my stop when drivers took alternative routes to avoid traffic, and found myself a victim of an elaborate scheme in which a collaborating driver and "passenger" colluded to steal some of my belongings while I was riding in what I thought was a shared taxi.

Older drivers, who began their work in the 1930s and 1940s, reported in interviews that it had not always been this way—that drivers had once been respected, and driving had been a profession that provided opportunities for young men to achieve success and prosperity outside of the networks of education, colonial administration, and Victorian-influenced respectability, which had served as a pathway for many members of the country's middle class. Inussa al-Haji noted that the change was one of respect: "Before, when I took the license and was driving, they respect drivers a lot. Not like now when people don't respect drivers. Sometimes when people want to join your car, they will even beg you before they join your car. That time, passengers are very respectful of drivers because they know that you are the one that is taking them to where they are going. Not that now if they are sitting in your car and they do something and you want to say it then they will start insulting you. If you no get heart, you will be doing something and it will turn to something else. At that time that we are driving at the olden time when I have my license, it is not like that." Many drivers also echoed al-Haji's sense of an evaporating respect between drivers and passengers, drawing implicit connections between the behavior of passengers and the changing material conditions of their work. The nostalgia in their accounts of a better time was palpable in the sharp contrasts they drew between "our time" and "these days." Of course, the reality was much more complicated, even during the "golden age" that drivers experienced between the 1930s and the 1960s. Motor transportation provided new social and economic opportunities, which drivers seized, using their vehicles to accumulate wealth, establish families, invest in property, and create identities as respectable, modern men. However, the practices and cultures of driving, which enabled their newfound status, were often subject to debate and critique. Drivers, passengers, and the state were part of an ongoing conversation about the meaning and significance of automobility in twentieth-century Ghana, and drivers regularly had to negotiate the demands of passengers as well as the consequences of regulation, road construction, and accidents.

And yet, in light of contemporary conditions, these early debates seem minor. "These days," driving represents not an alternative path toward prosperity and respectability, but rather an occupation of last resort. Motor transportation has become an occupation of refuge and survival, shaped by the realities of persistently high rates of unemployment and limited access to education. Many young men find themselves driving cars, bypassing the apprenticeship systems that trained skilled drivers and sometimes using bribes to obtain licenses without taking a test, all in the hopes of earning some income in the highly mobile country. Even older men, who have retired in other fields, find it necessary to enter the motor transport industry, purchasing cars to supplement pensions that fail to keep up with increasing inflation, driving the vehicles themselves in order to maximize profits. Particularly in urban centers, which house an increasing proportion of the country's population, young men transport people to work, home, church, and school, crowded into dilapidated vehicles that are both unpleasant and unsafe. Drivers queue at lorry parks waiting for their turn to load, often only a few times per day. Those who don't want to wait operate taxis outside of the union-controlled lorry parks as "floating cars," roaming city streets in search of passengers. On the roads and sidewalks, through broadcast media and newspapers, and in living rooms, restaurants, and bars across the country, people complain about the conditions of the roads, the traffic congestion of the city, and, most prominently, the dangerous practices of drivers who seem to regularly risk accidents in search of profit. One can, perhaps, understand the nostalgia.

The affection for the model mammy wagon expressed by such a wide swath of people on the streets of Accra suggests that this memory of a better time for both drivers and passengers was rooted not in nostalgia alone, but in a widely shared historical experience of mobility and the economic, social, and cultural opportunities as well as the debates and critiques that such mobility made possible. However, the realities of twenty-first-century motor transportation highlight the fact that the experience and significance of automobility have indeed changed. Drivers' transformation from indigenous entrepreneurs and modern men to criminals, cheats, and bad citizens was rooted not only in declining economic conditions, but also in a shifting discourse of autonomy and belonging, responsibility and prosperity, which had its roots in the nationalist period and came to full fruition in the years of political instability and economic decline after the fall of Kwame Nkrumah.

For drivers' lived realities, these changes are significant. Particularly for older drivers who remember earlier periods when driving work served as a pathway to prosperity, the relatively sharp decline in socioeconomic status has taken both a financial and psychological toll. Like many of us, their plans for the future assumed a kind of continuity that could not have predicted these changes in fortune. Drivers like Tawiah Adjetey, Tetteh, and Kobla mourned their inability to care for their children or pay for their schooling.[4] Many older drivers were heavily dependent on the younger drivers in their union for financial support, receiving small change for food and medicine in their retirement. These issues were exacerbated when older drivers were no longer able to maintain properties or spare vehicles that provided a source of income and retirement savings. For some, the struggles of old age led to regret over youthful spending and financial indiscretion.[5] But for others, their financial struggles represented relatively recent bad luck in the context of an ailing economy.

And yet, despite these changes, automobility remains central to life in twenty-first-century Ghana. While private car ownership has increased noticeably over the last twenty years, approximately 85 percent of the country's urban population still relies on commercial motor transportation. That number is undoubtedly higher in rural areas and smaller towns where income is generally lower. Likewise, the debates about the meaning, significance, organization, and practice of automobility persist. If colonial officials sought to control African mobility and road construction and postcolonial leaders grappled with the issues of fares and driver practice, twenty-first-century leaders are faced with this new problem of immobility. The physical immobility of urban residents is a symptom of broader systemic and infrastructural problems—an aging infrastructure, increasing urbanization, poor urban planning, and limited traffic regulation. But the growing number of cars on the road is also seen by many as a symbol of the widening income gap in contemporary Ghana, which has limited the possibilities for social and economic mobility among many of the country's citizens. Increasingly, these tensions have played out on the road, pitting the elite "myself" drivers with luxury SUVs and sedans against working-class urban residents crammed in dilapidated trotros and taxis, all asserting the rights to space, mobility, and opportunity in contemporary Ghana.

Development and the Tensions of Immobility

In their nostalgic longings for "our time," drivers do more than idealize the past. As Bissell argues, nostalgia is a form of "social practice that mobilizes various signs of the past (colonial or otherwise) in the context of contemporary struggles."[6] In other words, the appeal to "our time" and the comparison to "these days" is a contemporary manifestation of the vernacular politics or "endless self-fashioning" that have defined the culture and practice of automobility since the introduction of motor transportation technologies at the beginning of the twentieth century. In comparing the present with colonial and early postcolonial past, drivers seem to invoke the Akan notion of *sankofa*. Often glossed as "go back and fetch it," the proverb associated with the *sankofa adinkra* symbol—"*Se wo were fi na wosankofa a yenkyi*" ("It is not wrong to go back for that which you have forgotten")[7]—echoes the recollections of drivers who situate their current struggles within longer histories of respectability, professionalism, prosperity, and skill. As such, they speak to the growing insecurity and instability of driving work in the neoliberal age—a manifestation of a "millennium capitalism"[8] that has eroded "traditional paths to security"[9] and driven increasing numbers of people into the informal economy and the church in search of salvation and "fast money."[10] And yet, contemporary debates seem centered less on driver practice than the infrastructure and technology of automobility itself. In other words, the debates of the twenty-first century represent a new conversation about the "right to the road," framed around the crisis of immobility and the increasingly powerful demands of middle-class and elite private car owners.

In 2007, partially in response to public complaints, the World Bank approved $45 million in funding for a Bus Rapid Transit (BRT) system in Accra. The BRT, Ghanaian government officials argued, was part of a larger Urban Transport Project designed to "improve mobility in areas of participating metropolitan, municipal or district assemblies (MMDAs) through a combination of traffic engineering measures, management improvement systems, regulation of the public transport industry, and implementation of a Bus Rapid Transit (BRT) system."[11] The project was supposed to be implemented over the course of five years (2008–2012). By the time I arrived in Ghana in 2009, construction had begun on a pilot project that would operate along the Mallam Road. The Department of Urban Roads sought to extend the project with the support of an additional $50 million in funding from the International Development Association, the Global Environmental Facility, and the Agence Francaise de Developpement, building additional routes in and around the Central Business District.[12]

For twenty-first-century government officials, development experts, and planners, this project seems like an ideal solution to persistent problems of traffic congestion, poor vehicle conditions, high costs, and unpredictable schedules. However, for drivers in contemporary Ghana, this new form of urban planning and infrastructural development represented a fresh assault on the commercial motor transport industry. The BRT would fundamentally refigure the city's mobility system, restricting trotro drivers' access to main roads and funneling all passenger transport through BRT services, owned and operated by the government. Along main roads, BRT buses run on a set schedule in dedicated center lanes with a total of 27 bus stops. Passengers purchase tickets from automated machines. Transportation is, in effect, mechanized and regularized. That regulation extends to driver practice. The Urban Transport Project also created a regulatory framework that "provides the legal basis for the re-organization of the sector at the national level."[13]

The BRT is a clear attempt to respond to passenger complaints. Numerous studies have recorded what anyone on the streets of Accra already knows—passengers are discontented with the traffic congestion, high prices, and poor conditions of trotros and taxis.[14] In providing an alternative to trotros and taxis, the BRT not only seeks to decrease traffic congestion, but also to introduce new forms of competition and regulation, which its sponsors hope will improve conditions on the road. But the BRT is also a reflection of the interests of officials and institutions of foreign capital and development planning who see infrastructural reform as a means to an end—in this case, Millennium Development Goals—as well as a potentially lucrative investment. Scania, a Swedish auto company, signed an agreement with the Ghanaian government in 2014 to provide buses, ticketing machines, workshop services, operational support, and infrastructure. Fredrik Morsing, the regional director for Scania in West Africa, argued that, "The delivery to Accra marks a major step in increasing Scania's presence in West Africa and will also serve as an important reference project for other cities in the region."[15] In other words, Accra's attempts at infrastructural reform are supposed to be a model for regional development and a catalyst for capitalist expansion.

However, the drivers I interviewed in 2009 were skeptical, concerned about what seemed like inevitable restrictions on the autonomy, accessibility, and profitability of their work. The GPRTU directed its drivers not to engage in any form of negotiations or participate in BRT development until union officials could get a better sense of its impact. Union, officials like Al Haji Tetteh, chairman of the Accra branch of the GPRTU, traveled to Brazil and Britain to view other bus systems. Tetteh told me that he was reassured that the new system provided opportunities for drivers to continue their work. But, when I visited union "locals," drivers expressed anxiety over the impending changes in the nature of their work. Restrictions that banned trotros from major roads, new requirements for automated ticketing systems, and a new system of regulations and permits that would bring drivers under the authority of state and municipal authorities marked a fundamental reorganization of the driving profession. That reorganization was most obviously spatial, evidenced by the road construction that created new dedicated lanes for BRT buses. But it also reshaped the social and economic practices that had defined the motor transport industry for at least eighty years. Drivers feared that the BRT would turn them into salaried employees, eliminating their ability to collect profits daily—the "daily bread" that attracted young men to the profession and enabled drivers to support themselves and their families.

The BRT is not the first time that the state has attempted to reorganize and regulate the industry. The twentieth century was in many ways defined by debates about autonomy and mobility that played out through contestations over road construction, fares, driver practice, and public safety. Municipal bus systems, omnibus services, and even the colonial railway were all projects that sought to redefine and control African auto/mobility. That these earlier attempts largely failed highlights not only the strength of drivers as an occupational category, but also the degree to which the meaning and significance of auto/mobility was a subject of significant debate. In the twenty-first century, these debates have not fundamentally transformed. They have merely been refigured; new actors have entered the scene, but the motivations remain largely the same. And yet, drivers seem to wield less power in these debates than they did even in the difficult economic climate of the 1970s and 1980s. Drivers told me that strikes were no longer an option. Even if the union endorsed a strike, which drivers thought was unlikely given the close relationship between union officials and the government, the industry was simply too large to organize effectively and there were too many drivers who simply could not afford any loss in income.

More fundamentally, though, drivers seem to be caught up in a narrative of criminalization, which has its roots in the political instability and economic decline of the 1960s and 1970s, but which has now become reified, seemingly, in developmentalist discourses of informality, infrastructure, and urban planning. Despite the fact that trotros constitute only 35 percent of road traffic (while carrying at least 85 percent of all passengers), trotro drivers have received disproportionate blame for the traffic congestion common at major intersections.[16] And yet, as an attempt to solve traffic congestion, the BRT has sought to regulate and control the most efficient part of the motor transport system—an attempt that has been applauded by passengers, development officials, and foreign investors alike. Drivers remain understandably skeptical.

Vernacular Politics in the Postcolony

The politics of development, which shaped both government action and public response to the BRT project, suggest that the crisis of im/mobility is new—a manifestation of uniquely twenty-first-century challenges that require twenty-first-century solutions. Indeed, the rapid pace of urbanization, the expansion of the informal economy, and the growing income inequality of twenty-first-century Ghana provides new challenges, particularly as the promise of oil wealth fails to materialize. In 2015, the Ghanaian government struggled to address ongoing electricity shortages, known locally as *dumsor*, provoking public protest. As the value of the cedi deteriorated, Ghanaian President Mahama turned to the IMF for loans to stabilize the national currency. National debt ballooned. IMF loan conditions required that the government remove subsidies on petrol. For drivers, passengers, and government officials alike, im/mobility on the road was a symbol of broader socioeconomic crisis.

In the context of crisis, development and nostalgia appear to be two sides of the same coin. Government development strategies and the nostalgic longing of drivers both present alternative visions of the future: pathways out of the "crisis of the present."[17] And yet, drivers' nostalgia reminds us that the association between aspiration and automobility is far from new. Indeed, from the very earliest decades of the twentieth century, young men and women used auto/mobile technologies to engage with global debates about autonomy, mobility, and development—a form of vernacular politics that redefined twentieth-century African social, cultural, and economic life. Automobility provided a new pathway to respectability and prosperity for drivers and passengers in a country that was "on the go." Drivers built houses, educated their children, purchased cars, and established profitable businesses. Market women expanded their businesses, traveling over longer distances. Farmers asserted control over the transport and sale of their crops. Men and women from all walks of life traveled regularly between village and city, fulfilling family obligations, facilitating social, cultural, and economic exchange, and creating a community defined by periurban interaction. But in idealizing or romanticizing "our time," drivers also obscure the conflicts and contestations that shaped auto/mobile lives. Vernacular politics took shape within a larger technopolitical sphere, subject to government regulation, infrastructural development, and foreign investment, but contestation also came from within the auto/mobile population. Economic crisis shifted shared understandings about the value of accumulation, and both drivers and passengers negotiated the politics of criminalization even as they sought to protect the profitability of their own entrepreneurial mobility.

Debates about automobility, then, were debates about what it meant to be "on the go" in twentieth-century Ghana. At the most obvious level, motor transportation enabled new forms of physical mobility, but the movement of drivers and passengers was also part of a much larger system of social and economic interaction and exchange. That "mobility system" connected Ghanaian social and cultural practices of work, family, and leisure to global systems of capitalist exchange and political regimes of regulation and planning. The "mobile society" of twentieth-century Ghana was shaped by the infrastructures and technologies of motor transportation, but it was also shaped by the cultures and practices of technology-in-use, as drivers sought to secure the conditions of possibility for their own work, as well as that of their passengers. But auto/mobile Africans could not always realize their visions of autonomy and mobility. Economic decline, infrastructural failure, and technological breakdown all shaped a practice of automobility that was both full of promise and subject to the precarity and risks of the road.

Notes

Introduction

1. Moses Danquah, "The Romance of Our Roads," *Daily Graphic* 8/6/55; Simon Heap, "The development of motor transport in the Gold Coast, 1900–39," *Journal of Transport History*, 1990, 19–37; Komla Tsey, *From Head-Loading to the Iron Horse: Railway Building in Colonial Ghana and the Origins of Tropical Development* (Cameroon: Langaa RPCIG), 2012.

2. Moses Danquah, "The Romance of Our Roads," *Daily Graphic* 8/6/55.

3. Jan-Bart Gewald, "Missionaries, Hereros, and Motorcars: Mobility and the Impact of Motor Vehicles before 1940," *The International Journal of African Historical Studies* 35 (2/3) (2002): 257–285.

4. Brian Larkin, *Signal and Noise: Media, Infrastructure, and Urban Culture in Nigeria* (Durham, NC: Duke University Press), 2008: 20; Rudolf Mrazek, *Engineers of a Happy Land: Technology and Nationalism in a Colony* (Princeton, NJ: Princeton University Press), 2002: 3.

5. For a description of the new mobilities scholarship, see Clapperton Mavhunga, *Transient Workspaces: Technologies of Everyday Innovation in Zimbabwe* (Boston: MIT Press), 2014.

6. Rudolf Mrazek, *Engineers of Happy Land*, 34; Lindsey Green-Simms, "The Hum of Progress: Motorcars and the Modernization of West Africa," *Postcolonial Automobility: West Africa and the Road to Globalization*, forthcoming.

7. James Ferguson, *Expectations of Modernity: Myths and Meanings of Urban Life on the Zambian Copperbelt* (Los Angeles: University of California Press), 1999.

8. These processes have been well documented in the literature on Ghanaian social history and popular culture. See, for example: Stephanie Newell, *Literary Culture in Colonial Ghana: How to Play the Game of Life* (Bloomington, IN: Indiana University Press), 2002; Nathan Plageman, *Highlife Saturday Night: Popular Music and Social Change in Urban Ghana* (Bloomington, IN: Indiana University Press), 2012; T. C. McCaskie, *Asante Identities: History and Memory in an African Village, 1850–1950* (Bloomington: Indiana University Press), 2001; Jean Allman and Victoria Tashjian, *I Will Not Eat Stone: A Women's History of Colonial Asante* (Portsmouth, NH: Heinemann), 2000; John Parker, *Making the Town: Ga State and Society in Early Colonial Accra* (Portsmouth, NH: Heinemann), 2000; among others.

9. Michel de Certeau, *The Practice of Everyday Life* (Los Angeles: University of California Press), 2011.

10. John Urry, *Mobilities* (Cambridge: Polity Press), 2007: 118.

11. Mike Featherstone, Nigel Thrift, and John Urry, eds., *Automobilities* (New York: Sage Publications), 2005: 1.

12. Michael Adas, *Machines as the Measure of Man: Science, Technology, and Ideologies of Western Dominance* (Ithaca, NY: Cornell University Press), 1990.

13. Daniel Headrick, *Tools of Empire: Technology and European Imperialism in the Nineteenth Century* (Oxford: Oxford University Press), 1981.

14. Cotten Seiler, *Republic of Drivers: A History of Automobility in America* (Chicago: University of Chicago Press), 2008: 7.

15. Seiler, *Republic of Drivers*, 3.

16. Henri Lefebvre, *Everyday Life in the Modern World* (London: Allen Lane), 1971: 104.

17. Guy Debord, quoted in Kristin Ross, *Fast Cars, Clean Bodies: Decolonization and the Reordering of French Culture* (Boston: The MIT Press), 1996: 26.

18. Ross, *Fast Cars, Clean Bodies*, 19.

19. Paul Gilroy, *Darker than Blue: On the Moral Economies of Black Atlantic Culture* (Cambridge, Massachusetts: Belknap Press), 2011.

20. Lindsey Greene-Simms, *Postcolonial Automobility*, forthcoming.

21. Featherstone, et al, *Automobilities; Guillermo Giucci, The Cultural Life of the Automobile: Roads to Modernity* (Austin: University of Texas Press), 2012.

22. Gewald, "Missionaries, Hereros, and Motorcars," 260.

23. Gewald, "Missionaries, Hereros and Motorcars," 260; Michael Adas, *Machines as the Measure of Men*, 21–68, 221–36.

24. Michael Adas, *Machines as the Measure of Men*, 224.

25. Wolfgang Schivelbusch, *A Railway Journey: The Industrialization of Time and Space in the 19th Century* (Berkeley: University of California Press), 1987.

26. Brodie Cruickshank, *Eighteen Years on the Gold Coast of Africa* (London: Cass), 1966; Kwamina Dickson, *A Historical Geography of Ghana* (London: Cambridge University Press), 1971; Kwame Arhin, *West African Traders in Ghana in the Nineteenth and Twentieth Centuries* (New York: Prentice Hall Press), 1980. At least the gold-producing regions of the forest zone had also participated in the trans-Saharan trade for many centuries before the arrival of Europeans on the coast. While gold was an essential element in this trade, people of the forest zones were perhaps peripheral to the trade itself, providing raw materials. The arrival of Europeans on the coast gradually redirected trade from the interior forests to the south, placing these same communities in the forest, savannah, and coastal zones into positions as intermediaries between European coastal forts and deeper interior networks. These shifts in the direction of trade obviously built on older social and economic patterns and relationships; however, they also marked a significant change in the economic significance and centrality of states and economies of the southern Gold Coast. If they had once been peripheral to the dominant long-distance trade networks, they now controlled new networks. As a result, some states like the Asante rose significantly in power from the seventeenth century, as the extension of imperial borders went hand in hand with control over trade networks.

27. Allman and Tashjian, *I Will Not Eat Stone*, 12.

28. McCaskie, *Asante Identities*, 115.

29. Larkin, *Signal and Noise*, 7; Adas, *Machines as the Measure of Men*, 224.

30. McCaskie, *Asante Identities*, 124.

31. Penny Harvey and Hannah Knox, *Roads: An Anthropology of Infrastructure and Expertise* (Ithaca, NY: Cornell University Press), 2015: 7–8.

32. Nikhil Anand, "Pressure: The Politechnics of Water Supply in Mumbai," *Cultural Anthropology* 26(4): 2011, 542–564; quoted in Penny Harvey and Hannah Knox, *Roads: An Anthropology of Infrastructure and Expertise* (Ithaca, NY: Cornell University Press), 2015: 5.

33. Filip de Boeck, "Infrastructure: Commentary from Filip de Boeck," *Curated Collections, Cultural Anthropology Online*, November 26, 2012 http://production.culanth.org/curated_collections/11-infrastructure/discussions/7-infrastructure-commentary-from-filip-de-boeck, quoted in Harvey and Knox, *Roads*, 5.

34. Harvey and Knox, *Roads*, 7–8; Timothy Mitchell, *Rule of Experts: Egypt, Techno-Politics, Modernity* (Los Angeles: University of California Press), 2002; William Bissell, *Urban Design, Chaos, and Colonial Power in Zanzibar* (Bloomington, IN: Indiana University Press), 2010.

35. Jan-Bart Gewald, "Introduction," In *The Speed of Change: Motor Vehicles and People in Africa, 1890–2000*, eds. Jan-Bart Gewald, Sabine Luning, and Klaas van Walraven (Leiden: Brill), 2009.

36. John Iliffe, *Africans: The History of a Continent* (Cambridge: Cambridge University Press), 2007: 219–250.

37. Moses Danquah, "Transportation," *Daily Graphic*, 11/24/55.

38. Paul Edwards, "Infrastructure and Modernity: Force, Time, and Social Organization in the History of Sociotechnical Systems," in *Modernity and Technology*, eds. Thomas J. Misa, Philip Brey, and Andrew Feenberg (Cambridge: The MIT Press), 2003: 186.

39. For recent discussions of risk and the road, see *AFRICA* 83 (3) (2013).

40. Urry, *Mobilities*, 116.

41. Igor Kopytoff, "The Cultural Biography of Things: Commoditization as Process," in *The Social Life of Things: Commodities in Cultural Perspective*, ed. Arjun Appadurai (Cambridge: Cambridge University Press), 1986: 67.

42. Timothy Burke, *Lifebuoy Men, Lux Women: Commodification, Consumption, and Cleanliness in Modern Zimbabwe* (Durham, NC: Duke University Press), 1996: 3–4; Arjun Appadurai, *The Social Life of Things: Commodities in Cultural Perspective* (Cambridge: Cambridge University Press), 1986.

43. Larkin, *Signal and Noise*, 3; see also Daniel Miller, "Driven Societies," *Car Cultures*, Daniel Miller, ed. (New York: Berg), 2001: 1–34.

44. Urry, *Mobilities*, 115–116.

45. Mrazek, *Engineers of a Happy Land*, Mavhunga, *Transient Workspaces*. In many colonies, however, Europeans tended not to drive themselves, relying on "local" populations to serve as chauffeurs.

46. Lindsey Greene-Simms, *Postcolonial Automobility*.

47. Sara Abrevaya Stein, *Plumes: Ostrich Feathers, Jews, and a Lost World of Global Commerce* (New Haven, CT: Yale University Press), 2010.

48. Rudi Volti, *Cars & Culture: The Life Story of a Technology* (Baltimore: Johns Hopkins University Press), 2004: 63.

49. Schivelbush, *The Railway Journey*.

50. Ross, *Fast Cars, Clean Bodies*, 1–70.

51. Mavhunga, *Transient Workspaces*, 12.

52. Mavhunga, *Transient Workspaces*, 13.

53. Kwame Arhin, "Rank and Class among the Asante and Fante in the Nineteenth Century," *Africa* 53 (1983), 5.

54. Raymond Dumett, "Tropical Forests and West African Enterprise: The Early History of the Ghana Timber Trade," *African Economic History* 29 (2001), 79–116, 92.

55. Raymond Dummett, "African Merchants of the Gold Coast, 1860–1905: Dynamics of Indigenous Entrepreneurship," *Comparative Studies in Society and History* 25 (1983), 661–693, 662–664. For a more detailed discussion of these politics and the ways in which they influenced the politics of labor organization in the twentieth century, see Jennifer Hart, "Motor Transportation, Trade Unionism, and the Culture of Work in Colonial Ghana," *International Review of Social History* 29 (2014), Special Issue, 185–209.

56. Frederick Cooper, *Decolonization and African Society: The Labor Question in French and British Africa* (Cambridge: Cambridge University Press), 1996; Lisa Lindsay, *Working with Gender: Wage Labor and Social Change in Southwestern Nigeria* (Portsmouth, NH: Heinemann), 2003; Nathan Plageman, *Highlife Saturday Night*; Bianca Murillo, *Conditional Sales: Global Commerce and the Making of an African Consumer Society* (Athens, OH: Ohio University Press), forthcoming.

57. T. C. McCaskie, *Asante Identities*, 118.

58. Shadrak Yemo Odoi, Labadi, August 6, 2009, Interview by Author.

59. Shadrak Yemo Odoi, Labadi, August 6, 2009, Interview by Author.

60. Marian Aguiar, *Tracking Modernity: India's Railway and the Culture of Mobility* (Minneapolis: University of Minnesota Press), 2011, p. xviii. See also, Harvey and Knox, 7.

61. David Scott, *Conscripts of Modernity: The Tragedy of Colonial Enlightenment* (Durham, NC: Duke University Press), 2004.

62. Bissell, *Urban Design, Chaos, and Colonial Power in Zanzibar*; Mitchell, *Rule of Experts*; Timothy Mitchell, *Colonising Egypt* (Los Angeles: University of California Press), 1991; James Scott, *Seeing Like a State: How Certain Schemes to Improve the Human Condition Have Failed* (New Haven, CT: Yale University Press), 1999.

63. Brian Larkin, *Signal and Noise*, 4.

64. Here, I follow Brian Larkin, who defines infrastructure as the "totality of both technical and cultural systems that create institutionalized structures whereby goods of all sorts circulate, connecting and binding people into collectivities" (Larkin, *Signal and Noise*, 6).

65. Shack Marlow, Labadi, August 6, 2009, Interview by Author.

66. Abraham Tagoe, Teshie Linguist, Accra, August 5, 2009, Interview by Author.

67. George H. Lewis, "The Philosophy of the Street in Ghana: Mammy Wagons and Their Mottos—A Research Note," *The Journal of Popular Culture* 32(1) (Summer 1998): 165–171; Ato Quayson, "Signs of the Times: Discourse Ecologies and Street Life on Oxford St., Accra," *City and Society* 22 (1) (June 2010): 72–96; Sjaak van der Geest, "'Anyway': Lorry Inscriptions in Ghana," in *The Speed of Change: Motor Vehicles and People in Africa, 1890–2000*, eds. Jan-Bart Gewald, Sabine Luning, and Klaas van Walraven (Leiden: Brill), 2009: 253–293; Lawuyi, "The World of the Yoruba Taxi Driver: An Interpretive Approach to Vehicle Slogans," *AFRICA* 58 (1) (1988): 1–13.

68. Ato Quayson, "Signs of the Times."

69. Matteo Rizzo, "Being Taken for a Ride: Privatization of the Dar es Salaam Transport System, 1983–1998," *Journal of Modern African Studies* 40 (2002):133–157; Kenda Mutongi, "Thugs or Entrepreneurs?: Perceptions of *Matatu* Operators in Nairobi, ca. 1970 to Present," *Africa* 76(4) (2006): 549–568.

70. "Feel Free" (Mr. Musa), Madina Atomic Junction Driver. June 21, 2007.

71. Tim Ingold, *Lines: A Brief History* (New York: Routledge), 2007: 75.

72. Jean Allman, "Phantoms of the Archive: Kwame Nkrumah, a Nazi Pilot Named Hanna, and the Contingencies of Postcolonial History Writing," *American Historical Review* 118(1) (February 2013): 104–129.

73. Quayson, "Signs of the Times."

Chapter 1

1. The National Archives (TNA): Public Records Office (PRO) DO 35/359/7 Development of Transport Services in the colonies, 1930–1932.

2. Railroads and other transportation infrastructure were not developed with any intensity in the Northern Territories until at least the 1930s. As late as 1952, when a report on transportation in the Gold Coast was published, the Northern Territories still did not possess any major road or rail lines that would connect it to the southern half of the colonial territory, with the exception of the trunk road that connected Tamale and Kumasi.

3. The National Archives (TNA): Public Records Office (PRO) DO 35/359/7 Development of Transport Services in the colonies, 1930–1932.

4. William Bissell, *Urban Design, Chaos, and Colonial Power in Zanzibar* (Bloomington: Indiana University Press), 2010: 20.

5. Wolfgang Schivelbush, *Railway Journey: The Industrialization of Time and Space in the 19th Century* (Los Angeles: University of California Press), 1987; David Solkin, *Painting out*

of the Ordinary: Modernity and the Art of Everyday Life in Early Nineteenth Century Britain (London: Paul Mellon Center BA), 2008.

6. Schivelbush, *Railway Journey*; Marian Aguiar, *Tracking Modernity: India's Railway and the Culture of Mobility* (Minneapolis: University of Minnesota Press), 2011. What that interaction looked like, however, is debated. Jo Guldi argues that railways facilitated a breaking down of the sociability that developed on and along premodern road networks and introduced new forms and strategies of difference. Jo Guldi, *Roads to Power: Britain Invents the Infrastructure State* (Cambridge, MA: Harvard University Press), 2012.

7. Tim Ingold, *Lines: A Brief History* (New York: Routledge), 2007.

8. Aguiar, *Tracking Modernity*, 13.

9. Aguiar, *Tracking Modernity*, 10.

10. Helen Tilley, *Africa as a Living Laboratory: Empire, Development, and the Problem of Scientific Knowledge, 1870–1950* (Chicago: University of Chicago Press), 2011: 17.

11. Gabrielle Hecht, *Being Nuclear: Africans and the Global Uranium Trade* (Boston: The MIT Press), 2014.

12. Casper Andersen, *British Engineers and Africa, 1875–1914* (London: Pickering & Chatto, Ltd), 2011.

13. Bissell, *Urban Design, Chaos, and Colonial Power in Zanzibar*, 3.

14. Sara Berry, "Hegemony on a Shoestring: Indirect Rule and Access to Agricultural Land," *AFRICA* 62(3) (1992): 327–355.

15. Bruce Berman, "The Ordeal of Modernity in an Age of Terror," *African Studies Review* 49 (1) (2006): 1–14; Ato Quayson, *Oxford Street, Accra: City Life and the Itineraries of Transnationalism* (Durham, NC: Duke University Press), 2014; Bissell, *Urban Design, Chaos, and Colonial Power in Zanzibar*.

16. Denis Judd, "Diamonds Are Forever?: Kipling's Imperialism," *History Today*, 47 (6) (1997).

17. Clapperton Mavhunga, *Transient Workspaces: Technologies of Everyday Innovation in Zimbabwe* (Boston: The MIT Press), 2014.

18. Pieter de Marees, *Description and Historical Account of the Gold Kingdom of Guinea (1602)*, Albert van Dantzig and Adam Jones, trans and eds. (Oxford: Oxford University Press), 1987: 64.

19. John Parker, *Making the Town: Ga State and Society in Early Colonial Accra* (Portsmouth, NH: Heinemann), 2000: 195.

20. John Thornton makes compelling arguments about the sophistication of West African societies in the period around early European arrival. He argues that their technological, cultural, and economic sophistication surpassed that of Europeans in the late fifteenth century, which shaped the nature of their interaction. See, for example: John Thornton, *Africa and Africans in the Making of the Atlantic World, 1400–1800* (Cambridge: Cambridge University Press), 1998.

21. George Brooks, *Eurafricans in Western Africa: Commerce, Social Status, Gender, & Religious Observance* (Columbus, OH: Ohio University Press), 2003.

22. Kwame Arhin, *West African Traders in Ghana in the Nineteenth and Twentieth Centuries* (New York: Longman), 1979: 9–10.

23. Brooks, *Eurafricans in Western Africa*; Benjamin Lawrence, Emily Osborn, and Richard Roberts, eds., *Intermediaries, Interpreters, and Clerks: African Employees in Colonial Africa* (Madison, WI: University of Wisconsin Press), 2006.

24. Margaret Priestley, *West African Trade and Coast Society: A Family Study* (Oxford: Oxford University Press), 1969; Raymond E. Dumett, "John Mensah Sarbah, the Elder, and African Mercantile Entrepreneurship in the Gold Coast in the Late Nineteenth Century," *Journal of African History* 14(4) (1973): 653–679.

25. As Beverly Grier argues, in precolonial societies where land was abundant, but population densities were relatively low, "the struggle to control labor power was at the heart of social

and political organization." Beverly Grier, "Pawns, Porters, and Petty Traders: Women in the Transition to Cash Crop Agriculture in Colonial Ghana," *Signs* 17 (Winter 1992), p. 307.

26. Beverly Grier, "Pawns, Porters, and Petty Traders."

27. Jennifer Hart, "Motor Transportation, Trade Unionism, and the Culture of Work in Colonial Ghana," *International Review of Social History*, 29 (2014), 191; Kwame Arhin, "Trade, Accumulation and the State in Asante in the Nineteenth Century." *Africa*, 60 (1990): 524–537; J. H. Kwabena Nketia, *Drumming in Akan Communities of Ghana* (London, 1963). There are, of course, exceptions to this general statement, which Arhin discusses in "Trade Accumulation and the State in Asante in the Nineteenth Century."

28. Claire Robertson, *Sharing the Same Bowl: A Socioeconomic History of Women and Class in Accra, Ghana* (Ann Arbor: University of Michigan Press), 1990.

29. Kwamina Dickson, *A Historical Geography of Ghana*, (Cambridge: Cambridge University Press), 1971: 202, 214. Asante is included in this study under the category of "southern Gold Coast." As has been demonstrated by a number of scholars (See, for example, Jean Allman and Victoria Tashjian, *"I Will Not Eat Stone": A Women's History of Colonial Asante* [Portsmouth, NH: Heinemann], 2000; Kwame Arhin, *West African Traders in Ghana in the Nineteenth and Twentieth Centuries*; Kwame Arhin, "Trade, Accumulation and the State in Asante in the Nineteenth Century" *Africa* 60[4] [1990]: 524–537; Gareth Austin, "'No Elders Were Present': Commoners and Private Ownership in Asante, 1807–96," *Journal of African History* 37 [1996]: 1–30), Asante was inextricably linked to the trade and economy of coastal communities. Southern Ghana, it is argued here, represented a distinct and coherent commercial zone. As a result of these trading networks, this larger region—and not just the Gold Coast Colony—served as the forms of colonial economic and communication infrastructure policy. This differs profoundly from colonial attitudes toward and policies in the Northern Territories. Although recent studies have demonstrated the impact of colonial infrastructure and trade in the Northern Territories (See, for example: Samuel Ntewusu, *Settling In and Holding On: A Socio-Historical Study of Northern Trader and Transporters in Accra's Tudu, 1908–2008* [Dissertation: University of Lieden, Afrika Studies Centrum], 2011), colonial officials proved largely disinterested in investment in the Northern Territories, focusing financial investment and infrastructure construction on the Southern zones in which cash-cropping efforts (cocoa, kola, cotton, etc.) were focused.

30. A. G. Hopkins, *An Economic History of West Africa* (New York: Routledge), 1973.

31. Komla Tsey, *From Headloading to the Iron Horse: Railway Building in Colonial Ghana and the Origins of Tropical Development* (Cameroon: Langaa RPCIG), 2012: 13.

32. Tsey, *From Headloading to the Iron Horse*, 13.

33. Anderson, *British Engineers in Africa*.

34. Guldi, *Roads to Power*.

35. Naaborko Sackeyfio-Lenoch, *The Politics of Chieftaincy: Authority and Property in Colonial Ghana, 1920–1950* (Rochester, NY: University of Rochester Press), 2014: 30; Mahmood Mamdani, *Citizen and Subject: Contemporary Africa and the Legacy of Late Colonialism* (Princeton, NJ: Princeton University Press), 1995; Frederick Lugard, *The Dual Mandate in British Tropical Africa* (London: William Blackwood and Sons), 1922.

36. To see a thoughtful analysis of the ways in which these entrepreneurs influenced (and often constrained) colonial authority in the nineteenth century, see Trevor Getz, *Abina and the Important Men: A Graphic History* (Oxford: Oxford University Press), 2011.

37. Michael Adas, *Machines as the Measure of Men: Science, Technology, and Ideologies of Western Dominance* (Ithaca, NY: Cornell University Press), 1990: 4.

38. Hecht, *Being Nuclear*.

39. Quoted in Adas, *Machines as the Measure of Men*, 229.

40. Adas, Machines as the Measure of Men, 222–223.

41. Joseph Morgan Hodge, *Triumph of the Expert: Agrarian Doctrines of Development and the Legacies of British Colonialism* (Columbus, OH: Ohio University Press), 2007: 8.

42. Hodge, *Triumph of the Expert*, 8.

43. Daniel Headrick, *The Tools of Empire: Technology and European Imperialism in the Nineteenth Century* (Oxford: Oxford University Press), 1981: 9–13; Andersen, *British Engineers in Africa*, 12; Hodge, *Triumph of the Expert*, 8. Joseph Morgan Hodge argues that the railways were part of a broader process through which "science and technology had come to be seen as indispensable 'tools of empire,' tipping the scales in favor of European conquest and penetration of unprecedented expanses of the globe" (8).

44. Tilley, *Africa as a Living Laboratory*, 17. Tilley's "development state" is, she argues, one of many variants of the capitalist state. It also resonates with Jo Guldi's notion of Britain as an "infrastructure state," through which parliamentarians increasingly invested state resources in infrastructural development throughout the eighteenth and nineteenth centuries as a means of encouraging trade and consolidating political power. Guldi, *Roads to Power*.

45. Tsey, *From Headloading to the Iron Horse*, 4–6.

46. Schivelbusch, *The Railway Journey*, 17.

47. Tsey, *From Headloading to the Iron Horse*, 4–6.

48. Tsey, *From Headloading to the Iron Horse*, 4–6.

49. Hodge, *Triumph of the Expert*, 8.

50. Tsey, *From Headloading to the Iron Horse*, 6–7.

51. WTD Tudhope, "The Development of the Cocoa Industry in the Gold Coast and Ashanti," *African Affairs* IX(XXXIII) (1909): 34.

52. Arhin, *West African Traders in the Nineteenth and Twentieth Centuries*, 14.

53. Allman and Tashjian, *I Will Not Eat Stone*, pp. 3, 6.

54. Polly Hill, *Migrant Cocoa Farmers of Ghana: A Case Study in Rural Capitalism* (London: James Currey), 1997; Allman and Tashjian, *I Will Not Eat Stone*; Nathan Plageman, *Highlife Saturday Night: Popular Music and Social Change in Urban Ghana* (Bloomington, IN: Indiana University Press), 2012; Stephanie Newell, *Literary Culture in Colonial Ghana: How to Play the Game of Life* (Bloomington: Indiana University Press), 2002; Stephan Miescher, *Making Men in Ghana* (Bloomington: Indiana University Press), 2005.

55. Tsey, *From Headloading to the Iron Horse*, 3.

56. Ingold, *Lines*, 81.

57. Ingold, *Lines*, 81.

58. Tsey, *From Headloading to the Iron Horse*, 23.

59. Quoted in Tsey, *From Headloading to the Iron Horse*, 23.

60. Because of war and the global depression, however, the railway line was not completed until 1923 (Allman and Tashjian, "*I Will Not Eat Stone*," 9).

61. Dickson, *A Historical Geography of Ghana*, 218.

62. J.H.K., "Motor Transport on the Gold Coast," *The Commercial Motor* (17 August 1920), 10.

63. Quoted in Tsey, *From Headloading to the Iron Horse*, 3.

64. Public Records and Archives Administration Department (PRAAD): Accra *Debates of the Legislative Council*, September 30, 1870.

65. Guldi, *Roads to Power*; Anderson, *British Engineers in Africa*.

66. Guldi, *Roads to Power* 199.

67. TNA: PRO CO 100–52 1902 Gold Coast Blue Book of Statistics; Dickson, *Historical Geography of Ghana*, p. 220–221.

68. Traction engines were steam engines that ran on roads rather than rails. In effect, it was a road train.

69. PRAAD: Accra, *Minutes of the Gold Coast Legislative Council*, 16 January 1901. See also, Dickson, *Historical Geography of Ghana*, pg. 221.

70. Cited in Dickson, *A Historical Geography of Ghana*, pg. 221.

71. Guldi, *Roads to Power*.

72. Governor Nathan, on the advice of Prime Minister Joseph Chamberlain, imported the first motorcar in 1902.

73. Dickson, *A Historical Geography of Ghana*, p. 221.

74. Quoted in Hill, *The Migrant Cocoa Farmers of Southern Ghana*, 235, footnote 1.

75. Hill, *The Migrant Cocoa Farmers of Southern Ghana*, 235, footnote 1.

76. "Metalled roads" describe a gravel road covered with tarmac (a mixture of gravel and tar). In the United States this is often referred to as a "paved road."

77. Transportation maintenance costs were exacerbated by a lack of interchangeable parts in early motor vehicles and a lack of standardization of vehicles in the Gold Coast.

78. See for example, Hill, *The Migrant Cocoa Farmers of Southern Ghana*.

79. PRAAD: Accra CSO 14/1/72 1934–1935 Advances to purchase means of transport European staff, Public Works Dept.; PRAAD: Accra CSO 14/1/73 1937 Advances to purchase mean of Transport, European staff Public Works Dept.; PRAAD: Accra CSO 14/1/74a 1940 Advances to purchase means of transport European Staff, Public Works Dept. See also Georgine Clarsen, "Machine as the Measure of Women: Colony Irony in a Cape to Cairo Automobile Journey, 1930," *Journal of Transport History* 29(1) (2008): 44–63.

80. Hill argues that the increase in the numbers of imported vehicles resulted from improved shipping facilities in 1919 (*The Migrant Cocoa Farmers of Southern Ghana*, 235).

81. Guillermo Giucci, *The Cultural Life of the Automobile: Roads to Modernity* (Austin, TX: University of Texas Press), 2012: 2.

82. Governor Hugh Clifford, *Gold Coast Legislative Council, 1920–21* (Accra), 1921: 54. Quoted in Simon Heap, "The Development of Motor Transport in the Gold Coast, 1900–39," *Journal of Transport History* 11(2) (1990): 25.

83. The lorry is so important to the rise of cocoa that Polly Hill uses the advent of the lorry to establish periodization in her study of migrant Akwapim cocoa farmers. She argues that 1918 marked the end of the pre-lorry age, which corresponds with evidence of the increase in drivers post–WWI as well as the increased investment in road building as a result of Guggisberg's Ten Year Development Plan. See Hill, *The Migrant Cocoa Farmers of Southern Ghana*, p. 6.

84. Hill, *The Migrant Cocoa Farmers of Southern Ghana*, p. 190.

85. Tsey, *From Head-loading to the Iron Horse*, 131–133; TNA: PRO Transport—Road and Rail Competition, 1935; PRAAD: Accra CSO 14/2/23 1930–1931 Road and Rail Competition.

86. PRAAD: NAG (Accra) CSO 17/1/33 1933 Rail and Road Competition—Economic situation of the railway.

87. Tsey, *From Head-Loading to the Iron Horse*, 123–124.

88. Hill, *The Migrant Cocoa Farmers of Southern Ghana*, p. 234.

89. Arhin, *West African Traders in the Nineteenth and Twentieth Centuries*, 14.

90. PRAAD: NAG (Accra) CSO 14/2/23 Road and Rail Competition, letter from General Manager of the Gold Coast to the Colonial Secretary, 10 April, 1930).

91. PRAAD: NAG (Accra) CSO 14/2/23 Road and Rail Competition, Memo from the Director of Public Works to the Colonial Secretary, 19 March 1930.

92. Allman and Tashjian, *I Will Not Eat Stone*; Gracia Clark, *Onions Are My Husband: Survival and Accumulation by West African Market Women* (Chicago: University of Chicago Press), 1995. Although women had long been involved in local trade, Clark argues that women filled the places of male traders as large numbers of men left markets to engage in more lucrative cocoa farming. The ultimate dominance of women in long-distance trade, however, required

new technologies of mobility, which would enable women to spend less time traveling for their work in order to balance responsibilities and expectations both at home and in the market.

93. Tsey, *From Head-Loading to the Iron Horse*, 107, footnote 293; W. D. Waghon, *Report on the Gold Coast Railways*, 1912, 17.

94. Hill, *The Migrant Cocoa Farmers of Southern Ghana*, 234–235.

95. PRAAD: Accra CSO 14/2/329 Road Transportation Board—Formation of.

96. Giucci, *The Cultural Life of the Automobile*.

97. TNA: PRO CO 323/1339/8 Transport—Road and Rail Competition 1935
    "The crux of the whole question:—

    (a) It appears to be generally agreed that, for all the larger units, a railway is essential as the back-bone of the transport system.

    (b) If that is so, then it seems to me to follow that things must be so arranged that that essential back-bone is adequately protected. Failure to do so would mean direct loss to the community, and the disorganization of its whole economic life.

    (c) The railway is a cheaper means of transportation than the motor. (We may take it roughly as 4-6d per ton mile for the motor, as against 1d say for the railway—both figures being based on the assumption that all proper charges are taken into account in calculating the cost).

    (d) The railway depends for its very life upon a graduate rate system. Low value traffic is, broadly, carried at 'out-of-pocket cost'. High value traffic is charged a much higher rate. There is a complicated system of adjustment, the broad effect of which is that the railway just pays for its way—if that can be managed. No one wants to 'make a profit' out of it. If it just pays its way—costs, renewals interest on capital, sinking fund, etc.— everybody would be quite satisfied. But it cannot possibly be made to pay its way, in the world of to-day, unless it can count on the high-rate traffic.

    (e) If there is unregulated road competition, the motor can step in and pick its traffic. It can undercut the railway—not because it is a cheaper method of transport, but because it is under no obligation to carry everything. It can pick and choose. It won't look at the low-value traffic; but it can carry seasonal traffic where there are concentrated loads; it can carry high-value traffic; it can offer differential rates; and so on. The broad effect is to take from the railway the paying traffic on which the whole financial structure of the railway depends. The end, it would seem, must be the destruction of the railway as an efficient instrument of transportation. No Govt. can normally carry the loss which the working of such a system would lead to; nor could they allow the railway to force (or attempt to force) up the rates on the low-value traffic, which is usually so important to the life of the community, and which could not in fact 'bear' higher rates. That seems to me the essence of the affair. How to deal with the problem is a local question."

98. PRAAD: NAG (Accra) CSO 14/2/23 road and rail competition, "Letter to the Colonial Secretary, Accra from the General Manger of the Gold Coast Railway," 10 April 1930.

99. PRAAD: NAG (Accra) CSO 14/2/25 1933 Road, Rail and other System of Internal Communication, competition between; PRAAD: NAG (Accra) CSO 14/2/23 Road and Rail Competition.

100. PRAAD: NAG (Accra) CSO 14/2/123 1932–33 Scheduling of Roads.

101. Tsey, 131–133.

102. Tsey, 139–141.

103. Tsey, 131–133.

104. PRAAD: NAG (Accra) CSO 14/2/25 1933 Road, Rail and other System of Internal Communication, competition between.

105. Policies from the Gold Coast also influenced policy in other parts of Africa. See TNA: PRO CO 262/652 Sierra Leone Railway-road competition, Gold Coast Model 1936; TNA: PRO

CO 323/1339/8 Transport—Road and Rail Competition 1935; TNA: PRO CO 937/49/4 1947 Transport—Road and Rail Competition; TNA: PRO CO 323/1393/3 1936 Transport—Road and Rail Competition.

106. PRAAD: NAG (Accra) CSO 14/2/150 1929–1947 Road Policy: Gov. AR Slater formally discarded the use of road gaps in 1929, though no steps had been taken to bridge those gaps as of 1936.

107. PRAAD: NAG (Accra) CSO 14/2/123 1932–1933 Scheduling of Roads.

108. PRAAD: NAG (Accra) CSO 14/2/157 1935–1939 Accra-Sekondi Road; PRAAD: NAG (Accra) CSO 14/2/200 1939 Closing of roads in connection with control of transport and fuel supplies, "Letter from JB Danquah, General Secretary of the Gold Coast Youth Conference to the Colonial Secretary, 20th October 1939" and "Letter from Secretary of the Accra & Eastern Province Chamber of Commerce to the Colonial Secretary, 21 October 1939"; PRAAD: NAG (Accra) CSO 14/2/150 1929–1947 Road Policy.

109. Quoted in Tsey, 131–133.

110. PRAAD: Accra CSO 14/1/69 1932 Central Road Board Meeting 1931; CSO 14/1/70 1932 Central Road Board Meeting 1932; PRAAD: Accra CSO 14/2/126 1932–1933 Boundary road, Accra.

111. See Hill, *The Migrant Cocoa Farmers of Southern Ghana* for more information on the decline of cocoa prices in the 1930s and its effects on farmers.

112. Filip de Boeck, "Infrastructure: Commentary from Filip de Boeck," *Cultural Anthropology Online*, 2012.

113. Guldi, *Roads to Power*, 3–4.

114. Meeson, "Transport Experience: British West Africa," *The Commercial Motor*, 17 May 1927, 50–53.

115. PRAAD: NAG (Accra) CSO 14/2/123 1932–1933 Scheduling of Roads: "The minor points I raised as possible flaws in the scheme of scheduling roads were (a) It appeared to me likely that just one or two vehicles would pay the enhanced fee for the scheduled area and run a sort of shuttle service, the cacao being loaded and offloaded from ordinary lorries at each end of the area. (b) What is to prevent carriers being employed to transport loads of cacao through the scheduled areas to rejoin lorries on the other end."

116. See, for example, Hill, *The Migrant Cocoa Farmers of Southern Ghana*, p. 247.

117. Moses Danquah, "The Symbols of the People's Belief in Their Own Future," *Daily Graphic*, 9/3/55; Tsey; Hill, 247. Hill's recounting of this construction project comes from James Lawrence Tete's typescript book on the history of the Akwapim Hill estimates that construction likely took place between 1916 and 1926. Hill writes: "The three most important of these access roads were: that from Nsawam to Aburi (financed by Aburi farmers, at a cost, according to Tete, of £8,000—from another source it is learnt that the Aburi farmers had tried, unsuccessfully, to build a road down the scarp to Ayimensah); the Mamfe to Larteh road (recorded cost £3,300; and the spectacular hair-pinned road down the scarp which joins Larteh with Ayikuma—which, after many vicissitudes, involving changes in contractors, was ceremoniously opened in 1926 by Governor Guggisberg, who marked the occasion by presenting the Benkumhene of Akwapim (the chief of Larteh) with a Ford car." (Hill, *The Migrant Cocoa Farmers of Southern Ghana*, 247).

118. Particularly in the context of indirect rule, Mamdani argues, the devolution of authority to increasingly despotic indigenous rulers meant that rural residents were disconnected from the central institutions of control and colonial authority, which inhibited their participation in the colonial state. (Mamdani, *Citizen and Subject*).

119. Moses Danquah, "The Symbols of the People's Belief in Their Own Future," *Daily Graphic*, 9/3/55.

120. Hill, *The Migrant Cocoa Farmers of Southern Ghana*, 247.

121. Hill, *The Migrant Cocoa Farmers of Southern Ghana.*

122. Brian Larkin, *Signal and Noise: Media, Infrastructure, and Urban Culture in Nigeria* (Durham, NC: Duke University Press), 2008.

123. PRAAD: NAG (Accra) CSO 14/2/94 1929–1931 Public roads—statutory authority for the repair and maintenance of, "The Roads Ordinance, 1931 (Gold Coast Colony)"; CSO 14/2/150 1929–1947 Road Policy.

124. PRAAD: NAG (Accra) CSO 14/2/94 1929–1931 Public Roads—statutory authority for the repair and maintenance of.

125. PRAAD: NAG (Accra) CSO 14/2/95 1930–1931 Accra-Ada Road (Accra-Labadi-Dawa-Amlakpo-Ada). It is clear, however, that not all villages were interested in being connected to urban centers in the early 1930s, since these roads did not connect them to their markets inland. Such disinterest could hamper the construction of roads, when chiefs proved unwilling to provide land and labor to facilitate the construction of roads.

126. Despite slavery having been abolished in the Gold Coast in 1874, the transition from "slave trade" to "legitimate" trade was far from immediate, and the definitions and differences between "slave" and "free" were far from clear. Road construction was one sphere in which the difference between slave labor and free labor was less clear, and that ambiguity was manipulated by both "native authorities" and colonial officials. There is a rich literature on slavery and the slave trade in the Gold Coast/Ghana, as well as western Africa more generally, which highlights some of the difficulties and ambiguities involved in the shift between slave trade and legitimate trade. See, for example: Frederick Cooper, "The Problem of Slavery in African Studies," *The Journal of African History*, Vol. 20, No. 1. (1979) 103–125; Philip Curtin, *The African Slave Trade: A Census.* (Madison: University of Wisconsin Press), 1969; Allen Isaacman and Barbara S. Isaacman, *Slavery and Beyond: The Making of Men and Chikunda Ethnic Identities in the Unstable World of South-Central Africa, 1750–1920.* (Portsmouth, NH: Heinemann), 2004; Paul Lovejoy *Transformations in Slavery* (New York: Cambridge University Press), 2000; Joseph Miller, *Way of Death: Merchant Capitalism and the Angolan Slave Trade, 1730–1830* (Madison: University of Wisconsin Press), 1988; Joseph Miller, "The Paradoxes of Impoverishment in the Atlantic Zone" in *History of Central Africa* (I), ed. David Birmingham and Phyllis Martin (London: Longman), 1983: 118–159; Claire Robertson and Martin Klein (eds.). *Women and Slavery in Africa* (Madison: University of Wisconsin Press), 1997; Dickson, *Historical Geography of Ghana*, pg. 220–221. See also Kwabena Akurang-Parry, "Colonial Forced Labor Policies for Road-Building in Southern Ghana and International Anti-Forced Labor Pressures, 1900–1940," *African Economic History* 28 (2000): 1–25; Beverly Grier, "Pawns, Porters, and Petty Traders."

127. PRAAD: NAG (Accra) CSO 14/1/160 1931 Chiefs roads on which communal labor may be employed—list of, "List of roads gazetted under Cap. 149 which might be considered as exempt from the rule about paid labor" from Commissioner of the Western Province to the Colonial Secretary, 30 January 1931.

128. PRAAD: NAG (Accra) CSO 14/2/123 1932–1933 Scheduling of Roads.

129. Manche (sometimes Mashie or Mashe) is the Ga term for a chief. For a detailed discussion of the rights and responsibilities of the Manche, see Parker, *Making the Town.*

130. PRAAD: NAG (Accra) CSO 14/2/97 road to connect Tema with the Accra-Ada Road—petition for construction of, "Petition from the Temma Manche on behalf of the people of Temma to the Governor, Arnold Hodson," 12 December 1935.

131. PRAAD: NAG (Accra) CSO 14/2/151 Accra-Winneba Road. "Address of Ayirebi Acquah III, Omanhene-Effutu (Winneba) State to the Governor (Arnold Hodson)," 19 January 1935.

132. TNA: PRO CO 96/742/12 Townships Legislation, 1937 File Number: 31304 "The Townships Ordinance, 1937"; TNA: PRO CO 96/750/12 Townships Legislation, 1938 File Number: 31304.

133. PRAAD: NAG (Accra) CSO 14/2/115 Roads in Accra—Drainage and Maintenance of.

134. PRAAD: NAG (Accra) CSO 14/2/102 1931 Town Roads—payment by Town Councils toward upkeep of.

135. PRAAD: NAG (Accra) CSO 14/1/78 1934 Public Works Extraordinary Estimates 1935–1936; PRAAD: NAG (Accra) CSO 14/2/115 1932–1935 Roads in Accra—Drainage and Maintenance of.

136. PRAAD: NAG (Accra) CSO 14/2/126 1932–1933 Boundary Road—Accra.

137. PRAAD: NAG (Accra) CSO 14/2/115 1932–1935 Roads in Accra—Drainage and Maintenance of.

138. PRAAD: NAG (Accra) CSO 14/2/126 1932–1933 Boundary Road, Accra.

139. Parker, *Making the Town.*

140. See, for example, the list of commercial firms, merchants, and important figures in the Gold Coast of the 1920s in *The Red Book of West Africa: Historical and Descriptive, Commercial and Industrial, Facts, Figures, and Resources*, ed. Allister MacMillan (New York: Routledge), 1968.

141. PRAAD: NAG (Accra) NAG CSO 14/2/115 Roads in Accra—drainage and maintenance of, "Letter from Rumball Trading Company Limited to Colonial Secretary, 7th February, 1935."

142. PRAAD: NAG (Accra) CSO 14/2/115 Roads in Accra—drainage and maintenance of, "Letter from Rumball Trading Company Limited to Municipal Engineer, 7th January, 1935."

143. For information on sanitation in Accra in the 1910s–1930s, see John Parker, *Making the Town*, pp. 195–201.

144. PRAAD: NAG (Accra) CSO 14/1/75 1931 Public Works Extraordinary Estimates, 1932–1933; PRAAD: NAG (Accra) CSO 14/1/76 1933 Public Works Extraordinary Estimates, 1933–1934; PRAAD: NAG (Accra) CSO 14/1/79 1936 Public Works Extraordinary Estimates 1936–1937; PRAAD: NAG (Accra) CSO 14/2/205 1943–1944 Accra—Maintenance of town roads: Cost of maintenance of Winneba Road and Guggisberg Avenue, Accra.

145. Nate Plageman. "Colonial Ambition, Common Sense Thinking, and the Making of Takoradi Harbor, Gold Coast." *History in Africa* 40.1 (2013): 317–352; PRAAD: NAG (Accra) CSO 14/1/270 1938–1939 Lorry Parks, Accra.

146. Plageman, *Highlife Saturday Night*, 48; Parker, *Making the Town*, 195. See also PRAAD: NAG (Accra) CSO 14/1/76 1933 Public Works Extraordinary Estimates 1933–1934.

147. Parker, *Making the Town*, pp. 199–200; Sackeyfio-Lenoch, *The Politics of Chieftaincy*; TNA: PRO CO 1069-40.

148. "Tarmet" refers to *tar*red and *met*alled roads.

149. PRAAD: NAG (Accra) CSO 14/2/115 Roads in Accra—drainage and maintenance of, "Petition from Occupants of Kofi Oku Road," 24 June, 1932.

150. Sackeyfio-Lenoch, *The Politics of Chieftaincy*, 6.

151. Plageman, *Highlife Saturday Night*, 66.

152. For detailed accounts of the way these processes unfolded in other spheres of Gold Coast political, social, and cultural life, see Plagemen, *Highlife Saturday Night*; Sackeyfio-Lenoch, *The Politics of Chieftaincy.*

153. Tilley, *Africa as a Living Laboratory*; Monica van Beusekom, *Negotiating Development: African Farmers and Colonial Experts at the Office du Niger, 1920–1960* (Portsmouth, NH: Heinemann), 2001.

Chapter 2

1. Quarshie Gene (Chairman), P. Ashai Ollennu (Vice Chairman), and Simon Djetey Abe (Secretary), La Drivers' Union Officers Group, La, Accra, March 23, 2009, Interview by Author.

2. Many early drivers' unions or associations identified a "chief driver," but few other than La and Teshie elected "linguists" or possessed such an elaborate material and symbolic culture.

3. Jeremy Packer, *Mobility without Mayhem: Safety, Cars, and Citizenship* (Durham, NC: Duke University Press), 2008: 1–14.

4. Overspeeding is the British and/or Gold Coast/Ghanaian term for what is referred to as "speeding" in an American context.

5. Overloading refers to the practice in which drivers loaded a vehicle with more weight than a vehicle of its construction was designed to carry. In relation to goods transport, this was evaluated in terms of gross weight. In the realm of passenger transport, the number of passengers that a given vehicle was certified to safely carry was determined by certifying officers, testing officers, and police in relation to the size and type of the vehicle (three-ton, five-ton, ten-ton, private car, etc.). In practice, as will be discussed below, it proved more difficult to enforce these distinctions between goods and passenger transport than colonial officials and regulations predicted.

6. Packer, *Mobility without Mayhem*, 13; Adeline Masquelier, "Road Mythographies: Space, Mobility, and the Historical Imagination in Postcolonial Niger," *American Ethnologist* 29 (4) (2002): 831; Gabriel Klaeger, "Introduction: The Perils and Possibilities of African Roads," *Africa* 83 (3) (2013): 359.

7. Masquelier, "Road Mythographies," 832; Klaeger, "Introduction," 359.

8. Masquelier, "Road Mythographies," 836; Klaeger, "Introduction," 361.

9. Paul Schauert, *Staging Ghana: Artistry and Nationalism in State Dance Ensembles* (Bloomington, IN: Indiana University Press), 2015.

10. Packer, *Mobility without Mayhem*, 7; Mark Lamont, "Speed Governors: Road Safety and Infrastructural Overload in Post-Colonial Kenya, c. 1963–2013," *Africa* 83 (3) (2013): 368; Michael Mann, *The Sources of Social Power: A History of Power from the Beginning to AD 1760*, Vol. 1 (Cambridge: Cambridge University Press), 1986.

11. Packer, *Mobility without Mayhem*, 7.

12. Packer, *Mobility without Mayhem*, 1–14.

13. Albert Whitney, *Man and the Motorcar*, quoted in Packer, *Mobility without Mayhem*, 1.

14. Packer, *Mobility without Mayhem*, 1–2.

15. Joshua Grace, "Heroes of the Road: Race, Gender, and the Politics of Mobility in Twentieth Century Tanzania," *Africa* 83 (3) (2013): 403; Janet Roitman, *Fiscal Disobedience: An Anthropology of Economic Regulation in Central Africa* (Princeton, NJ: Princeton University Press), 2005: 136.

16. Lamont, "Speed Governors," 380.

17. Joshua Maama Larbi, Interview by Author.

18. Nate Plageman, *Highlife Saturday Night: Popular Music and Social Change in Urban Ghana* (Bloomington, IN: Indiana University Press), 2012.

19. Margaret Peil, "The Apprenticeship System in Accra," *Africa* 40(2) (April 1970): 139.

20. Akpeteshie is a type of local gin distilled from palm wine. For more information on the history of akpeteshie, see: Emmanuel Akyeampong, "What's in a drink?: Class Struggle, Popular Culture and the Politics of Akpeteshie (Local Gin) in Ghana 1930–67," *Journal of African History* 37(2) (1996): 215–236; Emmanuel Akyeampong, *Drink, Power, and Cultural Change: A Social History of Alcohol in Ghana, c. 1800 to Recent Times* (Portsmouth, NH: Heinemann), 1996.

21. Fufu is a local food staple, most commonly made by pounding cassava and plantain (though also sometimes with yam). Fufu is pounded with a large mortar and pestle and often requires two people to accomplish—one to pound and one to turn the product.

22. While these activities were essentially "women's work," it was not uncommon for men to engage in domestic work within households (Clark, *Onions Are My Husband*, 291). In the case of drivers, such work was expected as a subordinate apprentice and did not, in itself, diminish the status of apprentices or "mates," whose lower status was the result of their lack of training and knowledge.

23. Pierre Bourdieu, *The Logic of Practice* (Polity Press), 1990; Pierre de Certeau, *The Practice of Everyday Life* (Los Angeles: University of California Press), 2011.

24. Pierre Bourdieu, "The Forms of Capital." *Handbook of Theory and Research for the Sociology of Capital.* J. G. Richardson, ed. (New York, Greenwood Press), 1986: 241–58.

25. Shark Marlow, Interview by Author; Kanor Boye, Interview by Author; Steven Feld, "Liner Notes." *Por Por: Honk Horn Music of Ghana,* The La Drivers Union Por Por Group, (Washington, DC: Smithsonian Folkways Recordings), 2007; Steven Feld, *Jazz Cosmopolitanism in Accra: Five Musical Years in Ghana* (Durham, NC: Duke University Press), 2012; Ato Quayson, "Signs of the Times: Discourse Ecologies and Street Life on Oxford St., Accra," *City and Society,* 22 (1) (June 2010): 72–96. In Nigeria, see Damola Osinulu, "Painters, Blacksmiths and Wordsmiths: Building Molues in Lagos," *African Arts,* 41(3) (Autumn 2008): 44–53.

26. Kanor Boye, Interview by Author.

27. Gracia Clark, *Onions Are My Husband: Survival and Accumulation by West African Market Women.* (Chicago: University of Chicago Press), 1995; Claire Robertson, *Sharing the Same Bowl: A Socioeconomic History of Women and Class in Accra, Ghana.* (Ann Arbor: University of Michigan Press), 1990; Samuel Ntewusu, *Settling In and Holding On: A Socio-Historical Study of Northern Trader and Transporters in Accra's Tudu, 1908–2008.* (Dissertation: University of Lieden, Afrika Studies Centrum), 2011.

28. "Petition from Motor Transport Union of Ashanti (W. W. Taylor, Secretary) to the Chief Commissioner of Ashanti, 29th November, 1937" PRAAD: NAG (Accra) CSO 17/1/39 1935–38 Ashanti Motor Transport Union.

29. Ntewusu, *Settling In and Holding On.*

30. Joshua Maama Larbi, Interview by Author.

31. PRAAD-NAG (Accra) CSO 15/1/65 1932–40 Registration Statistics of Motor Vehicles Abroad—forms for.

32. PRAAD-NAG (Accra) CSO 17/4/9 1945 Vehicle Census.

33. Joshua Maama Larbi, Interview by Author.

34. PRAAD: NAG (Accra) CSO 17/1/92 1940–42 Motor Accidents. These numbers were significantly higher than in Britain itself, where there was approximately 1 accident per 290 vehicles in 1940. In the Gold Coast in the same year, by contrast, there was approximately 1 accident per 12 vehicles. See Department of Transport (2008), "Reported Road Casualties Great Britain: 2008 Annual Report," *Road Casualties Great Britain*; David Bayliss, Royal Automobile Club Foundation, "What Went Wrong? British Highways Development before Motorways," Background Paper No. 1, *Motoring Towards 2050—Roads and Reality* (March 2008): 7, Figure 3.

35. Ibrahim Ato, Anum Sowah, Yii O. Yem, J. F. Ocantey, La Drivers' Union Group Interview, Accra, March 26, 2009, Interview by Author.

36. Andrews A. C. Quaye (Chairman), Kobla, Tawiah Adjetey, and Tetteh, Tema Union Group, Accra, August 13, 2009, Interview by Author; Ibrahim Ato, Anum Sowah, Yii O. Yem, J. F. Ocantey, La Drivers' Union Group Interview, Accra, March 26, 2009, Interview by Author.

37. Ibrahim Ato, Anum Sowah, Yii O. Yem, J. F. Ocantey, La Drivers' Union Group Interview, Accra, March 26, 2009, Interview by Author.

38. As Steve Feld's work on *por por* music in Ghana has shown, drivers and passengers regularly sang songs and used available tools and horns to create music that would scare away curious animals while repairing vehicles in rural areas. See Steve Feld, *Jazz Cosmopolitanism in Accra: Five Musical Years in Ghana* (Durham, NC: Duke University Press), 2012; and Steve Feld, "Liner Notes," *Por Por: Honk Horn Music of Ghana,* The La Drivers Union Por Por Group.

39. Jonathan Sadowsky, *Imperial Bedlam: Institutions of Madness in Colonial Southwest Nigeria* (Los Angeles: University of California Press), 1999: 4–5.

40. PRAAD: NAG (Accra) CSO 15/7/94 1936–38 Motor Traffic Regulation No. 2 of 1934—Ashanti, Amendment to.

41. Lynn Thomas, *Politics of the Womb: Women, Reproduction, and the State in Kenya* (Los Angeles: University of California Press), 2003: 5.

42. PRAAD: NAG (Accra) CSO 14/2/176 1937, *Motor Traffic Ordinance* "Letter from Governor to WA Ormsby-Gore, 20 April 1937." See also PRAAD: NAG (Accra) CSO 15/7/104 1935 *Government transport work and motor traffic duties and appointment of certifying and examining officers.*

43. TNA: PRO CO 96/806/2 1946–47 *Ten Year Development Plan.*

44. TNA: PRO CO 96/806/2 1946–47 *Ten Year Development Plan.*

45. TNA: PRO CO 96/806/2 1946–47 *Ten Year Development Plan*; TNA: PRO CO 323/1654/1 1939 *Motor Vehicle Legislation in the Colonies*; TNA: PRO CO 852/1023/2 1949 *Gold Coast Development Road Project.*

46. PRAAD: NAG (Accra) CSO 14/1/81 1931 *Public Works Extraordinary Estimates 1938–39*; PRAAD: NAG (Accra) CSO 14/2/150 1929–47 *Road Policy.*

47. PRAAD: NAG (Accra) CSO 14/2/135 1933–34 *One-Way Traffic Road at Cantonments, Accra*; PRAAD: NAG (Accra) CSO 15/7/94 1936–38 *Motor Traffic Regulation No. 2 of 1934—Ashanti, Amendment to*; PRAAD: NAG (Accra) CSO 15/7/97 1937 *Regulation 21 of the Motor Traffic Ordinance, 1934—Amendment to*; PRAAD: NAG (Accra) CSO 15/7/93 1936 *Regulation 26 (6) of the Motor Traffic Regulation No. 31 of 1934—Amendment of.*

48. Gewald, Jan-Bart, Sabine Luning, and Klaas van Walraven, eds. *The Speed of Change: Motor Vehicles and People in Africa, 1890–2000* (Leiden: Brill), 2009.

49. This is certainly not unusual or particular to the Gold Coast or even to the various colonial projects in Africa. As Anne McClintock argues, "European imperialism was, from the outset, a violent encounter with preexisting hierarchies of power that took shape not as the unfolding of its own inner destiny but as untidy, opportunistic interference with other regimes of power. Such encounters in turn transformed the trajectories of imperialism itself. Within this long and conflictual engagement, the gendered dynamics of colonized cultures were contorted in such ways as to alter, in turn, the irregular shapes that imperialism took in various parts of the world." (Anne McClintock, *Imperial Leather: Race, Gender, and Sexuality in the Colonial Context* [New York: Routledge], 1995: 6).

50. PRAAD: NAG (Accra) CSO 17/1/39 1935–38 Ashanti Motor Transport Union.

51. PRAAD: NAG (Accra) CSO 17/1/39 1935–38 Ashanti Motor Transport Union.

52. PRAAD: NAG (Accra) CSO 17/1/39 1935–38 Ashanti Motor Transport Union; PRAAD: NAG (Accra) CSO 17/1/15 1934 *Motor Traffic Regulations, 1934.*

53. PRAAD: NAG (Accra) CSO 15/7/102 1938 *Legislation relating to the "governing" of motor vehicles—enquiry regarding.*

54. PRAAD: NAG (Accra) CSO 15/7/102 1938 *Legislation relating to the "governing" of motor vehicles—enquiry regarding.*

55. PRAAD: NAG (Accra) CSO 14/2/25 1933 *Road, Rail and other Systems of Internal Communication, Competition Between.* In fact, African drivers so dominated the system that in preparing for tests of a Leyland road train in the Gold Coast in 1933, the secretary of Oversea Mechanical Transport Directing Committee reported that "we have provided for an African driver and two mates in view of the fact that motor vehicles are not driven by Europeans in the Gold Coast" (PRAAD: NAG [Accra] CSO 17/1/32 1932–1938 *15 Ton unit of Oversea Mechanical Transport Directing Committee—Testing of, in the Gold Coast*). As late as 1932, however, colonial officials were still clearly underestimating the importance of these African owner-operators on the transport system as a whole: "At the end of the discussion it transpired that several present held the view that the small native owned lorry is not fully comparable

with the larger motor vehicles owned by the transport companies such as Swanzy's. The latter are concerned solely with transport and are run on commercial lines, the former are used as farm transport and for general utility purposes as well as longer distance running, e.g. to and from the sea ports. Moreover the vehicle is often family owned and the driver is not a salaried man." (PRAAD: NAG (Accra) CSO 14/2/123 1932–33 *Scheduling of Roads*).

56. PRAAD: NAG (Accra) CSO 14/2/23 1931 *Roads, Rail and other systems of internal communication, competition between*, "Letter from the Director of Public Works to the Colonial Secretary," 19 March 1930: "An enormous volume of road transport has been imported into this Colony and may be said to have captured the business. Transport owners cannot therefore afford to scrap their lorries and will presumably cut their prices to bone in an endeavour to hold on to some of this business."

57. PRAAD: NAG (Accra) CSO 15/7/37 1937 *A. T. Agbenyegah, Motor Driver petition praying for restoration of his driving license*; PRAAD: NAG (Accra) CSO 15/7/43 1937 *Mr. David Dafoe Corbla Avenor—petition praying for restoration of his driving license.*

58. PRAAD: NAG (Accra) CSO 15/7/11 1931 *Kofi Attah, Motor Driver—petition from for restoration of his driving license.*

59. "Driving without light" was particularly relevant through the early twentieth century when vehicles did not come with electric lights already affixed. Drivers were required to fix lanterns on both sides of the front of the vehicle. Later, the phrase referred to driving without the electric light switched on. PRAAD: NAG (Accra) CSO 15/7/11 1931 *Kofi Attah, Motor Driver—petition from for restoration of his driving license.*

60. TNA: PRO CO 554/324 1951–1953 *S&C: Enquiry into the Economics of the Gold Coast Transport Industry by MR Bonavia and CR Hayes of the British Transport Commission.*

61. Joshua Maama Larbi, Teshie, August 10, 2009, Interview by Author.

62. Anon, Circle Odawna Group, Accra, August 22, 2009, Interview by Author.

63. I follow Bourdieu's use of habitus as a form of embodied socialization. See Pierre Bourdieu "Structures, habitus, practices." In P. Bourdieu, *The Logic of Practice* (Stanford, CA: Stanford University Press), 1990: 52–79.

64. Inussa ("al Haji"), Circle Odawna Driver, Accra. August 27, 2009, Interview by Author.

65. PRAAD: NAG (Accra) CSO 15/7/43 1937 *Mr. David Dafoe Corbla Avenor—petition praying for restoration of his driving license*, Letter from Commissioner of Police to Colonial Secretary, 23 July 1937: "The offence of carrying passengers in insecure positions is a particularly dangerous one and is one which is in part responsible for the big loss of life in road accidents in the Gold Coast."

66. See, for example, PRAAD: NAG (Accra) CSO 15/7/25 1935 *Mr. J. B. Cobblah, Motor Driver—petition praying for refund of part of fine imposed on*; PRAAD: NAG (Accra) CSO 15/7/43 1937 *Mr. David Dafoe Corbla Avenor—petition praying for restoration of his driving license*, Letter from Commissioner of Police to Colonial Secretary, 23 July 1937.

67. PRAAD: NAG (Accra) CSO 15/7/16 1934 *Yaw Kumah, motor driver, petition praying for restoration of his driving license*, Report from H. M. Mitchell, Commissioner of Police Eastern Province to the Commissioner of Police, Criminal Investigation Department, 30 April 1929.

68. Klaeger, "The Perils and Possibilities of African Roads"; Masquelier, "Road Mythographies."

69. PRAAD: NAG (Accra) CSO 15/7/16 1934 *Yaw Kumah, motor driver, petition praying for restoration of his driving license*, Minute 13 from Acting Inspector General of Police to the Colonial Secretary, 19/3/36.

70. PRAAD: NAG (Accra) CSO 15/7/15 1935 *Erasmus Otutey Cournooh, motor driver—petition from, for restoration of his driving license*, Minute to the Acting Colonial Secretary, 6/9/34.

71. PRAAD: NAG (Accra) CSO 15/7/14 1933 *Davis Kofi, Motor Driver—petition for restoration of his driving license*, Letter from the Colonial Secretary to the Attorney General, 16 August 1933.

72. Emmanuel Akeampong, *Drink, Power, and Cultural Change: A Social History of Alcohol, c. 1800 to Recent Times* (Portsmouth, NH: Heinemann), 1996: p. 53.

73. Schnapps was only one part of a rather large compensation package, which often also included cigarettes, money, and sometimes also beer.

74. Nate Plageman, *Highlife Saturday Night: Popular Music and Social Change in Urban Ghana* (Indiana University Press), 2012. These dynamics are also depicted in the 1952 film *The Boy Kumasenu*, produced by the Gold Coast Film Unit (http://www.colonialfilm.org.uk /node/332).

75. PRAAD: NAG (Accra) CSO 15/7/27 1935 *John Kwadjo, Motor Driver—Petition praying for restoration of his driving license*, Letter from Inspector General of Police to Colonial Secretary, 8 July 1935. Heavy drinking had also long been associated in African societies throughout the southern Gold Coast with mental illness, madness, spiritual weakness, etc. See Akyeampong, *Drink, Power, and Cultural Change*, p. 154–155.

76. Instances of theft were similarly concerning, and reflected a disregard for the interests of passengers, on whom a drivers' business relies (PRAAD: NAG [Accra] CSO 15/7/13 1939 *Moses Acquaye, Motor Driver—request for restoration of his driving license*, Letter from the Acting Inspector General of Police to the Colonial Secretary, 21/3/33; PRAAD: NAG [Accra] CSO 15/7/78 1939 *Mr. Amewuda Kwao, motor driver—petition praying for restoration of his driving license*).

77. PRAAD: NAG (Accra) CSO 15/7/108 1935–38 *Motor Traffic on roads in Accra—control of*; PRAAD: NAG (Accra) CSO 15/7/108 1935–38 *Motor Traffic on roads in Accra—control of.*

78. Moses Ochonu, *Colonial Meltdown: Northern Nigeria in the Great Depression* (Athens, OH: Ohio University Press), 2009. These concerns also impinged on motor transport development in Britain itself. See Bayliss, "What Went Wrong?"

79. PRAAD: NAG (Accra) CSO 15/7/111 1938 *Speed limits, Motor Vehicles*; CSO 17/4/1 1940–1943 *Speed Limits, Motor Vehicles.*

80. PRAAD: NAG (Accra) CSO 14/2/150 1929–47 *Road Policy*, Letter from the Governor to the Colonial Secretary, 1 May 1937; PRAAD: NAG (Accra) CSO 14/2/262 1932 *Traffic Control*; TNA: PRO CO 554/324 1951–1953 *S&C: Enquiry into the Economics of the Gold Coast Transport Industry by MR Bonavia and CR Hayes of the British Transport Commission.*

81. PRAAD: NAG (Accra) CSO 15/7/107 1935 *Motor Traffic in Sekondi—speed limit for.*

82. PRAAD: NAG (Accra) CSO 15/7/94 1936–38 *Motor Traffic Regulation No. 2 of 1934, Ashanti—Amendment to*. It was suggested in 1936 and 1937 that a separate group of traffic police be established, though it seems that nothing came of that suggestion (TNA: PRO CO 96/725/4 1936 *Police Dept Staff—Establishment of Traffic Police*; PRAAD: NAG [Accra] CSO 14/2/176 *Motor Traffic Amendment Ordinance, 1937*).

83. In fact, questions about speed limits seemed to be at the core of the grievances expressed by lorry drivers in their 1937 strike. (PRAAD: NAG [Accra] CSO 15/7/94 1936–38 *Motor Traffic Regulation No. 2 of 1934, Ashanti—Amendment to*); PRAAD: NAG (Accra) CSO 17/1/39 1935–1938 *Ashanti Motor Transport Union.*

84. PRAAD: NAG (Accra) CSO 15/7/48 1937 *Raphael L. Lawson, Motor Driver—Petition praying for restoration of his driving license*, Opinions of Members of the Executive Council (Executive Council Paper), 11/12/37.

85. PRAAD: NAG (Accra) CSO 15/7/15 1935 *Erasmus Otuteh Cournooh, Motor Driver—Petition from, for restoration of his driving license.*

86. PRAAD: NAG (Accra) CSO 15/7/48 1937 *Raphael L. Lawson, Motor Driver—Petition praying for restoration of his driving license*, Opinions of Members of the Executive Council (Executive Council Paper), 11/12/37; PRAAD: NAG (Accra) CSO 15/7/21 1935 *Kofi Ewusie, Motor Driver—Petition Praying for restoration of his driving license*; PRAAD: NAG (Accra)

CSO 15/7/65 1938 *Mr. Aggrey Mensah, Motor Driver—Petition praying for restoration of his driving license*; PRAAD: NAG (Accra) CSO 15/7/76 1934–39 *Kwaku Jumfuor, motor driver—petition praying for restoration of his driving license.*

87. PRAAD: NAG (Accra) CSO 15/7/18 1934 Adjei Badoo, Motor Driver—complaint against ETO Mr. (Cruickshank).

88. PRAAD: NAG (Accra) CSO 15/7/20 1934 Kotey Nikoi, Motor Driver—prohibition for grant of driving license. In his reply to the chief transport officer after inquiry into the case, Cruickshank wrote: "With reference to the attached letter from Kotey Nikoi, our records show that he has been examined by me twice and failed both times. Re para (7) I have never heard of sparrows having anything to do with Cars; probably the applicant means spanners or spigots. From what I remember of this boy, I do not think he will ever be fit to drive a lorry on a public highway. It would be interesting to know if this boy has failed at other testing stations" (December 29, 1934).

89. PRAAD: NAG (Accra) CSO 15/7/45 1937 *Mr. Latouff Amin, Motor Transport owner—petition praying for issue to him of a driving license.*

90. Kanor Boye, Interview by Author; Shack Marlow, Interview by Author.

91. While the surname "Cruickshank" is associated with a prominent Afro-European family in the Gold Coast, it is not clear whether this colonial officer was a member of that family. Regardless, African drivers remember him as a "European" and, as a symbol of the colonial state, he certainly represented a European perspective.

92. Abraham Tagoe, Teshie Linguist, Accra, August 5, 2009, Interview by Author.

93. Anon, Circle Odawna Driver, Accra, August 27, 2009, Interview by Author.

94. Kanor Boye, Labadi, August 7, 2009, Interview by Author.

95. PRAAD: NAG (Accra) CSO 15/7/25 1935 Mr. J. B. Cobblah, motor driver—petition praying for refund of part of fine imposed on.

96. PRAAD: NAG (Accra) CSO 15/7/25 1935 Mr. J. B. Cobblah, motor driver—petition praying for refund of part of fine imposed on.

97. PRAAD: NAG (Accra) CSO 15/7/37 1937 A. T. Agbenyegah, motor driver—petition praying for restoration of his driving license; PRAAD: NAG (Accra) CSO 15/7/16 1934 Yaw Kumah, motor driver, petition praying for restoration of his driving license; PRAAD: NAG (Accra) CSO 15/7/15 1935 Erasmus Otutey Cournooh, motor driver—petition from, for restoration of his driving license; PRAAD: NAG (Accra) CSO 15/7/35 1936 Kwaku Buadee, motor driver—petition praying for restoration of his driving license.

98. PRAAD: NAG (Accra) CSO 15/7/38 1937 Kotey Neequaye, motor driver—petition praying for restoration of his driving license.

99. Shadrak Yemo Odoi, Labadi, August 6, 2009, Interview by Author; Abraham Tagoe, Teshie Linguist, Accra, August 5, 2009, Interview by Author.

100. Stephan Miescher, *Making Men in Ghana* (Bloomington: Indiana University Press), 2005: pp. 89–90.

101. Stephanie Newell, *Literary Culture in Colonial Ghana: How to Play the Game of Life* (Bloomington, IN: Indiana University Press), 2002; Nate Plageman, *Highlife Saturday Night: Popular Music and Social Change in Urban Ghana* (Bloomington, IN: Indiana University Press), 2012.

102. PRAAD: NAG (Accra) CSO 15/7/33 1936 Ismael Shah—petition requesting assistance in connection with grant of driving license.

103. PRAAD: NAG (Accra) CSO 15/1/224 1943–47 *Applications for driving license by unmechanical transport-drivers of the armed forces—appointment of board to consider.*

104. PRAAD: NAG (Accra) CSO 15/7/18 1934 *Adjei Badoo, Motor driver—complaint against ETO Mr. (Cruickshank).*

105. PRAAD: NAG (Accra) CSO 15/7/24 1935 *Alfred Ashong, motor driver and fitter—assistance required in connection with renewal of his driving license*; PRAAD: NAG (Accra) CSO 15/7/36 1937 *Quarmine Azumah, motor driver—petition praying for renewal of his driving license.*

106. PRAAD: NAG (Accra) CSO 15/7/46 1937 *Mr. S. K. Tsikudo, motor driver—petition praying for renewal of his driving license*; PRAAD: NAG (Accra) CSO 15/7/81 1939 *Mr. Kofi Baah—petition praying for grant of Gold Coast driving license.*

107. PRAAD: NAG (Accra) CSO 15/7/29 1935 *Okan Ngmashie—petition requesting assistance for the grant of his driving license by the police.*

108. PRAAD: NAG (Accra) CSO 15/7/110 1938–40 *Motor vehicles—examination and testing.*

109. PRAAD: NAG (Accra) CSO 15/7/89 1940 *Awuku Y. Nyangar, motor driver—petition praying for restoration of his driving license.*

110. PRAAD: NAG (Accra) CSO 15/7/7 1930 *Tetteh Amartey, motor driver—complaint by against confiscation of his driving license and 10- fee paid to licensing officer.*

111. "Letter from Headmaster of St. Nicholas' Grammar School (English Church Mission) to the Secretary for Native Affairs, April 13th, 1934, PRAAD: NAG (Accra) CSO 17/1/17 1934–1939 *Legislation regarding qualification desired of motor drivers—suggested enactment of.*

112. Still others viewed the literacy requirement as a helpful tool in weeding out the number of drivers. "Report from the Commissioner of Police to the Colonial Secretary, September 11, 1939": "There is no lack of suitable and competent literate applicants for Driving Licenses in the Gold Coast, and it is not proposed to lower the standard already obtained or to apply for the Regulations to be modified" (PRAAD: NAG [Accra] CSO 15/7/81 1939 *Mr. Kofi Baah—petition praying for grant of Gold Coast driving license*).

113. PRAAD: NAG (Accra) CSO 17/1/17 1934–1939 *Legislation regarding qualification desired of motor drivers—suggested enactment of,* "Minute 10 from Chief Transport Officer Cruickshank to the Colonial Secretary, August 25, 1939."

114. PRAAD: NAG (Accra) CSO 17/1/17 1934–1939 *Legislation regarding qualification desired of motor drivers—suggested enactment of,* "Minute 2, May 3, 1934."

115. PRAAD: NAG (Accra) CSO 17/1/17 1934–1939 *Legislation regarding qualification desired of motor drivers—suggested enactment of* (underlining in the original), "Minute 2, May 3, 1934."

116. PRAAD: NAG (Accra) CSO 17/1/39 1935–1938 *Ashanti Motor Transport Union,* "Petition from Motor Transport Union Ashanti (WW Taylor, Secretary) to the Chief Commissioner of Ashanti, November 29th, 1937." See also PRAAD: NAG (Accra) CSO 15/7/81 1939 *Mr. Kofi Baah—petition praying for grant of Gold Coast driving license:* "I have seen on many occasions that there are some lorry drivers who do not know how to read and write but are Drivers."

117. PRAAD: NAG (Accra) CSO 17/1/39 1935–1938 *Ashanti Motor Transport Union,* "Petition from Motor Transport Union Ashanti (WW Taylor, Secretary) to the Chief Commissioner of Ashanti, November 29th, 1937"; PRAAD: NAG (Accra) CSO 15/7/34 1936 *S. K. Mensah, driver—petition praying for issue to him of a driving license.*

118. PRAAD: NAG (Accra) CSO 15/7/75 1938–39 *Mr. Kwadwo Kroao—petition praying for assistance in securing a driving license.*

119. PRAAD: NAG (Accra) CSO 15/7/36 1937 *Quarmine Azumah, motor driver—petition praying for renewal of his driving license.*

120. PRAAD: NAG (Accra) CSO 15/7/42 1937 *Codjo Agbeti, motor driver—petition praying for issue to him of a driving license.* See also PRAAD: NAG (Accra) CSO 15/7/56 1937 *Tijani Belo, motor driver—petition praying for renewal of his driving license*; PRAAD: NAG (Accra) CSO 15/7/73 1938–39 *Mr. Hevor Ayao Paul—petition praying for a grant of 'Certificate of Competency' in motor driving.*

121. PRAAD: NAG (Accra) CSO 15/7/73 1938–39 *Mr. Hevor Ayao Paul—petition praying for a grant of 'Certificate of Competency' in motor driving.*

122. PRAAD: NAG (Accra) CSO 15/7/45 1937 *Mr. Latouff Amin, motor transport owner—petition praying for issue to him of a driving license*; PRAAD: NAG (Accra) CSO 17/1/17 1934–1939 *Legislation regarding qualification desires of motor drivers—suggested enactment of*.

123. PRAAD: NAG (Accra) CSO 17/1/17 1934–1939 *Legislation regarding qualification desired of motor drivers—suggested enactment of*.

124. PRAAD: NAG (Accra) CSO 17/1/17 1934–1939 *Legislation regarding qualification desired of motor drivers—suggested enactment of*.

125. PRAAD: NAG (Accra) CSO 15/7/89 1940 *Awuku Y. Nyangar, motor driver—petition praying for restoration of his driving license.*

126. David Killingray, "Repercussions of World War I in the Gold Coast," *Journal of African History*, 19(1) (1978): 39–59.

127. Killingray, "Repercussions of World War I in the Gold Coast."

128. PRAAD-NAG (Accra) CSO 17/1/24 1935–1937 Motor Traffic Ordinance and regulations 1934—petitions against.

129. Jennifer Hart, "Motor Transportation, Trade Unionism, and the Culture of Work in Colonial Ghana," *International Review of Social History*, 29 (2014), Special Issue, 185–209.

130. For a history of trade union activities in Ghana, see Richard Jeffries, *Class, Power, and Ideology in Ghana: The Railwaymen of Sekondi* (Cambridge: Cambridge University Press), 1978; Margaret Peil, *The Ghanaian Factory Worker: Industrial Man in Africa* (Cambridge: Cambridge University Press), 2009.

131. CSO 17/1/39 1935–1938 Ashanti Motor Transport Union. Emphasis by author.

132. CSO 17/1/39 1935–1938 Ashanti Motor Transport Union. "Ishmael" refers to the son of Abraham and Hagar. In the Biblical book of Genesis, Abraham fathers a son with the slave Hagar, with the permission of his wife Sarah. However, Hagar and Ishmael are later thrown out of Abraham's house. Ismael, as a result, has been used historically to represent an outcast, abandoned by his own father.

133. Ibrahim Ato, Anum Sowah, Yii O. Yem, J. F. Ocantey, La Drivers' Union Group Interview, Accra, March 26, 2009, Interview by Author.

134. Benjamin N. Lawrance, Emily Osborn, and Richard Roberts, eds. *Intermediaries, Interpreters and Clerks: African Employees in the Making of Colonial Africa* (Madison, WI: University of Wisconsin Press), 2015.

135. R. B. Davison, "Labor Relations in Ghana," *Annals of the American Academy of Political and Social Science* 310 (March 1957): 135.

136. Davison, "Labor Relations in Ghana," 135.

137. Davison, "Labor Relations in Ghana," 135; PRAAD-NAG (Accra) CSO 14/1/711 1940–46 Courses of Instruction in Labour Problems.

138. LaRay Denzer, "Wallace-Johnson and the Sierra Leone Labor Crisis of 1939," *African Studies Review*, 25 (June–September 1982): 162; Hart, "Honest Labour."

139. PRAAD-NAG (Accra) CSO 14/1/789 1943 The Bekwai Motor Transport Union.

140. PRAAD-NAG (Accra) CSO 25/3/132 1942–1946 Trade Unions—registration of.

141. Davison, "Labor Relations in Ghana," 133.

142. PRAAD-NAG (Accra) CSO 15/7/13 1939 Moses Acquaye--motor driver request for restoration of his driving license.

143. PRAAD-NAG (Accra) CSO 14/1/270 1938–39 Lorry parks, Accra.

144. This period also resulted in a noted shift in the gendered distribution of trading—from men to women, as men increasingly pursued wage labor work and cash crop farming that had increased throughout the 1910s and 1920s.

145. PRAAD-NAG (Accra) CSO 14/1/270 1938–39 Lorry parks, Accra; PRAAD-NAG (Accra) CSO 17/4/6 1940–1941 Native administration—lorry parks.

146. PRAAD-NAG (Accra) CSO 14/1/270 1938–39 Lorry parks, Accra; PRAAD-NAG (Accra) CSO 14/1/271 1938–39 Land at Salaga Market required for a lorry park—ownership of.

147. Joshua Maama Larbi, "Honest Labour."

148. Lisa Lindsay, *Working with Gender: Wage Labor and Social Change in Southwestern Nigeria* (Portsmouth, NH: Heinemann), 2003.

149. For more information about Ga governance structures and traditional offices, see John Parker, *Making the Town: Ga State and Society in Early Colonial Accra* (Portsmouth, NH: Heinemann), 2000.

150. Quarshie Gene (Chairman), P. Ashai Ollennu (Vice Chairman), and Simon Djetey Abe (Secretary), La Drivers' Union Officers Group, La, Accra, March 23, 2009, Interview by Author.

151. Quarshie Gene (Chairman), P. Ashai Ollennu (Vice Chairman), and Simon Djetey Abe (Secretary), La Drivers' Union Officers Group, La, Accra, March 23, 2009, Interview by Author; Abraham Tagoe, Teshie Linguist, Accra, August 5, 2009, Interview by Author.

152. Terence Ranger, "The Invention of Tradition in Colonial Africa," in *The Invention of Tradition*, Eric Hobsbawm and Terence Ranger, eds. (Cambridge: Cambridge University Press), 1992. For further information about chieftaincy and the okyeame, see Kwesi Yankah, *Speaking for the Chief: Okyeame and the Politics of Akan Royal Oratory* (Bloomington, IN: Indiana University Press), 1995; Steven J. Salm and Toyin Falola, *Culture and Customs of Ghana* (Westport, CT: Greenwood Press), 2002; Irene K. Odotei and Albert K. Awedoba, *Chieftaincy in Ghana: Culture, Governance and Development* (Sub Saharan Publishers and Traders), 2006. For discussions of chieftaincy outside of Akan communities, see Paul Stacey, *Traditional Uncertainty: Chieftaincy in Northern Ghana: Land Control and Ethnic Conflicts, 1901–1996* (VDM Verlag), 2009; John Parker, *Making the Town.*

Chapter 3

1. Inussa ("al Haji"), Circle Odawna Driver, Accra. August 27, 2009, Interview by Author.

2. Gracia Clark, "Consulting Elderly Kumasi Market Women About Modernization," *Ghana Studies* (12/13) (2009/2010): 97–119.

3. Steven Friedson, *Remains of Ritual: Northern Gods in a Southern Land* (Chicago: University of Chicago Press), 2009; Kathryn Linn Geurts, *Culture and the Sense: Bodily Ways of Knowing in an African Community* (Berkley: University California Press), 2003; Judy Rosenthal, *Possession, Ecstasy, and Law in Ewe Voodoo* (Charlottesville: University Press of Virginia), 1998. The ability to channel a spirit and achieve "eye-opening" is physically marked among Ewe people with scarification around the temples of the eyes. While there are obvious similarities between these concepts, drivers (as well as the traders interviewed by Clark) interpret "eye-opening" with an additional level of meaning. Here, wisdom or knowledge facilitates sophistication or cosmopolitanism. Similar concepts have been identified in other parts of Africa. In Nigeria, for example, JDY Peel (*Religious Encounter and the Making of the Yoruba* [Bloomington, IN: Indiana University Press], 2003) and Lisa Lindsay (*Working with Gender: Wage Labor and Social Change in Southwestern Nigeria* [Portsmouth, NH: Heinemann], 2003) have explored the idea of *olaju* as "enlightenment" or "civilization" in Yoruba communities. Much like *anibue*, *olaju* was associated at an early period with the "cultural package brought by European missionaries, including technical, medical, and clerical skills as well as Christianity" (Lindsay, *Working with Gender*, pp. 14–15). As Lindsay argues, "*Olaju* also referred to those who were not necessarily well educated, but who gained worldly knowledge by pursuing trading opportunities away from the hometown. Either way, the central idea was to use knowledge or experience derived from beyond the local community to advance individual

careers and, through the combined efforts of many, bring the material benefits of 'progress' back home" (pp. 14–15). Lindsay argues that the long history of *olaju* provided the foundation for African understandings of modernization "that the attributes of modernity did not form a 'package' to be adopted completely or not at all" (pp. 14–15). Rather, railway workers (who form the subject of Lindsay's study) drew on modernization, *olaju*, and new material circumstances to construct their experiences of both modernity and masculinity. Lindsay, however, argues that this results in the creation of "multiple modernities" that coincide or overlap with "multiple masculinities."

4. If modernity is aspirational, it is rooted in the willingness of individuals to embrace new technologies, commodities, and cultural influences and, more fundamentally, to challenge preexisting expectations and assumptions. This does not necessarily require foreign travel or even Westernization; modernity is not an inherently cultural or historical project, as implied in terms like "multiple modernities" or "alternative modernities." Rather, modernity—and its accompanying notions of cosmopolitanism and worldliness—imply an aspirational ontology, with individuals seeking out new opportunities and possibilities for engagement with/in the world. While "modernization" is often associated with a set of particular policies (and the historical period during which those policies played a central role in shaping economic development), Miescher and Tsikata argue that those modernization policies are, at heart, an extension of the aspirational ontology of "modernity." See Stephan Miescher and Dzodzi Tsikata, "Hydro-Power and the Promise of Modernity and Development in Ghana: Comparing the Akosombo and Bui Dam Projects," *Ghana Studies* (12/13) (2009/2010): 57–58. See also, Peter Bloom, Stephan Miescher, and Takyiwaa Manuh, "Introduction," *Modernization as Spectacle in Africa* (Bloomington, IN: Indiana University Press), 2014; Mikael Karlstrom, "Modernity and its Aspirants: Moral Community and Development Eutopianism in Buganda," *Current Anthropology* 45(5) (December 2004): 597.

5. J. D. Y. Peel, "Olaju: A Yoruba Concept of Development," *Journal of Development Studies* 14 (1978): 144 (quoted in Kate Skinner, "'It Brought Some Kind of Neatness to Mankind': Mass Literacy, Community Development and Democracy in 1950s Asant," *Africa* 79[4] [2009]: 482).

6. Many authors highlight cultural associations between "travel" and status, wealth, and/ or prestige—"been-tos" being the most famous example. The ability to travel and return has historically and culturally been understood as a symbol of an individual's access to resources and knowledge. See, for example, Axel Klein, "Trapped in the Traffick: Growing Problems of Drug Consumption in Lagos," *Journal of Modern African Studies* 32(4) (1994): 657–677; Ranu Samantrai, "Caught at the Confluence of History: Ama Ata Aidoo's Necessary Nationalism," *Research in African Literatures* 26(2) (Summer 1995): 140–157.

7. T. C. McCaskie, *Asante Identities: History and Memory in an African Village, 1850–1950* (Bloomington: Indiana University Press), 2001: 132–133.

8. Emmanuel Akyeampong, *Drink, Power, and Cultural Change: A Social History of Alcohol in Ghana, c. 1800 to Recent Times* (Portsmouth, NH: Heinemann), 1996: 13.

9. Stephan Miescher, *Making Men in Ghana* (Bloomington: Indiana University Press), 2005, 106; Kwame Gyekye, *An Essay on African Philosophical Thought: The Akan Conceptual Scheme* (Philadelphia, PA: Temple University Press), 1995.

10. Sara Berry similarly observed in Nigeria that "status and authority rested on achievement as well as on age or ancestry" (*Fathers Work for Their Sons: Accumulation, Mobility, and Class Formation in an Extended Yoruba Community* [Los Angeles: University of California Press], 1985: 9); Jane Guyer and Samuel M. Eno Belinga, "Wealth in People as Wealth in Knowledge: Accumulation and Composition in Equatorial Africa," *Journal of African History* 36 (1995): 91–120.

11. Akyeampong, *Drink, Power, and Cultural Change*, 15.

12. McCaskie, *Asante Identities*, 122–124.

13. Akyeampong, *Drink, Power, and Cultural Change*, pp. 43, 55.

14. Akyeampong, *Drink, Power, and Cultural Change*, 54.

15. Bianca Murillo, *Conditional Sales: Global Commerce and the Making of an African Consumer Society* (Athens, OH: Ohio University Press), forthcoming.

16. Stephanie Newell, *Literary Culture in Colonial Ghana: How to Play the Game of Life* (Bloomington, IN: Indiana University Press), 2002; Nate Plageman, *Highlife Saturday Night: Popular Music and Social Change in Urban Ghana* (Bloomington, IN: Indiana University Press), 2012.

17. Nate Plageman, *Highlife Saturday Night*.

18. McCaskie, *Asante Identities*, 125–126. These dynamics obviously varied based on local dynamics. Stephan Miescher, for example, distinguishes between conceptions of "Akan masculinity" and what he terms "Presbyterian masculinity," common among the Akuapem populations who serve as the primary subjects of his study and who were the primary targets of the Basel Mission Society, a protestant—and later explicitly Presbyterian—missionary group in the Gold Coast interior in the nineteenth century. See Miescher, *Making Men in Ghana* (Bloomington, IN: Indiana University Press), 2005: 2.

19. As Timothy Burke has argued, the growth of colonial capitalism and consumerism in the first half of the twentieth century (and particularly in the aftermath of the Second World War) was an experience that transcended colonial boundaries. Despite fundamental differences in colonial experience, Ghana was part of the broader transformations of consumerism and the cash economy on the continent, similar in many ways to Burke's description of twentieth-century Zimbabwe, or other studies of South Africa, Kenya, and Nigeria. See Timothy Burke, *Lifebuoy Men, Lux Women: Commodification, Consumption, and Cleanliness in Modern Zimbabwe* (Durham, NC: Duke University Press), 1996: 3.

20. See for example, Jean Allman, "Rounding Up Spinsters: Gender Chaos and Unmarried Women in Colonial Asante," *Journal of African History* 37(2) (1996): 195–214; Luise White, *Speaking with Vampires: Rumor and History in Colonial Africa* (Los Angeles: University of California Press), 2000; Dorothy Hodgson and Sheryl McCurdy, eds, *'Wicked' Women and the Reconfiguration of Gender in Africa* (Portsmouth, NH: Heinemann), 2001; Jean Allman, Susan Geiger, and Nakanyike Musisi, eds, *Women in African Colonial Histories* (Bloomington: Indiana University Press), 2002.

21. Emmanuel Akyeampong, *Drink, Power, and Cultural Change*.

22. Nate Plageman, *Highlife Saturday Night*.

23. McCaskie, *Asante Identities*, 127, 132–133.

24. Miescher, *Making Men in Ghana*, 12.

25. Miescher, *Making Men in Ghana*, 2.

26. James L. McLaughlin and David Owusu-Ansah, "Britain and the Gold Coast: The Early Years," *A Country Study: Ghana*, La Verle Berry, ed. (Library of Congress Federal Research Division), 1994.

27. Miescher, *Making Men in Ghana*, 2.

28. Miescher, *Making Men in Ghana*, 12; Plageman, *Highlife Saturday Night*.

29. There were some notable exceptions to this, particularly in government transportation work. See Figures 3.1 and 3.2.

30. Cobrah Antwi, Salaga-Mamprobi Taxi Driver, Accra, May 22, 2009, Interview by Author; Drivers in Tanzania justified the masculinization of their work in remarkably similar ways. See Joshua Grace, "Heroes of the Road: Race, Gender, and the Politics of Mobility in Twentieth Century Tanzania," *Africa* 83(3) (2013): 416.

31. Okan Tetteh, Tee, Nii Ayi Bule, Salaga-Chorkor Drivers' Union Group, Accra, May 13, 2009, Interview by Author.

32. For drivers, "bad behavior" covered a multitude of sins, including but not limited to: loud talking, violence, arguing, and insulting. Such activities were considered by drivers to be dangerous because they distracted the driver and made accidents more likely.

33. Gracia Clark, *Onions Are My Husband: Survival and Accumulation by West African Market Women* (Chicago: University of Chicago Press), 1995: 285–291. See also, Claire Robertson, *Sharing the Same Bowl: A Socioeconomic History of Women and Class in Accra, Ghana* (Ann Arbor: University of Michigan Press), 1990: 46.

34. Miescher, *Making Men in Ghana*, 20.

35. Miescher, *Making Men in Ghana*, 55.

36. Clark, *Onions Are My Husband*, 318.

37. Felicia, New Town Market Woman, Accra, August 18, 2009, Interview by Author.

38. It was also extremely uncommon to apprentice across gender lines (i.e., men and women being trained for the same work) (Clark, *Onions Are My Husband*, 201–211). As is noted above as well as in works discussing the history and culture of market women in Ghana, women did often receive training through more informal apprenticeships with relatives. This rarely required the investment of male apprenticeships, however. See Claire Robertson's *Sharing the Same Bowl*; Gracia Clark's *Onions Are My Husband*; Felicia, New Town Market Woman, Accra, August 18, 2009, Interview by Author.

39. Ibrahim Ato, Anum Sowah, Yii O. Yem, J. F. Ocantey, La Drivers' Union Group Interview, Accra, March 26, 2009, Interview by Author.

40. Ibrahim Ato, Anum Sowah, Yii O. Yem, J. F. Ocantey, La Drivers' Union Group Interview, Accra, March 26, 2009, Interview by Author.

41. According to drivers in La: "The first people who brought car is Bartholomew—the company is behind CMB (near Post Office). This company used to bring airport cars to Ghana, so if the airport car—they remove the back so you were left with the engine and the stand, so they have to get the driver who can drive to the shop so that they will fix the seat and the back on the car. And these cars—if they bring it—you can see the car, but you can't see if they (would) be in the car until they take it to the shop, so the first person who go into that work come from La. He went there to learn the driving, so if they bring the car, he took the car to the shop for the carpenters to fix the back on it. So if they said driving, La is the first place that recognized driving work in the whole of Accra. In La there is a man called Guggisberg who came as Governor and he's looking for a driver and he ask where he can find a good driver and they say Labadi. So Guggisberg sent people to La for this man who was working for the company. So this man leave the company to drive Guggisberg. After he was driving for Guggisberg, there is one man who is rich in La, and Djatey told the rich man that he should buy one car so that he be using it for a passenger's car for him. So this man bought one car and he need a driver. So he used to bring the car to Labadi, and you see people appreciating it. So that is the reason why the driving work has become their habit most in Labadi. The first driver who come from La is called Djatey. The first time that they're looking for drivers to come and learn the driving, all the people are afraid of the car because they don't know anything about the car, but this man went there and they took him and he learned the work, so that is the reason why La is the first place that if you want to talk about driving you should mention. People come from other places to learn driving in La—Teshie, Nungua, Tema, Ho—that's when it started spreading" (Ibrahim Ato, Anum Sowah, Yii O. Yem, J. F. Ocantey, La Drivers' Union Group Interview, Accra, March 26, 2009, Interview by Author). While there is no documentary confirmation of this story, it is often repeated within and outside of La among older drivers.

42. Ibrahim Ato, Anum Sowah, Yii O. Yem, J. F. Ocantey, La Drivers' Union Group Interview, Accra, March 26, 2009, Interview by Author.

43. Anon, Circle Odawna Driver, Accra, August 27, 2009, Interview by Author.

44. Abraham Tagoe, Teshie Linguist, Accra, August 5, 2009, Interview by Author; Anon, Circle Odawna Driver, Accra, August 27, 2009, Interview by Author.

45. Abraham Tagoe, Teshie Linguist, Accra, August 5, 2009, Interview by Author.

46. As David Killingray and others have noted, the appeal of travel and worldliness also attracted Gold Coasters to occupations in the colonial military (David Killingray, *Fighting for Britain: African Soldiers in the Second World War* [London: James Currey], 2012; Stephan Miescher, *Making Men in Ghana*).

47. Ibrahim Ato, Anum Sowah, Yii O. Yem, J. F. Ocantey, La Drivers' Union Group Interview, Accra, March 26, 2009, Interview by Author; Abraham Tagoe, Teshie Linguist, Accra, August 5, 2009, Interview by Author.

48. Ibrahim Ato, Anum Sowah, Yii O. Yem, J. F. Ocantey, La Drivers' Union Group Interview, Accra, March 26, 2009, Interview by Author.

49. Anon, Circle Odawna Driver, Accra, August 27, 2009, Interview by Author.

50. Akyeampong, *Drink, Power, and Cultural Change*, 16.

51. Moses Ochonu, *Colonial Meltdown: Northern Nigeria in the Great Depression* (Athens, OH: Ohio University Press), 2009.

52. Andrews A. C. Quaye (Chairman), Kobla, Tawiah Adjetey, and Tetteh, Tema Union Group, Accra, August 13, 2009, Interview by Author.

53. Andrews A. C. Quaye (Chairman), Kobla, Tawiah Adjetey, and Tetteh, Tema Union Group, Accra, August 13, 2009, Interview by Author; Shadrak Yemo Odoi, Labadi, August 6, 2009, Interview by Author; Ibrahim Ato, Anum Sowah, Yii O. Yem, J. F. Ocantey, La Drivers' Union Group Interview, Accra, March 26, 2009, Interview by Author; Quarshie Gene (Chairman), P. Ashai Ollennu (Vice Chairman), and Simon Djetey Abe (Secretary), La Drivers' Union Officers Group, La, Accra, March 23, 2009, Interview by Author.

54. Quarshie Gene (Chairman), P. Ashai Ollennu (Vice Chairman), and Simon Djetey Abe (Secretary), La Drivers' Union Officers Group, La, Accra, March 23, 2009, Interview by Author.

55. Quarshie Gene (Chairman), P. Ashai Ollennu (Vice Chairman), and Simon Djetey Abe (Secretary), La Drivers' Union Officers Group, La, Accra, March 23, 2009, Interview by Author.

56. Andrews A. C. Quaye (Chairman), Kobla, Tawiah Adjetey, and Tetteh, Tema Union Group, Accra, August 13, 2009, Interview by Author.

57. This song, regularly cited by older drivers during interviews to illustrate social attitudes toward drivers (particularly by women), was performed by Kakaiku's Band. Kakaiku's No. 1 Guitar Band, "Driver Ni na Meware No," *Adadam Paa Nie* (Kumasi: Ambassador Records). Lyrics and translation were generously provided by Nathan Plageman. For more information about the history of highlife music, see Nathan Plageman, *Everybody Likes Saturday Night: A Social History of Popular Music and Masculinities in Urban Gold Coast/Ghana, c. 1900–1970* PhD Dissertation (Bloomington, IN: Indiana University Press), 2008.

58. "Chop money" describes the money allocated by men for their wives, which is to be used to cover the costs of running the household and raising the children. As Claire Robertson and others have observed, the amount received for chop money varies greatly and has eroded significantly throughout the twentieth century to the point that women rely almost exclusively on their own income-generating activities as traders in order to pay for school fees and clothes for children, as well as food for the household. See Claire Robertson, *Sharing the Same Bowl*.

59. Apetsi Amenumey, Accra, July 22, 2009, Interview by Author; Kanor Boye, Labadi, Accra, August 7, 2009, Interview by Author; Andrews A. C. Quaye (Chairman), Kobla, Tawiah Adjetey, and Tetteh, Tema Union Group, Accra, August 13, 2009, Interview by Author.

60. Shadrak Yemo Odoi, Labadi, August 6, 2009, Interview by Author.

61. Stephan Miescher, *Making Men in Ghana*. As we will see in the next chapter, drivers were not immune to criticism; however, unlike in other countries within and outside of Africa,

drivers are not (and have not been, historically) explicitly associated with prostitution and the spread of HIV/AIDS. The practice among Gold Coast drivers to establish households and familial connections at regular intervals along regular long-distance routes might have served to limit their interactions with prostitutes.

62. Richard Rathbone, *Nkrumah and the Chiefs: The Politics of Chieftaincy in Ghana 1951–1960* (Athens: Ohio University Press), 2000: 23–24. See also Jeremy Pool, *Now is the Time of Youth: Youth, Nationalism and Cultural Change in Ghana, 1940–1966* (PhD Dissertation, Emory University), 2009.

63. Andrews A. C. Quaye (Chairman), Kobla, Tawiah Adjetey, and Tetteh, Tema Union Group, Accra, August 13, 2009, Interview by Author. Female traders who had also relocated to Accra for work purposes expressed a similar perspective: "When I was in Keta, that is where I used to go and dance and those things, but when I came to Accra, I came to work, so I didn't involve myself in those things" (Felicia, New Town Market Woman, Accra, August 18, 2009, Interview by Author).

64. Miescher, *Making Men in Ghana*, 33.

65. This discourse is common throughout Africa. See, for example, Andrew Burton, *African Underclass: Urbanization, Crime, and Colonial Order in Dar es Salaam, 1919–61* (Portsmouth, NH: Heinemann), 2005; Clive Glaser, *Bo Tsotsi: The Youth Gangs of Soweto, 1935–1976* (Portsmouth, NH: Heinemann), 2000.

66. Laura Fair, *Pastimes and Politics: Culture, Community, and Identity in Post-Abolition Zanzibar* (Columbus, OH: Ohio University Press), 2001; Phyllis Martin, *Leisure and Society in Colonial Brazzaville* (Cambridge: Cambridge University Press), 1996.

67. *The Boy Kumasenu*, Sean Graham: Director, The Gold Coast Film Unit (1952) (http://www.colonialfilm.org.uk/node/332); Peter Bloom and Kate Skinner, "Modernity and Danger: 'The Boy Kumasenu' and the Work of the Gold Coast Film Unit," *Ghana Studies*, 12/13 (2009): 121–153.

68. Akyeampong, *Drink, Power, and Cultural Change*, 57–60.

69. CSO 20/8/4 1940–47 Bye-laws for the regulations of Municipal bus service Accra, "Letter from PATC to CS," May 31, 1940.

70. Ibrahim Ato, Anum Sowah, Yii O. Yem, J. F. Ocantey, La Drivers' Union Group Interview, Accra, March 26, 2009, Interview by Author.

71. The Accra Municipal Omnibus Services Bye-laws of 1927 forbid other vehicles plying for passenger hire along Accra streets, which are covered by municipal buses. This restriction applied only to Accra, which had an Omnibus Authority, and was not a general authority of all Town Councils. CSO 17/1/172 1943–1944 bus services legislation regarding.

72. CSO 17/1/172 1943–1944 bus services legislation regarding.

73. These modernist visions are most completely laid out in: Minister of Housing, *Accra: A Plan for the Town* (Accra: Government of Ghana), 1958. This plan submitted by the newly independent Ghanaian government was heavily based on colonial-era urban planning schemes during this period, even as they were adapted to reflect the needs of the newly independent nation.

74. CSO 17/1/172 1943–1944 bus services legislation regarding. These regulations were never completely successful, as the police force was not large enough to enforce compliance at all times. But complaints decreased by 1945.

75. Tetteh, Okan, Tee, Nii Ayi Bule, Salaga-Chorkor Drivers' Union Group, Accra, May 13, 2009, Interview by Author; Antwi, Cobrah, Salaga-Mamprobi Taxi Driver, Accra, May 22, 2009, Interview by Author; Quarshie Gene (Chairman), P. Ashai Ollennu (Vice Chairman), and Simon Djetey Abe (Secretary), La Drivers' Union Officers Group, La, Accra, March 23, 2009, Interview by Author.

76. Ibrahim Ato, Anum Sowah, Yii O. Yem, J. F. Ocantey, La Drivers' Union Group Interview, Accra, March 26, 2009, Interview by Author.

77. Quarshie Gene (Chairman), P. Ashai Ollennu (Vice Chairman), and Simon Djetey Abe (Secretary), La Drivers' Union Officers Group, La, Accra, March 23, 2009, Interview by Author.

78. Similar passenger services do not seem to have developed in other urban areas (Kumasi, Sekondi-Takoradi, Cape Coast, etc.) until a much later period.

79. Andrews A. C. Quaye (Chairman), Kobla, Tawiah Adjetey, Tetteh, and Justice John Bay, Tema Union Group, Accra, August 13, 2009, Interview by Author.

80. Kwame Nkrumah, "The African Genius," Speech at the Opening of the Institute of African Studies, University of Ghana, Legon, October 25, 1963; Basil Davidson, *The African Genius* (Athens, OH: Ohio University Press), 2004.

81. Jean Allman, "Phantoms of the Archive: Kwame Nkrumah, a Nazi Pilot Named Hanna, and Contingencies of Postcolonial History-Writing," *American Historical Review*, 118(1) (February 2013): 118.

82. Andrews A. C. Quaye (Chairman), Kobla, Tawiah Adjetey, and Tetteh; Tema Union Group, Accra, August 13, 2009. Interview by Author.

83. Abraham Tagoe, Teshie Linguist, Accra, August 5, 2009. Interview by Author.

84. Abraham Tagoe, Teshie Linguist, Accra, August 5, 2009. Interview by Author.

85. Quarshie Gene (Chairman), P. Ashai Ollennu (Vice Chairman), and Simon Djetey Abe (Secretary), La Drivers' Union Officers Group, La, Accra, March 23, 2009, Interview by Author; Okan Tetteh, Tee, Nii Ayi Bule, Salaga-Chorkor Drivers' Union Group, Accra, May 13, 2009, Interview by Author; Shadrak Yemo Odoi, Labadi, August 6, 2009, Interview by Author; Quarshie Gene (Chairman), P. Ashai Ollennu (Vice Chairman), and Simon Djetey Abe (Secretary), La Drivers' Union Officers Group, La, Accra, March 23, 2009, Interview by Author; Andrews A. C. Quaye (Chairman), Kobla, Tawiah Adjetey, and Tetteh, Tema Union Group, Accra, August 13, 2009, Interview by Author; Anon, Circle Odawna Driver, Accra, August 27, 2009, Interview by Author; Felicia, New Town Market Woman, Accra, August 18, 2009, Interview by Author.

86. See, for example, Timothy Parsons, *Race, Resistance, and the Boy Scout Movement in British Colonial Africa* (Athens, OH: Ohio University Press), 2004.

87. While drivers did not explicitly identify it as a reason, it seems likely that the overlap between private cars and taxis motivated some of the suspicion about the skills and professionalism of taxi drivers.

88. Ibrahim Ato, Anum Sowah, Yii O. Yem, J. F. Ocantey, La Drivers' Union Group Interview, Accra, March 26, 2009, Interview by Author; Okan Tetteh, Tee, Nii Ayi Bule, Salaga-Chorkor Drivers' Union Group, Accra, May 13, 2009, Interview by Author; Quaye, Andrews A. C. (Chairman), Kobla, Tawiah Adjetey, and Tetteh; Tema Union Group, Accra, August 13, 2009, Interview by Author.

89. Some rumors suggested that the policy was, in fact, one result of Edusei's observations of taxi drivers on official foreign visits. While there is no evidence to support this argument, it seems likely, as Edusei had indeed been influenced by international practices during his many trips abroad.

90. Andrews A. C. Quaye (Chairman), Kobla, Tawiah Adjetey, and Tetteh, Tema Union Group, Accra, August 13, 2009, Interview by Author.

91. Jean Allman, "Let Your Fashion Be In Line With Our Ghanaian Costume," in *Fashioning Africa: Power and the Politics of Dress*, Jean Allman, ed. (Bloomington: Indiana University Press), 2004: 149; "Clean Up Accra," *Daily Graphic*, November 25, 1954.

92. Abraham Tagoe interview.

93. Jeffrey S. Ahlman, "A New Type of Citizen: Youth, Gender, and Generation in the Ghanaian Builders Brigade," *Journal of African History*, 53(2012): 98.

94. Quarshie interviews; Dennis Austen, *Politics in Ghana, 1946–1960* (Oxford: Oxford University Press), 1970.

95. Quarshie interviews; Dennis Austen, *Politics in Ghana, 1946–1960* (Oxford: Oxford University Press), 1970.

96. Anonymous, Ga Shifimo Kpee Taxi Driver, Salaga, Accra, May 22, 2009.

97. Abraham Tagoe interview.

98. Quarshie Gene (Chairman), P. Ashai Ollennu (Vice Chairman), and Simon Djetey Abe (Secretary), La Drivers' Union Officers Group, La, Accra, March 23, 2009, Interview by Author.

99. Margaret Field, *Search for Security: An Ethno-Psychiatric Study of Rural Ghana* (New York: W. W. Norton & Company), 1970.

100. Anon, Circle Odawna Driver, Accra, August 27, 2009, Interview by Author; Shadrak Yemo Odoi, Labadi, August 6, 2009, Interview by Author; Ibrahim Ato, Anum Sowah, Yii O. Yem, J. F. Ocantey, La Drivers' Union Group Interview, Accra, March 26, 2009, Interview by Author.

101. Tetteh, Okan, Tee, Nii Ayi Bule, Salaga-Chorkor Drivers' Union Group, Accra, May 13, 2009, Interview by Author.

102. Margaret Field, *Search for Security*.

103. Van Binsbergen and Geschiere, n.d., 3. Quoted in Jean and John Comaroff, "Millennial Capitalism: First Thoughts on a Second Coming," *Public Culture*, 12/2 (2000): 294.

104. McCaskie, *Asante Identities*, 189–190; Marshall Berman, *All That Is Solid Melts into Air: The Experience of Modernity* (New York: Penguin Books), 1988.

105. Gabriel Klaeger, "Religion on the Road: The Spiritual Experience of Road Travel in Ghana." In *The Speeds of Change: Motor Vehicles and People in Africa, 1890–2000* (Leiden: Brill Academic Publishers), 2009: 169–194; Margaret Field, *In Search of Security*.

106. Shadrak Yemo Odoi, Labadi, August 6, 2009, Interview by Author.

107. For example, during the course of fieldwork I was introduced to a family who was in the middle of mourning for their recently deceased son. The young man, only eighteen, had died only a day after his birthday. The doctor concluded that he had been poisoned. It was widely assumed that one of his "friends" had poisoned him during birthday celebrations due to jealousy.

108. Margaret Field, *Search for Security*.

109. Abu Maama ("Abayenie"), Accra New Town, March 5, 2009, Interview by Author.

Chapter 4

1. "The Exploitation Must Stop," *Daily Graphic* (Accra, Ghana, 7/24/62).

2. Ales Bulir, "The Price Incentive to Smuggle and the Cocoa Supply in Ghana, 1950–96," *International Monetary Fund Working Paper* (June 1998), 10.

3. Janet Roitman describes a similar process in postcolonial Cameroon, as the Biya regime attempted to respond to social and economic crisis by "posing the question of who is a legitimate citizen." See Janet Roitman, *Fiscal Disobedience: An Anthropology of Economic Regulation in Central Africa* (Princeton, NJ: Princeton University Press), 2005: 5.

4. Okan Tetteh, Tee, Nii Ayi Bule, Salaga-Chorkor Drivers' Union Group, Accra, May 13, 2009, Interview by Author.

5. Gracia Clark, *Onions Are My Husband: Survival and Accumulation by West African Market Women* (Chicago: University of Chicago Press), 1995.

6. Paul Nugent, *Big Men, Small Boys, and Politics in Ghana: Power, Ideology, and the Burden of History, 1982–1994* (London: Pinter Publishers, Ltd.), 1996.

7. For further information regarding the experiences of market women during this period, see Gracia Clark, *Onions Are My Husband: Survival and Accumulation by West African Market Women* (Chicago: University of Chicago Press), 1995; Claire Robertson, "The Death of Makola and Other Tragedies," *Canadian Journal of African Studies* 17, 3 (1983): 469–495; Claire

Robertson, *Sharing the Same Bowl: A Socioeconomic History of Women and Class in Accra, Ghana* (Ann Arbor: University of Michigan Press), 1990.

8. Deborah Pellow and Naomi Chazan, *Ghana: Coping with Uncertainty* (Boulder: Westview Press), 1986: 47.

9. While the question of their guilt or innocence might be intriguing, it is impossible to assess. And, furthermore, drivers' criminalization was not the result of significant changes in driver practice. Rather, it was a reflection of the ambiguous position of drivers in relation to an emerging social, political, and economic order. Gracia Clark, "Gender and Profiteering: Ghana's market women as devoted mothers and 'human vampire bats'" in D. Hodgson and S. McCurdy (eds), *'Wicked' Women and the Reconfiguration of Gender in Africa* (Portsmouth, NH: Heinemann), 2001.

10. "27,000 cars enter Accra Daily," *Daily Graphic*, 1-30-57.

11. Ahlman, "A New Type of Citizen," 88–89; Bill Freund, *The African City: A History* (Cambridge: Cambridge University Press), 2007: 66.

12. "Drivers' strike," *Daily Graphic*, 7-20-57.

13. "Drivers' strike," *Daily Graphic*, 7-20-57; "The Drivers' strike—thousands stranded as lorries stop work," *Daily Graphic*, 7-23-57.

14. Richard Jeffries, *Class, Power, and Ideology: The Railwaymen of Sekondi* (Cambridge: Cambridge University Press), 2009.

15. Felicia, New Town Market Woman, Accra, August 18, 2009, Interview by Author; Kanor Boye, Labadi, August 7, 2009, Interview by Author; Abu Maama ("Abayenie"), Accra New Town, March 5, 2009, Interview by Author; Okan Tetteh, Tee, Nii Ayi Bule, Salaga-Chorkor Drivers' Union Group, Accra, May 13, 2009, Interview by Author.

16. "Drivers' strike," *Daily Graphic*, 7-20-57.

17. "Drivers' strike," *Daily Graphic*, 7-20-57.

18. "Drivers' strike," *Daily Graphic*, 7-20-57.

19. "Drivers' strike," *Daily Graphic*, 7-20-57; Kanor Boye, Labadi, August 7, 2009, Interview by Author; Abu Maama ("Abayenie"), Accra New Town, March 5, 2009, Interview by Author; Okan Tetteh, Tee, Nii Ayi Bule, Salaga-Chorkor Drivers' Union Group, Accra, May 13, 2009, Interview by Author.

20. Tom McCaskie, "Accumulation, Wealth and Belief in Asante History II: The twentieth century," *Africa* 56, 1 (1986), 3–23.

21. Clark, "Gender and Profiteering," 299.

22. Clark, "Gender and Profiteering," 299; Patrick Chabal, *Africa: The politics of suffering and smiling* (London, UK: Zed Books, 2009), 119.

23. Roitman, *Fiscal Disobedience*, 12–13.

24. Clark, "Gender and Profiteering," 299. The association of magic and witchcraft with antisocial accumulation highlights the degree to which understandings of "legitimate prosperity" were wrapped up in larger notions of community welfare (Clark, "Gender and Profiteering," 299–301).

25. "Moses Danquah says . . . Stop this 'footsore' nuisance!," *Daily Graphic*, 7-29-57; Felicia, New Town Market Woman, Accra, August 18, 2009, Interview by Author.

26. "Those Death Traps," *Daily Graphic*, 7-23-57.

27. Kanor Boye, Labadi, August 7, 2009, Interview by Author; Felicia, New Town Market Woman, Accra, August 18, 2009, Interview by Author.

28. "TUC invites drivers," *Daily Graphic*, 7-24-57.

29. Kanor Boye, Labadi, August 7, 2009, Interview by Author.

30. Kanor Boye, Labadi, August 7, 2009, Interview by Author; Abu Maama ("Abayenie"), Accra New Town, March 5, 2009, Interview by Author; Okan Tetteh, Tee, Nii Ayi Bule, Salaga-Chorkor Drivers' Union Group, Accra, May 13, 2009, Interview by Author.

31. Kanor Boye, Labadi, August 7, 2009, Interview by Author; Abu Maama ("Abayenie"), Accra New Town, March 5, 2009, Interview by Author; Okan Tetteh, Tee, Nii Ayi Bule, Salaga-Chorkor Drivers' Union Group, Accra, May 13, 2009, Interview by Author.

32. Kate Skinner. "'It Brought Some Kind of Neatness to Mankind: Mass Literacy, Community Development, and Democracy in 1950s Asante," *Africa* 79(4) (2009): 479–499. For comparative perspectives on the ideological debates around self-reliance, see Priya Lal, "Self-Reliance and the State: The Multiple Meanings of Development in Early Post-Colonial Tanzania," *Africa* 82, 2 (2012), 212–234; Jeffrey Ahlman, "A New Type of Citizen: Youth, Gender, and Generation in the Ghanaian Builders Brigade," *Journal of African History* 53(2012): 87–105.

33. Sara Berry, *Chiefs Know Their Boundaries: Essays on Property, Power and the Past in Asante, 1896–1996* (Portsmouth, NH: Heinemann), 2001; Skinner, "It Brought Some Kind of Neatness to Mankind"; "Two Chiefs Lead in Self-Help on Schools and Roads," *Daily Graphic*, 2-22-61; "Road Transport—A Survey of Commercial Vehicles," *Daily Graphic* 11-2-62.

34. Jeffries, *Class, Power, and Ideology*; "Sacrifice for Greater Things Ahead Urges President Nkrumah," *Daily Graphic* 7-11-60.

35. "Sacrifice for Greater Things Ahead Urges President Nkrumah," *Daily Graphic*, 7-11-60.

36. Jeffrey Ahlman, *Living with Nkrumahism: Nation, State, and Pan-Africanism in Ghana*. PhD Dissertation (Urbana-Champaign: University of Illinois), 2011.

37. "Sacrifice for Greater Things Ahead urges President Nkrumah," *Daily Graphic*, 7-11-60.

38. Kwame Nkrumah, *Neocolonialism: The Last Stage of Imperialism* (London: Thomas Nelson & Sons, Ltd.), 1965.

39. "Cheating Drivers," *Daily Graphic*, 7-8-67; "Task for transport organizations," *Daily Graphic*, 1-23-68; "Transportation problem in Accra: The 'tro tro' drivers must be checked," *Daily Graphic*, 4-10-69.

40. "Trotro fares," *Daily Graphic*, 5-30-70.

41. "Our 'Tro Tro' Drivers Must Improve their service," *Daily Graphic*, 7-6-62.

42. "Careless Drivers—New Bill Soon," *Daily Graphic*, 7-25-64; "Wanted: a new taxi driver," *Daily Graphic*, 6-23-65.

43. "Punish them heavily," *Daily Graphic*, 1-7-65. These emerging attitudes toward drivers also found their way into other forms of cultural expression. See, for example, Ayi Kwei Armah, *The Beautyful Ones Are Not Yet Born* (Collier Books: Toronto, Canada), 1969; Benjamin Kwakye, *The Clothes of Nakedness* (Heinemann: London), 1998; and Nana Ampadu I and His African Brothers Band Int., "Adwuma Yi Ye De," *Double-Do: Oman Bo Adwo/Drivers* (originally released 1983).

44. "The False Ways to Get Rich Quick," *Daily Graphic*, 1-24-60.

45. "Sacrifice for Greater Things Ahead urges President Nkrumah," *Daily Graphic*, 7-11-60.

46. "Regulate Lorry Fares," *Daily Graphic*, 2-8-64; "Regulate Our Taxi Service," *Daily Graphic*, 7-10-63; "Transportation problem in Accra," *Daily Graphic*, 4-10-69.

47. "Drivers Support Kwame," *Daily Graphic*, 2-20-64; "Loyalty of our Drivers," *Daily Graphic*, 2-20-64.

48. "Help Develop the Country—Drivers Told," *Daily Graphic*, 3-24-64.

49. "DC appeals to drivers," *Daily Graphic*, 8-18-65.

50. See also Andrews A.C. Quaye (Chairman), Kobla, Tawiah Adjetey, and Tetteh; Tema Union Group, Accra, August 13, 2009, Interview by Author: "That time, we don't go to mechanic too much. Even though we wear the khaki-khaki and black and white, that time, you have to go under the car yourself and repair it, so we do all these things ourselves. By that time, every driver is a mechanic. So because we are repairing our car ourselves, it reach a time that we see that we dress very well and then the car spoils and we have to go under the car and become dirty, so we see that this thing is making us dirty, so we leave it and put it somewhere

and we stop wearing these things. What my brother here is saying is that even when you are traveling from here to Kumasi, you have to get spare parts and everything you need inside the car because car will spoil on the road, you and your mate will start to do it, get gear box, other items or inside your car, when something spoil, you can spend about two days or three days there while you are repairing it."

51. Driving had, in fact, emerged during the last depression experienced during the interwar period. As a result, professional driving developed in the context of broader conditions of want.

52. Anon, Circle Odawna Driver, Accra, August 27, 2009, Interview by Author.

53. "We'll stabilize our economy—Ankrah," *Daily Graphic*, 10-17-66.

54. "John Citizen and the Law," *Daily Graphic*, 8-1-67.

55. "Cheating Drivers," *Daily Graphic*, 7-8-67.

56. "High taxi fares—public help sought," *Daily Graphic*, 10-2-67.

57. "Ban all wooden mammy trucks," *Daily Graphic*, December 9, 1963. See also, "This is a death trap," *Daily Graphic*, September 19, 1972; "Death traps," *Daily Graphic*, April 18, 1973.

58. George H. Lewis, "The Philosophy of the Street in Ghana: Mammy Wagons and Their Mottos—A Research Note," *The Journal of Popular Culture* 32(1) (Summer 1998): 166.

59. Andrews A.C. Quaye (Chairman), Kobla, Tawiah Adjetey, and Tetteh, Tema Union Group, Accra, August 13, 2009, Interview by Author.

60. "Strikes have caused damage—Acheampong," *Daily Graphic*, 1-29-68.

61. "Trotro drivers need no strike," *Daily Graphic*, 11-14-68; Ame, Ayo, Mary Yemokae Laryea, Rita Akoko Laryea, Labadi Market Women Group, Accra, August 18, 2009, Interview by Author.

62. "Bid to solve transport problem," *Daily Graphic*, 12-6-67.

63. "Transportation problem in Accra: The 'tro tro' drivers must be checked," *Daily Graphic*, 4-10-69.

64. "Urban Transportation," *Daily Graphic*, 7-31-70.

65. "Insurance or Robbery?," *Daily Graphic*, 7-23-70. Aprankes or aplankes are drivers' mates or touts, who collect money, manage passengers, and load and unload vehicles.

66. "Insurance or Robbery?," *Daily Graphic*, 7-23-70. Tetteh's statement is both typical and extraordinary. Mammy lorries were nicknamed "boneshakers," an apt description for the bumpy ride and hard seats of the wooden vehicles. However, numerous drivers and passengers reported that many urban residents were relatively ambivalent about their mode of transportation, taking whatever was most convenient and available. Felicia, New Town Market Woman, Accra, August 18, 2009, Interview by Author; Ame, Ayo, Mary Yemokae Laryea, Rita Akoko Laryea, Labadi Market Women Group, Accra, August 18, 2009, Interview by Author.

67. "The 'Tro-Tro' System Must be Improved," *Daily Graphic*, 7-6-71; Felicia, New Town Market Woman, Accra, August 18, 2009, Interview by Author.

68. "Busia addresses transport owners," *Daily Graphic*, 2-27-71.

69. "Busia addresses transport owners," *Daily Graphic*, 2-27-71.

70. "Reorganize the omnibus service," *Daily Graphic*, 2-21-69.

71. "Urban Transportation," *Daily Graphic*, 7-31-70.

72. Alex Kwaku Danso-Boafo, *The Political Biography of Dr. Kofi Abrefa Busia* (Accra: Ghana University Press), 1996: 103–104; "Aliens answer questions on businesses," *Daily Graphic*, 9-26-69.

73. Even the widely respected Fattal Taxi Company was signed over to the Ghana National Trading Corporation: "GNTC to take over Fattal Taxis," *Daily Graphic*, 8-4-70; "New Company to run Fattal taxis," *Daily Graphic*, 8-7-70; "Fattal taxis sold," *Daily Graphic*, 8-11-70.

74. Danso-Boafo, *The Political Biography of Dr. Kofi Abrefa Busia*, 103–111.

75. "They Never Say Die (Mammy Trucks," *Daily Graphic*, 4-3-69.

76. "The problems with our transportation," *Daily Graphic*, 5-11-73.

77. Anon, Circle Odawna Driver, Accra, August 27, 2009, Interview by Author.

78. Andrews A.C. Quaye (Chairman), Kobla, Tawiah Adjetey, and Tetteh, Tema Union Group, Accra, August 13, 2009, Interview by Author.

79. Adu Boahen, *The Ghanaian Sphinx: Reflections on the Contemporary History of Ghana, 1972–1987* (Accra: Ghana Academy of Arts and Sciences), 1989.

80. The Ghanaian experience of early structural adjustment policies in the late 1960s and early 1970s corresponded with global patterns. Early structural adjustment reforms failed to account for the short-term consequences of devaluation and austerity policies on the general population. Such reforms prompted protests in many countries and the subsequent reversal of policies. When international financial institutions like the World Bank and the IMF resurrected structural adjustment reform as a condition for loans in the late 1970s and 1980s, they were soon accompanied by poverty-reduction strategies geared toward mitigating the short-term consequences of policies that were believed to have long-term benefits. See "The World Bank's Changing Discourse on Development: From Reliance on the State and 'Modernizing Elites' to 'Bypassing the State,' collage from World Bank texts, 1972–1989," In *Readings in Modernity in Africa* (Bloomington: Indiana University Press), 2008.

81. Danso-Boafo, *The Political Biography of Dr. Kofi Abrefa Busia*; Mike Oquaye, *Politics in Ghana, 1972–1979* (Accra: Tornado Publications), 1980.

82. "Workers in the Revolution, *Daily Graphic*, 9-6-72.

83. "Acheampong addresses workers," *Daily Graphic*, 9-4-72.

84. "The Budget—it is on self-reliance," *Daily Graphic*, 9-14-72.

85. "Let's Move Arm in Arm to Develop Ghana says Acheampong," *Daily Graphic*, 8-4-72.

86. Although *kalabule* was openly discussed as a general trend, it was only specifically associated with drivers in the pages of the *Graphic* in 1984: "Check on trotro cheats," *Daily Graphic*, 3-19-84.

87. Paul Nugent, *Smugglers, Secessionists & Loyal Citizens on the Ghana-Togo Frontier* (Athens, OH: Ohio University Press), 2002; Lauren M. Maclean, *Informal Institutions and Citizenship in Rural Africa: Risk and Reciprocity in Ghana and Cote d'Ivoire* (Cambridge: Cambridge University Press), 2010.

88. Paul Nugent, *Smugglers, Secessionists & Loyal Citizens on the Ghana-Togo Frontier* (Athens, OH: Ohio University Press), 2002: 264–265.

89. Paul Nugent, *Smugglers, Secessionists, and Loyal Citizens on the Ghana-Togo Frontier* (Athens, OH: Ohio University Press), 2002; Lauren Morris Maclean, *Informal Institutions and Citizenship in Rural Africa: Risk and Reciprocity in Ghana and Cote d'Ivoire.* Cambridge: Cambridge University Press), 2010; "What about the drivers?," *Daily Graphic*, 9-6-73; "Bid to stamp out smuggling: drivers urged to help," *Daily Graphic*, 2-17-75; "Drivers meet to end smuggling," *Daily Graphic*, 8-17-73.

90. "Ultimatum to trotro drivers," *Daily Graphic*, 3-21-72.

91. "Drivers to lose vehicles for charging exorbitant fare," *Daily Graphic*, 1-8-74.

92. "These unruly drivers must be disciplined," *Daily Graphic*, 6-22-74.

93. "Check these insolent drivers!," *Daily Graphic*, 6-22-73; Felicia, New Town Market Woman, Accra, August 18, 2009, Interview by Author; Ame, Ayo, Mary Yemokae Laryea, Rita Akoko Laryea, Labadi Market Women Group, Accra, August 18, 2009, Interview by Author.

94. "These unruly drivers must be disciplined," *Daily Graphic*, 6-22-74; "Transport Fares," *Daily Graphic*, 9-2-76; "FIRED!: Transport Union Taken to Task for Present High Cost of Living," *Daily Graphic*, 5-27-77.

95. "FIRED!," *Daily Graphic*, 5-27-77.

96. "Taxi Drivers," *Daily Graphic* (1977).

97. "Taxi drivers," *Daily Graphic* (1977).

98. "Taxi Drivers are exploiters," *Daily Graphic*, October 25, 1977.

99. This is a position that was reconsidered by the 1950s, when unions became important ways that individual Ghanaians organized around political movements for independence.

100. "Drivers to lose vehicles for charging exorbitant fares," *Daily Graphic*, January 8, 1974; "Drivers warned against arbitrary increases in fares," *Daily Graphic*, January 26, 1974; "Police to arrest no service drivers," *Daily Graphic*, February 21, 1974; "Ply the roads or lose vehicles RC warns drivers," *Daily Graphic*, March 14, 1974; "Policemen to check fares," *Daily Graphic*, March 15, 1974.

101. "Union to meet on new fares," *Daily Graphic*, March 25, 1974; "Drivers slash fares," *Daily Graphic*, March 30, 1974; "Drivers to check smuggling," *Daily Graphic*, December 2, 1974.

102. "GPRTU bans drug peddlers, preachers from vehicles," *Daily Graphic*, October 25, 1986.

103. "National Road Safety Campaign," *Daily Graphic*, December 3, 1975; "Contest to select oldest, best maintained vehicles starts soon," *Daily Graphic*, October 16, 1987; "Are you an accident free driver?," *Daily Graphic*, October 24, 1972; "Big Incentives to drivers," *Daily Graphic*, December 18, 1972.

104. "Warning to Motorists," *Daily Graphic* (1977).

105. "Warning to Motorists," *Daily Graphic*, May 27, 1977. See also "Bring Bookmen to book," *Daily Graphic*, October 26, 1973; "Leave Bookmen alone," *Daily Graphic*, September 17, 1973; "Ban bookmen from lorry parks," *Daily Graphic*, August 13, 1973; "Bookmen again," *Daily Graphic*, August 31, 1973; "Bookmen," *Daily Graphic*, July 28, 1976; "Bookmen are menace," *Daily Graphic*, June 14, 1976; "Bookmen to be hot," *Daily Graphic*, May 28, 1977.

106. "Protect Drivers from Thugs," *Daily Graphic*, September 19, 1974

107. The religious overtones here are obvious. J. J. Rawlings was nicknamed "Junior Jesus," and his second coup was known as a "second coming," implicitly labeling him as Ghana's savior, but also referring to the moral nature of his revolution. See chapter 5 for more discussion.

108. Rawlings and the Armed Forces Revolutionary Council (AFRC) had earlier taken over control in an initial coup in 1979, which overthrew the Supreme Military Council of Akuffo. After conducting initial "housecleaning" exercises, which were intended to seek out compensation for perceived corruption, the PNDC conducted democratic elections, which led to the election of Dr. Hilla Limann in 1979.

109. Gracia Clark, *Onions Are My Husband*.

110. Inussa ("al Haji"), Circle Odawna Driver, Accra. August 27, 2009, Interview by Author.

111. Andrews A.C. Quaye (Chairman), Kobla, Tawiah Adjetey, and Tetteh; Tema Union Group, Accra, August 13, 2009, Interview by Author.

112. Adu Boahen, *The Ghanaian Sphinx*, pg. 45.

113. Inussa ("al Haji"), Circle Odawna Driver, Accra. August 27, 2009, Interview by Author.

114. Andrews A.C. Quaye (Chairman), Kobla, Tawiah Adjetey, and Tetteh, Tema Union Group, Accra, August 13, 2009, Interview by Author.

115. Joshua Maama Larbi, Teshie, August 10, 2009, Interview by Author.

116. Paul Schauert, *Staging Ghana: Artistry and Nationalism in State Dance Ensembles* (Bloomington, IN: Indiana University Press), 2015.

117. Felicia, New Town Market Woman, Accra, August 18, 2009, Interview by Author.

118. "Callous Drivers," *Daily Graphic*, 9-30-83.

119. "Driver arrested for profiteering," *Daily Graphic*, 7-25-83; "Heed Govt Directives on Fares," *Daily Graphic*, 8-19-83.

120. "The Moral Aspect of Ghana's Revolution," *Daily Graphic*, 8-31-83.

121. "Check on trotro cheats," *Daily Graphic*, 3-19-84.

122. "Check overloading," *Daily Graphic*, 6-6-86.

123. Clark, *Onions Are My Husband*; Clark, "Gender and Profiteering"; Robertson, *Sharing the Same Bowl*; Robertson, "The Death of Makola and Other Tragedies."
124. Pellow and Chazan, *Ghana: Coping with Uncertainty*, 47.
125. "Achievements of the NLC since the Coup," *Daily Graphic*, 9-11-69.

Chapter 5

1. Inussa ("al Haji"), Circle Odawna Driver, Accra. August 27, 2009.
2. Inussa ("al Haji"), Circle Odawna Driver, Accra. August 27, 2009.
3. Paul Schauert, *Staging Ghana: Artistry and Nationalism in State Dance Ensembles* (Bloomington, IN: Indiana University Press), 2015: 5.
4. Schauert, *Staging Ghana*, 6; See also: Gracia Clark, *Onions Are My Husband: Survival and Accumulation by West African Market Women* (Chicago: University of Chicago Press), 1995; Jesse Weaver Shipley, *Living the Hiplife: Celebrity and Entrepreneurship in Ghanaian Popular Music* (Durham, NC: Duke University Press), 2013; John Chernoff, *Hustling is Not Stealing: Stories of an African Bar Girl* (Chicago: University of Chicago Press), 2003.
5. Ruth Marshall, *Political Spiritualities: The Pentecostal Revolution in Nigeria* (Chicago: University of Chicago Press), 2009: 9.
6. Frederick Cooper and Randall Packard, eds. *International Development and the Social Sciences: Essays on the History and Politics of Knowledge* (Los Angeles: University of California Press), 1998; Joseph Morgan Hodge, *Triumph of the Expert: Agrarian Doctrines of Development and the Legacies of British Colonialism* (Columbus, OH: Ohio University Press), 2007: 2–3.
7. Monica van Beusekom, *Negotiating Development: African Farmers and Colonial Experts at the Office du Niger, 1920–1960* (Portsmouth, NH: Heinemann), 2001; Hodge, *Triumph of the Expert*, 254; Percy Hintzen, "After Modernization: Globalization and the African Dilemma," In *Modernization as Spectacle in Africa*, Peter Bloom, Stephan Miescher, and Takyiwaa Manuh, eds (Bloomington: Indiana University Press), 2014: 28–32.
8. Hodge, *Triumph of the Expert*, 273–274.
9. Jean and John Comaroff, "Millennial Capitalism: First Thoughts on a Second Coming," *Public Culture* 12/2 (2000): 291–343.
10. Percy Hintzen, "After Modernization: Globalization and the African Dilemma," In *Modernization as Spectacle in Africa*, Peter Bloom, Stephan Miescher, and Takyiwaa Manuh, eds (Bloomington: Indiana University Press), 2014: 28–32.
11. Brenda Chalfin, "Cars, the Customs Service, and Sumptuary Rule in Neoliberal Ghana," *Comparative Studies in Society and History* 50(2) (April 2008): 424–453; Brenda Chalfin, *Neoliberal Frontiers: An Ethnography of Sovereignty in West Africa* (Chicago: University of Chicago Press), 2010.
12. Arturo Escobar, *Encountering Development: The Making and Unmaking of the Third World* (Princeton, NJ: Princeton University Press), 2011: 5.
13. Here I follow Monica van Beusekom, who "does not deny the powerful role of European institutions and scientific and social scientific disciplines, but in taking a close look at the experience of development at the Office du Niger, it reveals that development in practice was not merely conceptualized and imposed from above" (*Negotiating Development*, xx–xxi).
14. Chalfin, "Cars, the Customs Service, and Sumptuary Rule in Neoliberal Ghana," 425.
15. Andrew Apter, "The Pan African Nation: Oil Money and the Spectacle of Culture in Nigeria," *Public Culture* 8 (1996): 444.
16. Andrew Apter, "The Pan African Nation," p. 453. As Apter argues, "The magic of Nigeria's nascent modernity was based on unproductive accumulation that was controlled by the state" (453).

17. Comaroffs, "Millennial Capitalism."

18. Apter, "The Pan African Nation," 453.

19. James Scott, *Seeing Like a State: How Certain Schemes to Improve the Human Condition Have Failed* (New Haven, CT: Yale University Press), 1999: 4.

20. Paul Schauert, *Staging Ghana: Artistry and Nationalism in State Dance Ensembles* (Bloomington, IN: Indiana University Press), 2015; Jeffrey S. Ahlman, "A New Type of Citizen: Youth, Gender, and Generation in the Ghanaian Builders Brigade," *Journal of African History* 53(2012): 87–105; Jean Allman, "Phantoms of the Archive: Kwame Nkrumah, a Nazi Pilot Named Hanna, and the Contingencies of Postcolonial History Writing," *American Historical Review* 118(1) (February 2013): 104–129; Cati Coe, *Dilemmas of Culture in African Schools: Youth, Nationalism, and the Transformation of Knowledge* (Chicago: University of Chicago Press), 2005.

21. Scott, *Seeing Like a State*, 4.

22. Paul Nugent, *Big Men, Small Boys, and Politics in Ghana: Power, Ideology, and the Burden of History, 1982–1994* (London: Pinter Publishers, Ltd), 1996: 6–8. See also Patrick Chabal and Jean-Pascal Daloz, *Africa Works: Disorder as Political Instrument* (Bloomington, IN: Indiana University Press), 1999; J. P. Olivier de Sardan, "A Moral Economy of Corruption in Africa?" *Journal of Modern African Studies* 37(1) (1999): 25–52; M. G. Schatzberg, "Power, Legitimacy and 'Democratization' in Africa," *Africa* 63 (1993).

23. Paul Nugent, *Big Men, Small Boys, and Politics in Ghana*, p. 24; Minister of Housing, *Accra: A Plan for the Town* (Accra: Government of Ghana), 1958; Jeffrey S. Ahlman, *Living with Nkrumahism: Nation, State, and Pan-Africanism in Ghana*. PhD dissertation (Urbana-Champaign: University of Illinois), 2011. As Nugent argues, roads and transportation infrastructure were central ways in which the Nkrumah state redistributed wealth under a social contract that legitimized the political rule of elites through their functions as good patrons (34–35).

24. National Archives of Ghana (NAG): Record Center/Ministry of Transportation (RC/MT) 46/2/4 (02/02531) Public Reaction Reports, "Address by the General Secretary of the CEBCAG at the closing ceremony of a trade union seminar at Winneba on the theme 'The Challenges in the Construction Industry and Prospects for the 1990's,' Friday 29th September, 1989"; NAG: RC/MT 46/2/25 (02/02552) Urban Roads Dept—Establishment.

25. NAG: RC/MT 46/2/24 Urban Roads—General; NAG: RC/MT 46/2/25 (02/02552) Urban II Projects, vol. 2; NAG: RC/MT 46/2/25 (02/02552) Urban Roads Dept—Establishment; NAG: RC/MT (46/2/26 (02/02553) Accra District Management and Improvement Study; NAG: RC/MT 46/2/44 (02/02571) Lorry Fares and Charges.

26. Janet Roitman, *Anti-Crisis* (Durham, NC: Duke University Press), 2013: 12.

27. Stephan F. Miescher, "'No One Should be Worse Off': The Akosombo Dam, Modernization, and the Experience of Resettlement in Ghana," In *Modernization as Spectacle in Africa* (Bloomington, IN: Indiana University Press), 2014: 184–204.

28. Scott, *Seeing Like a State*, 3.

29. Stephan F. Miescher, Peter J. Bloom, and Takyiwaa Manuh, "Introduction," In *Modernization as Spectacle in Africa* (Bloomington, IN: Indiana University Press), 2014: 1–2.

30. See, for example, Stephan F. Miescher, "'No One Should be Worse Off.'"

31. Jeffrey Ahlman, "A New Type of Citizen: Youth, Gender, and Generation in the Ghanaian Builders Brigade," *Journal of African History* 53 (2012): 87–105.

32. "The Budget Speech: Emphasis on Self-Reliance," *Daily Graphic*, September 15, 1974.

33. "Graphic View: Feeder Roads," *Daily Graphic*, May 17, 1972.

34. "Graphic View: Feeder Roads," *Daily Graphic*, May 17, 1972.

35. "Graphic View: Feeder Roads," *Daily Graphic*, May 17, 1972.

36. Achille Mbembe, *On the Postcolony* (Los Angeles: University of California Press), 2001: 25.

37. Frederick Cooper, *Africa Since 1940: The Past of the Present* (Cambridge: Cambridge University Press), 2002: 5.

38. Chabal and Daloz, *Africa Works*, 103.

39. NAG: RC/MT 46/2/24 Urban Roads—General; NAG: RC/MT 46/2/25 (02/02552) Urban II Projects, vol. 2; NAG: RC/MT 46/2/25 (02/02552) Urban Roads Dept—Establishment; NAG: RC/MT (46/2/26 (02/02553) Accra District Management and Improvement Study.

40. Paul Nugent, *Big Men, Small Boys, and Politics in Ghana*, 17–18, 25–26.

41. For discussions of political change during the Rawlings regime, see: Paul Nugent, *Big Men, Small Boys, and Politics in Ghana*; Mike Oquaye, *Politics in Ghana, 1982–1992: Rawlings, Revolution, Popular Democracy*; Naomi Chazan, *An Anatomy of Ghanaian Politics: Managing Political Recession, 1969–1982* (Boulder: Westview Press), 1983.

42. Paul Nugent, *Big Men, Small Boys, and Politics in Ghana*, 27.

43. Kwame Boafo-Arthur, "Ghana: Structural Adjustment, Democratization, and the Politics of Continuity," *African Studies Review* 42 (2) (1999): 48.

44. Shadrak Yemo Odoi, Labadi, August 6, 2009, Interview by Author.

45. PNDC Committee of Secretaries Memorandum by PNDC Secretary for Transport and Communications, "Proposal for a Revision of Government's Road Transport Tariff Policy," NAG: RC/MT 46/2/44 (02/02571) Lorry Fares and Charges.

46. "Inaugural Address by the PNDC Secretary for the Ministry of Roads and Highways on the Inauguration of the Ghana Road Association," NAG: RC/MT 46/2/4 (02/02531) Ghana Road Association.

47. Paul Nugent, *Smugglers, Secessionists & Loyal Citizens on the Ghana-Togo Frontier* (Athens, OH: Ohio University Press), 2002.

48. Paul Nugent, *Big Men, Small Boys, and Politics in Ghana*, p. 90.

49. See NAG: RC/MT 46/2/44 (02/02571) Lorry Fares and Charges.

50. Boafo-Arthur, "Ghana: Structural Adjustment, Democratization, and the Politics of Continuity," 48.

51. Eboe Hutchful, *Ghana's Adjustment Experience: The Paradox of Reform* (Portsmouth, NH: Heinemann), 2002; Boafo-Arthur, "Ghana: Structural Adjustment, Democratization, and the Politics of Continuity," 46.

52. See Paul Nugent, *Big Men, Small Boys, and Politics in Ghana*, 90–92. For a demonstration of the transformations in World Bank rhetoric from the 1950s/60s–1990s, see "The World Bank's Changing Discourse on Development: From Reliance on the State and 'Modernizing Elites' to 'Bypassing the State,' collage from World Bank texts, 1972–1989," In *Readings in Modernity in Africa*.

53. Paul Nugent, *Big Men, Small Boys, and Politics in Ghana*, pp. 111–112.

54. Boafo-Arthur, "Ghana: Structural Adjustment, Democratization, and the Politics of Continuity," 49.

55. "Project Document for GHA/84/007, Ministry of Roads and Highways Reorganization Study," NAG: RC/MT 46/2/8 (02/02535) Organization of—Min of Roads and Highways. See also 46/2/4 (02/02531) Ghana Road Association; NAG: RC/MT 46/2/25 (02/02552) Urban II Projects, vol. 2.

56. NAG: RC/MT 46/2/44 (02/02571) Transport Development in Ghana.

57. NAG: RC/MT 46/2/25 (02/02552) Urban II Projects, vol. 2. See also NAG: RC/MT 46/2/44 (02/02571) Transport Development in Ghana.

58. "Achimota Road Rehabilitation Project, Ministry of Roads and Highways, 19th May 1988," NAG: RC/MT 46/2/26 (02/02553) Achimota Road Project-37 Roundabout-Dimples Inn.

This initial development plan was supplemented throughout the 1980s and 1990s by additional externally funded projects, incorporating feeder roads, urban roads, and motorways (both maintenance/reconstruction and construction).

59. As of 1988, the country had approximately 14,000 km of roads, 6,000 km of which were tarred.

60. "Inaugural Address by the PNDC Secretary for the Ministry of Roads and Highways on the Inauguration of the Ghana Road Association," NAG: RC/MT 46/2/4 (02/02531) Ghana Road Association. Despite this significant funding, the secretary notes that funding remains inadequate "set against the task of road construction and maintenance," for which "there is a back log of over 10 years maintenance work to be done."

61. NAG: RC/MT 46/2/21 (02/02548) Accra-Tema Motorway; NAG: RC/MT 46/2/26 (02/02553) Accra District Management and Improvement Study.

62. "Address by the General Secretary of the CEBCAG at the closing ceremony of a trade union seminar at Winneba on the theme 'The Challenges in the Construction Industry and Prospect for the 1990's,' Friday 29th September, 1989," NAG: RC/MT 46/2/24 (02/02531) Public Reaction Reports.

63. NAG: RC/MT 46/2/25 (02/02552) Urban II Projects, vol. 2.

64. NAG: RC/MT 46/2/24 (02/02551) Urban Roads-General, "Programme for Accelerated Maintenance of Roads in Four Urban Centres."

65. NAG: RC/MT 46/2/44 (02/02571) Lorry Fares and Charges, "PNDC Committee of Secretaries Memorandum by PNDC Secretary for Transport and Communications (Proposal for a Revision of Government's Road Transport Tariff Policy)." This policy represents a degree of continuity from older government approaches to urban transport, dating as far back as the colonial period. By the late 1980s, however, this approach increasingly began to be seen as an ineffective investment, since private road transport regularly outperformed state services and had effectively pushed state services out of the transportation system.

66. Naaborko Sackeyfio-Lenoch, *The Politics of Chieftaincy: Authority and Property in Colonial Ghana, 1920–1950* (Rochester, NY: University of Rochester Press), 2014.

67. NAG: RC/MT 46/2/24 (02/02531) Public Reaction Reports, "Letter from the chiefs of the Eastern Region to PNDC Secretary for the Ministry of Roads and Highways, 24th February 1992."

68. Paul Nugent, *Big Men, Small Boys, and Politics in Ghana*, 116–121.

69. NAG: RC/MT 46/2/24 (02/02531) Public Reaction Reports, Memorandum from PRO to PNDC Secretary, "Fill the Hole Near the Stairs of the Kaneshie Market Overbridge."

70. NAG: RC/MT 46/2/24 (02/02531) Public Reaction Reports, Memorandum from PRO to PNDC Secretary, "Fill the Hole Near the Stairs of the Kaneshie Market Overbridge."

71. NAG: RC/MT 46/2/24 (02/02531) Public Reaction Reports, "Public Reaction Report, Information Services Department, Ministry of Information, 'Feeder Roads in the Wa District,'" 25th April, 1991. See also "Public Reaction Report, Information Services Department, Ministry of Information, 'Poor State of Roads,'" 20th August, 1990.

72. "Public Reaction Report, Information Services Department, Ministry of Information, 'Poor State of Roads,'" 20th August, 1990.

73. NAG: RC/MT 46/2/24 (02/02531) Public Reaction Reports, "Public Reaction Report, Information Services Department, Ministry of Information, 'Feeder Roads in the Wa District,'" 25th April, 1991. See also "Public Reaction Report, Information Services Department, Ministry of Information, 'Poor State of Roads,'" 20th August, 1990: "The laudable efforts of the people to improve the condition of the road through communal labor has not yielded much result since the whole stretch is muddy. The poor state of the road has made it virtually impossible for the farmers to send their foodstuffs and other crops to the urban centres for sale."

74. NAG: RC/MT 46/2/4 (02/02531) Public Reaction Reports, "Report on Evaluation of Work done on Sunyani-Buoko Jn. Road"; NAG: RC/MT 46/2/8 (02/02535) Organization of—Min of Roads and Highways.

75. NAG: RC/MT 46/2/4 (02/02531) Public Reaction Reports, "Report on Evaluation of Work done on Sunyani-Buoko Jn. Road"; NAG: RC/MT 46/2/8 (02/02535) Organization of—Min of Roads and Highways.

76. NAG: RC/MT46/2/21 (02/02548) Accra-Tema Motorway, "Danger on Motorway—A Rejoinder": "What is even worse is that, the mushrooming of a number of access roads to factory buildings and farms has now become a common feature along the motorway. The Ministry of Roads and Highways, and for that matter the Ghana Highway Authority, has had occasions to issue warnings through the radio and the newspapers against the construction of these access roads because of the danger they pose to motorists, but the warnings have been ignored. Much as the Ghana Highway Authority would not want the motorway to be obstructed by the linkage of access roads, the agencies responsible for the construction of these access roads have not only ignored all previous warnings but they have also displayed a complete lack of sense of cooperation with the Authority to protect and preserve the motorway to its expected standard. . . . In light of these circumstances, perhaps, a new legislation on obstruction to the motorway will be needed so that people who construct access roads to the motorway can be punished with heavy fines, and or, imprisonment. When that is done, we will expect all agencies, especially the law enforcement agencies, to cooperate in order to make the lives of motorists using the motorway safe."

77. NAG: RC/MT 46/2/4 (02/02531) Public Reaction Reports.

78. NAG: RC/MT 46/2/4 (02/02531) Public Reaction Reports, Letter from Michael Dollah (Nima) to PNDC Chairman Rawlings, 25th November 1991.

79. NAG: RC/MT 46/2/4 (02/02531) Public Reaction Reports Letter from Michael Dollah (Nima) to PNDC Chairman Rawlings, 25th November 1991.

80. In some cases, the consequences of construction (and related demolition) challenged the policies of the government itself, as in the case of Model Nursery School. When the government demolished a school block in order to make way for a new road, and then failed to reconstruct the school block as promised, the Parent-Teacher Association for the school petitioned the Ministry on the basis of its avowed commitment to the principle, adopted at the World Summit for Children, that "every child in Ghana has a right to an education" (NAG: RC/MT 46/2/25 [02/02552] Urban II Projects vol. 2, Letter from The Parent-Teacher Association of Model Nursery School to the Ministry of Roads and Highways, 19th March 1993).

81. NAG: RC/MT 46/2/4 (02/02531) Public Reaction Reports, Letter from Monomanye Area Residents to the PNDC Secretary for the Ministry of Agriculture, 29th April 1992.

82. NAG: RC/MT 46/2/4 (02/02531) Public Reaction Reports.

83. When asked "who did the most for drivers," most older drivers noted Rawlings' commitment to road construction and recognized that he "did something for drivers." Such a phrase was a recognition not only of road construction efforts but also of broader institutional and political support, as we shall see below.

84. NAG: RC/MT 46/2/45 (02/02572) Ghana Private Road Transport Organizations.

85. NAG: RC/MT 46/2/45 (02/02572) Ghana Private Road Transport Organizations.

86. NAG: RC/MT 46/2/44 (02/02571) Lorry Fares and Charges, PNDC Committee of Secretaries Memorandum by PNDC Secretary for Transport and Communications, "Proposal for a Revision of Government's Road Transport Tariff Policy."

87. NAG: RC/MT 46/2/44 (02/02571) Lorry Fares and Charges, PNDC Committee of Secretaries Memorandum by PNDC Secretary for Transport and Communications, "Proposal for a Revision of Government's Road Transport Tariff Policy."

88. NAG: RC/MT 46/2/4 (02/02531) Public Reaction Reports, Public Reaction Report, Information Services Department, Ministry of Information, "The Ban on the Use of Mammy Trucks," 10th July, 1991.

89. NAG: RC/MT 46/2/4 (02/02531) Public Reaction Reports, Public Reaction Report, Information Services Department, Ministry of Information, "The Ban on the Use of Mammy Trucks," 10th July 1991.

90. NAG: RC/MT 46/2/25 (02/02552) Urban II Projects, vol. 2, "Urban Transport Project, Letter of Urban Transport Policy."

91. NAG: RC/MT 46/2/21 (02/02548) Accra-Tema Motorway.

92. Inussa ("al Haji"), Circle Odawna Driver, Accra. August 27, 2009.

93. NAG: RC/MT 46/3/12 (03/05292) Petitions and Complaints—General, Letter from McAshley's Memorial School of Driving to the Chief Executive of the Accra Metropolitan Assembly, 16th February 1995.

94. NAG: RC/MT 46/3/12 (03/05292) Petitions and Complaints—General, Letter from McAshley's Memorial School of Driving to the Chief Executive of the Accra Metropolitan Assembly, 16th February 1995.

95. Joshua Maama Larbi Teshie, August 10, 2009, Interview by Author.

96. NAG: RC/MT 46/2/44 (02/02571) Lorry Fares and Charges, PNDC Committee of Secretaries Memorandum by PNDC Secretary for Transport and Communications, "Proposal for a Revision of Government's Road Transport Tariff Policy."

97. The deregulation of petroleum prices was gradual—petrol was in fact one of the last imports to still benefit from price controls and government subsidies.

98. The distribution of inputs was also gradually phased out as the government relinquished control over the input and distribution of all imports and essential commodities during the 1990s.

99. Letter from Emmanuel Narh to PNDC Secretary of Transport and Communication, 25th April, 1984, 46/2/44 (02/02571) Lorry Fares and Charges. See similar complaints recorded in the same file: "Information Services, Public Reaction Report, June 30, 1983."

100. NAG: RC/MT 46/2/45 (02/02572) Ghana Private Road Transport Organizations.

101. In fact, the number of complaints was so large that complaints about STC alone took up two enormous files. NAG: RC/MT 46/2/43 (02/02570) Petitions and Complaints—STC A; NAG: RC/MT 46/2/43 (02/02570) Petitions and Complaints—STC B; NAG: RC/MT 46/2/44 (02/02571) Lorry Fares and Charges.

102. NAG: RC/MT 46/2/44 (02/02571) Lorry Fares and Charges.

103. NAG: RC/MT 46/2/43 (02/02570) Petitions and Complaints—STC B.

104. NAG: RC/MT 46/2/43 (02/02570) Petitions and Complaints—STC A.

105. NAG: RC/MT 46/2/24 (02/02551) Urban Roads—General, Terms of Reference: Preparation of an Urban Transport Policy Action Programme.

106. Quarshie Gene (Chairman), P. Ashai Ollennu (Vice Chairman), and Simon Djetey Abe (Secretary), La Drivers' Union Officers Group, La, Accra, March 23, 2009, Interview by Author.

107. As seen below, the GPRTU represented 85 percent of all drivers in the 1990s.

108. Paul Nugent, *Big Men, Small Boys, and Politics in Ghana*, 61–68, 117–119.

109. Paul Nugent, *Big Men, Small Boys, and Politics in Ghana*, 61–68.

110. Although the GPRTU was the largest union, it was not the only one. PROTOA (Progressive Transport Owners Association) and Co-Operative Drivers' Union both split off of the GPRTU in disagreements over leadership and discipline. Disagreements between the GPRTU and its rival unions occasionally influenced national-level discussions, but the dominance of the GPRTU, in reality, made it the government's preferred negotiating partner and most

important and influential ally. See Quarshie Gene (Chairman), P. Ashai Ollennu (Vice Chairman), and Simon Djetey Abe (Secretary), La Drivers' Union Officers Group, La, Accra, March 23, 2009, Interview by Author; NAG: RC/MT 46/2/45 (02/02572) Ghana Private Road Transport Organisations.

111. NAG: RC/MT 46/2/45 (02/02572) Ghana Private Road Transport Organisations.

112. NAG: RC/MT 46/2/45 (02/02572) Ghana Private Road Transport Organisations.

113. Okan Tetteh, Chorkor, May 13, 2009, Interview by Author.

114. NAG: RC/MT 46/2/45 (02/02572) Ghana Private Road Transport Organisations; NAG: RC/MT 46/3/10 (03/05290) lorry fares and charges.

115. By 1995, the union was solely responsible for establishing responsible fares. NAG: RC/MT 46/3/10 (03/05290) Lorry Fares and Charges; NAG: RC/MT 46/2/45 (02/02572) Ghana Private Road Transport Organisations; NAG: RC/MT 46/3/10 (03/05290) lorry fares and charges.

116. NAG: RC/MT 46/2/45 (02/02572) Ghana Private Road Transport Organisations; NAG: RC/MT 46/3/10 (03/05290) lorry fares and charges.

117. NAG: RC/MT 46/2/45 (02/02572) Ghana Private Road Transport Organisations.

118. NAG: RC/MT 46/2/45 (02/02572) Ghana Private Road Transport Organisations.

119. NAG: RC/MT 46/2/45 (02/02572) Ghana Private Road Transport Organisations; NAG: RC/MT 46/3/8 (03/05288) Ghana Private Road Transport Union (GPRTU).

120. Quarshie Gene (Chairman), P. Ashai Ollennu (Vice Chairman), and Simon Djetey Abe (Secretary), La Drivers' Union Officers Group, La, Accra, March 23, 2009, Interview by Author; NAG: RC/MT 46/2/45 (02/02572) Ghana Private Road Transport Organisations.

121. NAG: RC/MT 46/2/45 (02/02572) Ghana Private Road Transport Organisations.

122. In fact, in many cases, the police would bring offenders to the union offices directly to allow them to punish and lecture the driver rather than taking him to court. This happened several times while I was conducting interviews, most memorably at the Achimota GPRTU branch office.

123. "Draveni e wo mfomsɔ a wobɛyɛ no sɛ onyame ampata a wobɛhwere ɔkra bi nkwa." Nana Ampadu I and His African Brothers Band Int., "Adwuma Yi Ye Den" *Double-Do: Oman Bo Adwo/Drivers* (originally released 1983). Transcribed and Translated by Kofi Agyekum and Jennifer Hart.

124. Nana Ampadu I and His African Brothers Band Int., "Adwuma Yi Ye Den" *Double-Do: Oman Bo Adwo/Drivers* (originally released 1983). Transcribed and Translated by Kofi Agyekum and Jennifer Hart.

125. "Draevani biara pɛ "laif," Draevani biara pɛ "show" Woasɔre anɔpa akɔtena wo sitia anim. Woasɔre anɔpa akɔtena wo sitia anim. Obiara hu wo a, na wafrɛ wo na wo nso woayi no nsa. ɛba no saa a, na wo tirim ayɛ wo dɛ. Wo nso woyɛ "popular," wo nso woyɛ "somebody."" Nana Ampadu I and His African Brothers Band Int., "Adwuma Yi Ye Den" *Double-Do: Oman Bo Adwo/Drivers* (originally released 1983). Transcribed and Translated by Kofi Agyekum and Jennifer Hart.

126. Okan Tetteh, Tee, Nii Ayi Bule, Salaga-Chorkor Drivers' Union Group, Accra, May 13, 2009, Interview by Author.

127. Birgit Meyer (with Jojada Verrips) Kwaku's Car. The Struggles and Stories of a Ghanaian Long-Distance Taxi Driver. In *Readings in Modernity in Africa*, Peter Geschiere, Birgit Meyer & Peter Pels, eds. (Bloomington: Indiana University Press), 2008: 155–165 (Reprint of Kwaku's Car. In: Daniel Miller [ed.], *Car Cultures*. Oxford: Berg Publishers. Pp.153–184).

128. There are many problems with the application of this term to motor transportation, the least of which is that "informal economy" implies that such an economy operates outside of the structures of government regulation (though this, in itself, is a matter of some debate among scholars who have been unable to agree on a definition of the informal economy, which most

often continues to be referred to vaguely). While that is truer of motor transportation than wage labor occupations (and government and union officials note the difficulty of implementing any sort of regulation or taxation across a mobile, fluid, and independent occupational population), drivers are still required to obtain various licenses and certificates in order to operate. Regardless, both the government and the unions identify driving as lying within the "informal sector."

129. By the 1990s, it was even possible to operate as a professional driver without a license. The culture of bribery and corruption that invaded the system (both governmental and union) meant that one only needed to have a vehicle to drive.

Epilogue

1. Homi Bhabha, *The Location of Culture* (London: Routledge), 1994.

2. These questions are increasingly being taken up by anthropologists, historians, and others. See, for example, the work of Gabriel Klaeger, Joshua Grace, and Lindsey Green-Simms. A summary of some of these issues, organized around the theme of risk, is explored in a special issue of *Africa* 83 (3) (2013).

3. Meyer and Verrips, "Kwaku's Car: The Struggles and Stories of a Ghanaian Long-Distance Taxi Driver," in *Car Cultures,* ed. Daniel Miller (London: Bloomsbury), 2001: 154–155.

4. Andrews A. C. Quaye (Chairman), Kobla, Tawiah Adjetey, and Tetteh, Tema Union Group, Accra, August 13, 2009, Interview by Author.

5. Ayi Addo, J. K. Mills, K. B., Salaga-Chorkor Drivers' Union, Accra, May 25, 2009.

6. William Bissell, "Engaging Colonial Nostalgia," *Cultural Anthropology* 20(2) (May 2005): 218.

7. Julia Stewart. *African Proverbs and Wisdom* (New York: Carol Publishers), 1997.

8. Jean and John Comaroff, "Millennial Capitalism: First Thoughts on a Second Coming," *Public Culture* 12/2 (2000): 291–343.

9. Brian Larkin, *Signal and Noise: Media, Infrastructure, and Urban Culture in Nigeria* (Durham, NC: Duke University Press), 2008: 169–170; James Ferguson, *Expectations of Modernity: Myths and Meanings of Urban Life on the Zambian Copperbelt* (Los Angeles: University of California Press), 1999. For a summary of global patterns, see Guy Standing, *The Precariat: The New Dangerous Class* (London: Bloomsbury), 2014; Franco Barchiesi, *Precarious Liberation: Workers, the State, and Contested Social Citizenship in Postapartheid South Africa* (New York: State University of New York Press), 2011.

10. Larkin, *Signal and Noise,* 169–170; Abdoumaliq Simone, "On the Worlding of African Cities," *African Studies Review* 44(2) (2001): 15–41; Charles Piot, *Nostalgia for the Future: West Africa after the Cold War* (Chicago: University of Chicago Press), 2010: 20; Brad Weiss, *Producing African Futures: Ritual and Reproduction in a Neoliberal Age* (Leiden: Brill Academic Press), 2004; Ato Quayson, *Oxford Street, Accra: City Life and the Itineraries of Transnationalism* (Durham, NC: Duke University Press), 2014; Comaroffs, *Millennium Capitalism*; Ruth Marshall, *Political Spiritualities: The Pentecostal Revolution in Nigeria* (Chicago: University of Chicago Press), 2009; Birgit Meyer, "Pentecostalism and Neo-Liberal Capitalism: Faith, Prosperity, and Vision in African Pentecostal-Charismatic Churches," *Journal for the Study of Religion* 20(2) (2007): 5–28.

11. "Ghana Urban Transport Project," *The World Bank: Projects and Operations.* Accessed July 10, 2014. <http://www.worldbank.org/projects/P100619/ghana-urban-transport-project?lang=en>.

12. "Project Update: Accra Bus Rapid Transit, Ghana, Africa," *Global Mass Transit Report.* Accessed July 10, 2014. <http://www.globalmasstransit.net/archive.php?id=11546>.

13. "Case Study: Accra, Ghana," *The World Bank: Toolkit on Intelligent Transport Systems for Urban Transport*. Accessed on July 10, 2014. http://www.ssatp.org/sites/ssatp/files/publications /Toolkits/ITS%20Toolkit%20content/case-studies/accra-ghana.html.

14. Victoria Okoye, Jahmal Sands, and C. Asamoah Debrah, "The Accra Pilot Bus-Rapid Transit Project: Transport-Land Use Research Study," *Millennium Cities Initiative (MCI)*, Earth Institute at Columbia University, October 2010. Accessed on July 11, 2014. http://victoriaokoye .files.wordpress.com/2010/02/mci_urbantransport_finaldraft.pdf.

15. "Scania to deliver bus rapid transit system to Ghana," *Scania Group: Media—Press Releases*. Accessed on July 11, 2014. http://www.scania.com/media/pressreleases/N14020EN .aspx.

16. Victoria Okoye, Jahmal Sands, and C. Asamoah Debrah, "The Accra Pilot Bus-Rapid Transit Project: Transport-Land Use Research Study," *Millennium Cities Initiative (MCI)*, Earth Institute at Columbia University, October 2010. Accessed on July 11, 2014. http://victoriaokoye .files.wordpress.com/2010/02/mci_urbantransport_finaldraft.pdf.

17. Marshall, *Political Spiritualities*, 9.

Bibliography

Interviews

Abayenie, Abu Maama, Accra New Town, March 5, 2009.

Abe, Simone Djetey, La Secretary. Accra. April 2, 2009.

Addo, Ayi, J. K. Mills, K. B., Salaga-Chorkor Drivers' Union, Accra, May 25, 2009.

Adu, Madina Old Road Market Driver, June 21, 2017.

Afum, Joseph Agye, New Town Company Driver. Accra. August 12, 2009.

Ahama, Madina, Accra, June 12, 2007.

Ama, Ibrahim ("Go Slow"), Kotobobi Down, March 10, 2009.

Ame, Ayo, Mary Yemokae Laryea, Rita Akoko Laryea, Labadi Market Women Group, Accra, August 18, 2009.

Amenumey, Apetsi, Accra, July 22, 2009.

Ametefe, Ferdinand, Kokolemle, March 10, 2009.

Amoah, Victoria Aku, Chief Driver's Daughter, Labadi, August 11, 2009.

Ampadu, Nana, Lapaz, Accra, June 21, 2007.

Anatsui, Mechanic, Accra, August 4, 2009.

Andrews, Margaret, Ebony Workers Brigade Member, Accra, August 5, 2009.

Antwi, Cobrah, Salaga-Mamprobi Taxi Driver, Accra, May 22, 2009.

Anon, Korlebu Peugeot Drivers' Chairman and Secretary, Accra, August 24, 2009.

Anon, Achimota Minister, Accra. April 17, 2009.

Anon, Achimota Secretary, Accra. April 17, 2009.

Anon, Frytol, Accra. April 18, 2009.

Anon, Accra, April 23, 2009.

Anon, Tudu Station, Accra, April, 29, 2009.

Anon, Ewe Driver, Korlebu, Accra. May 6, 2009.

Anon, New Town, May 8, 2009.

Anon, Tudu Station (Aflao), Accra, May 12, 2009.

Anon, Former General Secretary, Madina, May 14, 2009.

Anon, GPRTU Official, Accra, May 14, 2009.

Anon, Ga Shifimo Kpee Taxi Driver, Salaga, May 22, 2009.

Anon, Driver, New Town, August 12, 2009.

Anon, Circle Odawna Group, Accra, August 22, 2009.

Anon, Circle Odawna Protoa Vice Chairman, Accra. August 26, 2009.

Anon, Koforidua Driver/Policeman, Accra, August 26, 2009.

Anon, Korlebu Chairman, Accra, August 26, 2009.

Anon, Korlebu Peugeot Driver, Accra, August 26, 2009.

Anon, Circle Odawna Driver, Accra, August 27, 2009.

Anon, Lapaz Policeman, Accra, September 12, 2009.

Anon, Salaga Mamprobi Taxi Station Chairman, Accra, August 25, 2009.

Asore, Kofi, Madina, Accra, June 12, 2007.

Ato, Ibrahim, Anum Sowah, Yii O. Yem, J. F. Ocantey, La Drivers' Union Group Interview, Accra, March 26, 2009.

Awudaman, Agbogbloshie, August, 24, 2009.

Ayette ("Think Twice"), Accra, April 24, 2009.

Binghi Man, Madina, Accra, June 12, 2009.

Boye, Kanor, Labadi, August 7, 2009.

Bruburo Kesuo, Madina Old Road Market Driver, June 12, 2007.

Buedu, Circle Odawna Driver, Accra, August 28, 2009.

Darko, Vincent, Member of New Town-Lapaz Driver's Union, Accra. August 20, 2009.

Destiny, Madina, Accra, June 12, 2007.

"Feel Free" (Mr. Musa), Madina Atomic Junction Driver. June 21, 2007.

"Feel Free" (Mr. Musa), Madina, March 16, 2009.

Felicia, New Town Market Woman, Accra, August 18, 2009.

Fening, Prof. Addo, Accra, November 4, 2009.

Gene, Quarshie (Chairman), P. Ashai Ollennu (Vice Chairman), and Simon Djetey Abe (Secretary), La Drivers' Union Officers Group, La, Accra, March 23, 2009.

Glover, Ablade, Artists' Alliance (Omanye House), Accra, July 8, 2007.

Godwin, Madina, Accra, June 12, 2007.

GPRTU General Secretary, Trades Union Congress Headquarters, Accra, May 6, 2009.

Inussa ("al Haji"), Circle Odawna Driver, Accra. August 27, 2009.

Isaac, Madina Atomic Junction Driver, June 21, 2007.

Krakadoh, A. B, New Town, March 12, 2009.

Kwaku, Accra, June 11, 2007.

Larbi, Joshua Maama, Teshie, August 10, 2009.

Laye, Samuel and Foli Kuma, Accra, March 23, 2009.

Mensah, Jacob, Circle Odawna Taxi Driver, Accra. August 21, 2009.

Mensah, David O., Salaga, Accra. August 25, 2009.

Miregah, Ibrahim, Madina Atomic Junction Driver. June 21, 2007.

Odoi, Shadrak Yemo, Labadi, August 6, 2009.

Okantom, Emmanuel, Lapaz, Accra, April 17, 2009.

Oso, Madina Old Road Market Driver, June 21, 2007.

Quarshie, Attoh, Accra, August 24, 2009.

Quarshie, Attoh, Accra, October 17, 2009.

Quaye, Andrews A. C. (Chairman), Kobla, Tawiah Adjetey, and Tetteh; Tema Union Group, Accra, August 13, 2009.

Sarbah, Robert, GRPTU Regional Chairman, Accra, January 28, 2009.

Tagoe, Abraham, Teshie Linguist, Accra, August 5, 2009.

Tetteh, Al Haji, GRPTU Regional Secretariat Chairman (Accra), Accra, May 18, 2009.

Tetteh, Okan, Tee, Nii Ayi Bule, Salaga-Chorkor Drivers' Union Group, Accra, May 13, 2009.

Tetteh, Ebenezer Agyin, Agbogbloshie, August 28, 2009.

Published Sources

"Case Study: Accra, Ghana," *The World Bank: Toolkit on Intelligent Transport Systems for Urban Transport*. Accessed on July 10, 2014. http://www.ssatp.org/sites/ssatp /files/publications/Toolkits/ITS%20Toolkit%20content/case-studies/accra-ghana .html.

"Ghana Urban Transport Project," *The World Bank: Projects and Operations.* Accessed July 10, 2014. http://www.worldbank.org/projects/P100619/ghana-urban-transport -project?lang=en.

"Project Update: Accra Bus Rapid Transit, Ghana, Africa," *Global Mass Transit Report.* Accessed July 10, 2014. http://www.globalmasstransit.net/archive.php?id=11546.

"The World Bank's Changing Discourse on Development: From Reliance on the State and 'Modernizing Elites' to 'Bypassing the State,' Collage from World Bank Texts, 1972–1989." In *Readings in Modernity in Africa.* (Bloomington: Indiana University Press), 2008.

Adas, Michael. *Machines as the Measure of Man: Science, Technology, and Ideologies of Western Dominance* (Ithaca, NY: Cornell University Press), 1990.

Aguiar, Marian. *Tracking Modernity: India's Railway and the Culture of Mobility* (Minneapolis: University of Minnesota Press), 2011.

Ahlman, Jeffrey S. "A New Type of Citizen: Youth, Gender, and Generation in the Ghanaian Builders Brigade." *Journal of African History.* 53(2012): 87–105.

———. *Living with Nkrumahism: Nation, State, and Pan-Africanism in Ghana.* PhD dissertation (Urbana-Champaign: University of Illinois), 2011.

Akurang-Parry, Kwabena. "Colonial Forced Labor Policies for Road-Building in Southern Ghana and International Anti-Forced Labor Pressures, 1900–1940." *African Economic History* 28(2000): 1–25.

Akyeampong, Emmanuel. *Drink, Power, and Cultural Change: A Social History of Alcohol in Ghana, c. 1800 to Recent Times* (Portsmouth, NH: Heinemann), 1996.

———. "What's in a Drink?: Class Struggle, Popular Culture and the Politics of Akpeteshie (Local Gin) in Ghana 1930–67." *Journal of African History* 37(2) (1996): 215–236.

Allman, Jean and Victoria Tashjian. *I Will Not Eat Stone: A Women's History of Colonial Asante* (Portsmouth, NH: Heinemann), 2000.

Allman, Jean, Susan Geiger, and Nakanyike Musisi, eds. *Women in African Colonial Histories* (Bloomington: Indiana University Press), 2002.

Allman, Jean. "Rounding Up Spinsters: Gender Chaos and Unmarried Women in Colonial Asante." *Journal of African History.* 37(2) (1996): 195–214.

———. "Let Your Fashion Be in Line with Our Ghanaian Costume." In *Fashioning Africa: Power and the Politics of Dress.* Jean Allman, ed. (Bloomington: Indiana University Press), 2004.

———. "Phantoms of the Archive: Kwame Nkrumah, a Nazi Pilot Named Hanna, and the Contingencies of Postcolonial History Writing," *American Historical Review* 118(1) (February 2013): 104–129.

Ampadu I, Nana and His African Brothers Band Int., "Adwuma Yi Ye De," *Double-Do: Oman Bo Adwo/Drivers* (originally released 1983).

Anand, Nikhil. "Pressure: The Politechnics of Water Supply in Mumbai." *Cultural Anthropology.* 26(4): 2011, 542–564.

Andersen, Casper. *British Engineers and Africa, 1875–1914* (London: Pickering & Chatto, Ltd), 2011.

Appadurai, Arjun, ed. *The Social Life of Things: Commodities in Cultural Perspective* (Cambridge: Cambridge University Press), 1986.

Apter, Andrew. "The Pan-African Nation: Oil-Money and the Spectacle of Culture in Nigeria" *Public Culture* 8(1996): 441–466.

Arhin, Kwame. "Rank and Class among the Asante and Fante in the Nineteenth Century." *Africa*. 53(1) (1983): 2–22.

———. *West African Traders in Ghana in the Nineteenth and Twentieth Centuries* (New York: Prentice Hall Press), 1980.

———. *West African Traders in Ghana in the Nineteenth and Twentieth Centuries* (New York: Longman), 1979.

———. "Trade, Accumulation and the State in Asante in the Nineteenth Century." *Africa*. 60(1990): 524–537.

Armah, Ayi Kwei. *The Beautyful Ones Are Not Yet Born* (Collier Books: Toronto, Canada), 1969.

Arnold, David. *Everyday Technology: Machines and the Making of India's Modernity* (Chicago: University of Chicago Press), 2013.

Austen, Dennis. *Politics in Ghana, 1946–1960* (Oxford: Oxford University Press), 1970.

Austin, Gareth. "'No Elders Were Present': Commoners and Private Ownership in Asante, 1807–96." *Journal of African History*. 37(1996): 1–30.

Barchiesi, Franco. *Precarious Liberation: Workers, the State, and Contested Social Citizenship in Postapartheid South Africa* (New York: State University of New York Press), 2011.

Bayart, Jean Francois. *The State in Africa: The Politics of the Belly* (London: Longman), 1993.

Berman, Bruce. "The Ordeal of Modernity in an Age of Terror." *African Studies Review*. 49(1) (2006): 1–14.

Berman, Marshall. *All that Is Solid Melts into Air: The Experience of Modernity* (New York: Penguin Books), 1988.

Berry, Sara. *Fathers Work for Their Sons: Accumulation, Mobility, and Class Formation in an Extended Yoruba Community* (Los Angeles: University of California Press), 1985.

———. "Hegemony on a Shoestring: Indirect Rule and Access to Agricultural Land." *Africa*. 62(3) (1992): 327–355.

———. *Chiefs Know Their Boundaries: Essays on Property, Power and the Past in Asante, 1896–1996* (Portsmouth, NH: Heinemann), 2001.

Bhabha, Homi. *The Location of Culture*. (London: Routledge), 1994.

Bissell, William. "Engaging Colonial Nostalgia." *Cultural Anthropology*. 20(2) (May 2005): 215–248.

———. *Urban Design, Chaos, and Colonial Power in Zanzibar* (Bloomington, IN: Indiana University Press), 2010.

Bloom, Peter and Kate Skinner, "Modernity and Danger: 'The Boy Kumasenu' and the Work of the Gold Coast Film Unit," *Ghana Studies*, 12/13(2009): 121–153.

Bloom, Peter, Stephan Miescher, and Takyiwaa Manuh, "Introduction," *Modernization as Spectacle in Africa* (Bloomington, IN: Indiana University Press), 2014.

Boafo-Arthur, Kwame. "Ghana: Structural Adjustment, Democratization, and the Politics of Continuity." *African Studies Review*. 42(2) (1999): 41–72.

Boahen, Adu. *The Ghanaian Sphinx: Reflections on the Contemporary History of Ghana, 1972–1987* (Accra: Ghana Academy of Arts and Sciences), 1989.

Bourdieu, Pierre. "Structures, habitus, practices." In P. Bourdieu, *The Logic of Practice* (Stanford, CA: Stanford University Press), 1990: 52–79.

———. "The Forms of Capital." In *Handbook of Theory and Research for the Sociology of Capital*. J. G. Richardson, ed. (New York, Greenwood Press), 1986: 241–58.

———. *The Logic of Practice* (Cambridge: Polity Press), 1990.

Brooks, George. *Eurafricans in Western Africa: Commerce, Social Status, Gender, & Religious Observance* (Columbus, OH: Ohio University Press), 2003.

Bulir, Ales. "The Price Incentive to Smuggle and the Cocoa Supply in Ghana, 1950–96." *International Monetary Fund Working Paper* (June 1998).

Burke, Timothy. *Lifebuoy Men, Lux Women: Commodification, Consumption, and Cleanliness in Modern Zimbabwe* (Durham, NC: Duke University Press), 1996.

Burton, Andrew. *African Underclass: Urbanization, Crime, and Colonial Order in Dar es Salaam, 1919–61* (Portsmouth, NH: Heinemann), 2005.

Chabal, Patrick and Jean-Pascal Daloz. *Africa Works: Disorder as Political Instrument* (Bloomington, IN: Indiana University Press), 1999.

Chabal, Patrick. *Africa: The Politics of Suffering and Smiling* (London, UK: Zed Books, 2009).

Chalfin, Brenda. *Neoliberal Frontiers: An Ethnography of Sovereignty in West Africa* (Chicago: University of Chicago Press), 2010.

———. "Cars, the Customs Service, and Sumptuary Rule in Neoliberal Ghana." *Comparative Studies in Society and History* 50(2) (April 2008): 424–453.

Chazan, Naomi. *An Anatomy of Ghanaian Politics: Managing Political Recession, 1969–1982* (Boulder: Westview Press), 1983.

Chernoff, John. *Hustling Is Not Stealing: Stories of an African Bar Girl* (Chicago: University of Chicago Press), 2003.

Clark, Gracia. "Consulting Elderly Kumasi Market Women About Modernization." *Ghana Studies* (12/13) (2009/2010): 97–119.

———. *Onions Are My Husband: Survival and Accumulation by West African Market Women* (Chicago: University of Chicago Press), 1995.

———. "Gender and Profiteering: Ghana's market women as devoted mothers and 'human vampire bats.'" In D. Hodgson and S. McCurdy, eds. *'Wicked' Women and the Reconfiguration of Gender in Africa* (Portsmouth, NH: Heinemann, 2001).

Clarsen, Georgine. "Machine as the Measure of Women: Colony Irony in a Cape to Cairo Automobile Journey, 1930." *Journal of Transport History* 29(1) (2008): 44–63.

Coe, Cati. *Dilemmas of Culture in African Schools: Youth, Nationalism, and the Transformation of Knowledge* (Chicago: University of Chicago Press), 2005.

Cole, Catherine, *Ghana's Concert Party Theater* (Bloomington, IN: Indiana University Press), 2001.

Comaroff, Jean and John Comaroff. "Millennial Capitalism: First Thoughts on a Second Coming." *Public Culture* 12(2) (2000): 291–343.

Cooper, Frederick and Randall Packard, eds. *International Development and the Social Sciences: Essays on the History and Politics of Knowledge* (Los Angeles: University of California Press), 1998.

Cooper, Frederick. *Decolonization and African Society: The Labor Question in French and British Africa* (Cambridge: Cambridge University Press), 1996.

———. "The Problem of Slavery in African Studies." *The Journal of African History* 20(1) (1979): 103–125.

———. *Africa Since 1940: The Past of the Present* (Cambridge: Cambridge University Press), 2002.

Cruickshank, Brodie. *Eighteen Years on the Gold Coast of Africa* (London: Cass), 1966.

Curtin, Philip. *The African Slave Trade: A Census* (Madison: University of Wisconsin Press), 1969.

Danso-Boafo, Alex Kwaku. *The Political Biography of Dr. Kofi Abrefa Busia* (Accra: Ghana University Press), 1996.

Davidson, Basil. *The African Genius* (Athens, OH: Ohio University Press), 2004.

Davison, R. B. "Labor Relations in Ghana." *Annals of the American Academy of Political and Social Science* 310 (March 1957): 133–141.

de Boeck, Filip. "Infrastructure: Commentary from Filip de Boeck." *Curated Collections. Cultural Anthropology Online* (November 26, 2012). Accessed August 26, 2015. http://production.culanth.org/curated_collections/11-infrastructure/discussions /7-infrastructure-commentary-from-filip-de-boeck.

de Certeau, Michel. *The Practice of Everyday Life* (Los Angeles: University of California Press), 2011.

de Marees, Pieter. *Description and Historical Account of the Gold Kingdom of Guinea (1602).* Albert van Dantzig and Adam Jones, trans and eds. (Oxford: Oxford University Press), 1987.

de Sardan and J. P. Olivier. "A Moral Economy of Corruption in Africa?" *Journal of Modern African Studies* 37(1) (1999): 25–52.

Denzer, LaRay. "Wallace-Johnson and the Sierra Leone Labor Crisis of 1939." *African Studies Review* 25 (June–September 1982): 159–183.

Dickson, Kwamina. *A Historical Geography of Ghana* (London: Cambridge University Press), 1971.

Dumett, Raymond. "African Merchants of the Gold Coast, 1860–1905: Dynamics of Indigenous Entrepreneurship." *Comparative Studies in Society and History* 25(4) (1983): 661–693.

———. "John Mensah Sarbah, the Elder, and African Mercantile Entrepreneurship in the Gold Coast in the Late Nineteenth Century." *Journal of African History* 14(4) (1973): 653–679.

———. "Tropical Forests and West African Enterprise: The Early History of the Ghana Timber Trade." *African Economic History* 29 (2001), 79–116.

Edwards, Paul. "Infrastructure and Modernity: Force, Time, and Social Organization in the History of Sociotechnical Systems." In *Modernity and Technology.* eds. Thomas J. Misa, Philip Brey, and Andrew Feenberg. (Cambridge: The MIT Press), 2003.

Fair, Laura. *Pastimes and Politics: Culture, Community, and Identity in Post-Abolition Zanzibar* (Athens, OH: Ohio University Press), 2001.

Featherstone, Mike, Nigel Thrift, and John Urry, eds. *Automobilities* (New York: Sage Publications), 2005.

Feld, Steven. "Liner Notes." *Por Por: Honk Horn Music of Ghana.* The La Drivers Union Por Por Group. (Washington, DC: Smithsonian Folkways Recordings), 2007.

———. *Jazz Cosmopolitanism in Accra: Five Musical Years in Ghana* (Durham, NC: Duke University Press), 2012.

Ferguson, James. *Expectations of Modernity: Myths and Meanings of Urban Life on the Zambian Copperbelt* (Los Angeles: University of California Press), 1999.

Field, Margaret. *Search for Security: An Ethno-Psychiatric Study of Rural Ghana* (New York: W. W. Norton & Company), 1970.

Friedson, Steven. *Remains of Ritual: Northern Gods in a Southern Land* (Chicago: University of Chicago Press), 2009.

George, Abosede A. *Making Modern Girls: A History of Girlhood, Labor, and Social Development in Colonial Lagos* (Athens, OH: Ohio University Press), 2014.

Getz, Trevor. *Abina and the Important Men: A Graphic History* (Oxford: Oxford University Press), 2011.

Geurts, Kathryn Linn. *Culture and the Sense: Bodily Ways of Knowing in an African Community* (Berkley: University California Press), 2003.

Gewald, Jan Bart. "Introduction." In *The Speed of Change: Motor Vehicles and People in Africa, 1890-2000*. eds. Jan-Bart Gewald, Sabine Luning, and Klaas van Walraven (Leiden: Brill), 2009.

———. "Missionaries, Hereros, and Motorcars: Mobility and the Impact of Motor Vehicles before 1940." *The International Journal of African Historical Studies* 35 (2/3) (2002): 257–285.

Gilroy, Paul. *Darker than Blue: On the Moral Economies of Black Atlantic Culture* (Cambridge, MA: Belknap Press), 2011.

Giucci, Guillermo. *The Cultural Life of the Automobile: Roads to Modernity* (Austin: University of Texas Press), 2012.

Glaser, Clive. *Bo Tsotsi: The Youth Gangs of Soweto, 1935–1976* (Portsmouth, NH: Heinemann), 2000.

Grace, Joshua. "Heroes of the Road: Race, Gender, and the Politics of Mobility in Twentieth Century Tanzania." *Africa* 83(3) (2013): 403–425.

Graham, Sean, director. *The Boy Kumasenu*. The Gold Coast Film Unit. (1952) Accessed August 26, 2015. http://www.colonialfilm.org.uk/node/332.

Grier, Beverly. "Pawns, Porters, and Petty Traders: Women in the Transition to Cash Crop Agriculture in Colonial Ghana." *Signs* 17 (Winter 1992): 304–328.

Guldi, Jo. *Roads to Power: Britain Invents the Infrastructure State* (Cambridge, MA: Harvard University Press), 2012.

Guyer, Jane and Samuel M. Eno Belinga. "Wealth in People as Wealth in Knowledge: Accumulation and Composition in Equatorial Africa." *Journal of African History* 36 (1995): 91–120.

Gyekye, Kwame. *An Essay on African Philosophical Thought: The Akan Conceptual Scheme* (Philadelphia, PA: Temple University Press), 1995.

Hart, Jennifer. "Motor Transportation, Trade Unionism, and the Culture of Work in Colonial Ghana." *International Review of Social History*. 29 (2014), Special Issue, 185–209.

Harvey, Penny and Hannah Knox. *Roads: An Anthropology of Infrastructure and Expertise* (Ithaca, NY: Cornell University Press), 2015.

Headrick, Daniel. *The Tools of Empire: Technology and European Imperialism in the Nineteenth Century* (Oxford: Oxford University Press), 1981.

Heap, Simon. "The development of motor transport in the Gold Coast, 1900–39." *Journal of Transport History*. (1990): 19–37.

Hecht, Gabrielle. *Being Nuclear: Africans and the Global Uranium Trade* (Boston: The MIT Press), 2014.

Hill, Polly. *Migrant Cocoa Farmers of Ghana: A Case Study in Rural Capitalism* (London: James Currey), 1997.

Hintzen, Percy. "After Modernization: Globalization and the African Dilemma."
In *Modernization as Spectacle in Africa*. Peter Bloom, Stephan Miescher, and
Takyiwaa Manuh, eds. (Bloomington: Indiana University Press), 2014.

Hodge, Joseph Morgan. *Triumph of the Expert: Agrarian Doctrines of Development
and the Legacies of British Colonialism* (Columbus, OH: Ohio University Press),
2007.

Hodgson, Dorothy and Sheryl McCurdy, eds. *"Wicked" Women and the Reconfiguration
of Gender in Africa* (Portsmouth, NH: Heinemann), 2001.

Hopkins, A. G. *An Economic History of West Africa* (New York: Routledge), 1973.

Hutchful, Eboe. *Ghana's Adjustment Experience: The Paradox of Reform* (Portsmouth,
NH: Heinemann), 2002.

Iliffe, John. *Africans: The History of a Continent* (Cambridge: Cambridge University
Press), 2007.

Ingold, Tim. *Lines: A Brief History* (New York: Routledge), 2007.

Isaacman, Allen and Barbara S. Isaacman. *Slavery and Beyond: The Making of Men and
Chikunda Ethnic Identities in the Unstable World of South-Central Africa, 1750–1920*
(Portsmouth, NH: Heinemann), 2004.

J. H. K. "Motor Transport on the Gold Coast." *The Commercial Motor* (17 August 1920).

Jeffries, Richard. *Class, Power, and Ideology in Ghana: The Railwaymen of Sekondi*
(Cambridge: Cambridge University Press), 1978.

Judd, Denis. "Diamonds Are Forever?: Kipling's Imperialism." *History Today* 47 (6)
(1997).

Karlstrom, Mikael. "Modernity and its Aspirants: Moral Community and Development
Eutopianism in Buganda." *Current Anthropology* 45(5) (December 2004): 595–610.

Killingray, David. *Fighting for Britain: African Soldiers in the Second World War*
(London: James Currey), 2012.

———. "Repercussions of World War I in the Gold Coast." *Journal of African History*
19(1) (1978): 39–59.

Klaeger, Gabriel. "Introduction: The Perils and Possibilities of African Roads." *Africa*
83(3) (2013): 359–366.

———. "Religion on the Road: The Spiritual Experience of Road Travel in Ghana." In
The Speeds of Change: Motor Vehicles and People in Africa, 1890–2000. (Leiden:
Brill Academic Publishers), 2009: 169–194.

Klein, Axel. "Trapped in the Traffick: Growing Problems of Drug Consumption in
Lagos." *Journal of Modern African Studies* 32(4) (1994): 657–677.

Kopytoff, Igor. "The Cultural Biography of Things: Commoditization as Process." In *The
Social Life of Things: Commodities in Cultural Perspective.* ed. Arjun Appadurai.
(Cambridge: Cambridge University Press), 1986.

Kwakye, Benjamin. *The Clothes of Nakedness* (Heinemann: London), 1998.

Lal, Priya. "Self-Reliance and the State: The Multiple Meanings of Development in Early
Post-Colonial Tanzania." *Africa* 82, 2 (2012), 212–234.

Lamont, Mark. "Speed Governors: Road Safety and Infrastructural Overload in Post-
Colonial Kenya, c. 1963–2013." *Africa* 83(3) (2013): 367–384.

Larkin, Brian. *Signal and Noise: Media, Infrastructure, and Urban Culture in Nigeria*
(Durham, NC: Duke University Press), 2008.

Lawrence, Benjamin, Emily Osborn, and Richard Roberts, eds. *Intermediaries, Interpreters, and Clerks: African Employees in Colonial Africa* (Madison, WI: University of Wisconsin Press), 2006.

Lawuyi, Olatunde. "The World of the Yoruba Taxi Driver: An Interpretive Approach to Vehicle Slogans." *Africa* 58 (1) (1988): 1–13.

Lefebvre, Henri. *Everyday Life in the Modern World* (London: Allen Lane), 1971.

Lewis, George H. "The Philosophy of the Street in Ghana: Mammy Wagons and Their Mottos—A Research Note." *The Journal of Popular Culture* 32(1) (Summer 1998): 165–171.

Lindsay, Lisa. *Working with Gender: Wage Labor and Social Change in Southwestern Nigeria* (Portsmouth, NH: Heinemann), 2003.

Lovejoy, Paul. *Transformations in Slavery* (New York: Cambridge University Press), 2000.

Lugard, Frederick. *The Dual Mandate in British Tropical Africa* (London: William Blackwood and Sons), 1922.

Maclean, Lauren M. *Informal Institutions and Citizenship in Rural Africa: Risk and Reciprocity in Ghana and Cote d'Ivoire* (Cambridge: Cambridge University Press), 2010.

MacMillan, Allister, ed. *The Red Book of West Africa: Historical and Descriptive, Commercial and Industrial, Facts, Figures, and Resources* (New York: Routledge), 1968.

Mamdani, Mahmood. *Citizen and Subject: Contemporary Africa and the Legacy of Late Colonialism* (Princeton, NJ: Princeton University Press), 1996.

Mann, Michael. *The Sources of Social Power: A History of Power from the Beginning to AD 1760*, Vol. 1. (Cambridge: Cambridge University Press), 1986.

Marshall, Ruth. *Political Spiritualities: The Pentecostal Revolution in Nigeria* (Chicago: University of Chicago Press), 2009.

Martin, Phyllis. *Leisure and Society in Colonial Brazzaville* (Cambridge: Cambridge University Press), 1996.

Masquelier, Adeline. "Road Mythographies: Space, Mobility, and the Historical Imagination in Postcolonial Niger." *American Ethnologist* 29(4) (2002): 829–856.

Mavhunga, Clapperton. *Transient Workspaces: Technologies of Everyday Innovation in Zimbabwe* (Boston: MIT Press), 2014.

Mbembe, Achille. *On the Postcolony* (Los Angeles: University of California Press), 2001.

McCaskie, T.C. "Accumulation, Wealth and Belief in Asante History II: The twentieth century." *Africa*. 56, 1 (1986), 3–23.

———. *Asante Identities: History and Memory in an African Village, 1850–1950* (Bloomington: Indiana University Press), 2001.

McClintock, Anne. *Imperial Leather: Race, Gender, and Sexuality in the Colonial Context* (New York: Routledge), 1995.

McLaughlin, James L. and David Owusu-Ansah, "Britain and the Gold Coast: The Early Years," *A Country Study: Ghana*. La Verle Berry, ed. (Library of Congress Federal Research Division), 1994.

Meeson, "Transport Experience: British West Africa." *The Commercial Motor* 17 May 1927, 50–53.

Meyer, Birgit (with Jojada Verrips). "Kwaku's Car. The Struggles and Stories of a Ghanaian Long-Distance Taxi Driver." In *Readings in Modernity in Africa* Peter

Geschiere, Birgit Meyer & Peter Pels, eds. (Bloomington: Indiana University Press), 2008: 155–165 [Reprint of "Kwaku's Car." In: Daniel Miller (ed.), *Car Cultures*. Oxford: Berg Publishers. Pp.153–184.].

———. "Pentecostalism and Neo-Liberal Capitalism: Faith, Prosperity, and Vision in African Pentecostal-Charismatic Churches." *Journal for the Study of Religion* 20(2) (2007): 5–28.

Miescher, Stephan and Dzodzi Tsikata, "Hydro-Power and the Promise of Modernity and Development in Ghana: Comparing the Akosombo and Bui Dam Projects." *Ghana Studies* (12/13) (2009/2010): 15–53.

Miescher, Stephan. "No One Should Be Worse Off": The Akosombo Dam, Modernization, and the Experience of Resettlment in Ghana." In *Modernization as Spectacle in Africa*. Peter Bloom, Stephan Miescher, and Takyiwaa Manuh, eds. (Bloomington, IN: Indiana University Press), 2014: 184–204.

———. *Making Men in Ghana* (Bloomington: Indiana University Press), 2005.

Miller, Daniel. "Driven Societies." In *Car Cultures*. Daniel Miller, ed. (New York: Berg), 2001: 1–34.

Miller, Joseph. "The Paradoxes of Impoverishment in the Atlantic Zone" In *History of Central Africa* (I), ed. David Birmingham and Phyllis Martin (London: Longman), 1983: 118–159.

Miller, Joseph. *Way of Death: Merchant Capitalism and the Angolan Slave Trade, 1730–1830* (Madison: University of Wisconsin Press), 1988.

Minister of Housing. *Accra: A Plan for the Town* (Accra: Government of Ghana), 1958.

Mitchell, Timothy. *Colonising Egypt* (Los Angeles: University of California Press), 1991.

———. *Rule of Experts: Egypt, Techno-Politics, Modernity* (Los Angeles: University of California Press), 2002.

Moorman, Marissa. *Intonations: A Social History of Music and Nation in Luanda, Angola, from 1945 to Recent Times* (Athens, OH: Ohio University Press), 2008.

Mrazek, Rudolf. *Engineers of a Happy Land: Technology and Nationalism in a Colony* (Princeton, NJ: Princeton University Presss), 2002.

Murillo, Bianca. *Conditional Sales: Global Commerce and the Making of an African Consumer Society* (Athens, OH: Ohio University Press), forthcoming.

Mutongi, Kenda. "Thugs or Entrepreneurs?: Perceptions of *Matatu* Operators in Nairobi, ca. 1970 to Present." *Africa* 76(4) (2006): 549–568.

Newell, Stephanie. *Literary Culture in Colonial Ghana: How to Play the Game of Life* (Bloomington, IN: Indiana University Press), 2002.

Nketia, J. H. Kwabena. *Drumming in Akan Communities of Ghana* (London, 1963).

Nkrumah, Kwame. *Neocolonialism: The Last Stage of Imperialism* (London: Thomas Nelson & Sons, Ltd.), 1965.

Ntewusu, Samuel. *Settling In and Holding On: A Socio-Historical Study of Northern Trader and Transporters in Accra's Tudu, 1908–2008* (Dissertation: University of Lieden, Afrika Studies Centrum), 2011.

Nugent, Paul. *Big Men, Small Boys, and Politics in Ghana: Power, Ideology, and the Burden of History, 1982–1994* (London: Pinter Publishers, Ltd, 1996).

———. *Smugglers, Secessionists & Loyal Citizens on the Ghana-Togo Frontier* (Athens, OH: Ohio University Press), 2002.

Ochonu, Moses. *Colonial Meltdown: Northern Nigeria in the Great Depression* (Athens, OH: Ohio University Press), 2009.

Odotei, Irene K. and Albert K. Awedoba. *Chieftaincy in Ghana: Culture, Governance and Development* (Sub Saharan Publishers and Traders), 2006.

Okoye, Victoria, Jahmal Sands, and C. Asamoah Debrah, "The Accra Pilot Bus-Rapid Transit Project: Transport-Land Use Research Study." *Millennium Cities Initiative (MCI)*, Earth Institute at Columbia University, October 2010. Accessed on July 11, 2014. http://victoriaokoye.files.wordpress.com/2010/02/mci_urbantransport_finaldraft.pdf.

Oquaye, Mike. *Politics in Ghana, 1972–1979* (Accra: Tornado Publications), 1980.

Osinulu, Damola. "Painters, Blacksmiths and Wordsmiths: Building Molues in Lagos." *African Arts* 41 (3) (Autumn 2008): 44–53.

Packer, Jeremy. *Mobility without Mayhem: Safety, Cars, and Citizenship* (Durham, NC: Duke University Press), 2008.

Parker, John. *Making the Town: Ga State and Society in Early Colonial Accra* (Portsmouth, NH: Heinemann), 2000.

Parsons, Timothy. *Race, Resistance, and the Boy Scout Movement in British Colonial Africa* (Athens, OH: Ohio University Press), 2004.

Peel, J. D. Y. "Olaju: A Yoruba Concept of Development." *Journal of Development Studies* 14(1978): 139–165.

———. *Religious Encounter and the Making of the Yoruba* (Bloomington, IN: Indiana University Press), 2003.

Peil, Margaret. "The Apprenticeship System in Accra." *Africa* 40(2) (April 1970): 137–150.

———. *The Ghanaian Factory Worker: Industrial Man in Africa* (Cambridge: Cambridge University Press), 2009.

Pellow, Deborah and Naomi Chazan. *Ghana: Coping with Uncertainty* (Boulder: Westview Press), 1986.

Piot, Charles. *Nostalgia for the Future: West Africa after the Cold War* (Chicago: University of Chicago Press), 2010.

Plageman, Nathan. "Colonial Ambition, Common Sense Thinking, and the Making of Takoradi Harbor, Gold Coast." *History in Africa.* 40(1) (2013): 317–352.

———. *Everybody Likes Saturday Night: A Social History of Popular Music and Masculinities in Urban Gold Coast/Ghana, c. 1900–1970.* PhD Dissertation (Bloomington, IN: Indiana University Press), 2008.

———. *Highlife Saturday Night: Popular Music and Social Change in Urban Ghana* (Bloomington, IN: Indiana University Press), 2012.

Pool, Jeremy. *Now is the Time of Youth: Youth, Nationalism and Cultural Change in Ghana, 1940–1966.* PhD Dissertation (Emory University), 2009.

Priestley, Margaret. *West African Trade and Coast Society: A Family Study* (Oxford: Oxford University Press), 1969.

Quayson, Ato. "Signs of the Times: Discourse Ecologies and Street Life on Oxford St., Accra." *City and Society* 22 (1) (June 2010): 72–96.

———. *Oxford Street, Accra: City Life and the Itineraries of Transnationalism* (Durham, NC: Duke University Press), 2014.

Ranger, Terence. "The Invention of Tradition in Colonial Africa." In *The Invention of Tradition.* Eric Hobsbawm and Terence Ranger, eds. (Cambridge: Cambridge University Press), 1992.

Rathbone, Richard. *Nkrumah and the Chiefs: The Politics of Chieftaincy in Ghana 1951–1960* (Athens: Ohio University Press), 2000.

Rizzo, Matteo. "Being Taken for a Ride: Privatization of the Dar es Salaam Transport System, 1983–1998." *Journal of Modern African Studies* 40(2002): 133–157.

Robertson, Claire and Martin Klein (eds). *Women and Slavery in Africa* (Madison: University of Wisconsin Press), 1997.

Robertson, Claire. *Sharing the Same Bowl: A Socioeconomic History of Women and Class in Accra, Ghana* (Ann Arbor: University of Michigan Press), 1990.

———. "The Death of Makola and Other Tragedies." *Canadian Journal of African Studies.* 17, 3 (1983): 469–495.

Roitman, Janet. *Anti-Crisis* (Durham, NC: Duke University Press), 2013.

———. *Fiscal Disobedience: An Anthropology of Economic Regulation in Central Africa* (Princeton, NJ: Princeton University Press), 2005.

Rosenthal, Judy. *Possession, Ecstasy, and Law in Ewe Voodoo* (Charlottesville: University Press of Virginia), 1998.

Ross, Kristin. *Fast Cars, Clean Bodies: Decolonization and the Reordering of French Culture* (Boston: The MIT Press), 1996.

Sackeyfio-Lenoch, Naaborko. *The Politics of Chieftaincy: Authority and Property in Colonial Ghana, 1920–1950* (Rochester, NY: University of Rochester Press), 2014.

Sadowsky, Jonathan. *Imperial Bedlam: Institutions of Madness in Colonial Southwest Nigeria* (Los Angeles: University of California Press), 1999.

Salm, Steven J. and Toyin Falola. *Culture and Customs of Ghana* (Westport, CT: Greenwood Press), 2002.

Samantrai, Ranu. "Caught at the Confluence of History: Ama Ata Aidoo's Necessary Nationalism." *Research in African Literatures* 26(2) (Summer 1995): 140–157.

Schatzberg, M. G. "Power, Legitimacy and 'Democratization' in Africa." *Africa.* 63 (1993).

Schauert, Paul. *Staging Ghana: Artistry and Nationalism in State Dance Ensembles* (Bloomington, IN: Indiana University Press), 2015.

Schivelbusch, Wolfgang. *A Railway Journey: The Industrialization of Time and Space in the 19th Century* (Berkeley: University of California Press), 1987.

Scott, David. *Conscripts of Modernity: The Tragedy of Colonial Enlightenment* (Durham, NC: Duke University Press), 2004.

Scott, James. *Seeing Like a State: How Certain Schemes to Improve the Human Condition Have Failed* (New Haven, CT: Yale University Press), 1999.

Seiler, Cotten. *Republic of Drivers: A History of Automobility in America* (Chicago: University of Chicago Press), 2008.

Shipley, Jesse Weaver. *Living the Hiplife: Celebrity and Entrepreneurship in Ghanaian Popular Music* (Durham, NC: Duke University Press), 2013.

Simone, Abdoumaliq. "On the Worlding of African Cities." *African Studies Review* 44(2) (2001): 15–41.

Skinner, Kate. "'It Brought Some Kind of Neatness to Mankind: Mass Literacy, Community Development, and Democracy in 1950s Asante." *Africa* 79(4) (2009): 479–499.

Solkin, David. *Painting out of the Ordinary: Modernity and the Art of Everyday Life in Early Nineteenth Century Britain* (London: Paul Mellon Center BA), 2008.

Stacey, Paul. *Traditional Uncertainty: Chieftaincy in Northern Ghana: Land Control and Ethnic Conflicts, 1901-1996* (VDM Verlag), 2009.

Standing, Guy. *The Precariat: The New Dangerous Class* (London: Bloomsbury), 2014.

Stein, Sara Abrevaya. *Plumes: Ostrich Feathers, Jews, and a Lost World of Global Commerce* (New Haven, CT: Yale University Press), 2010.

Stewart, Julia. *African Proverbs and Wisdom* (New York: Carol Publishers), 1997.

Thomas, Lynn. *Politics of the Womb: Women, Reproduction, and the State in Kenya* (Los Angeles: University of California Press), 2003.

Thornton, John. *Africa and Africans in the Making of the Atlantic World, 1400-1800* (Cambridge: Cambridge University Press), 1998.

Tilley, Helen. *Africa as a Living Laboratory: Empire, Development, and the Problem of Scientific Knowledge, 1870-1950* (Chicago: University of Chicago Press), 2011.

Tsey, Komla. *From Head-Loading to the Iron Horse: Railway Building in Colonial Ghana and the Origins of Tropical Development* (Cameroon: Langaa RPCIG), 2012.

Tudhope, W. T. D. "The Development of the Cocoa Industry in the Gold Coast and Ashanti." *African Affairs* IX(XXXIII) (1909).

Urry, John. *Mobilities* (Cambridge: Polity Press), 2007.

van Beusekom, Monica. *Negotiating Development: African Farmers and Colonial Experts at the Office du Niger, 1920-1960* (Portsmouth, NH: Heinemann), 2001.

van der Geest, Sjaak. "'Anyway': Lorry Inscriptions in Ghana." In *The Speed of Change: Motor Vehicles and People in Africa, 1890-2000.* eds. Jan-Bart Gewald, Sabine Luning, and Klaas van Walraven (Leiden: Brill), 2009: 253-293.

Volti, Rudi. *Cars & Culture: The Life Story of a Technology* (Baltimore: Johns Hopkins University Press), 2004.

Weiss, Brad, ed. *Producing African Futures: Ritual and Reproduction in a Neoliberal Age* (Leiden: Brill Academic Press), 2004.

White, Luise. *Speaking With Vampires: Rumor and History in Colonial Africa* (Los Angeles: University of California Press), 2000.

Yankah, Kwesi. *Speaking for the Chief: Okyeame and the Politics of Akan Royal Oratory* (Bloomington, IN: Indiana University Press), 1995.

Index

JENNIFER HART is an assistant professor of African history at Wayne State University. She received her PhD from Indiana University in 2011, MA from Indiana University in 2007, and BA from Denison University in 2005. She teaches courses in African history, comparative colonial history, British imperial history, and world history.

Printed and bound by CPI Group (UK) Ltd, Croydon, CR0 4YY

23/04/2025

14661012-0001